D1430807

AMULETS AND SUPERSTITIONS

AMULETS AND SUPERSTITIONS

THE ORIGINAL TEXTS WITH TRANSLATIONS AND DESCRIPTIONS OF A LONG SERIES OF EGYPTIAN, SUMERIAN, ASSYRIAN, HEBREW, CHRISTIAN, GNOSTIC AND MUSLIM AMULETS AND TALISMANS AND MAGICAL FIGURES, WITH CHAPTERS ON THE EVIL EYE, THE ORIGIN OF THE AMULET, THE PENTAGON, THE SWĂSTIKA, THE CROSS (PAGAN AND CHRISTIAN), THE PROPERTIES OF STONES, RINGS, DIVINATION, NUMBERS, THE ĶABBÂLÂH, ANCIENT ASTROLOGY, ETC.

BY

Sɪʀ E. A. WALLIS BUDGE, Kᴛ.
M.A., Lɪᴛᴛ.D., D.Lɪᴛᴛ., D.Lɪᴛ., F.S.A.

SOMETIME KEEPER OF THE EGYPTIAN AND ASSYRIAN ANTIQUITIES IN THE BRITISH MUSEUM, SCHOLAR OF CHRIST'S COLLEGE, CAMBRIDGE, AND TYRWHITT HEBREW SCHOLAR

With Twenty-two plates and three hundred illustrations in the text

DOVER PUBLICATIONS, INC.
NEW YORK

Published in Canada by General Publishing Company, Ltd., 30 Lesmill Road, Don Mills, Toronto, Ontario.
Published in the United Kingdom by Constable and Company, Ltd., 10 Orange Street, London WC2H 7EG.

This Dover edition, first published in 1978, is an unabridged republication of the work originally published by Oxford University Press, London, in 1930. This edition is published by special arrangement with Oxford University Press, Oxford.

International Standard Book Number: 0-486-23573-4
Library of Congress Catalog Card Number: 77-086708

Manufactured in the United States of America
Dover Publications, Inc.
180 Varick Street
New York, N.Y. 10014

CONTENTS

LIST OF PLATES

LIST OF ILLUSTRATIONS

PAGE

PREFACE

EARLY in the year 1873 the late Dr. Samuel Birch, Keeper of Oriental Antiquities in the British Museum, gave me permission to copy cuneiform tablets in his private study, and to use the Departmental Library. His study, which was entered from the Ḳûyûnjik Gallery and no longer exists, was a comparatively small room, and he was obliged to transact his business, both official and private, in the presence of the few students whom he allowed to work in it. These were accommodated at a table and a desk which stood under the north and west windows respectively. Day by day there came to him antica dealers and amateur collectors, who wished to show him objects which they possessed or were about to acquire, and to know what purpose they had served, what the marks or inscriptions on them meant, and what their pecuniary value was. The objects brought were usually Oriental, papyri, Egyptian and Coptic, cuneiform tablets, figures of gods, palm-leaf manuscripts, rings, pendants, necklaces, amulets of all kinds, inscribed metal plaques, Chinese pottery and seals, etc. But no matter what the object put before him was, Birch always seemed to know something about it, and to be able to refer his visitors to authoritative books, or to living scholars, for further information. That he was the greatest Egyptologist in England, and that officials from the

Chinese Embassy in London came to him for information about ancient Chinese history and the old forms of Chinese pictographs we all knew, but one could only listen and wonder at the encyclopaedic character of his general knowledge. Naturally he was consulted by many members of the general public on matters dealing with Egyptology and Assyriology, for the greater number of the antiquities under his charge came from Egypt, Babylonia and Assyria. But some of his visitors asked him for information, and usually got it, about the Moabite Stone, the Cyprian inscriptions (which were at that time undeciphered), the Massorah, the Ḳabbâlâh, the Sinaitic inscriptions, the monuments of Susa and Persepolis, the inscriptions of Mal Amir, the Himyaritic inscriptions, astrology, the ritual of fire-worship, the rites of the Yazîdîs or Devil-worshippers, etc. His answers and short dissertations were always interesting, and that we, *i.e.* Naville, Strassmaier, W. H. Rylands and myself, more often listened to them than worked need not be wondered at.

One day, when he seemed to have a little leisure, I ventured to ask him if members of the public ever put to him questions which he could not answer? and he replied, " Yes, often." Said I, " Then what happens ? " He answered promptly, " I confess my ignorance, and refer the visitor to another member of the staff. When the enquirer has gone I at once write down the question he has asked on a slip of paper, and as soon as I can I try to obtain the information necessary to answer the question. And if the day ever comes when you are an Assistant in this Department I recommend you to write all the sensible questions which you are asked upon slips of paper and search out the answers to them. Many members of the public ask the same question, especially about matters of general interest."

Ten years later I had the good fortune to become one of Dr. Birch's Assistants, and in due course I was asked many questions by the public which I could not answer satisfactorily. Therefore I adopted Dr. Birch's plan and wrote such questions on slips of paper, and I continued to do this during the years of my long service in the British Museum. When I resigned in 1924 and left my official residence I brought away with me a very thick bundle of slips with questions written on them. During the first years of my service the questions were of a very miscellaneous character and dealt with a great variety of subjects. But when Dr. Birch's successor found that the answering of questions orally and by letter took up so much of his time daily, he moved the Trustees to change the title of the Department to that of " Department of Egyptian and Assyrian Antiquities." This change limited the scope but not the number of enquiries, and little by little the questions chiefly concerned Egyptian and Assyrian, Babylonian and other Semitic antiquities.

As opportunity offered, after my retirement I read over the mass of slips which I had collected, and discovering by the letters sent to me that the public were asking much the same kinds of questions which their fathers and mothers had asked me thirty and forty years ago, I determined to deal with the questions, as far as possible comprehensively, and to write a book which in a series of chapters would supply answers to them ; and the present volume is the result. As at least three-fourths of the questions concerned amulets and the beliefs which they represented I have called it "AMULETS AND SUPERSTITIONS," though perhaps a more correct title would have substituted "Magic" for "Superstitions." But the reader must note that in this book no attempt has been made to deal with amulets in general, for the writing of a history of the amulets which have been and still are in use throughout the world is beyond the power of any one man. Such a work would fill many thick volumes, and only a syndicate of specialists working together could produce the necessary " copy " for the printer. The use of amulets is the result of the belief in the power of the EVIL EYE in man and beast, and a proof of the vastness of the literature of this subject, which is growing daily, is furnished by the fact that the " Quellen-Register " in DR. SELIGMANN'S *Der Böse Blick* (Berlin, 1910) contains nearly 2,500 entries. And in his *Die Zauberkraft der Auges* (Hamburg, 1922) the authorities quoted number many hundreds more.

In this volume I have described the principal amulets which were used by the Semitic peoples of Western Asia, Egypt, Nubia and Ethiopia, beginning with those of the third millennium B.C. from Sumer and Elam. I have given many illustrations of them, reproduced photographically from the collections in the British Museum, and from those which are in the hands of private collectors, including my own. The description of the actual amulet is a comparatively simple matter, for in most cases the object explains itself. But when we come to the inscriptions on amulets, which consist of symbols, sacred and divine names used as words of power,

spells, etc., explanations of some length are necessary
of the ideas and beliefs which they represent.
Therefore I have added a series of short chapters
in which I have tried to set forth the principal
theories about the powers of " working " amulets, and
the meaning of the inscriptions and symbols inscribed
on them, and to indicate the beliefs concerning
them which were held by the ancient Babylonian
and Egyptian magicians, and by the later Ḳabbalists, Gnostics, both pagan and Christian, and
astrologers. And I have incorporated in them
many of the views of the astrologers, makers of
horoscopes, casters of nativities, diviners, crystal-
gazers, palmists and fortune-tellers with whom I
came in contact in Egypt, the Sûdân and Mesopotamia during my official Missions to those countries.

The use of amulets dates from the time when
animism or magic satisfied the spiritual needs of
man. Primitive man seems to have adopted them
as a result of an internal urge or the natural instinct
which made him take steps to protect himself and
to try to divine the future. He required amulets
to enable him to beget children, to give him strength
to overcome his enemies, visible and invisible, and
above all the EVIL EYE, and to protect his women
and children, and house and cattle ; and his descendants throughout the world have always done
the same. When the notion of a god developed
in his mind, he ascribed to that god the authorship
of the magical powers which he believed to be
inherent in his amulets, and he believed that his
god needed them as much as he himself did. He
did not think it possible for his god to exist without
the help of magical powers. At a later period he

regarded his god as the bestower of magical powers on men, and we find this view current among the civilized priests of Egypt, Sumer and Babylonia. These priests did not reject the crude magical beliefs and practices of their predecessors, whether savage or semi-savage; on the contrary they adopted many of them unaltered, and they formed an integral part of the mystery of the RELIGION which they formulated. Henceforth magic and religion went hand in hand. The gods became magicians, and employed magic when necessary, and dispensed it through their priests to mankind.

The Jewish Rabbis and some of the Christian Fathers condemned the use of amulets, some because they associated them with magic, and some because they regarded their use as an indication of distrust in the wisdom and arts of Divine Providence. But their condemnation had no lasting effect except to incite men to do what was arbitrarily forbidden, and the making and wearing of amulets went on as before. Men have always craved for amulets and the priests, both Pagans and Christians, should have taken steps to satisfy this craving. In this way they could have more or less controlled the use of amulets of every kind. The ancient literature of Babylonia and Egypt makes it clear that magic was believed to be an essential part of the equipment of the gods, who used it to help themselves and each other, and when they willed transmitted it to men.

In a papyrus at St. Petersburg[1] there is a remark-

---

[1] Published by W. GOLÉNISCHEFF, *Les Papyrus hiératiques No.* 1115, 1116A and 1116B *de l'Ermitage imperial à St. Pétersbourg*, 1913. The papyrus is not older than the XVIIIth Dynasty, but the work itself was written under the IXth or Xth Dynasty.

able passage in which it is stated that the great god, presumably Rā, created magic for the benefit of man. It occurs in a work written by a king called KHATI, who reigned during the troublous times between the downfall of the VIth Dynasty and the rise of the Theban Kingdom, in the third millennium before Christ. This work contains a series of "Teachings," which the king advised his son MERI-KA-RĀ to follow closely. In section XXVIII the king enumerates the great things which God has done for men and women, whom he describes as the "flocks and herds of God," and says, "He made heaven and earth for their pleasure ; He dissipated the darkness of the waters (*i.e.* the primeval ocean) ; He made the breezes of life for their nostrils ; they (*i.e.* men and women) are the images of Him and they proceeded from His members ; He rises in the sky to gratify them ; He made fruits and vegetables and flocks and herds, and feathered fowl and fish for their food ; He slew his enemies, he destroyed his own children when they murmured against him and rebelled ; He made the daylight to gratify them ; and

He made for them　　　magic　　　for a weapon

for resisting the power　of [evil] happenings [and] the dream (*sic*)

of the night　as well as　of the day."

The word *ḥekau* here rendered "magic," includes in its meaning, spells, incantations, words of power, and all the arts of the witch and sorcerer. The word *Kheprit* must mean unlucky or untoward, or evil happenings. And the kind of dream is not indicated ; the writer may mean the dream which terrifies, or the dreams in which the dreamer is shown future events, and is enabled in consequence to arrange or rearrange his affairs in respect of them. If it is the latter kind of dream which is referred to by the king, we have a proof that dreams were often employed by the gods in making their will known to the Egyptians. And this proves that the art of divining by means of dreams was commonly practised.

The literature of Babylonia also gives instances of the use of magic by the gods themselves. Thus when the Abyss-god Apsû rebelled against his overlord Ea, he had no opportunity of fighting him, for Ea first cast a mighty spell on him which made him fall into a heavy sleep, and then he killed him and seized his habitation ; and Mummu, the commander-in-chief of the forces of Apsû, was overpowered or bewitched by the same means and rendered impotent. When the gods found that they were to be attacked by Tiâmat, the personification and mother of all evil, and by all the powers of darkness under the leadership of her son Kingu, they selected Marduk, the son of Ea, as their champion, and endowed him with the power which they believed would enable him to avenge their cause effectively. But before he set out on his mission, they felt it necessary to make quite sure that his power as a magician was adequate for his task. They caused a cloak to appear in their midst, and said to him, " Thou shalt be chief among the gods, to cause the overthrow [of Tiâmat] and the reconstruction [of creation], and it shall come to pass. Nevertheless speak one word only and let the cloak disappear. Speak a second [word] and let the cloak reappear uninjured." Thereupon Marduk uttered a word of power and the cloak disappeared ; he uttered a second and the cloak reappeared. When the gods saw that their champion was able to invest his words with magical power they were satisfied and gave him the sceptre and throne and other symbols of sovereignty and the invincible weapon with which he was to slay Tiâmat.

An instance of the invincible magical power attributed to the great god Neb-er-djer (*i.e.* the Lord to the limit) or Khepera is furnished by an Egyptian papyrus in the British Museum (No. 10188). In the *Book of Knowing the Generations of Rā* it is stated that the god existed by himself in the primeval ocean in name only. In some way not described by the use of *ḥeka* or magic, he worked on his heart (*i.e.* mind) and so became a being, whom the Egyptians knew as Khepera or Rā. That the god existed by means of his name only is proved by the well-known legend in which the god reveals the secret name to Isis, who craved to know it so that she might rule over the whole world. Through her knowledge of magic Isis was able to construct a venomous reptile and to make it bite the god with such terrible effect that he nearly died. When death stared him in the face, he revealed his secret name to Isis, and she recited a spell which healed him. Thus Isis was skilled in the art of Black Magic as well as White. The idea of a god existing in name only is also found in Ethiopic literature, and some native writers have gone so far as to state that the Three Persons of the Trinity at first existed in name only in the primeval ocean, and that their existence is maintained by the use of words of power, *i.e.* magic.

And the ancient gods of Babylonia also used amulets. A most interesting example of this fact is given in the Creation Epic. When the great god Marduk, the son of Ea, the champion of the gods, set out to fight Tiâmat, he was heavily armed and carried invincible weapons ; but he carried between his lips an amulet made of red paste, or red stone, in the form of an eye, and he held in one hand a bunch of herbs which was intended to protect him from any magical influence which would be hostile to him.[1] And there is no doubt that Tiâmat, the " mother of everything," the fomenter and leader of rebellion against the gods, also possessed a remarkable object, which seems to have been of the nature of an amulet and which, in any case, was the source of all her power. In the texts this object is called " DUPPU SHEMATI," which is usually translated " Tablet of Destinies," but no detailed description of it is extant. Whence she obtained it is not known, and whether she carried it on her head or wore it on her breast is not clear.

Tiâmat created a number of horrible creatures of monstrous shape and form, to help her in her fight against the gods, and she made her first born son Kingu the commander-in-chief of her forces. In one place she calls Kingu " my only spouse." She bestowed upon him all the power which she could, and she gave him the Tablet of Destinies and fastened it to his breast, though a variant

---

[1] Meissner, *Altorientafesche Texte*, II, 41, 44, line 61 f.

(line 105, Third Tablet of Creation) says that she placed it on his head. When Marduk had defeated Kingu and his host, he took from him the Tablet of Destinies " which should never have been his," and sealed it with his seal, which showed that he regarded the Tablet as being legally his, and fastened it on his breast. This action suggests that the Tablet was, like the Pâizah of the Mongols, a sign of authority, which was worn on the breast, being suspended from the neck by a chain. In this case also we must ask, How did Tiâmat get it ? Was it given to her, and if so by whom ? It is evident from the narrative of the Creation Texts that the Tablet was the source of Tiâmat's power, and that her spells and incantations enabled her to use it in producing evil results, *i.e.* to work Black Magic with it. In itself it cannot have been a thing of evil, for when Marduk obtained possession of it he fastened it to his breast. Therefore it seems that we must regard the Tablet of Destinies as an amulet.

The whole of the Babylonian story of the Creation shows that men believed that all the great works of the gods and devils were performed by magic. The magic of Marduk was more powerful than that of Tiâmat, and his spells and incantations were more powerful than hers and therefore made her curses and spells to have no effect.

Some form of the belief that the gods of the Sumerians, Babylonians and Egyptians made use of amulets as protectors on urgent occasions made its way, probably at a very early date, into Ethiopia. In the *Book of the Mysteries of Heaven and Earth* we find an account of the rebellion of Satan against the Almighty. The Prince of Darkness mustered his troops and engaged in battle with the hosts of God. Twice the divine armies were repulsed and over-thrown and Satan was about to assume the position of the conqueror of God. The Almighty reformed His armies and sent them forth a third time to destroy Satan and his followers, but on this occasion He sent forth with them a Cross of Light on which the Names of the Three Persons of the Trinity were written. When Satan saw the Cross and the Three Names of Power, his boldness and courage forsook him, his arms lost their strength and the weapons which he was wielding fell from them and he and his hosts turned their backs and were hurled down into the abyss of hell by the now invincible angels of God. The Abyssinian belief in the power of the Cross to vanquish evil spirits and the diseases caused by them is based on this Legend ; and from early Christian times the Cross has been regarded as the amulet and talisman *par excellence* throughout Ethiopia.

Since the oldest civilized ancient nations believed that their gods had need of and made use of magic, it is not surprising that men and women had recourse to magic in periods of stress and difficulty. What was good for the gods was good also for man. Men made and used amulets to protect themselves, and the fundamental idea in their minds was to safe-guard the life and strength which had been given to them by the gods, although the divine powers seemed inattentive to them; each generation in every country borrowed something from its pre-decessors, but, apparently, abandoned no essential part of the tradition, belief or teaching concerning amulets. It was always assumed that materials from which amulets were made possessed certain qualities or attributes or powers which were beneficial to man. The influence of the inscription or device or name or word of power which was written upon the amulet, supplemented and perhaps increased the innate power in the material. To this power belief added that of the good will or affection or love of the giver of the amulet. When to these was added the firm belief of the wearer of the amulet in the qualities of the material it is clear that no amulet could be regarded as a piece of inert and dead matter. It became, in fact, a " working " amulet. A dose of medicine might be regarded as an amulet applied internally, and the effect of the matter which composed the dose was supplemented by the spell of the pagan, or the prayer of the Christian. The good will of both, AND THE FAITH of the patient joined to them, healed him and saved his life. The power and effect of FAITH in all such matters cannot be over-estimated.

Looking back over the history of amulets it is difficult to understand why ecclesiastical and other bodies condemned their use. The universal use of the amulet was, and still is, due to an instinct of the race, viz., that of self-preservation, and has nothing evil connected with it ; it has never been, and never can be, connected with what is commonly called " Black Magic." If we examine carefully the groups of amulets and amuletic inscriptions described and translated in this book, we find that each and all of them was believed to derive its protective powers from figures of the gods either engraved or drawn, and from the great names of the gods and of their divine attributes and the figures of sacred animals, and from inscriptions which contain divine names in various forms. All these amulets base their appeal to the Divine Powers for virility, fecundity, preservation of the family, success and well-being on the belief of their makers and wearers in the triumph of the Power of God over the Satans of every age and country, and the victory of Good over Evil, Law over Chaos, and Light over Darkness. The wearers of many of them may be said to have performed acts of worship when they wore them, and should have won the approval of their spiritual pastors and masters. It is probable that in Babylonia, Assyria and Egypt amulets were designed and made by workmen attached to the great temples, and that the inscriptions on them were drafted by the priests and engraved by employés in the temples.

From the Babylonian and Egyptian inscriptions we know that amulets made of certain kinds of stones secured for their wearers the presence of gods and goddesses, and brought them into daily contact with divine beings. Men possessing these had no need to have recourse to any system of divination in order to find out what the will of the gods was in respect of themselves, for no man " whose god was always with him " could come to harm. The insatiable desire to know the future was and still is a deep-rooted instinct in man, and many kinds of divination were practised in the earliest times. Some amulets were believed to make the wearer dream dreams in which his future would be revealed to him, but as few men were satisfied with their own interpretations of their dreams, a class of professional interpreters of dreams came into being.

The interpreters of dreams and omens were usually members of the priesthoods of the temples, and were men of solid learning, but in country villages impostors and charlatans were many. The ancient Asiatic peoples seem to have had three methods of divination, viz., by lots, by the pronouncements of astrologers, and by oracles which were given by the priests of the great temples. And among many peoples the " seer " was commonly consulted about the future. Ordinary folk cast lots and though their kind of divination was denounced by both the Hebrews and the Christians, it was often resorted to by them when other means of divination failed. Balaam, the diviner, was slain by the Israelites (Joshua xiii. 22), but Matthias was chosen to be an apostle by the casting of lots (Mark xv. 24) ! The astrologer and the " seer " (especially the latter) were likewise denounced, because their prophetic ecstacy or frenzy was regarded as madness and delirium.

The most reputable form of divination was enquiry by oracle. Shamash was the " Lord of Oracles," but many other great Babylonian gods were givers of oracles ; the first man in Babylonia to enquire by oracle was Enmeduranki, the king of Sippar, who reigned in prehistoric times. The goddess Ishtar of Arbela, too, gave oracular responses to Esarhaddon, King of Assyria. In Egypt the great giver of oracles was Rā, the Sun-god, or Amen-Rā. In Israel God gave His oracles through Aaron and his successors, but the story of Saul shows that there were occasions when He would give no oracle. " Saul asked counsel of God, . . . but He answered him not that day " (1 Sam. xiv. 37). And again,

" When Saul enquired of the Lord, the Lord answered him not, neither by dreams, nor by Urîm, nor by prophets " (1 Sam. xxviii. 6). In desperation Saul consulted the witch of Endor and a day or so later met his fate. The witch herself, before she obeyed his commands, reminded him that he had " put away those who had familiar spirits, and the wizards out of his land " (1 Sam. xxviii. 3).

Now although the Law decreed that there should not be in Israel any one who used divination, or observed times, or who was an enchanter, or a witch, or a charmer, or a consulter with familiar spirits, or a wizard or a necromancer (Deut. xviii. 10, 11), we find that one kind of divination was permitted by the Law, namely, the enquiry by Urîm and Tummîm, and that Moses gave very careful directions for the preparation of the means by which it could be carried out. Urîm and Tummîm were the names of two small pebbles, or plaques, or bits of wood, which were used much as we use dice. They were kept in a small pocket or pouch which was made at the back of the " breast-plate of judgment " (Exod. xxviii. 30 ; Lev. viii. 8), and it was the duty of Aaron and his successors to keep them there in safety, and to produce them when men wished to enquire of them. It is quite clear that the use of these two little objects for divining purposes was very ancient, and that Moses, being unable to suppress entirely the arts of divining which were among the Israelites, adopted this the oldest and most reputable form of divination and kept it under the control of himself and the priests of the Levites. In short, he regularized the use of Urîm and Tummîm and made enquiry by them a semi-religious ceremony ; and naturally he condemned all other forms of divination just as he condemned the use of all other amulets except the Phylacteries or frontlet bands which were worn between the eyes, the Mezûzâh or door-post amulet, and the Ṣîṣîth, *i.e.* tassel or fringe.

The object of all systems of divination was to compel the gods and the Deity to make their wills in respect of certain matters known to earnest, and it may be added, lawful enquirers, and Moses in common with pagan priests considered that there were occasions when the orthodox Israelite might be assisted in his quest.

Chrysostom and many other Christian Fathers condemned the use of amulets and systems of divination because of their connection with magic, but it is quite clear that the Christians of the Orient clung to many practices of pagan magic long after they had ceased to exist among European Christians. To the latter FAITH in God's Government was sufficient, and systems of divination were therefore unnecessary, and their priests were not called upon to be as tolerant as their brethren in the European parts of Asia Minor, Egypt, Nubia, Palestine, and Syria. Evidences of this are given in the New Testament. The story of the Star which led the Magi (Matt. ii. 2) shows that astrology was regarded with toleration by St. Matthew and his readers ; the mention of the dream of Joseph (Matt. ii. 12, 13, 19, 22) and the dream of Pilate's wife proves that dreams were still regarded as legalized forms of divination. The waking dreams or trance of Peter (Acts x. 10) and Paul (Acts xxii. 17) were thought of in the same light by the early Christians. The pagan belief in the virtue which is latent in the shadow of a holy man is referred to in Acts v. 15, where we are told that the sick folk and demoniacs on whom the shadow of Peter fell " were healed every one." The belief was common that there were healing powers in the apparel of holy men, and when the " handkerchiefs and aprons " of Paul were brought and laid upon the sick, " the diseases departed from them, and the evil spirits went out of them " (Acts xix. 12).

Soon after the close of the IVth century of our Era a sort of revival in the use of amulets began, and the Christians began to make use of amulets which were connected with their religion. First and foremost was the Cross, which appeared in various forms, and the sign of the Cross, which was commonly used by the clergy and laity alike to drive away devils and disease-producing spirits. Then came pictures of the Virgin Mary, and pictures and figures of the Archangels and the great saints, and the cult of the relics of the martyrs who were the victims of the numerous persecutions which took place in the first four centuries of our Era. Untanned leather and parchment and papyrus and stones were also inscribed with extracts from the Scriptures, and finally, after the invention of paper, amulets and talismans of paper became common. And a species of Christian Magic came into being. The greatest Name and word of power was Jesus, and the Host and sacramental oil and incense became to many amulets of invincible power, and the Sacred Elements were actually called " immortal medicine."

Oriental magic of every kind made its way into Europe in the Middle Ages, and traces of it are recognizable throughout the West, even at the present day. The mathematician and the astronomer and the physician have founded their sciences on the lore of the Sumerians and Babylonians and Assyrians, and believe that they have taken from the arithmetic and astrological and medical tablets everything there is of value in them, but in this they are mistaken. Astrology, divination, the use of numbers, and the system of medicine which were in use in Mesopotamia in the third millennium before Christ are as much alive and as active in that country as ever, and are held by the natives in far higher esteem than the exact sciences which Europeans have derived from them. And even in England and America at the present time large numbers of people are influenced by beliefs which were common in Babylonia four or five thousand years ago. No amount of development, culture or education will make men abandon wholly the use of amulets and systems of divination. For amulets give their wearers a sense of comfort, and protection and well-being, and they harm no one. And he who practises the arts of divination can harm nobody but himself.

Writers of books and articles on occult matters in encyclopaedic works frequently refer to astrology and divination and kindred subjects as if they were products of the ages of ignorance and are rapidly becoming non-existent ; but if they really believe this they have fallen into grievous error. We are told that ASTROLOGY is a pseudo-science, although it has been developed entirely on the lines of experiment and experience, and accurate records of facts. This development does not make it an exact science, but it is impossible not to be struck with the general accuracy of the readings of a large number of the characters of men and women which are based upon the readings of horoscopes. There are living among us parents who have had horoscopes made immediately after births of their children, and who bring up their children according to the directions supplied by the horoscopist. Similarly there are medical practitioners who have horoscopes of their patients made, and who use the information derived from them as a guide to the treatment which they eventually prescribe for their patients. Among one's friends and acquaintances are many men and women who have their horoscopes made annually, and who plan their work and travel and pleasure in accordance with the positions of the planets and the Signs of the Zodiac at the Vernal Equinox. The publication of the astrological works by Mr. Waite and " Sepharial " and Miss Adams and others proves that the number of astrologers and amateur astrologers in our country must be very great. Men have always believed that their lives are directed by the stars, and among a large proportion of the dwellers on the earth it will never die. The results which astrologers obtain sometimes are so remarkable, and their prognostications are so often fulfilled to the letter by subsequent events, that even the unbeliever is compelled to admit that there must be " something in it."

PALMISTRY likewise is dubbed a pseudo-science. It grew up in the East and made its way into Europe via India and Mesopotamia and Egypt. The Oriental experts in palmistry are usually learned and able men who are shrewd and wise judges of character, and they can undoubtedly give accurate estimates as to the nature of the past and present of men's lives by examining the lines of the hand. When palmistry came into being is unknown, but it seems to have been used as a means of divination by the earliest inhabitants of our earth. Parsee friends assert that the face and the palms of the hands supply a key to the true nature, character and disposition of every man. And every one who has seen the Parsee expert handling this key, and been able to check his statements subsequently, must admit that his character sketches are accurate, and that the fulfilment of his prophecies is so exact as to be uncanny. He can literally read faces and hands and the ability to do so enables him to avoid contact with bad and vicious men.

The art of CRYSTAL-GAZING, or " Scrying," is practised by many men and women, and some " gazers " obtain very remarkable results. There is no imposture when the " gaze " is honest, for the staring into the crystal globe hypnotizes the "gazer," and his mind falls into the state of the " seer " of old, who saw visions which he was unable to describe. In short, he goes into a sort of trance, which causes the optic nerve to stimulate the brain, and makes it dispatch visions along it into the eye. Excessive " Scrying " is harmful to the sight, and excess in the use of the ball of crystal should be carefully avoided. The skilled " gazer " can obtain just as good results for the enquirer by gazing into a mirror, or into water or a cup or bowl, or pail, or a pond, or water or ink cupped in the hand.

The belief in the existence of WITCHES has perished in our land, although at a few outlying districts in Western Scotland and Ireland " spae women " (or " wise women ") are said still to be found. But it must not be thought that the belief in WITCHCRAFT has died out, for such is not the case. There are in all large towns numbers of women who earn quite good livings by fortune-telling by cards and by trances in which they claim to hold converse with the dead, and to be able to bring the living and the dead together. These women make no pretence to read the past in the lives of their clients, but claim to foretell the futures of some of them, and it must be admitted that their efforts are sometimes extraordinarily successful, that is to say their prognostications are often fulfilled literally. An experienced and discreet clairvoyante numbers her clients by the score, and they belong to all classes— soldiers, sailors, politicians, civil servants, and ecclesiastics, besides a considerable number of women, titled and untitled. The wish to divine the future seems to be as general now as ever. Divining by means of trance is described as very exhausting for the diviner, and conscientious clairvoyantes say that they can only " work " for a limited number of hours each day, and that these hours must not be consecutive. The modern witch, male or female, no longer dispenses " hell broth " and decoctions of drugs, and philtres made from bats' eyes, and the insides of reptiles, and human fat, and the juice of adders, because the Law stands in the way, and she no longer travels through the air astride of a besom or broomstick. But there is little doubt that she still exercises her traditional wiles and crafts among civilized folk who pay her well for her trouble. It is only fair to say that she deceives herself as well as her clients.

The witch man of the West is much less to be feared or concerned about than his colleague in the

East. No one who has lived among Sûdânî peoples
and the Fâng people of West Africa and the devil-
ridden natives of the swamps of Lower Babylonia
can help believing that their witch-doctors possess
some kind of psychic power unknown to us. They
seem to kill their own enemies, and for payment
other people's enemies, by SUGGESTION, that is to
say, the witch doctor goes to a man and tells him
that he should die on or before a certain day, and
he follows this up by wishing intensively for the
man's death, and at length the man does actually
die. The witch doctor also seems to have the power
of " suggesting " blindness or rheumatism, or some
wasting disease which will cause the victim to
welcome death. The only answer that anyone who
has seen the witch-doctors of the East work can give
to the question, " Is it possible for any man, black
or white, to possess such a power of suggestion ? " is
" I do not know." When in the East the traveller
believes that it is possible and goes delicately, and is
afraid ; in the West he still believes but is unafraid.

Against the wearing of amulets little objection,
it seems to me, can be made. It may be foolish or
superstitious to wear and treasure inanimate objects,
even thought they be made of gold or silver or plati-
num or precious stones. The wearers gain from them
feelings of comfort and protection, and they often
represent the affection and love of friends. And
beautiful amulets evoke the admiration of their
wearers and their friends, and frequently satisfy
the lust of the eye for beauty. In the Near East
amulets are used universally and unashamedly. The
old camel postman who guided me from Damascus
to Baghdâd attributed our safe arrival to the five

blue beads which were fastened on the foreheads of
each of his camels. Such success as I had in collecting manuscripts in the Tiyârî country was also
attributed to the blue beads, and the Ḳur'ân amulets
which I bought there. Under the protection of a
small bag of dust from the tomb of Rabban Hôrmîzd
our caravan travelled from Môṣul through the country
of the Yazîdîs or Devil-worshippers, and under the
protection of a bag of dust from Ḳubbah Idrîs our
boat sailed in safety from Dulgo to Kôshah in the
Third Cataract. When the Shammar Arabs pillaged
our caravan and stole our food and clothes and
carried off our beasts they discussed the question
as to whether they should cut our throats or strip
us naked and turn us loose into the desert for God
to kill by thirst and cold. They did neither, but
Muḥammad Amîn assured me that we escaped only
because he was wearing on his breast an agate
plaque engraved with the Throne Verse from the
Ḳur'ân, and I had another in my cigar case. From
this it seems that Muslim amulets are tolerant of
Christians. The same authority assured me that
we were able to shoot two of the thieves who came
to steal two cases of indigo from our raft at Ḳal'ah
Sherḳât, and to slit our sheep skin bags and sink us,
because we had those two amulets in our possession.
To him the wearing of orthodox amulets was a species
of worship. It was the same in Egypt. The acrobats
refused to exhibit their sword dance until we gave
them time to put on their amulets, and the dancing
women of Ḳana and Mansûrah cheerfully divested
themselves of everything except the little neck
bands on which they wore their amulets. Dozens
of instances of a similar character might be quoted.

In the West, too, many great and distinguished
men had a firm belief in the power of their amulets
to protect them. The late Czar of Russia attached
great value to a ring which contained a piece of the
wood of the True Cross ; the ring had protected his
grandfather, but on the day in which he forgot
to take the ring with him he was assassinated
(SHARPER KNOWLSON, *Origins of Popular Superstitions*, p. 156). Mr. J. D. Rockefeller, a Non-
conformist, has for years carried in his pocket an
" eagle stone " in a hollow in which there are con-
cretions which rattle when the stone is shaken.
He regarded it as a charm against disease, shipwreck
and other calamities (*ibid.*, p. 10). The late Prof. W.
Wright, of Cambridge, a very hard-headed Scotsman,
wore by day and night a gold ring from Loango on
which were worked in wire the Twelve Signs of the
Zodiac. He used to say that he could never work
unless he had it on his finger. A colleague at
Cambridge being worsted in an official dispute with
him, cursed him by the ineffable Name of God,
and Wright believed that the fatal disease which
attacked him was due to this curse.

During the last fifty years the Egyptian scarab has
become a very favourite and popular amulet or
mascot because of the ideas of new life and resurrection which the Egyptians associated with it. But one
lady paid £50 for a pretty blue glazed porcelain scarab
of Queen Ḥatshepsut because she believed that she
was a reincarnation of the Great Queen, and had
in herself the divinity of the god Amen her father.
And another lady paid a large sum for a pretty
scarab of Queen Tî because she believed that she
was a reincarnation of that beautiful woman, whom

in features she thought she resembled. On the other hand many owners of scarabs have changed their opinions, and because they regarded them as sources of ill-luck and misfortune have presented them to the British Museum.

Paragraphs in the daily press often contain interesting reading about the objects which are chosen as mascots. The late Sir Henry Segrave always carried with him a rabbit's paw, which the negroes say is the luckiest thing in the world. The paw was with him at Daytona when he made all his great successes as the speed king. But when calamity overtook his boat and death claimed him the rabbit's paw was not with him ! (*Evening Standard*, June 14, 1930). The Australian cricketers had a large rubber kangaroo mascot, which one of their number knocked over and broke. Mr. Woodfull had it repaired and set up at once (*Evening Standard*, June 16, p. 11). Eight people killed an octopus near Corbière lighthouse in Jersey ; they took it back to their hotel and set it up as a mascot (*Daily Express*, June 17, p. 11). An instance of how the rabbit's paw saved the life and the money of a man is told in Mr. Ernest Poole's excellent story, *The Car of Croesus*, p. 164. When Hobbs went in to play he wanted 16 runs to beat Grace's record of 54,896 runs, and with him went a white sparrow ; the sparrow stayed until he scored 40 runs and then flew away. The bystanders said " Hobbs' luck has gone," and three balls later Hobbs was bowled (*Sunday Graphic*, August 10, 1930, p. 2). Surely one of the strangest mascots ever placed on a motor car is that of Mr. Somerset Maxwell : this is a tiny figure of a huntsman in pink, holding up a dead fox (*Evening Standard*, Oct. 15, p. 1).

" Fear," the Wisdom of Solomon saith, " is nothing else but a betraying of the succours which reason offereth " (xvii. 12). It is impossible not to conclude that it was man's fear which brought amulets into being, and that it is only his belief which endows them with power, and his implicit and invincible FAITH which makes them operative.

My grateful thanks are due to the Trustees of the British Museum for their permission to photograph extracts from—1, Mandaean, Samaritan and Syriac manuscripts ; 2, diagrams from MSS. of the Ḳabbâlâh ; 3, amulets and drawings from printed books, including the rare Book of Râzîêl ; and 4, a comprehensive collection of Sumerian, Babylonian, Assyrian, Phoenician, Pehlevi and other amulets. This work has been greatly facilitated through the kindness of my former colleagues, Dr. L. O. BARNETT, Keeper of the Department of Oriental Printed Books and Manuscripts, and Mr. J. D. LEVEEN, B.A., and their staff of Clerks. The selection of the amulets from Babylonia and Elam for publication was made by Mr. SIDNEY SMITH, of the British Museum. His translation of the texts explaining the use of the prophylactic and atropopaeic figures which Mr. WOOLLEY excavated at Ur of the Chaldees and described in a learned paper in the *Journal* of the Royal Asiatic Society, have brought to light many fundamental facts concerning early Mesopotamian religion. The co-operation of the trained philologist and the expert excavator has produced most excellent results. To Mr. C. J. GADD, of the British Museum, I am indebted for many facts concerning ancient Babylonian beliefs about precious stones, and for the information about the clay model of a sheep's liver in the British Museum, which his researches have made available. Further, I am greatly indebted to Dr. MOSES GASTER, Chief Rabbi of the Sephardic Communities in England, for permission to publish several extracts from the *Corpus* of his works which he published this year under the title of *Studies and Texts in Magic, Folklore, Samaritan Archaeology*, 3 vols., 1923-28. Much has been written by commentators and others about the phylacteries which are mentioned in the New Testament, what they were and what they were not, etc., but Dr. Gaster was the first to publish phylactery-texts, and to translate and explain not only the language of the Samaritans, but also their philosophy and their religion.

During the writing of this book I have consulted many works on the so-called " Occult Sciences," and read many scores of papers and articles on the various subjects which I have dealt with in the following pages. The more useful to the student are undoubtedly the volumes of Dr. S. SELIGMANN. This distinguished author has shown that amulets and amuletic objects are the result of the belief of man in the EVIL EYE, and its far-reaching and terrible power. This he has made clear in his works, *Der böse Blick und Verwandter*, 2 vols., 1910, and *Die Zauberkraft der Auges*, 1922, and they will form the standard works on the subject for many years to come. The Kabbâlâh is a great fount of occultism and mysticism as well as forming a great system of religious philosophy. The *Kabbala Denudata* by Baron von ROSENROTH (1677-78), and the *Kabbâlâh* by Ginsburg (1865), and the works of Mr. WAITE are very useful books on the subject, but the practical

side of Ḳabbâlâh is very successfully handled by
Dr. ERICH BISCHOFF, a skilled Hebraist, in his
Die Kabbalah (Einführung), Leipzig, 1923, and more
fully in his larger work, *Die Elemente der Kabbalah*,
2 vols., 1920. The student will also find much of
interest in the German translations of the old books
of magic by PETER of Abano, PICTORIUS of Villingen,
GERHARD of Cremona, in LINDEN'S edition of
CORNELIUS AGRIPPA, 3 vols., Berlin, 1921. The
extracts from Mr. MONTGOMERY'S translations of the
texts on the terra-cotta " devil-traps " found at
Babylon and Niffar well illustrate the character of
the magic of the MANDAEANS.

The addition of a Bibliography to a volume already
bulky was unnecessary, because the works of the
principal authorities are named in the various
chapters. Those who wish to explore occult literature, both ancient and modern, more fully should
consult the lists of books and papers given by
Dr. Seligmann, and the invaluable SUBJECT-Index
volumes published by the British Museum. The
long and very full Index which I have added
will, I hope, make reference to this book easy.
My thanks are also due to Messrs. G. A. Crane,
S. J. Wadlow and the Readers of the staff of
Messrs. Harrison & Sons, Ltd., for many practical
suggestions which I have gladly adopted.

E. A. WALLIS BUDGE.

21st October, 1930.

48, BLOOMSBURY STREET,
    BEDFORD SQUARE, W.C.1.

AMULETS AND
SUPERSTITIONS

CHAPTER I.

THE UNIVERSAL USE OF AMULETS DUE TO MAN'S BELIEF IN THE EXISTENCE OF DEMONS AND EVIL SPIRITS.

IN every place in our own country and in foreign lands where excavations on the sites of ancient cities have been made, the spade of the excavator has brought to light a number of objects of various kinds and sizes which we may call generally AMULETS and TALISMANS, and regard as the works of men who were believers in MAGIC. The use of these objects was not confined to any one place, or people, or period, and the great mass of the evidence about the matter now available justifies the statement that the use of amulets and talismans was and, it may be added, still is, universal. We may even go further and say that it is coeval with the existence of *Homo sapiens* on the earth. It is natural to ask why amulets and talismans are so numerous, and so widely distributed over the earth, and what purpose they served? The answer to these questions is not far to seek. Early man lived days of misery and nights of anxiety and fear, not to say terror. To feed himself and his woman and their children was often difficult, and to avoid or overcome the beasts and reptiles which were his natural enemies must have taxed his wit and strength to the uttermost ; and the fear of the unknown dangers of the darkness and night, when

the beasts of prey were prowling round his cave
or his thicket, added greatly to his misery. In
some places the vicissitudes of climate laid an

Face of the very early Babylonian demon Humbaba, whose voice was like
that of a storm, and whose breath was like a hurricane. He was con-
quered by Gilgamish, King of Erach, and Enkidu. The face is formed of
a single raised line, the twistings of which represent the convolutions of
the entrails, and form the features. How the demon came to have his
face represented thus is discussed by SIDNEY SMITH in the Liverpool
Annals, vol. xi. p. 107 f.

The above rough tracing made from Plate V of the *Journal of the
Royal Asiatic Society*, July, 1926, is published with the kind permission
of the Council of the Society. The original is in the British Museum,
No. 116737.

additional burden upon him and he had to be ever
on the watch in order to frustrate the attacks of
his human enemies. The physical difficulties which

he faced and triumphed over were indeed sufficient to trouble and exhaust him; but, though *why* he did so is inexplicable, he proceeded to fashion in his mind a whole host of invisible, hostile beings, DEVILS, DEMONS and EVIL SPIRITS. These, he believed, not only had the power to curse him and everything he had, but also to cast upon him and his woman and beasts the EVIL EYE, and he went daily and hourly in terror lest they should do so. He attributed all his bodily ills and ailments to the operations of the evil spirits, and any and every misfortune that might befall any member of his family and his servants and other possessions. He attributed horrible forms to them, and thought them capable of assuming any disguises, animal or human, which would enable them to work their wicked wills on him. The men and women who openly made themselves servants of the evil spirits he regarded as MAGICIANS and WITCHES, and he believed that they as well as the evil spirits could, at will, do him incalculable harm, and compass his death. As time went on his fear of evil spirits did not diminish; on the other hand, it increased, and each generation became more devil-ridden than its predecessor. The civilized Sumerians, Babylonians, and Egyptians, like the savages or half-civilized peoples who were their neighbours, were as much obsessed by the fear of evil spirits as their savage ancestors who had lived in Mesopotamia and Egypt some thousands of years before them. This, in the case of the Sumerians and Babylonians, is made quite clear by the great Legend of the Creation, written in cuneiform, which has come down to us.

THE EVIL SPIRITS OF BABYLONIA.

According to this Legend the great primeval, watery abyss called APSÛ was the home of both devils and gods, *i.e.* evil spirits and good spirits ; the abyss and its inhabitants had existed from everlasting. The evil spirits had hideous forms, part animal, part bird, part reptile and part human ; the good spirits were in the image of men. After a countless series of aeons had passed two gods appeared, ANSHAR and KISHAR, and they performed some preliminary act of creation, and after another very long period of time had elapsed the great gods of Babylonia, among them ANU, the Sky-god, BÊL, the Earth-god, and EA, god of the watery abyss, came into being. These gods began the work of ordering Creation, and in so doing caused APSÛ to be greatly troubled. This god saw with dismay that chaos, of which he was the symbol and type, was doomed to disappear as a result of the operations of the gods, and he took counsel with TIÂMAT and began to evolve plans to destroy the works and powers of the gods. Tiâmat is shown by native reliefs and figures to have had the scaly body of a Typhonic animal or serpent, and to have possessed wings and claws. She was the personification of all evil, yet, strange to say, she was the " mother of everything," and was the keeper of the TABLET of DESTINIES, probably a sort of talisman by means of which she preserved her being. APSÛ and TIÂMAT sent forth an envoy called MUMMU to obstruct the work of EA, but in the fight which followed EA was the conqueror, and TIÂMAT'S plan was defeated and APSÛ was slain. Then TIÂMAT spawned a brood of devilish monsters, and she and her male counterpart KINGU collected their hosts of evil beings, and made ready to fight the gods ; and the TABLET of DESTINIES was transferred to KINGU by TIÂMAT to assist him in gaining the victory over them.

The gods, feeling themselves unable to cope with TIÂMAT, nominated MARDUK, their champion, and having bestowed upon him all their powers this god armed himself with a bow, spear, a club and a net, and set out to do battle with TIÂMAT. When KINGU saw MARDUK arrayed in his terrible panoply of war, he was terrified and stumbled about and took refuge in the body of TIÂMAT, and all his allies became stupefied with fear. When MARDUK approached TIÂMAT she recited the spells and incantations which she believed to render him powerless, but they had no effect upon him. Straightway he cast his net over her, and blew a gale of wind into her through her mouth, and as soon as her body was blown up like a bladder he drove his spear through her hide, and she split asunder and her womb fell out from her. He took the TABLET of DESTINIES from Kingu's breast, and then one by one he caught the Eleven Allies of Tiâmat in his net and trampled upon them. He smashed in the skull of TIÂMAT with his club and, having split her body into two parts, he fashioned the vault of heaven out of one of them, and out of the other he constructed the abode of EA or the World-Ocean.

This done, MARDUK set to work to arrange the heavens and the earth and everything which is in them in the order in which they now are. As the gods complained to him that there was no one to worship them or to bring offerings to them, MARDUK, after consultation with the other gods, determined to create man. He proposed that one of the gods should be sacrificed, so that the others might be rendered free of service, and the gods decided that KINGU should suffer death because he had been the commander-in-chief of the forces of evil which had opposed MARDUK. Thereupon KINGU was seized and bound in fetters, and slain, and EA fashioned man from his blood for the service of the gods. Man therefore had in him the taint of evil which always prompted him to evil ways and deeds.

The Babylonian story of the Creation makes it quite clear that MARDUK conquered all the ringleaders of the revolt against the gods, but he did not destroy the hosts of evil utterly, and these remained in existence to vex and harass and injure men who were descended from the man who had been made from the evil blood of Kingu. Thus MARDUK'S victory was not complete and absolute, for he did not destroy evil once and for all. He safeguarded himself and his fellow-gods, but men were left by him to be the prey of the evil spirits which had escaped from his wrath. The enormous number of clay tablets in the great Museums of the world, inscribed in cuneiform with spells and incantations against devils and evil spirits, prove that the Babylonians were far more afraid of evil spirits than of their gods.

THE EVIL SPIRITS OF EGYPT.

The Literature of Ancient Egypt does not supply us with any detailed account of the Creation, but the texts state briefly that there was a time when nothing existed except a mass of dark and inert water, of great and indefinite extent, called

Nu or Nenu. It was covered by dense darkness, and was the abode of a god called Neberdjer, who existed there either in the form of a liquid or essence, or in *name* only, and of a host of creatures in Typhonic forms who are called " *Mesu Beṭshu*,"

The god Khepera, *i.e.* the " Generator," in the form of a beetle-headed man, seated in his phantom or " spirit " boat, which is sailing over the waters of the primeval Ocean called Nu or Nenu. Motion was given to the boat by the hawk-headed paddle which possessed magical power.

i.e. spawn of rebellious malice. The god took counsel with his heart, and possessing magical power (*heka*), he uttered his own name as a spell or word of power, and he straightway came into being under the form of the god Khepera, and began the work of creation. The inert powers of evil were disturbed by his actions and at once began to oppose him actively. The making of light was the first act of creation, and the fight between SET, the personification of darkness and night and evil, and ḤER-UR, the personification of light and day and night, began. The Day was established, but so was the Night, and thus matters stood for a long period. KHEPERA next created a god, SHU, and a goddess, TEFNUT, from matter ejected from his body, and thus was formed the first triad or TRINITY. The work of creation proceeded rapidly and the heavens and the earth were fashioned ; the sun, moon, and stars were assigned their places in the sky, men and women were formed from the tears which dropped from the eyes of KHEPERA, and animals, birds and reptiles appeared on the earth. Then SET collected his powers of darkness and evil, and waged war against the Sun-god Rā and was defeated. He next set the monster ĀPEP in the eastern part of the sky so that he and his allies might destroy the Sun-god Rā, and prevent him rising upon our world. Rā sent forth his rays and darts of fire and scattered the allies of ĀPEP, and he cast a spell upon ĀPEP himself which paralysed him and reduced him to impotence. The Sun-god rose in the heavens triumphantly and continued his course across the sky until the evening, when he disappeared into the darkness of night. But when he wished to rise on the following morning he found all his enemies lying in wait for him, for ĀPEP had recovered his strength and surrounded himself with his old allies, and the fight with the Sun-god was renewed and enacted daily. Thus Rā never gained an absolute victory over Āpep, and he failed to slay him, and as a result his evil spirits were able to attack men and to harm them spiritually and physically.

In spite of the high character of their religion, the Egyptians found it necessary to burn daily a wax figure of ĀPEP in the great temple of AMEN-Rā at Thebes, and to recite numerous spells in order to prevent that monster from obstructing the course

Rā, the self-created, self-existent, and everlasting Sun-god, who caused his material body to come into being by pronouncing his own secret NAME, which was unknown to mortal ever.

THOTH, the mind and tongue of Rā, the Word-god, through whose utterances all things material come into being. He invented writing and was the first writer of magical and religious books, and the author of spells, incantations, etc.

of the Sun-god and from working destruction upon themselves through the operations of the spirits of evil. The Egyptians embraced Christianity in the first century of our Era, but retained their belief in evil spirits and in the efficacy of amulets and talismans, and magic, as means of defence against them ; and they believe this at the present day. The greater number of the modern Egyptians are

MUHAMMADANS, but though they confess many times daily their belief in the almightiness of ALLÂH, their fear of evil spirits is very great, and they resort to many forms of magic for protection for themselves and their families and their beasts and cattle.

EVIL SPIRITS IN CHRISTIAN LANDS.

Several Christian Apocrypha contain the statement, based upon Hebrew traditions written after the Captivity, that God created nine classes of angels who were divided into three groups, viz. :— 1. Cherubim, Seraphim and Thrones. 2. Lords, Powers and Rulers. 3. Principalities, Archangels and Angels. The Egyptian and Ethiopian Churches hold the view that MICHAEL, " the angel of the Face," was the commander-in-chief of all these angels, and that he and all the angels of his class were created during the first hour of the sixth day of Creation, *i.e.* on Friday. But another class of angels, the tenth, was created on that day, towards the evening, and its commander was SATNÂÊL or SATAN. The creation of ADAM followed that of the angels, and when Satan saw the great honour which GOD bestowed upon the first man he was filled with wrath. A week later he usurped the honour due to God, and declared war on the hosts of the Almighty. These consisted of horsemen, shield-bearers, charioteers, torch-bearers, dagger-bearers, axe-bearers, cross-bearers, lamp-bearers and slingers, in number about 4,100,000 beings of fire. The angels uttered their battle cries and prepared to fight, but Satan charged them and put them to flight ; the divine hosts reformed and renewed the fight, but Satan charged them and put them to flight a second time.

God then sent to His hosts a Cross of Light on which was inscribed the names of the Three Persons of the Trinity, and when Satan and his devils saw this, their strength oozed out of them and they became faint, and turned their backs and fled. MICHAEL and the angels pursued them, and drove them down into hell, where they are still believed to dwell by many Christian peoples. None of the founders of the great religions of the world have attempted to teach their followers that the Devil, by whatever name he may be called, and the spirits of evil have been destroyed. In some religious systems the Devil and God have been regarded as almost equal though opposing powers, and there have not been wanting peoples, *e.g.* the YAZÎDÎS, who worshipped the Devil. And even in Europe there are many more adherents to Satanism than is commonly thought.

The mind of primitive man was not sufficiently advanced to enable him to understand stories of the fight between the Devil and God, *i.e.* Darkness and Evil, and Good and Light, such as have been described in the preceding paragraphs, still less to invent them. It seems to have been instinct rather than reason which directed him to the use of amulets and talismans as a means of defence against the Evil Eye and the attacks of evil spirits, and which induced him to believe that the things which he chose as amulets possessed some innate power to protect him. But before further consideration of this question we must try to find out what the words " amulet " and " ṭalismân " really mean and, supposing we can find their correct, or even probable, meanings, whether they will tell us what was the idea in the mind of primitive man which underlay his use of amulets.

" AMULET " AND " TALISMÂN."

The word AMULET is borrowed from the Latin AMULÊTUM, which we find in PLINY, who uses the word to indicate (1) an object which preserves a man from some trouble ; (2) medical or prophylactic treatment ; and (3) a substance used in medicine. He says that the European cyclamen prevents all magical arts from coming near the place where it is planted, and that it is therefore called " amulet " (*Nat. Hist.*, xxv. p. 115) ; that if a living bat be carried round the house, and nailed to a window with its head downwards, it will act as an " amulet " (*ibid.*, xxix. p. 83) ; the large, indented horns of the scarabaeus, attached to the bodies of infants, have all the virtues of an " amulet " (*ibid.*, xxx. p. 130) ; it is useful to tie a piece of amber to delicate children as an " amulet " (*ibid.*, xxvii. p. 51) ; all over the East men wear jasper as an " amulet " (*ibid.*, xxvii. p. 117) ; in connection with the use of another " amulet " the user had to spit upon urine and into the shoe of the right foot (*ibid.*, xxviii. p. 88) ; the blood of the basilisk is regarded as a remedy for various diseases, and as an " amulet " which will protect a man from spells and incantations (*ibid.*, xxix. p. 66) ; the gall of a black dog is an " amulet " for the whole house, if it be cleaned or fumigated therewith (xxxi. p. 82). One ancient writer thought that " amulet " was equivalent to " phylactery," and according to another it meant something which drove away the Evil Eye ; but no one seems to have known the exact meaning of the word. Some have connected " amulet " with the sacramental vessel called ἄμη and others with ἅμμα, a knot

or band, and ἄμυλον, or amylum, but it is unlikely
that any one of these suggested derivations, except
the last, will be accepted. In many books it is
stated that " amulet " is derived from the Arabic
ḥimâla, which the lexicographer DOZY says is the
word for the cord by which an amulet is suspended
from the neck, as well as for the amulet itself.
HÖFLER thought that " amulet " was derived from
some lost Etruscan word, or from an Etruscan word
to which the Latin suffix ĕto was added. SELIGMANN
(Heil und Schutzmittel, Stuttgart, 1920, p. 26) is
of opinion that " amulet " is derived from the Old
Latin AMOLETUM, i.e. a " means of defence," and
this derivation seems to me to be the best of those
which have been suggested.

We shall never know exactly what meaning was
attached to the word " amulet " by its inventor, or
by those who first used one, or even by PLINY, but
clearly it was different from the meaning which we
attach to it to-day. To us an " amulet " is an object
which is endowed with magical powers, and which of
its own accord uses these powers ceaselessly on behalf of the person who carries it, or causes it to be
laid up in his house, or attaches it to some one of his
possessions, to protect him and his belongings from
the attacks of evil spirits or from the Evil Eye.

As for " TALISMAN," the derivation and meaning
of this strange word are difficult to determine.
It is found in Arabic under the forms ṭilasm and
ṭillasm, plural ṭalâsim, ṭilasmât and ṭilassamât, and
the root ṭalisam means " to make marks like a
magician." But there is little evidence that the
Arabs borrowed the word from the Greek τέλεσμα,
one of the meanings of which is a " consecrated

religious object." The object of the talisman is quite different from that of the amulet. The amulet is supposed to exercise its protective powers on behalf of the individual or thing continually, whereas the talisman is only intended to perform one specific task. Thus a talisman may be placed in the ground with money or treasure, which it is expected to protect and to do nothing else. But the line which divides the amulet from the talisman has rarely been observed by any people who regard such things as parts of the machinery of magic, and in modern times the use and meanings of the two objects are generally confounded, even by educated folk who are superstitious. And the experts are not agreed on the subject.

BULLA, FASCINUM AND FETISH.

BULLA was the name given to a certain kind of amulet by the Romans and Christians during the early centuries of our Era ; its primary meaning is some object which is rounded and inflated or swollen, e.g. a bubble, the boss of a shield, a metal stud, the head of nail or door-bolt, etc. This amulet was made of wood or metal, and was worn by the living as an ornament, and also buried with the dead ; in shape it resembled a flat, rounded capsule, with a little loop at the top. When made of metal it was often engraved with magical figures and inscriptions, and it was filled with some substance to which magical powers and properties were attributed, this substance being the real amulet. Thus the complete Bulla was an amulet in its case. The substance in the case was called *praebia*, and was composed of various ingredients, each of which was believed to drive away evil from the wearer and to defeat the machinations of witches and magicians. The Christians (Copts) of AKHMÎM in Upper Egypt tied bullae to the necks of their dead, and they contained dust from a saint's tomb, or dust made from saints' bones, or some small bone or other sacred relic.

The Greeks and Romans believed firmly that certain men had the power to harm their fellows, and even to kill them, and to destroy cattle by looking at them. The Greek βασκαινειν means to "kill with a glance of the eye." The amulet used against the Evil Eye ὀφθαλμὸς βάσκανος was called BASKANION or PROBASKANION, and FASCINUM, and it was usually in the form of the PHALLUS. As children were specially liable to be attacked by the Evil Eye, models of the phallus were hung round their necks (Varro, De Lingua Lat., vii. pp. 97, 107). It was used as a house-amulet and was also placed in gardens, and in front of blacksmiths' forges, and even under chariots. Other names of the phallus amulet were mutonium, scaevola, and Satyrica signa; for the last name see Pliny, Nat. Hist., xix. p. 19, §1.

FETISH.

The word FETISH is of Portuguese origin. Some derive it from " feitiço," i.e. something which is made by the hand, and is therefore regarded as artificial, and unnatural, and later the word comes to mean magical ; others derive it from " faticeira," i.e. " witch," or from " faticaria," i.e. " witch- craft." The word was, as DR. NASSAU says, originally applied to the amulets and talismans, e.g. crucifixes, crosses, rosaries, images of saints, relics, etc., which

were in use among the Roman Catholic natives on
the west coast of Africa in the XVth and XVIth
centuries. The natives themselves used quite other
words to describe their amulets and talismans which
they regarded as " Medicine," because they healed
sicknesses as well as warded off evils. Thus
we have " Gri-gri," " Juju," " Wong," " Monda,"
" Mkissi," " Biang," etc.

The religions of the negro peoples on the west
coast of Africa and elsewhere is commonly known
as FETISHISM. According to some travellers and
students, the natives believe that the fetish contains a god or spirit which the priest can keep
there and command to do his will ; but such
is not the case. This view is the result of a
misconception, and is due to the teachings of the
Christian missionaries who did not understand the
natives' views about the fetish, or realize the fact
that it only contained MEDICINE. There is no doubt,
as SELIGMANN says, that there are two kinds of
fetishes, viz. the natural or *simple fetish*, and the
artificial fetish, which is either charged or impreg-
nated with " medicine," *i.e.* some substance which
is supposed to possess magical properties and to be
also prophylactic in character. The *simple fetish*
corresponds roughly to our amulets and talismans,
and the objects forming them are simple in nature,
and are easily made, and they produce their effects
by means of the native power which dwells in them.
They are commonly employed for household purposes. The *artificial fetish* contains two substances,
viz. the substance which possesses magical powers,
and the " medicine," which is really an extract, or a
decoction, or an essential form of some well-known

medicine. The choice of the magical substance is the secret of the medicine man, and he alone decides what magical substance and what " medicine " to mix together in order to obtain the result desired by the man or woman who wants the fetish. Like modern physicians in England and Europe, each medicine man has his own particular methods in the making of fetishes, and there are fetish specialists in Africa as there are specialist physicians in Harley Street.

The medicines used by the medicine man are substantially the same as those mentioned in Egyptian Medical Papyri, and medical tablets written in cuneiform, and in Arabic and Ethiopian Books of Medicine. One of the most complete lists of such medicines is given by PECHUËL-LOESCHE, who enumerates :—Leaves, flowers, juices, fruits, roots, rinds of fruits and vegetables, bushes, trees, and climbing plants ; the gall, whiskers and dung of leopards, the gall of the crocodile, heads of snakes, frogs, lizards, turtles, and fish ; crabs, scorpions, and all kinds of reptiles, the eyes, brains, livers and feathers of certain birds ; hides, hair, paws, and dung of beasts which are swift, strong and courageous ; teeth, horns and bones ; resin, coloured earths, spittle, salt, powder of red-wood, the milk of women and the urine of virgins. No part of a man or a pig is used in " medicine " for fetish purposes. The substance possessing the magical powers may be laid upon objects of dress, or placed in a purse or bag, or laid up for safety in the figure of a man or animal ; and it is believed that the " medicine " administered will be more efficacious if it also contains the personal strength of the medicine man himself.

The objects with which the medicine man surrounds himself or hangs upon his person are very
numerous, and among them may be mentioned :—
Mussel-shells, talons of birds and claws of animals,
teeth, horns, feathers, locks or tufts of hair, strips
of leather, cords, string, rags, bags, pieces of earth,
balls of resin, leaves, fruits, plates, dishes, bottles,
pots, chains, baskets, stumps of wood, rolls of cloth,
bits of sacking, boxes, images made of wood, metal,
bones, ivory, figures of apes, leopards, serpents,
crocodiles, hippopotami, elephants, men, etc. Many
of the fetishes on the west coast of AFRICA are
decorated with pieces of looking-glass or mirrors,
which are placed on the body, back or front, or on
the face, and sometimes mirrors take the places of
eyes in the large fetish figures. Mirrors were
introduced into the country by the Christian
EUROPEANS, and the natives at once associated
them with " white man's magic," and made use of
them in the way here stated in order to increase
the power of their own magic. Another form of the
fetish figure also seems to be due to the missionaries
who brought with them pictures of the Crucifixion.
On the coast of LOANGO the natives made a wooden
figure in the form of a man, and drove nails into it
until the whole body was covered with nails and
fragments of iron ; one such " nail-fetish " mentioned
by Seligmann had a crown of thorns fixed on its
head, and small box-shaped attachments in which
the " medicine " was placed. Some authorities
think that the medicine man who made such figures
borrowed the idea of the box-shaped attachments
from the reliquaries of the Roman Catholic missionaries.

THE ORIGIN AND DEVELOPMENT OF THE AMULET.

The amulets worn by primitive men and women were made of simple natural substances, and at first were chosen simply because they were of unusual form and colour, or because their substance was new to them. The oldest amulets were the objects which roused man's curiosity, or excited his wonder and admiration, and his natural love of possession led him to make them his own property, and to take them to his dwelling. Among such objects were leaves of unusual form and colour, berries, nuts, and fruits, and the seeds and roots of trees and plants. Any strange vegetable growth, *e.g.* mandragora roots, always possessed a strong fascination for him. In the same way stones of unusual colours, or having markings on them, or veins of different colours running through them, *e.g.* the marbles and the agates, or containing pyrites, or having striae in them, were promptly taken possession of by him, and carried home. A stone which had become perforated naturally was especially prized by him, and to the first man who threaded such a stone on grass, or on a thong cut from the skin of some animal, and then hung it round his neck, belongs the credit of having introduced the wearing of amulets into the world. The perforated stone suggested to him the boring of other stones which he used as amulets, and which he could then hang on his body, and next the perforation of the beads which his women up to that time had attached to their bosoms by means of mud. At a very early period the properties of rock-salt, rock-alum, and rock-crystal would add to the attraction of their appearance, and the sparkle in them probably suggested dimly to him that they possessed life like himself. The portions of their bodies with which animals and reptiles slew their prey also attracted his attention, and hence the horns, claws, teeth and tails of animals, and the skin of serpents, were used as amulets at a very early period. The dwellers on the sea-coast, and on lakes filled with fish, made amulets of shells and parts of fishes ; and little fingers, toes, eyes, phalli and hair of human beings have been regarded as powerful amulets in many countries. Objects coloured white, blue, red and yellow have more often been chosen as amulets than those which were grey or brown or black. As soon as man learned the art of working in metals he made many amulets, in many forms, in gold, silver, copper and iron. When he had learned to write figures of men, animals, birds, fish, trees and plants cut in stone or wood, or drawn upon some substance which served as a writing material, were also used by him as amulets ; and at length large stones covered all over with inscriptions, pyramids, the walls of the corridors and chambers of which were covered with hundreds of lines of text, tombs, inscribed coffins and rolls of papyri, volumes of sacred writings, obelisks, colossal stone figures, etc., were considered as amulets, and were expected to protect in one way or another those who caused them to be made.

We shall never know accurately what primitive man expected his various amulets to do for him, or how he thought they worked for his good, but it is quite clear from the number and variety of them that there was no one amulet which he believed to be capable of protecting him from *every* danger.

We may divide amulets into two classes :
(1) PERSONAL and INDIVIDUAL, and (2) GENERAL.
The most important of the personal class were those
which protected a man from sickness and disease,
and preserved and increased his natural strength
and virility, especially in the procreation of children.
Another important group comprised those which
protected the pregnant woman and preserved her
from miscarriages, and gave her easy delivery, and
a full and regular supply of milk when nursing her
children. The male child was protected by amulets
either attached to his neck or hidden in some portion
of his apparel, and the female child by amulets laid
upon or tied to various parts of her body. Special
dangers, e.g. plague, pestilence, sun-stroke, death
by lightning and the attacks of wild beasts, scorpion
stings, snake-bite, wounds inflicted in battle, drown-
ing, etc., had to be guarded against by special
amulets. The mariner carried amulets to preserve
him from shipwreck and death by sea-monsters, the
business man relied on amulets to give him success
in his trafficking, and in amulets the caravan man
sought safety for himself and his asses or camels.
The crops of the farmer were protected by amulets
placed either in the earth or hung above them, and
amulets were attached to the horns or foreheads
of prominent beasts in his herds, and amuletic
signs were marked on certain members of his flocks
to frighten wild beasts away from them. It was
necessary for every amulet to be powerful enough
to overcome the influence of the Evil Eye, and every
attack of the evil spirits which were regarded as the
instigators of every sickness, disease, accident, misfortune and calamity.

Among GENERAL AMULETS may be included those which were hidden in the walls of houses or under them, and those which were placed at the entrances to the villages, and in certain parts of them. Primitive man judged the potency of an amulet by results. If, having adopted a certain object as an amulet, his affairs prospered and he remained in good health, his belief in it was increased and he regarded it as a precious possession, and his neighbours congratulated him on his good fortune. But if his affairs did not prosper and trouble came upon him, his belief in the amulet ceased, and he abandoned it in favour of another. Amulets might be lost or stolen, and in such cases, it seems, they either lost their beneficent powers or withheld them from their finders or new owners.

Why certain objects were chosen as amulets is quite clear in some cases, but in others we can only guess at the reasons. Thus a man carried the claws and teeth of lions and tigers and other savage and powerful animals because he believed they would add to his strength in fighting wild beasts and human foes. He thought that the feathers of birds would add to the rapidity of his movements, and swiftness in attacking man and beast, and make his eyesight more keen. An amulet of serpent skin would add to his craftiness and cunning in the chase and so on. Some amulets may be described as HOMOEOPATHIC, for " medicine " made from yellow coloured plants and flowers, and water in which yellow stones had been washed, was given to patients suffering from jaundice, and red stones were worn to stop bleedings, blood fluxes and wounds from bleeding overmuch.

In other words, it was believed that there was some intimate connection or relationship between the yellow plant and stone and the yellow colour of the body afflicted with jaundice. Similarly, the red colour of the stone and blood were thought to be connected, and so on. Various explanations of the use of homoeopathic and other amulets by savages and semi-civilized peoples have been given by scientific anthropologists, but none of them can be made to explain the use of all the known kinds of amulets, and it is more than probable that all are wrong.

The truth seems to be that primitive man believed that every object which he used as an amulet possessed, either as a result of its natural formation or through the operation of some supernatural spirit which had incorporated itself in it, a power which to him was invisible. It was this power, which existing in everything, animate and inanimate, turned every object into an amulet, and as such it became a prized possession. This power was, so to speak, brought into activity or operation by the person who carried it, and then it performed his wish and will. The amulet was no longer merely passive matter, but an operating force. This force or power is called by the Melanesians and Polynesians " Mâna," and the greatest authority on magic and religion in the Pacific, the Rev. R. H. CODRINGTON, describes it thus : " Mâna is a power or influence, not physical, and in a way supernatural ; but it shows ïtself in physical force, or in any kind of power or excellence which a man possesses. This Mâna is not fixed in anything, and can be carried in almost anything ; but spirits, whether disembodied souls or supernatural beings, have it and can impart it, and it essentially belongs to personal beings to originate it, though it may act through the medium of water, or a stone, or a bone " (*The Melanesians*, Oxford, 1891, p. 119). It works to affect everything which is beyond the ordinary power of men, outside the common processes of nature, it is present in the atmosphere of life, attaches itself to persons and to things, and is manifested by results which can only be ascribed to its operation. Wizards, doctors, weather mongers, prophets, diviners, dreamers, all alike, everywhere in the islands work by this power (*ibid.*, p. 192). " Mâna is the stuff through which magic works ; it is not the trick itself, but the power whereby the sorcerer does the trick " (E. CLODD, *Magic in Names*. London, 1920, p. 3).

From the practical point of view Mâna may be used either for good or evil, and healing medicine and poison are alike regarded as Mâna. In short, all traffickings with the unseen and occult, whether licit or illicit, involve Mâna. As regards the meaning to be attached to Mâna from a scientific point of view, Dr. R. R. MARETT says: " There is no reason why, for the general purposes of comparative science, Mâna should not be taken to cover all cases of magico-religious efficacy, whether the efficacy be conceived as automatic or derived, *i.e.* as proceeding immediately from the nature of the sacred person or thing, or mediately because a ghost or spirit has put it into the person or thing in question " (HASTINGS' *Encyclopaedia*, vol. viii. p. 377, col. 2). We may then say that every effective amulet was believed to possess Mâna, which re-acted to the Mâna and will or wish of its possessor, and that it is this belief, whether formulated or not, which has induced man in all ages to rely upon amulets for protection and assistance. This belief was the outcome of men's fear of unseen evil spirits and their works, and the Evil Eye, and this fear is as real and powerful in some countries at the present day as it was in primitive times.

We may rest assured that as soon as the medicine man, or magician, saw that his fellow men needed amulets, he promptly took means to supply them, and that he spared himself no pains in proving to them that he alone was able to supply them with " genuine " amulets, *i.e.* those which contained Mâna and were able to fulfil their owner's desires. He claimed that he himself was filled with Mâna, which had been incorporated in him by his ancestral spirits, that he was able to hold converse with every kind of spirit, good and bad, and that he knew their wills and was able to influence their actions; and in addition to this he claimed to have special knowledge of the various natural objects which contained Mâna, and how to add to that Mâna the Mâna which was inherent in himself. And when the medicine man, or magician, died his colleagues or successor proclaimed that magic could be worked not only by parts of his body, but also by his apparel and possessions, and even by the earth or dust from the place where he was buried. In fact, each and every object that had belonged to him or was connected with him possessed Mâna, and was a powerful amulet. It is this belief that makes the boatman on the NILE in NUBIA tie a little bagful of dust

from ḲUBBAH IDRÎS to the bows of his boat to save
him from shipwreck in the Third Cataract. The
Nestorian caravan-men at MÔṢUL and in its neighbourhood carry with them dust from the tomb of
Rabban HORMÎZD at AL-ḲÔSH, and the Jacobites
seek protection in the dust from the tomb of MÂR
MATTAI. The Persian Muslims carry away dust
from the tomb of their saints at KARBALA, and the
Arabs make amulets of the dust from the tomb of
MUḤAMMAD the Prophet. The cult of the relics of
saints springs from the belief that their bodies,
whether living or dead, possessed Mâna, and in
the Middle Ages at least men did not seem to care
whether the relics were genuine or " faked." This
is proved by SELIGMANN, who states (*op. cit.*, p. 49)
that the praeputium Christi is shown in ROME,
CHARROUX, ANTWERP, PARIS, BRÜGGE, BOULOGNE,
BESANÇON, NANCY, METZ, LE PUY, CONQUES,
HILDESHEIM and CALCUTTA, and is venerated as a
genuine relic.

The Mâna which existed naturally in objects
which were chosen for amulets was, so to speak,
increased and " fixed " by the formulas or spells
which the magician pronounced over them. In
other words, the spell itself was Mâna, and if the
objects were without Mâna before its utterance, from
the moment the words were spoken they became
" working " amulets. Words, like blood and hair,
and saliva, contained Mâna and without the utterance of the formula or spell no " medicine " had
or could have any good, still less full, effect. When
the priest, in course of time, superseded the
magician, the prayer superseded the spell. The
spell was a command, the prayer an entreaty. We

are justified in assuming that spells were transmitted orally from one generation of magicians to another for many centuries, and even after men learned the art of writing the conservative magician would cling to the methods of his predecessors and refuse to make use of the new-fangled invention. But at length he realized that his spells were made permanent by the written characters, and the inscribed amulet, or " CHARM," as it is often called, came into being.

The SUMERIANS, BABYLONIANS and ASSYRIANS wrote their spells on clay tablets, which were often baked in furnaces ; the EGYPTIANS wrote them on papyri, slabs of calcareous stone, potsherds (ostraka), and figures of wood, stone and wax, and cut them on wooden tablets and on large stone stelae, e.g. the Metternich stele ; the JEWS wrote them on parchment and, in the Middle Ages, on paper and on terra-cotta bowls ; the GNOSTICS and GREEKS cut them on semi-precious stones ; the PERSIANS and ARABS[1] cut them on tablets of agate, onyx, carnelian and schist, and wrote them on the skin of the unborn gazelle and on parchment and paper ; the JAPANESE burnt them into wood ; the CHINESE wrote them on silk paper ; and the INDIANS inscribed them on plates of copper and wrote them on palm leaves and bark paper. Copies of magical texts are now multiplied by means of the printing press, and the ordinary paper of commerce has

---

[1] The Arabs wrote copies of some of the Sûrahs of the Ḳur'ân on the flat bones of sheep and oxen, and fine examples of these, with legible Arabic inscriptions on them, are preserved in the British Museum (in the Department of Oriental Manuscripts).

superseded parchment, wood, palm leaves and bark paper.

The INK which the ancient writers of magical formulas used was generally black or red. In copies of the Egyptian Book of the Dead, which are written in hieroglyphs, the instructions concerning the performance of rites and ceremonies which follow certain Chapters, and are usually called " Rubrics," are written in red ink. In the BOOK OF OVER-THROWING ĀPEP it is ordered that the name of this fiend is to be written in green ink.

AMULET CASES.

In many countries the possessor of an amulet carries his treasure in a box made of precious metal, or in a little bag made of silk, or linen, or cloth or leather, his idea in the first place being to protect it from injury and contamination, and in the second place to keep it out of the sight of evil spirits and men and women possessing the Evil Eye. This is also the case when a book containing magical or sacred texts was regarded as an amulet. The Egyptian inserted his papyrus Book of the Dead in a painted wooden figure of the god Osiris, and a short extract from it in the wooden bases of figures of PTAḤ-SEKER-ĀSÁR ; gold figures of the gods when worn as amuletic pendants were enclosed in cases of silver or some other metal. The extracts from the Ḳur'ân, which were written on long strips of paper and were worn by Persian women as pendants on their necklaces, were inserted in oblong silver cases inscribed with amuletic texts. The ARABS and PERSIANS, whether nomads or dwellers in towns and villages, always keep their

Ḳur'âns in cases, some of them being studded with jewels, and the ABYSSINIAN wraps up his Psalter, and his Book of the Praises of Mary, and his amulets in many thick sheets of leather.

Modern Oriental authorities on amulets impress upon their clients the necessity of possessing many amulets, for according to them an amulet should only be expected to protect its owner from one danger. Certain kinds of amulets should always be in contact with the skin, and should only be worn on parts of the body where this is possible. These may be placed on the scalp, or forehead, or fastened to the ears, or set in necklaces and pectorals which lie on the breast, or fixed by cords over the umbilicus and genital organs, or tied on the upper part of the left arm, or on the wrist, or at the base of the spine, or on the leg below the knee. Amulets of a more general character may be carried in the turban, or fastened to the *tarbûsh* or to the hat of the European, or in a pocket or stitched into some part of the apparel near the heart. The latter class may be used with advantage for the protection of the house or of any special chamber in it by hanging them on the walls. If they be tied to the bed of a sick man, or placed in some position where he can see them, they will bring about his recovery. It is good for a sick man to drink the water in which they have been dipped or washed. Tied to a pole set up in an orchard they will increase the fruit-bearing power of the trees, and prevent the fruit from being eaten by birds and slugs and caterpillars ; if a pole with the proper kind of amulets tied to it be set up in a field where crops are growing, the crops will ripen satisfactorily. To protect horned cattle tie the amulets to the horns, or fasten them in holes drilled in the horns ; to protect sheep, goats and pigs, tie the amulets to their heads, or to that part of their bodies where the tails join the back. Amulets intended to avert the Evil Eye from animals or children must be large, and either made of some bright coloured substance, or painted a bright colour. In the bazârs of CAIRO and ṬANṬṬAH large blue-glazed pottery beads, fully half an inch in diameter, used to be sold to caravan men, who made bandlets of them and tied them to the foreheads of their camels before they set out on their journeys across the desert. The natives believed that the baleful glances of the Evil Eye would be attracted to the beads, and averted from the animals ; strips of red and green cloth and bits of polished brass are often used as amulets against the Evil Eye instead of the blue beads. It is tolerably certain that the brass bosses and ornaments which decorate the harness of cart horses and shire-stallions were, like the great brass horns which rise from their collars, originally intended to protect the animal from the Evil Eye ; but this fact has been forgotten, and amulets have degenerated into mere ornaments. Similarly the long fringes and tassels which are now fastened to saddle-bags as ornaments in the East, represent the long, knotted thongs of leather which were tied to the saddle-bags so that the sound of their striking together when the horseman was riding fast might frighten away evil spirits. In these, as in many other cases, the true meanings of the ornaments have been forgotten.

FAKED AMULETS.

It follows from the nature of the case, that in countries where everyone wishes to possess an amulet of one kind or another, or many amulets, that the magician must often find it difficult to meet all the demands made upon him. It is then that the pseudo-magician finds his opportunity, and he makes and sells what the natives call " dead " amulets. All over the East forged amulets are common. In PERSIA and 'IRÂḲ we find forged seal-cylinders and engraved stones, inscribed divining bowls and tablets and reliefs, and in Egypt forged scarabs, rings, figures, jewellery, gems, papyri, etc., have been made and sold to both natives and travellers for the last 150 years. During the rebellion of the Mahdî in the Sûdân thousands of his soldiers bought amulets purporting to contain magical texts from the Ḳur'ân, and magical prayer which, they believed, would protect them and give them victory. The writer has seen many of their leather cases cut open, and they contained nothing but carefully folded blank sheets of paper, wrapped in an outer sheet inscribed " Bismillâh," *i.e.* " in the Name of God." And the Abyssinian peasant is often cheated in the same way.

In connection with amulets may be mentioned a series of objects which are regarded as bringers of luck and are known as " MASCOTS." The word is also applied to men and women who are supposed to be lucky in themselves and to bring luck to others ; it is derived from the French *mascotte* and is probably cognate with the Provençal *masco*, " witch."

It came into general use through the Comic Opera of ANDRAUS called " La Mascotte," where we have the following :—

Un jour, le diable, ivre d'orgueil :
Choisit dans sa grande chaudière
Des démons qu'avaient l'mauvais oeil
Et les envoya sur la terre !
Mais le bon Dieu, not' protecteur
Quand il l'apprit, créant de suite
Des anges qui portaient bonheur,
Chez nous les envoya bien vite !
Ces envoyés du paradis.
Sont des mascottes, mes amis,
Heureux celui que le ciel dote
D'une mascotte !
(Quoted by Seligmann, *op. cit.*, p. 30.)

Nearly every large motor car is provided with a mascot fixed on the bonnet of the radiator, and nearly every famous regiment has its mascot, a goat, or a bear, etc. The TEDDY-BEAR is also regarded as a luck bringer. It made its first appearance in an American toy factory, and was called " Teddy " in honour of ROOSEVELT, then President of the American Republic.

CHAPTER II.

The Arabs in all periods of their history have worn amulets and talismans to protect their bodies and cattle and houses from the attacks of evil spirits, and especially against the Evil Eye. The amulets of the primitive Arabs, *i.e.* those who lived before the Christian Era, were made of stone, wood, and probably bone, and were, it would seem from the few scattered notices about them which have come down to us, uninscribed. The pagan Arabs of the first six centuries of our Era followed the example of their ancestors and wore and made use of many kinds of amulets and talismans, but they associated with them ideas which were borrowed from Hebrew, Egyptian, and Gnostic writings. Muḥammad himself sanctioned such borrowings, and in the Ḳur'ân passed on to his followers the history of Solomon as a magician, and a belief in the magical names of Allâh.

The simplest form of amulet worn by the Arabs and Persians in modern times consists of a piece of paper on which is written a short prayer, or spell, or verse from the Ḳur'ân, or a magical name or names. The inscription must be written by a holy man of some kind, on material chosen by him, with black ink. The Cairenes and others prefer to have the inscription written with ink made in France or England because it " bites " into the paper deeply. Native ink, charcoal and water, or burnt sheep's wool and water, washes off the paper easily. When written upon the paper, which is believed to have acquired the magical qualities which the native to this day associates with writing, is folded up and laid flat in a cardboard, or cheap leather, case. A cord is attached to the case, which is either tied under the left arm or hung round the neck. People of means and position cause the magical texts, even Sûrahs from the Ḳur'ân, to be written on gazelle skin, preferably on the skin of the unborn animal, and in such cases the amulet is rolled up and carried in a metal tube, made usually of silver. A portion of a very elaborate amulet written on the skin of an unborn kid is reproduced on Plate I, No. 1 ; the original is in my possession. The upper end is illuminated in bright colours, in the style of the early nineteenth century. The blocks of text are Sûrahs of the Ḳur'ân, written in red and black, with their titles in blue. No. 2 on the same plate is a reproduction from the first part of a paper amulet which was rolled up and carried in a silver case. This amulet was written in Persia and, judging by the paper, some time in the second half of the XVIIth century. Though small, the writing is very clear and the floral design is well executed. Mirza Khân, a Persian diplomatist, for some years resident in London, from whom I purchased both amulets, said that he had never seen a finer specimen of amuletic calligraphy.

Amuletic texts, or talismans, were sometimes written on thin sheets of lead which were folded up flat and carried in metal cases, but examples of such are very rare. Fragments of such amulets have been found among the ruins of Babylon, side by side with thin leaves of lead inscribed in Greek.

PLATE I

No. 1.
Amulet made of the skin of
an unborn kid.

No. 2.
Amulet made of paper.

PLATE II

Silver amulet case inscribed on both sides with a series of short texts from the Ḳur'ân. (From Baghdâd, XVIIth century.)

The cases in which girls and women wear their amulets are often of a very elaborate character and a good, characteristic example is shown on Plate II. Here we have a silver amulet case, the outside of which is covered with texts from the Ḳur'ân, and the long chain by which it was suspended from the neck. The owner of the case withdrew the amulet and kept it as a means of protection for himself, but he sold the case willingly! On Plate III is a necklace with two rows of ornaments. In the upper row are twelve hollow silver plaques, joined by rings, each of which contained a small piece of paper on which a magical name was written. The lower row consists of twleve small silver cases, pointed at both ends, which are attached by rings to the twelve plaques above them, and have silver pendants, some two and some three. Each tube originally contained a small roll of paper inscribed with verses from the Ḳur'ân. Each roll of paper was supposed to afford protection to the wearer during one month, and as the necklace contains twelve rolls, she was protected during the whole year.

The inscriptions which are found on Arab amulets to-day may be divided into two classes : (1) those which are composed of characters borrowed from the Hebrews, Egyptians and Gnostics, and of which the phonetic values and meanings are unknown. The following are examples of these :—

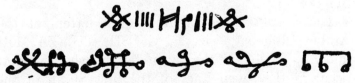

Both these are given in the autographed book of AL-BÛNÎ, from whom they are quoted by DOUTTÉ, pp. 155, 158.

(2) Inscriptions which consist of series of unknown
signs or characters, series of letters of some known
alphabet, rows of figures or numbers, magical
names, names of the planets, names of the days of
the week, names of angels, devils, fiends, etc.,
names of God, and Sûrahs of the Ḳur'ân. An
example of the amulet in which both classes of
inscriptions appear is given by DOUTTÉ in his *Magie
et Religion dans l'Afrique du Nord*, Algiers, 1908,
p. 154. This is known as the " SEVEN SEALS," and
appears in the form of a rectangle containing 7 × 7
squares, arranged in seven lines, and each line has
in it seven signs, or letters, or names. The first line
has these seven signs :—

Now the FIRST of these is the well-known pentacle
which is frequently confounded with the hexagon

, and is a design which is said to have been

cut on the bezel of King Solomon's ring. But the
pentacle is many centuries older than the hexagon,
for it is found drawn on pots from ancient Babylonian sites. The pentacle and the six other signs
in the first line are the Seven Seals in the amulet,
and they either represent the great Names or
Symbols of God.

The SECOND line contains seven letters of the
Arabic alphabet, viz. F, G, SH, TH, ZA, KH
and Z. These are the seven letters which do not
occur in the seven lines of the first Sûrah of the
Ḳur'ân, and they begin the seven names of God

PLATE III

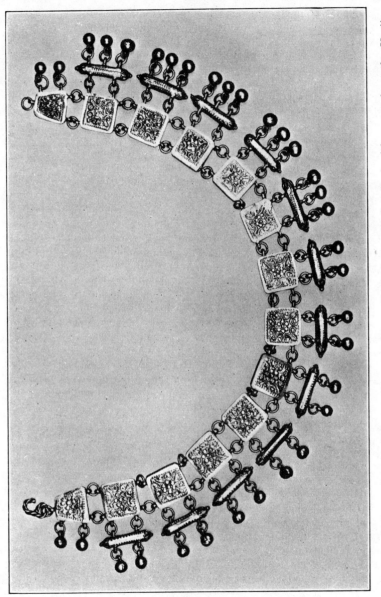

Silver necklace with plaques and tubes to hold small amuletic rolls inscribed with verses from the Ḳur'ān. (From Ḥillah.)

which we find in the THIRD line of the amulet :—
Fard, Gabbâr, Shakûr, Thabit, Zahîr, Khabîr,
Zakî.

The FOURTH line contains the names of seven
angels, viz. Rûkyâîl, Gabriel, Samsamâîl. Michael,
Ṣarfyâîl, 'Anyâîl, and Kasfyâîl. The names of all
these angels, or rather archangels, are of Hebrew
origin.

The FIFTH line contains the names of the Seven
Kings of the Genii :—Mudhhib, Marra (?), Akhmar,
Buskân, Shamḥûrash, Ibyaḍ and Mîmûm. These
names are of Arab origin, and some of them seem
to describe the outward appearances of the kings,
e.g. the White One, the Golden One, the Red One,
the Lightning One.

The SIXTH line contains the numbers of the days
of the week, the first, the second, etc., and the
SEVENTH line gives the names of the five planets—
Mars, Mercury, Jupiter, Venus, Saturn, and the
Sun and Moon. Thus we see that the amulet of the
Seven Seals was believed to carry with it the protection of God, by whatever name called, and of the
archangels, and the kings of the spirits, the Jinn and
the Jann, and the five planets and the sun and moon,
and the days of the week, and the seven letters.
In fact, the wearer of the amulet was believed to be
protected by God and His creation generally. The
seven letters, each written seven times and arranged
in seven lines containing forty-nine squares, also
form a powerful amulet. The wearer is even more
protected if it be written on some part of the wearer,
which seems to suggest that the figures and signs
which men had tattooed on their bodies carried
with them some magical protection. The " tribal

marks " which are seen on the faces of Arabs at the present day are probably the remains of amuletic signs or names.

Groups of LETTERS of the alphabet play a prominent part in amuletic inscriptions. The earlier magicians arranged them in an order, which was not necessarily alphabetic ; to some of them they assigned meanings or symbolisms, but of others they regarded the meanings as incomprehensible to the human understanding. The twenty-eight letters are connected directly with the twenty-eight stations of the moon, and with the heavenly bodies, and the Signs of the Zodiac and the Dekans. Letters to the early Hebrews were the essence of things and, as Doutté has observed (*op. cit.*, p. 172), the Romans described all human knowledge as " letters," using the word as the peoples of the North used " runes." The Arabs, like the Hebrews, attributed greater powers to some letters than to others, and a proper knowledge of the use of these formed a separate branch of the study of magic. Each letter had its special powers, and a single letter might be developed into a design which would in itself form an effective amulet.

The powers of the LETTERS are intimately associated with NUMBERS, for each letter in the Arabic alphabet has a numerical value. No. 1 = God. No. 2 is important because it is said in the Ḳur'ân, "And of everything have we created two kinds " (Sûrah, li, verse 49) [*i.e.* male and female, heaven and earth, sun and moon, light and darkness, plains and mountains, winter and summer, sweet and bitter, JALÂL UD-DIN]. No. 3 is important. No. 4 is very important, for there are 4 archangels, 4 chief devils,

4 elements, 4 seasons, 4 cardinal points, and an amulet must be a square. No. 5 has always possessed a special significance, perhaps of completeness. The Arabs pray 5 times daily, and they have 5 fundamental dogmas, and 5 "pillars" of religion. No. 6 has no special importance. No. 7 plays a very prominent part in Arab magic. Of the amulet of the Seven Seals mention has already been made. God created seven heavens, seven earths, seven seas, seven hells with seven doors, the seven members of the body used during the ceremonies of prayer, the seven periods of life, the seven Climes, the seven days of the week, and the seven Prophets who preside over the seven days of the week, viz. Moses, Jesus, David, Solomon, Jacob, Adam, and Muḥammad. No. 8 is divisible by 2 and 4, both important numbers. No. $9 = 8 + 1$ and 3×3, and 3 is a specially magical number. Nos. 10, 12, 40, 50, 100, 110 and 1,000 have their magical powers increased by adding or subtracting 1.

Now, as letters possess magical powers and have numerical values, amuletic inscriptions can be composed of letters only or numbers only ; both letters and figures are often arranged in lines, each containing three or four letters or figures, and three or four lines form a MAGICAL SQUARE. Here is a simple square, quoted by Doutté, containing the numbers 1 to 9. Whether these are added up

4	9	2
3	5	7
8	1	6

perpendicularly, or horizontally, or diagonally, the total is always 15. An example of the four-lined

square, each line containing four numbers, is here
given ; the numbers given are 1–16. Whether

4	14	15	1
9	7	6	12
5	11	10	8
16	2	3	13

these are added up perpendicularly, or horizontally,
or diagonally, the total is always 34. The knowledge of arithmetic required by those who constructed such squares was considerable, and it
seems to have formed the foundation of the Arab
science of mathematics. The Arabs thought that
the magical powers of some of the 28 letters were
greater than those of others ; thus *Alif*, the first
letter of the Arabic alphabet, is also the first letter
of the name of Allâh, and as its numerical value
was *one* it represented Allâh the One God. The
names of God, the Archangels, etc., might be written
with letters or with the numerical values of the
letters which formed the names, and in either form
they made a protective amuletic inscription.

Many amulets contain the Hebrew names of God
and the Archangels, but the names which the Arabs
believe to possess the greatest magical power are
the names of the *attributes* of God. The title ALLÂH,
the meaning of which is unknown, is called " Ismu
az-Zât," *i.e.* the " essential name," and these
attributes are known as " Asmâu aṣ-Ṣifât." In
alluding to them Muḥammad the Prophet spoke of
them as " Al-Asmâu al-ḥusnâ," *i.e.* the " Beautiful
Names " (Ḳur'ân, Sûrah vii. verse 179), and to
this day they are known as the " Beautiful or

Excellent Names of God." Abu Hurairah said
that the " Names of God were ninety-nine in number,
and that he who recites them shall enter Paradise."
The commentators say that Muḥammad had no
intention to limit the names of God to ninety-nine,
and that all he wished the orthodox Muslims to do
was to recite this number daily. The lists of the
names given by the traditionalists do not agree.
Some lists begin with the name ALLÂH and others
end with it ; and some begin with AL-AḤAD, *i.e.*
" the One," and others end with it. The following
list of the Ninety-nine Names is that of TIRMIDHI
(see DOUTTÉ, *op. cit.*, p. 200) and HUGHES (*Dict.
Islâm*, p. 141) :—

1. Ar-Raḥmân	..	The Merciful.
2. Ar-Raḥim	..	The Compassionate.
3. Al-Malik ..	..	The King.
4. Al-Ḳuddûs	..	The Holy.
5. As-Salâm	..	The Peace.
6. Al-Mu'mîn	..	The Faithful.
7. Al-Muhaimin	..	The Protector.
8. Al-'Azîz ..	..	The Mighty.
9. Al-Jabbâr	..	The Repairer.
10. Al-Mutakabbir	..	The Great.
11. Al-Khâliḳ	..	The Creator.
12. Al-Bârî ..	..	The Maker.
13. Al-Muṣawwir	..	The Fashioner.
14. Al-Ghaffâr	..	The Forgiver.
15. Al-Ḳahhâr	..	The Dominant.
16. Al-Wahhab	..	The Bestower.
17. Al-Razzâḳ	..	The Provider.
18. Al-Fattâḥ	..	The Opener.
19. Al-Alîm ..	..	The Knower.
20. Al-Ḳâbiẓ ..	..	The Restrainer.

21. Al-Bâsiṭ ..	..	The Spreader.
22. Al-Khâfiẓ ..	..	The Abaser.
23. Ar-Râfiʻ ..	..	The Exalter.
24. Al-Muʻizz	..	The Honourer.
25. Al-Muzîl ..	..	The Destroyer.
26. As-Samîʻ ..	..	The Hearer.
27. Al-Baṣir ..	..	The Seer.
28. Al-Hâkim	..	The Ruler.
29. Al-ʻAdl ..	..	The Just.
30. Al-Laṭîf ..	..	The Subtle.
31. Al-Khabîr	..	The Aware.
32. Al-Ḥalîm	..	The Clement.
33. Al-ʻAzîm ..	..	The Grand.
34. Al-Ghafûr	..	The Forgiving.
35. Ash-Shakûr	..	The Grateful.
36. Al-ʻAlî ..	..	The Exalted.
37. Al-Kabîr ..	..	The Great.
38. Al-Ḥafîẓ ..	..	The Guardian.
39. Al-Muḵît ..	..	The Strengthener.
40. Al-Ḥasîb ..	..	The Reckoner.
41. Al-Jalîl ..	..	The Majestic.
42. Al-Karîm	..	The Generous.
43. Ar-Raḵîb	..	The Watcher.
44. Al-Mujîb ..	..	The Approver.
45. Al-Wâsiʻ ..	..	The Comprehensive.
46. Al-Ḥakîm	..	The Wise.
47. Al-Wadûd	..	The Loving.
48. Al-Majîd ..	..	The Glorious.
49. Al-Baiṣ ..	..	The Raiser.
50. Ash-Shahîd	..	The Witness.
51. Al-Ḥaḵḵ ..	..	The Truth.
52. Al-Wakîl ..	..	The Advocate.
53. Al-Ḵawî ..	..	The Strong.
54. Al-Matîn ..	..	The Firm.

55. Al-Walî ..	..	The Patron.
56. Al-Hamîd	..	The Laudable.
57. Al-Muhsî ..	..	The Counter.
58. Al-Mubdî	..	The Beginner.
59. Al-Mu'îd ..	..	The Restorer.
60. Al-Muhyî	..	The Quickener.
61. Al-Mumît..	..	The Killer.
62. Al-Hayy ..	..	The Living.
63. Al-Kaiyûm	..	The Subsisting.
64. Al-Wâjid	..	The Finder.
65. Al-Majîd ..	..	The Glorious.
66. Al-Wâhid..	..	The One.
67. As-Samad	..	The Eternal.
68. Al-Kâdir ..	..	The Powerful.
69. Al-Muktadir	..	The Prevailing.
70. Al-Mukaddim	..	The Bringer Forward.
71. Al-Mu'akhkhir	..	The Deferrer.
72. Al-Awwal	..	The First.
73. Al-Âkhir ..	..	The Last.
74. Az-Zâhir ..	..	The Evident.
75. Al-Bâtin ..	..	The Hidden.
76. Al-Wâlî ..	..	The Governor.
77. Al-Muta'âlî	..	The Exalted.
78. Al-Barr ..	..	The Righteous.
79. At-Tawwâb	..	The Accepter of Repentance.
80. Al-Muntakim	..	The Avenger.
81. Al-'Afûw ..	..	The Pardoner.
82. Ar-Ra'uf ..	..	The Kind. [dom.
83. Mâlik ul-Mulk	..	The Ruler of the King-
84. Dhu'l-Jalâh wa'l-Ikrâm		The Lord of Majesty and Liberality.
85. Al-Muksit	..	The Equitable.
86. Al-Jâmî' ..	..	The Collector.

87.	Al-Ghanî	The Independent.
88.	Al-Mughnî ..	The Enricher.
89.	Al-Mu'tî	The Giver.
90.	Al-Mâni'	The Withholder.
91.	Az-Zarr	The Distresser.
92.	An-Nâfi'	The Profiter.
93.	An-Nûr	The Light.
94.	Al-Hâdî	The Guide.
95.	Al-Badî'	The Incomparable.
96.	Al-Bâḳî	The Enduring.
97.	Al-Wârith ..	The Heir.
98.	Ar-Rashîd ..	The Director.
99.	Aṣ-Ṣabûr ..	The Patient.

Muslim sages have agreed that God has one great and exalted name, which is above all others. Muḥammad himself declared that it was to be found in the Second or Third Sûrahs of the Ḳur'ân, and as the only names of God given in these are Ar-Raḥman, Ar-Raḥîm, Al-Hayy and Al-Ḳaiyûm, it should be one of these four names. The importance of the Ninety-Nine Names of God from a magical point of view is that when God is adjured by any one of them He is bound to fulfil the wish or prayer of the person who addresses Him by it. The idea that the great and ineffable name of God has only been known to the high priests is borrowed from the Jews, who believed that it was known only to Moses and his successors who used it only once a year, when they went into the Holy of Holies to plead for forgiveness for Israel. Most of the names of God are taken from the Ḳur'ân, and every large amulet is inscribed with several of them. These were carefully chosen by the man or woman for whom the amulet was made, and they give the attributes of

God which endear Him to him or her, and to which
it was thought He would certainly make answer.
As so many of the texts found on amulets are
taken from the Ḳur'ân, or are based upon it, the
following description of that famous work may be
found useful.
AL-ḲUR'ÂN, or " The Ḳur'ân," *i.e.* " the reading "
or " what ought to be read," is the name given by
the Muslims to the collection of " revelations " or
" instructions " which Muḥammad the Prophet
declared had been sent to him from God by the hand
of the Archangel Gabriel. These revelations were,
during the Prophet's lifetime, written upon skins,
palm leaves, slices of stone, and bones of sheep and
oxen. Specimens of these inscribed bones are
preserved in the Department of Oriental Manuscripts
in the British Museum. At the suggestion of 'Omar
in the year 633 all these " revelations " were collected by Abu Bakr's orders into one book, and a
fair copy of them was made by Zaid ibn-Thâbit, a
former secretary of Muḥammad, who knew both
Hebrew and Syriac. 'Omar gave this copy to his
daughter Ḥafsah, who was one of the widows of
Muḥammad. Extracts and copies were made from
this, but so many mistakes and interpolations
crept into the text that the Khalîfah 'Othmân
ordered Zaid and three scholars of the Koraish tribe
to make a new Recension of the Ḳur'ân. This was
done, and copies of it having been sent to Kûfah on
the Euphrates, Baṣrah on the Shaṭṭ al-'Arab, Damascus, Cairo, Makkah and Madînah, every other version
of every " revelation " which could be found was ruth-
lessly burnt. Subsequently even Ḥafsah's copy was
destroyed by Marwân, the governor of Madînah.

Learned Muḥammadans assert that the Ḳur'ân
existed in heaven from all eternity in a form which
they call the " Mother of the Book " or the " Preserved Tablet," which is a part of the essence of
God, who was its Creator. A copy of this was made
on paper in heaven and it was bound in silk and
ornamented with the gold and precious stones of
Paradise. This was committed to the care of the
Archangel Gabriel, who revealed it to the Prophet
piecemeal, but allowed him to see the complete
book once a year. The Ḳur'ân contains 114 sections,
each of which is called a Sûrah. Some were revealed
at Makkah, others at Madînah, and others partly
at Makkah and partly at Madînah. The number of
verses in the whole book is given as 6,000, or 6,214,
or 6,219, or 6,225, or 6,226, or 6,236 ; the number of
words in it is 77,639, or 99,464 ; and the number of
letters is 323,015, or 330,113. Each section is
introduced by the words " In the Name of Allâh,
the Merciful, the Compassionate." The Arabs regard
the Ḳur'ân as the source of all knowledge and
wisdom ; they think its language is the purest Arabic
in the world, and the most beautiful, and that its
eloquence is incomparable. In spite of all the care
which the Arabs have lavished on the preservation
of the text, a few slight variations in it exist, but
these are held to be due to the fact that the " revelations " were made to the Prophet in seven distinct
dialects of Arabic. At one time a woman was not
allowed to possess a copy of the Ḳur'ân, and when
a man died his copy was buried with him. But when
I was in the Tiyârô district on the Persian border,
I bought several copies wrapped up in earth-stained
pieces of linen, and reeking with damp, and even

mildew, which starving women dug up out of their husbands' graves and were only too thankful to find a purchaser.

The Arabs regard the whole Ḳur'ân as a powerful amulet, and many of them never travel without it In recent years miniature copies of it have been made by photo-lithography and enclosed in small

The Ḳur'ân Amulet, which is frequently carried or worn by the members of the caravans which travel from Persia to Ḥillah, Kûfa, Karbala and carry dead Shiah Muslims to the last-named city for burial.

metal cases (with rings for attachment to necklaces, etc.), in one side of which little lenses have been fixed to be used as magnifying glasses. The whole book measures 1 inch × $\frac{3}{4}$ inch × $\frac{7}{16}$ inch, and the little lens in the case is sufficiently strong to enable the traveller to read his favourite chapters by the light of the camp fire. A photograph of the amulet and its case is given above.

But although the whole Ḳur'ân is regarded as a powerful amulet, there are certain chapters in it which the Arabs have always considered to be of more importance than the others, and these are frequently written upon skin or paper, or engraved on semi-

Âyat al-Kursî.

precious stones of a special shape. One of the most beautiful passages, which Muḥammadans greatly admire and recite in their prayers and wear as an amulet, is the following extract from Sûrah ii, verse 256:—

" GOD! there is no GOD but HE; the living the self-subsisting;

Neither slumber nor sleep seizeth Him ;
To Him [belongeth] whatsoever is in heaven,
and on earth,
Who is he that can intercede with Him but
through His good pleasure ?
He knoweth that which is past, and that which
is to come unto them ;
And they shall not comprehend anything of His
knowledge, but so far as He pleaseth.
His throne is extended over heaven and earth,
and the preservation of both is no burden
unto Him.
He is the High, the Mighty."

(Sale's translation.)

This beautiful passage is known as ÂYAT AL-KURSÎ,
i.e. the " Throne Verse." The word " Throne " is an
allegorical description of the Divine Providence which
sustains all creation and is incomprehensible to
human beings.

There is another very important text which is
also known as a Throne Verse, and is called AYAT
AL-'ARSH. It is formed by the two last verses (Nos.
129 and 130) of Sûrah x, and reads :

" Now hath an apostle come unto you of our
own nation, an excellent [person] ;
It is [grievous] unto him that ye commit
wickedness.
[He is] careful over you, [and] compassionate
and merciful towards the believers.
If they turn back, say, God is my support :
There is no GOD but HE.
On Him do I trust ; and He is Lord of the
Magnificent Throne." (Sale's translation.)

The Magnificent, or Sublime, Throne here referred to is the Imperial Throne of God, on which He sits. It is situated in the heavens high above the Kursî.

More important still as an amulet is the Sûrah of the Ḳur'ân which is the " Beginning of the Book." This is the famous " Fâtiḥat," which is a prayer and which is held in the greatest veneration by Muslims all over the world. It is to them what the

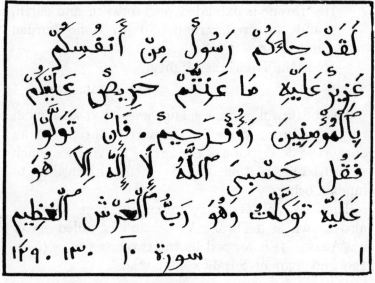

Ayat al-'Arsh.

Lord's Prayer and the Sign of the Cross are to Christians. It stands by itself at the beginning of the Book, and is always carefully and beautifully written. It is often enclosed within decorated borders full of rich designs and colour, and lavishly ornamented with burnished gold. The general character of the designs and the elaborate decorations which are found in modern manuscripts of the Ḳur'ân are well illustrated (except in the matter of

PLATE IV

Mirza Khân's Ḳur'ân amulet.

colours) by the reproduction of the two first pages
of a small copy which was obtained for me from
Persia by Mirza Khân.   The Mullah who paid for the
production of the book carried it as an amulet in an
elaborate gold case.   This later he was obliged to sell to
obtain money to enable him to return to Persia when
the war broke out in 1914 (Plate IV).   The titles of the
Sûrahs are written in red upon gold.   Every column

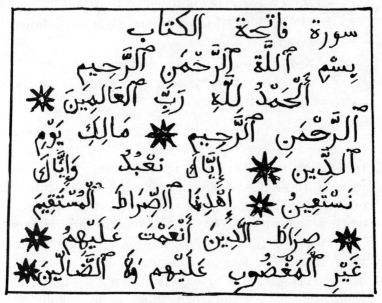

The Fâtiḥat al-Kitâb.

of text is enclosed within a gold border, and there is
a line of gold under every line of text.   Each column
of text contains 21 lines.   This copy measures
4 inches × 2⅜ inches × ⅝ inch, and is dated Anno
Hijra 1289 = A.D. 1872.   The paper is thin and
very tough and is parchment-like in colour.

The Fâtiḥat, like every other Sûrah or Chapter
except the ninth, is preceded by the words, " In the

Name of Allâh, the Merciful, the Compassionate,"
and may be thus translated :—

1. Praise be unto Allâh, the Lord of the worlds.
2. The Merciful, the Compassionate.
3. King of the Day of Judgment.
4. Thee do we worship, of Thee we entreat for help.
5. Direct us in the path which is straight.
6. The path of those on whom Thou hast shown favour.
7. Not of those with whom Thou art angry. Nor those who wander (*i.e.* stray from the Straight Path).

The prayer in lines 5–7 has been much discussed by commentators, both Muslim and Christian. Sale translated it : " Direct us in the right way, in the way of those to whom thou hast been gracious ; not of those against whom thou art incensed, nor of those who go astray." Al-Zamakhshari renders lines 6 and 7 thus : " The way of those to whom thou hast been gracious, against whom thou art not incensed, and who have not erred." In other words, he makes the three lines apply wholly to Muslims, whilst Sale thinks that "those to whom God had been gracious " were the Prophets, and that "those against whom he was incensed " were the Jews, and " those who go astray " to the Christians.

There are several shorter extracts from the Ḳur'ân which are very popular as amuletic inscriptions, and among these of special interest is the short Sûrah (No. CXII), which contains the declaration of the Unity of Allâh.

In the Name of Allâh, the Merciful, the Compassionate.

1. Say : He Allâh [is] One.
2. Allâh the self-subsisting.
3. He begetteth not, and He was not begotten.
4. And there is no one like unto Him.

The recital of this Sûrah is supposed to confer upon a man the decree of merit which he would acquire if he recited one-third of the whole Ḳur'ân.

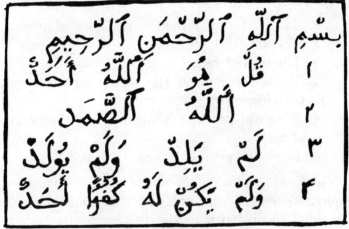

The Sûrah of the Unity of God.

It is held in great veneration by the Muslims and, naturally, detested by Christians.

The following are Sûrahs directed against witchcraft and the Devil:—

I. SURAH CXIII. THE CHAPTER OF THE DAYBREAK.

In the Name of God the Merciful, the Compassionate.

1. Say : I fly for refuge to the Lord of the Daybreak.
2. From the evil things which He hath created.

3. And from the evil of the night when it hath come.
4. And from the evil of [women who] are blowers on knots.
5. And from the evil of the envious man when he hath envied.

II. SURAH CXIV. THE CHAPTER OF MAN.

In the Name of God the Merciful, the Compassionate.

1. Say : I fly for refuge to the Lord of men.
2. The king of men.
3. The God of men.
4. From the evil of the whisperer who slyly withdraweth.
5. Who whispereth evil words into the breasts of men.
6. From the genii and men.

The words " blowers on knots " refer to magicians, male and female, who recite incantations which are intended to do harm to the fellows whilst they tie knots in a string—in other words, " weave spells." These two Sûrahs were revealed to Muḥammad at the same time, and must be regarded as forming one whole ; and the Prophet used them for a very special service. The commentators say that a Jew called Lubaid and his daughters bewitched Muḥammad by tying eleven knots in a cord which they hid in a well. The result was that the Prophet fell seriously ill and would undoubtedly have died had not God intervened. He sent down these Sûrahs to him, and also instructed the Archangel Gabriel to tell him how to use them, and where the cord was

PLATE V

Persian agate amulet inscribed with texts from the Kur'án.   Dated A.H. 1113.   (From Baghdád.)

PLATE VI

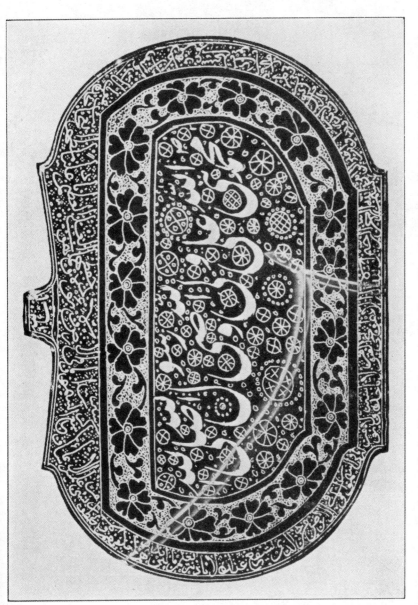

Persian agate amulet inscribed with texts from the Ḳurʼân. The original is 4 inches long and is 2¾ inches in the widest part. Undated. (From Karbala on the Euphrates.)

hidden. Muḥammad sent 'Alî to fetch the cord, and when it was brought he recited over the eleven knots the eleven verses in the two Sûrahs, and as he recited each line one of the knots untied itself ; as soon as the last knot was loosed Muḥammad was freed from his bewitchment, and recovered his normal health.

In the Arabic treatises which deal with amulets and talismans and supply the reader with magical texts, we find that little drawings or vignettes are mingled with the texts. These are of many kinds, Thus we find grotesque figures of men and animals, figures of archangels, the Signs of the Zodiac, the Sun and Moon and the five planets, mythological beasts, linear designs and geometrical patterns, and very frequently the human hand stretched out flat with the fingers well apart, or all close together. All these drawings are borrowed from the Egyptians, Copts, Gnostics and Hebrews, for the Arab is a better borrower of such things than inventor. The Sunni Arabs, or traditionalists, only employ some of these, but the Shiahs, or " free thinkers " adopt them all. As a rule, Persian amulets are more artistic than those of the Arabs. Two of the finest Persian or Shiah amulets known to me are reproduced on Plates V and VI.

The first is a rectangular slice of Persian agate bevelled at the corners. And it seems to have been made in the year 1113 of the Hijra, *i.e.* A.D 1701. It was made for a follower of 'Alî, the son-in-law of the Prophet, and to him the text in the centre, written in large Arabic letters, refers. At each corner is a circle containing a divine name, and the first border, *i.e.* that with diamond-shaped ornaments, contains forty-eight of the ninety-nine " Beautiful Names " of God. The second and fourth borders, which are separated by an ornamental border, contains extracts from the Ḳur'ân, viz. the Fâtiḥah, and the Throne Verses, the Declaration of the unity of God, etc. The texts, decorated border, etc., were inscribed on the stone by the fumes of acid and are therefore very difficult to read, even in the reproduction which is nearly double the size of the original. And the manner in which the scribe found it necessary to break up the words increases the difficulty. This amulet formed the centre-piece of a very elaborate necklace of amulets, and was mounted in a heavy silver frame. It is in fact a " House-amulet." The second amulet is in the form in which the Shiahs or free-thinking Muslims of Karbala prefer to make their amulets. It was set in a silver frame and was hung on the wall of a house in Karbala on the Euphrates by means of a chain which passed through the projection on the upper edge. The texts inscribed on the edge are the Fâtiḥah and the Throne Verses. The decorated centre is of an unusual character, for the field is filled up with annules, circles divided into 4, or 8, or 16 sections, and circles surrounded with annules or filled with crosses.

From what has been said above it is clear that the wearing of amulets bearing texts from the Ḳur'ân may be regarded as a religious exercise, for their sole object is to put the wearer into communication with Allâh, so that He may afford His protection. And most Arabs regard the practice of wearing amulets of this kind not only as harmless, but even as meritorious, and the science of them is a branch of White Magic.

In Arabia and Mesopotamia and Syria the common words for amulet are TAMÎMAH and 'ÛDZAH and TA'WÎDZAH, and in Egypt and North Africa KHURZA. The stones used for amulets are usually choice agates across which run white bands, or the dark grey semi-transparent agates which are brought from India. These are carefully cut into the required shapes and highly polished, and then the inscriptions are either cut with a lapidary's wheel or a graver's tool. As engraving on stone is a very costly matter, even in the East, another method of inscribing the stone amulet has been found. The slice of agate, or carnelian, or chalcedony having been chosen, the amulet maker covers it all over with a thin layer of wax. Care is taken that the wax touches the surface of the stone everywhere, and that there are no air bubbles between the wax and the stone. The waxed stone is then handed over to the skilled scribe, who writes the inscription in the wax with a sharp-pointed graver, taking care that the tool touches the stone as each letter of the inscription is written. The waxed stone is then exposed to the fumes of hydrochloric acid, which eat into the stone wherever its surface has been laid bare by the scribe's graver. When the fumes of the acid have done their work, the stone is cleared of wax, and the inscription stands out clearly on the stone. The writing lacks the beauty and character of that cut with a wheel or graver, but the cheapness of amulets which are made in this way brings them within the reach of many who cannot afford those which are engraved. Among the officials of the great mosques at Baghdâd, Kazmain, Karbala, Damascus, Cairo, and Persia there were men who specialized in the making of amulets, but during the last forty years these men, and their successors, have devoted themselves to making imitations of Persian and Babylonian antiquities, which they sell to travellers and the uninitiated. The amulets bought in the mosques, and those which were specially made there for private individuals, were usually blessed by a Mullah. The engraver on stone, or the scribe who wrote on paper or leather, began his work by pronouncing the words " Bism Illâh," *i.e.* " in the Name of God." As the Name of God was regarded as God Himself, the engraver or the scribe were sure of God's help when he pronounced His Name. These words are said to have been written on Adam's side, and on the wings of Gabriel, and on the seal of Solomon, and on the tongue of Jesus (see Doutté, *op. cit.*, p. 211). The ink used by the scribe was sometimes perfumed with musk, or oil of roses, or extract of saffron, and sometimes sticks of incense were kept burning whilst he was copying certain texts.

Though the greater number of Persian and Arab amulets are made of agate and carnelian because of the magical power which was believed to exist in these stones, other substances were often used by amulet manufacturers in places where limestone formations did not exist. Thus on the coasts of the Red Sea and in Palestine amulets made of mother-of-pearl shell are found. Examples of such are reproduced on Plate VII, Nos. 1 and 2. No. 1 is inscribed in Arabic with a prayer that the wearer may be defended from internal troubles and

PLATE VII

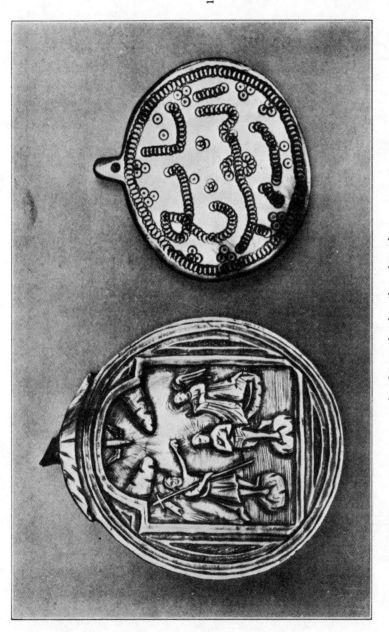

Amulets made of mother-of-pearl.

2. The Baptism of Christ in the Jordan by John the Baptist. Bought at the Fords of the Jordan.

1. Amulet worn by unmarried girls.

has a pierced projection by which it was hung by a
cord from the neck ; its owner was a little girl who
was wearing it over the umbilicus. I obtained it
at Suez. The Christians in Palestine and Syria
also wore, and still wear, amuletic plaques made
of mother-of-pearl shell, and a good example of
the class is reproduced on Plate VII, No. 2. The
scene cut on this plaque represents the baptism
of Christ by St. John the Baptist, who stands
upon a stone in the Jordan. He holds a long cross-
headed staff in his right hand and pours water on
the head of our Lord with his left hand. Above is
a dove symbolizing the Holy Ghost descending
through an opening in the clouds. On the right
is an angel.

The ancient Egyptians appear to have used
large shells from the Red Sea as amulets, and
these were held to be more effective when the
nomens and prenomens of kings were cut upon
them. Thus we have in the British Museum
shells inscribed with the nomen and prenomen of
Usertsen I (XIIth Dynasty), and the prenomen
of Amenemḥat II (XIIth Dynasty), and the pre-
nomen of Rameses II the Great (Nos. 15423, 20744,
29434, etc.).

The Muslim soldier has always felt that he needed
the protection of amulets, and he always provided
himself with as many as he could get before he set
out on the march. The commonest military amulet
is a strip of paper inscribed with an extract from
the Ḳur'ân, or with the Name Allâh, and the names of
Muḥammad and 'Alî, and those of some or all of the
Seven Archangels. Sometimes the strip developed
into a long roll of paper, which was tied to the

breast or body of the warrior. The Turkish soldiers who during the reign of 'Abd al-Hamîd fought in Southern Arabia wore amulets made of stone and metal. A specimen of a brass amulet is given on Plate VIII, No. 3. This is a curved, rectangular shield-shaped plaque with rounded corners and two pierced projections by which it was sewn to the tunic of the soldier. On the upper part is an extract from the Ḳur'ân, and below this are two magical designs with conical tops and two magical squares. On the back of a similar plaque in my possession is a magical square filled with numbers which represent the names of celestial beings. The desert Arabs in the Yaman regarded these brass amulets as objects of very great value, and there is no doubt that they murdered many of the Turkish soldiers in order to cut the brass amulets from their jackets. An amulet which was taken from the left arm of a Turkish officer is shown on Plate IX. It is formed of three oval agate plaques, mounted in thick silver cases, and inscribed with texts from the Ḳur'ân, viz. the declaration of the Unity of Allâh, the opening prayer, etc. On the stone to the right is the name of Muḥammad, which is here regarded as a word of power. The cord by which these stones were fastened to the left arm of their owner is made of silk, and the eyelets at the ends of the cord are bound round with wire.

Among objects which are believed to carry with them magical protection must be mentioned what may be called the " Dust Amulet," the dust being earth, or sand, or dust taken from the tomb of a saint. For many centuries the pilgrims to Makkah (Mecca), the birthplace of Muḥammad the Prophet,

PLATE VIII

Miscellaneous amulets in silver and brass.

1 and 2. Silver amulets worn by Indian Muslim women who are about to become
  mothers. (From the west coast of India.)
3. Brass shield-shaped amulet from the strap of the left shoulder of a soldier who
  fought in the Yaman.   On it are inscribed two magical squares of figures and
  passages from the Ḳur'ân. (From Aden.)
4. Hebrew amulet inscribed with the hexagon of Solomon, and Shaddai, a name
  of God.
5 and 6. Silver amulets inscribed in Arabic with prayers for the well-being of
  their wearers, who were women about to become mothers. (From the Sûdân.)

PLATE IX

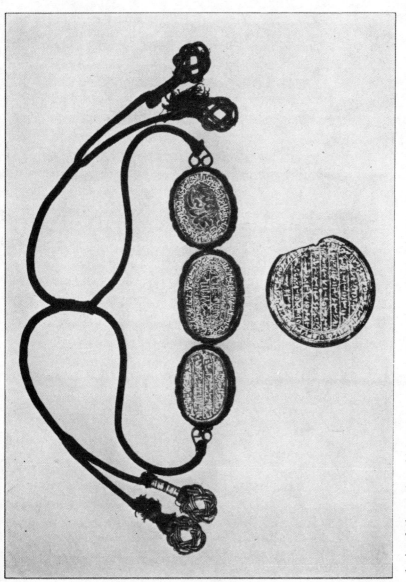

1. Amuletic armlet which was found on the left arm of a Turkish officer during a fight with the Sinaitic Arabs at al-Kanṭarah on the Suez Canal.

2. Slate amulet inscribed with a magical inscription formed wholly of Arabic numerals, found at Ḳurnah on the Shaṭṭ al-ʿArab.

have carried away from the mosque pinches of dust which they tied up in little bags and hung round their necks. The boatmen on the Nile above the Second Cataract tie little bags containing dust from the tomb of Ḳubbah Idrîs, a famous Murghânî shaikh, in the belief that it will procure them a safe passage through the Cataract. And when I visited the Monastery of Rabban Hormizd at Alḳôsh I saw men scraping up the dust from the ground close to the Saint's tomb, to carry away with them in little bags and boxes as a protection against the dangers of the desert.

Here for convenience sake may be mentioned the string of ninety-nine beads, and a " pillar," which is commonly called the " Muḥammadan Rosary." It must not be confused with the string of 165 beads which Christians use in keeping count of the Aves, Paternosters and Glorias of the form of prayer which constitutes the " Rose-garden [of Mary]." Early Christian monks and anchorites were in the habit of repeating the Lord's Prayer a great number of times daily, and the story of Paul the anchorite shows that some of them kept count of their prayers by means of pebbles. The monk Paul collected three hundred pebbles in his gown, and when he finished a prayer he threw out a pebble ; when the pebbles came to an end, he knew that he had said the full number of prayers. There is no evidence that the monks used *strings* of pebbles, and when the Christian and Muḥammadan rosaries first came into use is not known. The Arabs have a tradition that the early Muslims counted the praises of Allâh by means of pebbles, or on their fingers, but they think that Muḥammad did not use a rosary. The

Buddhists used a rosary containing 100 or 108 beads, and carried it on their wrist like a bracelet, or wore it as a necklace (see WADDELL, *The Buddhism of Tibet*, London, 1895). On the whole it seems probable that the Muslims borrowed the rosary from the Buddhists, and that the Crusaders borrowed it from the Saracens and introduced it into Europe. Some think that it was introduced into Christendom by Domenic, the founder of the Black Friars, about A.D. 1221, with the sanction of Pope Pius V.

The Muḥammadans call their Rosary " SUBḤAH," because it is used for the " praise " of Allâh. Each of its 99 beads is associated with one of the " beautiful names " of Allâh, and the " pillar " or elongated bead which completes the 100 is reserved for the ineffable Name of God. Dividing marks, made usually of bone or ivory, are placed after the 33rd and 66th beads, so that the devotee may rest at these points. The beads are usually made of wood, acacia-sycamore, *sunt*-wood, *shâj*-wood, and sandal wood, but coloured glass beads are very popular among the *fallaḥîn*, or peasants. Beads are also made of ivory or bone and the grey, smoke-coloured agates found in Arabia. The beads of the rosaries carried by men are small, but on days of festival the girls and women wear rosaries made of large wooden beads coloured red. Large numbers of these are brought from Makkah by pilgrims who have made the *ḥajj* or journey to the sacred city of the Muslims. Before colouring the beads are dipped in water from the holy well of Zemzem, which was shown to Hagar by the angels, and from which she gave her son Ishmael to drink. And a *subḥah* which has been blessed by a holy man is supposed to bring a blessing on the user of it. A tassel made of some brightly coloured stuff is generally attached to the cord on which the " pillar " is strung, and Egyptians have told me that it is intended to keep off the Evil Eye, and that evil spirits dislike tassels and fringed objects. The leather fringes attached to saddle bags are said to serve the same purpose, especially when the animal carrying them is in motion. In ancient Pentateuch rolls some of the letters have fringes attached to them, presumably with the same object.

CHAPTER III.

BABYLONIAN AND ASSYRIAN AMULETS.

The literature of the Sumerians and Babylonians which has come down to us proves that the peoples who occupied Mesopotamia from about 3000 B.C. downwards attached very great importance to magic in all its branches, and that they availed themselves of the services of the magician on every possible occasion. This is probably true also of the pre-Sumerïan inhabitants of the country, but as they had not acquired the art of writing, we have no means of knowing exactly what they thought or believed. The Sumerians invented and developed a system of writing, and the inscriptions which they wrote on tablets of clay and stone suggest that they lived anxious lives and were in perpetual fear of the attacks of hosts of hostile and evil spirits which lost no opportunity of attempting to do them harm. To protect themselves against these they employed charms and spells and incantations, and in order to destroy the operations of the Evil Eye they wore amulets of various kinds, both inscribed and un-inscribed. And to protect their houses they buried little clay figures in the foundations or embedded them in the walls. We will consider first the AMULETS in the forms of animals, birds, fish, etc. Among the early amulets in the British Museum the following are of special interest, for they are ARCHAÏC, that is to say they were made before 2500 B.C. (Plate X).

PLATE X

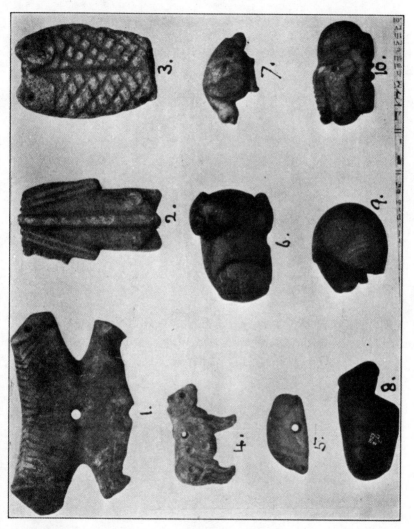

Archaic Babylonian and Assyrian amulets.

1. The fore-parts of two animals (bulls or lions ?) united [No. 116709] ; symbolic of two-fold strength. [Compare the two Lion-gods of Yesterday and To-day, seated, back to back, supporting the horizon. Book of the Dead Papyrus of Ani, sheet 7. The double Lion-god mentioned in Chapter III = Shu and Tefnut.] All animals were thus treated, and the device persisted through the, ages.

2. The frog, symbolic of fertility, as in Egypt, in glazed clay [No. 116913].

3. Two fish, side by side, symbolic of fertility [No. 120089]. These may represent the Sign of the Zodiac, Pisces, and possess an astral significance. [Compare the Egyptian mythological fishes, the Ānt and the Ábṭu.]

4. The bull, symbol of strength and virility [No. 116711]. Compare the Egyptian royal title "mighty bull."

5. The sow (?), probably symbolic of fecundity [No. 118529]. Compare the Egyptian figure of a sow with young in the British Museum [No. 11976] and the figures [Nos. 1700 and 1795].

6. The ram, symbol of virility [No. 118530]. Compare the Ram of Amen and the Ram of Mendes.

7. A bird of prey (?). Signification unknown [No. 118020].

8. A sacred bull [No. 116355]. Sometimes the figure is marked on the forehead with a triangle. Herodotus says (iii. 28) that the Apis Bull has on the forehead a white triangle, and in the bronze figures of Apis, or sacred Bull of Memphis, this white blaze is represented by a triangular piece of silver inlaid in the forehead. This figure is of the shape of an Apis Bull mummified. Its exact signification is unknown.

9. A lion's head, symbolic of strength [No. 118527].

10. A horse : symbolism unknown [No. 118019].

The ape. The oldest known specimen of this amulet is made of gold and was found at Ur of the Chaldees. It probably symbolized virility and fecundity. Amuletic figures of the goat and calf are fairly common, and a civet-cat is cut on a seal in the possession of Captain Spencer Churchill.

No. 118529.   No. 118527.

No. 118530.

Figures of animals which were used as amulets were sometimes engraved on their bases with protective designs, animals, men, etc. Examples of these designs are given above. On No. 118529 is the figure of a man, on No. 118527 are scorpions (?) and on No. 118530 are three animals.

Amulets in the form of CYLINDER-SEALS are a large and important class, and these are of special interest. The cylinder-seal was made of precious and semi-precious stones, *e.g.* agate, amethyst, carnelian, chalcedony, crystal, emerald (root of), haematite, jade, jasper, lapis lazuli, marble, onyx, sand, steatite, topaz, etc. There is little doubt that each kind of stone was believed to possess qualities peculiar to itself, and to have the power to protect the wearer from certain evils and troubles. This is proved by a text to which Mr. C. J. Gadd has been so kind as to call my attention (No. 185 in Ebeling's *Keilschrift texte aus Assur, religiösen Inhalts*). From this we learn that a seal made of KA-GI-NA stone (haematite ?) will help a man to destroy his enemy. A seal made of lapis lazuli will possess a god, and " his god will rejoice in him." A seal made of DU-SHI-A, *i.e.* rock crystal, will extend the possessions of a man, and its name is good, *i.e.* auspicious. A man possessing a seal made of TU-UD-ASH stone will walk in joy of heart. Wheresoever a man carrieth a seal made of ZA-TU-MUSH-GIR, *i.e.* green serpentine, " blessing and blessing shall be given to it." And he who possesses a seal made of GUG stone, *i.e.* red jasper or carnelian, will never be separated from the protection of his god.

The cylinder-seal was used both as a seal and as an amulet. When used as a seal it was rolled over the moist clay of the tablet in a space which was provided for it. When this was done the design on the seal and the name of its owner stood up above the surface of the tablet in relief. The witnesses to the contract, which was written both on the clay case and the tablet inside it, affixed their seals to the document, and on some of the " case-tablets " in the British Museum as many as ten or a dozen impressions of the seals of the contracting parties and their witnesses will be found. The designs on cylinder-seals were cut in outline by a metal graver, and a drill was used in producing the deeper parts. There seems to be little doubt that the cylinder-seal was introduced into Egypt from Babylonia at a very early period, and the hieroglyph ⌒ shows that it was attached to a cord or chain by which it might be hung round the neck. In Egypt the cylinder-seal was made of wood, bronze or copper, bone or ivory, blue glazed porcelain, etc. Its use ceased in Egypt before the rise of the New Kingdom, and in Babylonia before the conquest of Alexander the Great took place. The names cut on cylinder-seals are of various kinds, and the common scene of the type usually called " Gilgamish and Enkidu fighting beasts " almost certainly represents the combat of good genii against the assault of evil and hostile monsters.

The series of typical cylinder-seals reproduced on Plate XI may now be described.

1. Cylinder-seal of Adda the scribe, about 2500 B.C. The scene represents the Sun-rise, and was intended to relieve the wearer from fears of the powers of darkness. The Sun-god is rising between two mountains on one of which grows the sacred tree. On the right stands Ea, the Water-god, with the river of fish flowing about him. On the left is the goddess Ishtar, who is helping Shamash, the Sun-god, to emerge from the mountain. On the right and left are attendant deities [No. 89115].

2. Scene from a cylinder-seal representing the Judgment of Zu (?) before Ea. An ancient legend says that Zu coveted the sovereignty of Enlil, and that one morning when Enlil was taking his seat

PLATE XI

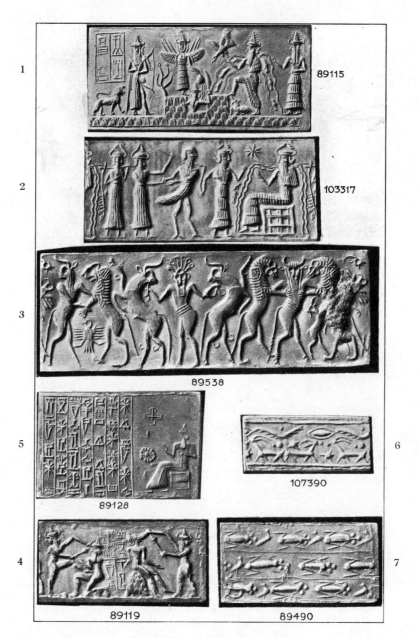

Babylonian cylinder-seal amulets.

on his throne, he seized the Tablet of Destiny of the Gods, and carried it off to a mountain where he hid himself. The gods were in great distress at the theft, and Anu, the Sky-god, entreated them to select a champion and to send him forth to punish Zu and recover the Tablet. The god Adad was chosen, but he refused to fight, and several other gods did the same. The text describing the end of the matter is wanting, but it seems that Zu was captured and brought before Ea, who pronounced judgment upon him. The value of this seal as an amulet depended upon the moral teaching of the myth. About 2500 B.C. [No. 103317].

3. Scene from a cylinder-seal representing early heroes fighting wild animals. It was also used to drive away from a man the demons which produce sickness and disease. Archaïc period [No. 89538].

4. Scene from a cylinder-seal representing the gods fighting the gods of evil and the slaughter of the demon-gods, whose skulls are being smashed by the divine maces. Period doubtful [No. 89119].

5. Scene from a characteristic cylinder-seal of the Kassite Period. On the right is a figure of Shamash the Sun-god, seated, and before him is a rosette. Above this is a form of the Kassite CROSS. The inscription is a prayer to the Sun-god for the life and prosperity of the owner [No. 89128].

6. Scene from a cylinder-seal of the Archaïc period, with a representation of a row of horned animals with an eye above them. The eye symbolized divine protection [No. 107390].

7. Scene from a cylinder-seal of the Kassite period, representing nine frogs. The frog was a fertility amulet [No. 89490].

8. (See below.)   Scene from a cylinder-seal representing the adoration of a god by a worshipper who is
accompanied by a priest and an attendant bringing an
animal as an offering.   Before the god are the solar
disk and crescent moon, symbols which were adopted
by the Himyarites, and later by Arabs and Turks,
and behind him is a naked goddess or woman whose
presence is difficult to explain.   The following illustration is made from a plaster cast of the seal in the
British Museum.

Sometimes the cylinder-seal was engraved with
a wholly religious scene and a prayer, *e.g.* that of
Shuanishuria (B.M. No. 89001), which reads, " O
Marduk, thou [great] Lord, thou Ruler of the Judg-
ments of Heaven and of Earth, unto Shuanishuria
thy servant who feareth thee, may thy countenance
be favourable." A fine selection of cylinder-seals
is exhibited in the British Museum, and descriptions of them will be found in the *Guide to the
Babylonian and Assyrian Antiquities*, 3rd edit.,
London, 1922, p. 223 f.

As examples of inscribed stone amulets of a later
date may be mentioned :—

I. A memorial tablet in the form of an amulet
inscribed with the name and titles of Esashaddon,
King of Assyria, about 680 B.C.   It was worn to
give protection from the demon Lamashtu, of which

PLATE XII

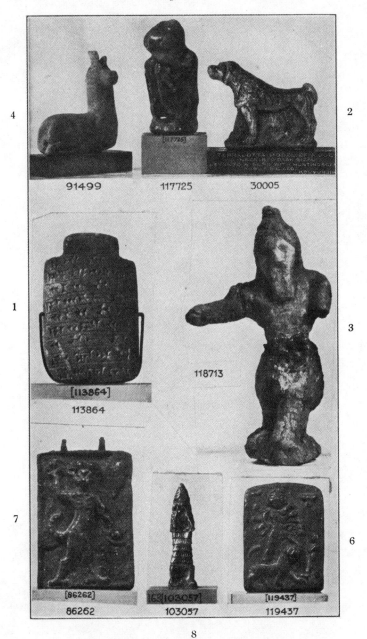

Sumerian, Babylonian and Assyrian amulets.

PLATE XIII

102. [22464]
LIMESTONE AMULET
INSCRIBED WITH A FIGURE OF
A GODDESS AND AN
INVOCATION TO HER.
[ABOUT B.C. 650]

[117759]
AMULET INSCRIBED ON ONE SIDE WITH
AN INCANTATION TO THE FEMALE DEMON
LAMASHTU. THE DEMON IS SHOWN STANDING
ON A WILD ASS, GRASPING SERPENTS AND
SUCKLING A JACKAL AND A WILD PIG.
FROM CARCHEMISH.

1   2   3

Babylonian amulets.

more will be said later. Whether the name of the king was regarded as a " word of power," or whether the king himself was held to be a magician, like Solomon, is uncertain ; in either case it is interesting to find him associated with Lamashtu [No. 113864, Plate XII, No. 1]. Amulets in this form, with the names of gods upon them, and belonging to Minaean times are found in South Arabia.

2. A limestone amulet similar in shape to the preceding. On one side is the figure of a goddess seated on a throne with her feet resting on the back of an animal. She has a star on her head, and holds a circular object in her right hand ; above her is a disk, solar or lunar, and before her an offering stand (?). The inscription is an invocation to her [No. 22464, Plate XIII, No. 1].

3. Amulet inscribed on one side, with an incantation to the female devil Lamashtu. On the other is a figure of Lamashtu, who is standing on the back of a wild ass. She is grasping a serpent in each hand, and is suckling a jackal and a wild pig [No. 117759, Plate XIII, No. 2].

4. A house-amulet. On the upper half are cut in outline figures of four gods, who are probably Marduk, who is standing on a magical beast, Ishtar, Nabû, who is standing on a magical beast, and Tashmetum [No. 118796; see page 98].

In addition to the amulets in the form of animals, cylinder-seals, tablets, plaques, etc., the Sumerians, Babylonians and Assyrians sought to protect themselves and their houses from sickness and evil spirits by the use of PROPHYLACTIC FIGURES of gods and men, goddesses and women, animals, reptiles, etc. That they did so has been known for many years, for

George Smith tells us in his *Assyrian Discoveries* (p. 78) that he found a brick box below a late pavement containing six terra-cotta figures which he described as having human bodies, and the heads of lions and large wings. The five small terra-cotta dogs, with their names inscribed on their left sides, which have

118796

been exhibited in the British Museum for the last forty years (see *Guide*, p. 221, Nos. 65–69), were for long thought to be models of the hunting dogs of Ashur-bani-pal.[1] But we now know that the

---

[1] One of these dogs is figured on Plate XII, No. 2. His name was " Dân-rigishshu," *i.e.* the " Loud-Bayer " [No. 30005].

Assyrians were in the habit of burying figures of dogs of different colours under the thresholds of their houses, so that the spirits of the dogs might repel the attacks of such evil spirits as tried to make an entry into the houses. The number of figures of dogs buried under a house was usually ten, and they were arranged five on each side of the door-way. Dr. Koldewey found under the pavements of buildings at Babylon small unbaked clay figures of gods, and groups of statuettes lying in small brick boxes.

In 1924–26 Mr. C. Leonard Woolley found at Ur of the Chaldees among the ruins of a building which probably dated from about the middle of the VIIth century B.C. a series of boxes formed of three bricks of the plano-convex type, one of the four sides of the square being open. The cover of each box was a pavement brick. In each box was usually a single figure or statuette. The boxes were lined up all round the rooms against the walls, the open side of each box facing towards the centre of the chamber ; the figures stood in their boxes like sentries and guarded the area of the room. With the figure in each box were found remains of food-stuffs, such as grain and the bones of a pigeon or some small bird, and generally a broken fragment of pottery. All the figures were made of unbaked clay, and were covered with a thin layer of lime, on which details of the form and dress were roughly sketched in black. A large number of these pro-phylactic figures have been discussed and figured by Mr. C. L. Woolley in his article, " Babylonian Prophylactic Figures," in the *Journal Royal Asiatic Society*, October, 1926, p. 689 f. In this paper are included several translations from cuneiform

inscriptions which explain the use of these figures by
Mr. Sidney Smith of the British Museum. These
prove that the figures were used in rituals in order
to avert evil hap, sickness, disease, and calamities of
all kinds. The selection of these figures for illustration in this book was made for me by Mr. Sidney

No. 90996.   No. 91837.

Smith, and the principal types are reproduced by
the illustrations here given.

1. Human figure wearing a fish skin robe. The
head of the fish forms a high pointed cap, and the
body of the fish hangs down behind. The special
function of this figure is unknown [B.M., No. 91837].

2. Bearded male figure wearing a horned head-dress and a long plain garment reaching to the feet ; the Papsukkal type of Koldewey [B.M., No. 90996].

3. A human figure naked down to the waist, with the feet and claws of an eagle, and wearing a horned cap [B.M., No. 118713], Plate XII, No. 3.

No. 118714.   No. 103225.

4. Bear standing on its hind legs. The right arm is raised, and the club which was in the hand is broken away [B.M., No. 118714].

5. The Ṣirrush or Mushrush, an animal con-quered by Marduk ; it was buried under floors or affixed to walls. A large figure of this animal was

found on the Ishtar Gate at Babylon [B.M., No. 103381] (see below). For another example see Plate XII, No. 4 [B.M., No. 91499].

6. Figure of a being, half man and half animal, holding a magical staff ; figures of this being were placed behind walls to repel the attacks which devils might make on the building [B.M., No. 103225].

7. Plaque with figures of two men fighting, and two men beating a drum ; it was used to repel the attacks of devils [B.M., No. 91906].

THE ṢIRRUSH, No. 103381.

8. A fish which was dedicated to a god during the recital of a ritual [B.M., No. 102986].

9. Figure of a monkey, in blue glaze with black lines ; its significance is unknown [B.M., No. 117725], Plate XII, No. 5.

10. Plaque with a figure of the goddess Ishtar standing on a lion and astral symbols [B.M., No. 119437], Plate XII, No. 6.

11. Plaque with a figure of a scorpion-man to avert the attacks of demons [B.M., No. 86262], Plate XII, No. 7.

12. Figure of a bird-headed winged being holding a pot similar to the beings represented on the sculptures of Ashur-naṣir-pal. This class of figure was

No. 91906.

[102986]

buried under the floor of the *Kummu*, or room in the temple in which the sick were tended [B.M., No. 90998], Plate XIII, No. 3.

13. The wild boar. " On the 29-feet level among fragments of the painted Jemdal Nasr pots there was found a steatite figure of a wild boar, $4\frac{1}{2}$ inches long and carved in the round. The whole character of the crouching brute is rendered with amazing

skill, but more marked than the realism of the work is its curious style.   It is the oldest piece of sculpture that we have from Ur, and it implies the apprentice-ship of many generations " (Woolley, in *The Times*, February 11, 1930, p. 13).

14. Bronze plaque used for averting the attacks of devils.   On one side is a figure of the devil Pazuzu, and on the other the head of Nergal.   In the third register a sick man lying on a couch is represented, and above and below are rude figures of the animals which it was the object of the priest to placate by means of prayers and offerings [B.M., No. 108979], Plate XIV.   The finest known example of this class of amulet is described in the following paragraphs.

LABARTU OR LAMASHTU.

Among all the devils and fiends of which the Mesopotamians lived in terror, the one that seems to have been the most dreaded was Labartu (or, as the name is now read, Lamashtu), a she-devil, and the daughter of the great god Anu.   She lived in the mountains, and deserts, and cane brakes in the marshes, and the magicians composed a whole series of incantations and spells against her.   She attacked pregnant women and young children with such dire results to them that people were terrified at the mere mention of her name.   Many texts of the Lamashtu Ritual have been published by Campbell Thompson, Myhrman and Thureau Dangin, but it seems that the whole of the series has not come down to us.   Stones played a very prominent part in the ritual, and it is clear that each kind of stone possessed its special magical powers ; and many of

[108979]

Reverse.

108979
1914
4-7
145

[108979]

Obverse.

Bronze Pazuzu-Nergal plaque.   [Brit. Mus., No. 108979.]

PLATE XV

Labartu or Lamashtu plaque.
(Obverse.)
Reproduced from the *Catalogus* of the De Clercq Collection
(vol. ii. plate xxxiv).

the stones used were in the form of cylinders. Some stones were male and others female. They were tied to various parts of the body by knotted cords of different colours, and sometimes had to remain in position for lengthy periods, even 100 days. The goddess Lamashtu was a violent, raging devil of terrifying aspect. In form she resembled a leopard (?), her face was that of a lion, and her feet were like those of the Storm-god Zu. With her hair tossed about wildly, and her breasts uncovered she burst out of the cane brakes like a whirlwind and chased the ox and the sheep and thrust her hands into their flesh and blood. She glided like a serpent into the houses, and went in and came out at her own good pleasure. All miscarriages among women, and all droppings of their young by animals, were attributed to her and her baleful influences operating through objects animate and inanimate.

Lamashtu is figured on a series of plaques in metal and stone which have, for the most part, been discussed by Karl Frank (see his *Babylonische Beschworungs reliefs*) and Thureau Dangin in *Revue d'Assyriologie,* vol. xviii. No. IV, p. 171 f, " Rituel et amulettes contre Labartu." The finest example of these is reproduced on Plates XV and XVI. It is a rectangular bronze plaque measuring $5\frac{1}{4}$ inches in height by $3\frac{1}{4}$ inches in width. It was bought in Syria in 1879 by M. Pérétié, and was acquired by De Clercq, and published by Clermont Ganneau in the *Revue archéologique* (" L'enfer Assyrien "), December, 1879, and republished in the *Catalogus De Clercq* (vol. ii. Plate xxxiv). On the back of the plaque is the figure of an animal demon, standing upright with the two fore-paws resting on the upper edge of the plaque, which also supports the head of the monster, which is in the round. The face looks down on the figures, etc., on the front of the plaque. The body is that of a lion, and is covered with scales and has four wings. The head has a pair of ram's horns, which lie flat on

Pazuzu, son of Ḫanpu, King of the air devils.

the sides of the head, the eyes are round and fierce, and the shape of the mouth shows that the lion is supposed to be roaring. His tail is a scorpion, and the phallus, which lies along the lower part of the belly, terminates in a snake's head. His hind legs have the claws of a bird of prey instead of feet,

PLATE XVI

Labartu or Lamashtu plaque.
(Reverse.)
Reproduced from the *Catalogus* of the De Clercq Collection
(vol. ii. plate xxxiv).

and they rest on the lower projecting border of the plaque. The name of this animal demon is PAZUZU. An inscription published by Thureau Dangin (*Revue,* p. 190) makes him say, " [I am Pazuzu, the son of Ḥanpu, king of the evil spirits of the air ; I go forth from the mountains raging like a whirlwind.]" The British Museum possesses several heads of figures of Pazuzu, chiefly in stone. The one in bronze, No. 93089, has been published by Layard ; No. 22459 (stone), by L. W. King, *Babylonian Religion,* p. 189 ; and Nos. 91873–91876 (stone), by Campbell Thompson, *Devils,* vol. i. Plate II.

The front of the plaque is divided into four registers, the largest of which is at the bottom. REGISTER I contains ten emblems which are, beginning on the left side, viz. (1) a cylindrical crown with several pairs of horns ; (2) a ram-headed staff ; (3) a thunder-bolt ; (4) a lance ; (5) two reeds bound together ; (6) an eight-rayed star on a disk ; (7) a disk with the wings and tail of a bird ; (8) a crescent ; (9) seven globes ; (10) a lamp.

REGISTER II contains figures of seven demons, each facing to the right and wearing a long fringed garment held in position by a belt round the waist. Their right arms are raised, and their clenched hands, ready to strike, are behind their heads, and their left arms are extended a little in front of them, the hands being clenched. The first has the head of a panther, the second the head of a lion, the third the head of a wolf, the fourth the head of a ram, the fifth the head of an ibex, the sixth the head of a bird, the seventh the head of a serpent. REGISTER III : Here we see a draped man lying at full length on a cushion, with his right arm raised and the palm of the hand turned towards his face. The cushion rests on a bier with one end rounded and bent upwards ; the legs of the bier are round and are fastened together by cords. At each end of the bier stands a bearded man wearing the skin of a fish, the head of which serves as a covering for the man's head, and the tail reaches the ground behind him. The right hand of each man is raised, and in his left he holds a small vessel or bucket ; his right leg is extended in front of him. On the left is a lamp which rests on a flat tablet which is tied to a tripod. On the left are two lion-headed beings facing each other, with legs terminating in the claws of birds of prey. Each wears a short tunic which is held in position by a fillet and a belt, and has a dagger in his belt. Each grasps the clenched left hand of the other, and the right hand of each is raised behind his head. The last figure in this Register has his face turned away from the bier. He is bearded, and wears an ordinary head cloth and a short tunic with a belt.

REGISTER IV : Here we have represented a river bank with reeds and a stream in which five fish are swimming to the right. The central figure is that of a devil with a woman's body which is covered with hair ; her head, which is cased in a rounded cap (?) of unusual shape, is that of a roaring lioness. Her arms are raised, and in each hand, which is on the level of her face, she holds a two-headed serpent. A small dog is sucking at her right breast and a pig at her left breast ; and her legs terminate in the claws of a bird of prey. She kneels on the back of an ass with her right knee, and her left claw rests on the ass's

head.   In the space between her legs and the back of
the ass is a scorpion.   The ass is placed in a boat,
the bow of which ends in the head of a serpent, and
the stern in the head of a bull.   The ass has one
hind leg fastened by a rope to the boat or the bank
of the stream.   Standing on the bank to the left is
a hairy monster with his arms in the same position
as those of the beings in the Second Register.   He
is perhaps the king of the evil spirits PAZUZU.   In
the space to the right are nine objects which are
difficult to identify.

The general meaning of the group of scenes
depicted on this bronze amulet is quite clear.   The
female devil in the boat is Lamashtu, whose home
is the infernal regions whence she comes when she
arrives on the earth to carry out her campaign of
slaughter and death.   The only way to stop her
from carrying out her baneful plans is to get her
back again in the Underworld, and it is necessary
to coax her to leave this earth by promising to give
her gifts.   What these gifts are is duly set out in
the incantations which are engraved on Lamashtu
amulets, and they include jewels, a spindle, a cloak
for her journey from earth to hell, provisions of
various kinds, e.g. cakes of bread baked on hot
cinders, malt, bread soaked in beer, drink necessary
to keep her from thirsting, a flask of choice oil,
sandals which will not wear out on the journey,
roasted grain packed in four leather bags, and all
these are to be stowed in four clay vessels.   In short,
she must be provided with oil to anoint herself,
apparel in which to dress herself, water and grain
with which she can make beer, and means of trans-
port, viz. a suitable boat and receptacles for her

provisions. The texts go on to say that she is to set out on her westward journey through the desert to hell at a certain time before the sun sets, and that she must go direct to the place of sunset. She must then make her way over the mountains which block the road to hell, and when this is done she must cross the river of hell, which is no other than the great World-Ocean Nâr Marratu.

The scenes on the Lamashtu amulets and the texts of the incantations agree closely, and the following prayer, which was published by L. W. King (*Babylonian Magic*, Plates 67 and 68) and translated in full by Thureau Dangin, shows that men really carried out the regulations concerning offerings to Lamashtu : " O Shamash, the *etimmu* devil which terrifieth me, who hath clung to me for several days past, and will not leave me, who doggeth my steps by day, and terrifieth me all night long, who maketh the skin of my body to rise up, and the hair of my head to stand up, who constraineth my forehead, and maketh my face feverish, and drieth up my palate, and poisoneth my flesh, and parcheth all my members, whether it be a ghost of my family and of my ancestor, or the ghost of some man who hath died a violent death, or whether it be a homeless ghost— it may or may not be one of these. O Shamash, in thy presence, I have sought for a garment with which to clothe it, and sandals for its feet, and a belt of leather for its waist, and a pot of water from which it may drink, I have given it the flour of malt, and I have supplied it with food for the journey. May it depart to the West ; may he be committed to the care of Ne-Gab, the great gatekeeper of hell ; may Ne-Gab, the great gatekeeper of hell, keep him in strict custody. May his key lock fast the lock."

The following are specimens of the shorter incantations :—

I.—(1) INCANTATION : (2) Lamash, daughter of Anu ; (3) Whose name has been uttered by the gods ; (4) Innin, queen of queens ; (5) Lamashtu, O great lady ; (6) Who seizes the painful *Asakku* ; (7) Overwhelming the '*Alû* ; (8) Come not nigh what belongeth to the man ; (9) Be conjured by Heaven ; (10) Be conjured by the Earth ; (11) Be conjured by Enlil ; (12) Be conjured by Ea.

II.—(1) INCANTATION : Lamashtu, " Daughter of Anu " ; (2) is thy first name. The second is, " Sister of the gods of the streets " ; (3) The third is, " Sword which splitteth the skull " ; (4) The fourth is, " She who kindleth a fire " ; (5) The fifth is, " Goddess [the sight] of whose face causeth horror " ; (6) The sixth is, " Committed to the hands."

Returning to the figures which were used as amulets and the incantations which were recited in connection with them, a specimen incantation may now be given :—

1. INCANTATION, that a . . . demon and an evil demon (*utukku* ?) may not [dwell] in the house of a man.

2. RITUAL.—On seven figures of the *apkallu* (*i.e.* the teachers who lived before the Flood) made of the wood of the bay-tree (?) which are crowned with the head-dress proper to each of them, and wear the apparel proper to each of them.

3. And carry in their right hand a [piece of] bay-tree (?) wood which has been burned in the fire at the top and bottom and place their left hands on their chests.

4. Write their names on their left hip. On the first image, covered in red paste for its outer garment,

5. Write, " Day of life, born of Ur." On the second, covered in gypsum,

6. Write, " Day of plenty, gracious son of Nippur." On the third, covered in gypsum and with water drawn on him in black wash,

7. Write, " Day of delight grown up in Eridu." On the fourth, covered with black wash, write, " Fortunate day, created in Kullah."

8. On the fifth, covered with IM·KAL·LA· write, " Day of bright face, nursling of Kesh." On the sixth, covered in green paste,

9. Write, " Lucky day, exalted judge of Lagash." On the seventh, wearing IM·KAL· of carnelian (?),

10. Write, " Day that has given life to him who is smitten protection of Shuruppak."

11. Bury at the head of the bed. Recite before them the incantation, " O you seven eldest (or, leading) APKALLU."

---

12. Seven clay figures of the *apkallu*, which have faces of birds and wings fitted, and carry a *mulilu* (cleansing implement ?) in their right hands.

13. And a wooden bucket in their left hands, covered in gypsum, cloaked with a bird's wings on the *teqeti*.

14. Bury in the second pavement of the house at the head of the bed. Recite before them the incantation, " You are the figures of the guardian *apkallu*."

---

15. Seven clay figures of the *apkallu*; covered in gypsum, cloaked in the skin of a fish of black paste, carrying in their right hands the same thing, and in their left hands the same thing,

16. Bury in the frieze on the wall of the *kummu* chamber. Their incantation as before.

---

17. Seven clay figures of the *apkallu*, covered in gypsum, cloaked in the skin of a fish, grasping in their right hands the date-spathe, with their left hands

18. Their breasts, bury facing the door behind the chair. Incantation as before.

19. Seven clay figures of the *apkallu*, covered in gypsum, cloaked in the skin of a fish,

20. Carrying in their right hands the *urigallu* reed (standard ?), grasping their breasts with their left hands, bury in the middle of the house in front of the chair.

---

21. Seven tamarisk figures of the divine Seven, crowned with the head-dress proper to each of them, wearing the apparel proper to each of them,

22. Standing on a base of *p(b)uridu* (reed matting), covered with red paste, carrying in their right hands a *kultu* of copper,

23. In their left hands a copper dagger, their waists girdled with a band of copper, caps of copper on their heads . . .

24. With horns of copper fitted, bows and quivers stand at their sides,

25. Bury opposite the figure of tamarisk. Recite before them the incantation, " You are the figures of the divine Seven, the great gods."

The text then goes on to speak of a tamarisk figure of the goddess Narudu which is to be buried in the *kamu* gate (*i.e.* the principal gate), seven figures of weapon-men or " club-bearers " which are to be buried in the same gate behind the dagger-bearers ; a tamarisk figure inscribed " Over-thrower of evil deeds " and " Introducer of the good *shedu* and good *lamassu* " ; a tamarisk figure of the god of the house ; clay figures of the Fish-man ; of the Scorpion-man, male and female ; of Latarak in green and black paste ; of the Lion-man ; of ten dogs. The figures of the dogs, which were to be painted in different colours, were to be buried in the *kamu* gate. For the complete translation from which the above extracts are taken, see Sidney Smith, *Journal Royal Asiatic Society*, 1926.

Some details of the Ritual of prophylactic and evil-averting figures are supplied in the following extract published by Zimmern, No. 54, and rendered into English by Sidney Smith (*Journal Royal Asiatic Society*, 1926, p. 205).

INCANTATION : For the raising up of their arms I have stretched out a red cloth above, I have hung a spotted cord round, in their hands I have set the date-spathe. I have made the *usurtu* perfect, I have put a wash of gypsum round them. At the head of the seven of them, of those with terrible wings, I have set Nergal. I put Nusku at their head in the furnace. Two figures, twins, bound together, whose form is complete " overthrowers of wicked devils," I set at the sick man's head, right and left. The figure of LUGAL·GIR·RA· who has no equal, I set on the *riksu* of the house: the figure of SHIT·HAM·TA·E·A· who has no rival, the figure of Narudu, the sister of the great gods, I set at the bottom of the bed. That nought evil might approach, I set Latarak and Latarak in the gate. To drive away everything evil I set up a *hulduppu* opposite the gate. Fighting twins of gypsum I drew on the door. Fighting twins of the enclosure, of bitumen, I set up in the gateway wings, right and left. Two figures of the guardians of Ea and Marduk I set up in the gate, right and left. The incantation is the incantation of Marduk. The magician is the figure of Marduk. Repeat for so-and-so the son of so-and-so, whose god is so-and-so, whose goddess is so-and-so, in whose body there is sickness, the incantation, " When the cattle come home, when the cattle go out, do you, offspring of the sweet water, holy sons of Ea, eat what is good, drink honey, may nought that is evil approach the place you guard."

———————————

When you have recited this before the seven figures of those with wings, in front of whom Nergal stands, recite the following before the seven figures of the divine Seven, made of wood of the bay-tree (?)

which carry clubs. INCANTATION : " Beating down the evil *rabisu*, sparing life, exercising force, turning back the breast of the evil, preserving the oracular utterances of Enlil, fire that overwhelms the unfriendly dagger that overbears fate . . . that lights up mankind, divine Seven that destroy the wicked."

The following illustrates the symbolism of the objects which were used in the Ritual :—

14. The gypsum and bitumen which they smear on the gate of the sick man's house.

15. The gypsum is the god Ninurta, the bitumen is the *utukku* demon. Ninurta pursues the *utukku* demon.

16. The two *zisurru* which surround the sick man's bed are the gods LUGAL·GIR·RA· and SHIT·HAM·TA·E·A·

17. The three meal-heaps which are thrown down are Anu, Enlil and Ea.

18. The *usurtu* which they drew in front of the bed, that is the net ; it surrounds everything bad.

19. The skin of the *gugallu*, and the *URUDU· NIG·KAL·GÂ* which they . . . at the head of the sick man.

20. The skin of the *gugallu* is Anu, and the *URUDU·NIG·KAL·GÂ* is Enlil ; the *urigallu* reeds.

21. Which are set up at the head of the sick man are the divine Seven, the great gods, the sons of Ishara.

22. The *hulduppu* goat which is set at the head of the bed of the sick man is the god Nin. AMASH· KU·GÂ·

23. The shepherd of Enlil. The censer and torch which are put in the sick man's house.

24. The censer is the god KU·BU· the torch is Nusku.

See Sidney Smith in *Journal Royal Asiatic Society*, 1926, p. 205 f.

CYLINDER-SEALS AS VOTIVE OFFERINGS.

In the observations on the cylinder-seal printed above we have only dealt with it as an amulet ; but it seems that the cylinder-seal was sometimes used as a votive offering, and was laid before the god, and was thereafter regarded as the property of the god. Sidney Smith has called attention (*Journal Royal Asiatic Society*, 1926, p. 444) to the fact that among the large number of cylinder-seals now known, whilst the greater number of them show marks of hard wear, and cleaning and of being worn as amulets, many are in such an excellent state of preservation that they look as if they had only just left the hands of their makers. Basing his opinion on a tablet in the British Museum (No. 117666), he thinks that this is due to the fact that cylinder-seals which were " before " a divine statue or symbol would not be continually used, and that they were thus enabled to retain their pristine clearness. The tablet to which he refers, and the text of which he translates, is inscribed with a royal command in which an official is ordered to search for a certain cylinder-seal, and to take it and bring it to him. The correctness of this view is proved by two cylinder-seals which were found at Babylon, the one bearing the image of Marduk, and the other that of Adad ; both seem to have belonged to the " treasure of Marduk."

THE CYLINDER-SEAL IN ASSYRIA, PERSIA AND PHOENICIA.

The Babylonians of the late Empire used cylinder-seals in the same way as the early Babylonians, but as a rule they are much smaller, though the traditional scenes and figures are found on them. The Assyrians also used cylinder-seals and introduced on them the characteristic figures of their gods, and figures of men grouped about the sacred tree. The Cappadocians and Hittites also adopted the cylinder-seal, but the scenes found on them are arranged differently from those found on Babylonian cylinder-seals. Figures of gods standing upon lions appear for the first time. The Phoenicians borrowed Assyrian designs for their cylinder-seals, but wrote the names of their owners with Phoenician letters. About the time of the downfall of the Assyrian Empire after the destruction of Nineveh (612 B.C.), the place of the cylinder-seal for sealing clay tablets was taken by CONE-SEALS, in sard, carnelian, agate, chalcedony, etc., and they were used for this purpose throughout the Persian Period down to about 350 B.C. The favourite stone for seals of this period was chalcedony, and on these were cut symbols of the gods Shamash, Sin, Adad, Marduk and Nabû ; mythical beasts and winged demons ; men standing by the sacred tree above which is the symbol of the god Asshur ; scenes from the Gilgamish legend ; man-headed goat-fish, man-headed birds, cock, crescent ; hunting scenes, etc. The scenes on two chalcedony cones are here reproduced. In the first (B.M., No. 115604) we see three bulls' heads created in a disc formation. This device was magical, and it appears in many forms during the Achaemenian

No. 115604.   No. 119919.

Period, and after down to the Middle Ages. In the second (B.M., No. 119919) we see a mounted horseman engaged in conflict with some animal ; perhaps the foundation of the legend of St. George and the Dragon.

SASSANIAN AMULETS AND SEALS.

Here for convenience sake may be mentioned the large class of amulets and amuletic seals which were used in Western Irân or Persia during the period of the rule of the Sassanides, *i.e.* from about A.D. 226–632. They are commonly known as " Pehlevi gems," because the inscriptions upon them, which are usually the names of the owners or gods, are written in Pehlevi characters. These characters were derived from a Semitic alphabet, which was probably Syriac. Pehlevi seals are made of different kinds of stone, agate, lapis lazuli, sard, carnelian, chalcedony, and variegated hard stones. The larger specimens are rounded and pierced and were threaded on string or wires and carried like cylinder-seals, or attached to the body like amulets ; the smaller ones, which are flat, formed the bezels of rings. On the largest of them, which resemble oval plaques, we find busts of governors and women. Favourite representations on them are :—Palm branches and flowers held in hands, animals, especially the winged horse (Pegasus ?), birds, reptiles, mythological creatures, and elaborate linear devices. Six characteristic specimens from the British Museum Collection are here given. (1) Three little men and an indeterminate object ; this scene is very

No. 119382.   No. 119351.   No. 119392.

No. 119979.   No. 119983.   No. 119971.

common and probably illustrates some legend [No. 119382]. (2) Three lions' heads in disc form [No. 119351]. (3) A palm branch and a man worshipping a star and the crescent moon [No. 119392]. (4) A symbol which was probably supposed to possess magical powers [No. 119979]. (5) A semi-human figure grasping the symbols of the Beginning and the End ; between his legs is the figure of an animal (mouse ?) [No. 119983]. (6) A hand with the thumb and index-finger touching [No. 119971].

CHAPTER IV.

According to the Life of St. ANTHONY, the Great, of EGYPT, the Egyptians were in the habit of embalming the bodies of the saints and martyrs, and of placing them not in graves but in their houses so that they might do honour to them. ANTHONY had entreated the bishops to order the people not to do this, but the custom continued. When he was dying he commanded those who were about him, saying : " Dig a grave then, and bury me therein, and hide my body under the earth. And let these my words be observed carefully by you, and tell ye no man where ye lay me ; [and there I shall be] until the Resurrection of the dead, when I shall receive [again] this body without corruption " (BUDGE, *Paradise of the Fathers*, Vol. i. p. 72). This passage makes it quite clear that the Egyptian Christians continued to mummify their dead long after their conversion to Christianity, and the tombs of *Egypt* of the early Christian period support ANTHONY'S statement. Anthony died about A.D. 360, and thus it is certain that the Egyptian Christians had been mummifying their dead for at least 260 years, for the introduction of Christianity into EGYPT cannot be placed later than about A.D. 100. There is no satisfactory evidence showing under whose auspices the Christianizing of Egypt took place, though it is generally attributed to ST. MARK, who began to preach in Alexandria about A.D. 69. Though the form of the Egyptian Religion which was in use between 200 B.C. and A.D. 100, with its doctrine of a Last Judgment and its fastings and prayers and asceticism generally, was an excellent preparation for the reception of Christianity by the Egyptians, when once their conversion was effected, they determined to break absolutely with the old pagan religion and its cults. They discarded the hieroglyphic, hieratic and demotic scripts, and formulated an alphabet for themselves, which included the Greek alphabet and a number of conventional forms of old Egyptian characters ; in this mixed alphabet they wrote the Coptic version of the Scriptures. They rejected the spells and the Vignettes of the Book of the Dead, and abandoned the use of the funerary amulets of the ancient Egyptians, and all their amuletic symbols save one, viz. the sign ☥ *ānkh* which means " life, living." What object this sign represented cannot be said, but as to the idea which both pagans and Egyptians associated with it there is no doubt. Gods and goddesses, and men and women, are seen holding it, and it seems that the life of every being, divine or human, depended upon his or her possession of it. From first to last the gods are seen carrying it in their right hands, and they gave life to their kings and servants presenting it to them. It has been suggested that ☥ is a conventional representation of some organ of the human body connected with procreation, and this view is probably correct. But be this as it may, the Egyptian Christian adopted it as an equivalent of the Cross of Christ, and it symbolized to them life everlasting. On the stele of ABRAHAM

(B.M., No. 1257) we have it in this form

with the letters ⋋ and Ω. On the stele of PLÊINÔS (B.M., No. 679) we have the ordinary Greek cross

, the and two *ānkh* crosses .

On the stele of SABINOS (B.M. 1352) we have ,

and ⋋ and Ω. On another stele are cut figures of doves holding ⳨ (B.M., 1327). NAVILLE found a mummy with the *suwastika* drawn on the left shoulder (see *Deir el-Bahari*, ii, p. 5), but there is no proof that the mummy was that of a Christian. There is in the British Museum (No. 54051) a mummy of a child of the early Christian or late Roman period ; the hands are crossed over the breast,

and in one he holds a cross and in the other

a flower (lotus (?) which suggests that the mummy is that of a girl). On a portion of a mummy swathing found at LYCOPOLIS is painted a Christian cross (No. 55056). On a very rare amulet which was given to the British Museum by Sir RIDER HAGGARD, the Birth of Christ is represented

(No. 469) ; Mary is seated under a tree and she holds ♀ in one hand ; on the reverse is the sign ♀ and the legend, " One God in heaven." As the woman is seated under a tree and not in a cave, it has been suggested that it is the birth of the Buddha which is represented.

The amuletic signs ♀ and ☧ which are seen on Coptic monuments older than the time of Constantine the Great, have not been found in the form of amulets. Attempts have been made to show that the sign ☧ is derived from ♀, but they appear to the writer to be unsuccessful. The sign 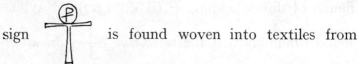 is found woven into textiles from Akhmîm. From the excavations of Coptic sites at Akhmîm and elsewhere the following amulets have been recovered :—

1. The Cross, both in the Greek and Coptic forms, made of bronze, sometimes inlaid with paste or stones, bone, ivory (?), mother-of-pearl, iron, glass.

2. The Dove, symbolic of the Holy Ghost, in mother-of-pearl.

3. Pendants in mother-of-pearl ; significance unknown.

4. Bone figures of the Virgin Mary seated in a shrine.

5. Bone plaques carved with figures of ST. GEORGE spearing a dragon ; the spear is cross-headed, and the saint holds a cross in his left hand.

6. Plaques of shell inscribed and .

Saint George of Lydda.

7. Terra-cotta bottles stamped with a cross.

8. The FISH, a symbol of Christ. The fish became a very popular amulet when it was pointed out that the letters of ἰχθὺς = Ἰησους χριστὸς θεοῦ υἱὸς σωτήρ, " Jesus Christ, son of God, the Saviour." The cross resting on a fish, and a cross with a fish on each side of it are found cut upon gems. See FORRER, *Reallexikon*, Strassburg, 1907, p. 427, Tafel 109.

9. Terra-cotta oil flasks from the tomb of St. MENAS, on which are stamped figures of the saint, camels, etc. See BUDGE, *Texts relating to Saint Mêna*, London, 1909, p. 33 f. The dolphins which protected the saint's body at sea are often sculptured on funerary Coptic stelae.

10. Large crosses made of lead and stone, which were used as funerary monuments. (See B.M., Nos. 46708 and 1339.)

Among the Copts the amulets which were intended to protect the dead took the form of sheets of inscribed papyrus ; many of these are preserved in the British Museum. One contains a copy of the apochryphal letter of King Abgar to Christ, and the first words of each of the Four Gospels (Oriental 4919 (2)). Another is inscribed " Lord God Almighty help me ! " and a third is inscribed with some of the vowels, each seven times repeated and in separate lines (Crum, *Catalogue*, p. 175).

CHAPTER V.

EGYPTIAN AMULETS.

The Egyptians in all periods of their history were lovers of amulets, and they placed them under and in their houses and tombs, and set them up in their temples, and wore them when living, and caused them to be placed on their bodies when dead. They made them of many kinds of stones, both common and semi-precious, various kinds of wood, gold, copper, silver-gold, ivory, bone, shell, wood, wax, faïence, etc. The common word for *amulet* in the dynastic period was *mk-t*, 𓅓𓎡𓏏, which means "protector"; a synonym frequently used in the texts is *udjau*, 𓎗𓂝𓎗𓊁, *i.e.* "the thing which keeps safe," the "strengthener." Many of the substances of which amulets were made were believed to possess influence or properties which could be absorbed by the wearers. Amulets with names of gods or words of power inscribed upon them were held to be more powerful than those which were uninscribed, and those which had been "blessed" by the magician, and therefore contained a portion of his spiritual power, were the most powerful of all. Most of the Egyptian amulets known have come from the tombs of Egypt, and were "protectors" worn by the dead; it is probable that they are identical with those which were worn by the living.

The oldest amulets from Egypt belong to the Neolithic period. Among them are figures *in flint* of the crocodile, some horned animal (goat ?), the head of a cow with a woman's face (the goddess HATHOR ?), the hippopotamus, the cuttle-fish (?), and the objects 𝖸 and 𝖯; the first of the two objects may be the *Kef-pesh*, an instrument used in connection with birth ceremonies, and the second may be a feather. All these were worn to give the wearers virility and fecundity, and the last two mentioned are probably models of some human

The great amulet of the Sun-gods of sunrise and sunset in the form of a lion with a head at each end of his body.

organ of generation. The flint arrow heads were also used as amulets. To the same period belong the green slate models of tortoises or turtles, rams, stags, bears, birds (bats ?), which are exhibited in the British Museum (see *Guide to the 4th, 5th and 6th Egyptian Rooms*, p. 281 f).

The oldest AMULETIC SIGN used by the dynastic Egyptians is ☥, to which they assigned the phonetic value of *ānkh* or *ānḫ*. What object it represents is not known, but it was probably some part of the human body which the Egyptians believed to be intimately connected with generation and with the maintenance of life. The meaning of the word *ānkh* is " life," " living," in fact " everlasting life " and the " life which cannot die." Every god and goddess and divine being possessed it, and by it their life was maintained. They bestowed it on kings and also on the souls who were acquitted in the Hall of Judgment, and those who received it lived for 𓆓𓏤𓆓, *i.e.* " one hundred thousand millions of years." When the Egyptians embraced Christianity in the Ist century they adopted the sign ☥, though of pagan origin, and its meaning, and it appears on funerary monuments side by side with the Christian Cross. The *amulet* ☥ was made of wood, wax, metal, stones of various kinds, faïence, etc. ; this fact proves that the Egyptians did not know what object the sign ☥ represented. The principal funerary amulets were :

1. The SCARAB, *scarabaeus sacer*, 𓆣, one of the class of the dung-eating beetles. This beetle collects a mass of dung, lays in it one egg, and then kneads the dung together and finally makes it into a round ball about 2 inches in diameter. This done, it turns its head away from the ball, and with its hind legs rolls the ball along the ground into some sunny place, where under the influence of the heat of the sun, the egg is hatched, and the little beetle lives and flourishes on the excrement with which the egg has been surrounded. For a naturalist's description of the beetle, see J. H. FABRE, *The Sacred Beetle and others*, London, 1919. From the earliest times the Egyptians associated this beetle with the god of creation, and its egg-ball with the sun ; the god was

believed to roll the ball of the sun across the sky even as the beetle rolled its ball over the ground. And heat and life came from the sun, just as the larva of the beetle, hatched in the egg-ball and nourished on its substance, proceeded from the egg-ball. The god who rolled the solar ball across the sky was called *Kheperà, i.e.* " the Roller," and in the Book of Àmmi Ṭuat we see him pushing the sun into the sky at dawn. The Egyptians wore models of the beetle when living to give them the life and strength of the god of creation. They placed in their mummies models in green stone or black basalt or haematite of the *Goliathus Atlas* beetle, to effect the RESURRECTION of their dead kinsfolk. These are the well-known " heart sca-rabs," on which copies of Chapter xxx*b* of the Book of the Dead are inscribed.

Colossal models of the scarab were set up upon pedestals in the temples, *e.g.* the example which was found by Legrain in the temple of Àmen-Rā at Karnak, and was made in the reign of Àmenḥetep III. The largest known temple scarab is in the British Museum (Central Saloon, No. 965). It is uninscribed, is 5 feet long, 3 feet wide and weighs over two tons ; it was brought from Constantinople by Lord Elgin. Àmenḥetep III had many hundreds of large scarabs made, and recorded on them the events of his reign which he deemed noteworthy, viz.: 1. His marriage with the lady Tî. 2. His Wild-Cattle Hunt in the second year of his reign. 3. The genealogy of Queen Tî. 4. The slaughter of 102 lions when hunting during the first 10 years of his reign. 5. The digging of a lake in Western Thebes. His son Àmenḥetep IV (Àakhunàten) also made use of large scarabs to commemorate important events (see B.M., No. 51084). For texts describing these events and translations (see BUDGE, *The Mummy*, 2nd edit., p. 298). Scarab amulets were made of almost every kind of material, and they vary in length from half an inch to 2 inches. They did not come into general use until the XIth or XIIth Dynasty, and their vogue ceased about 550 B.C. They have been found in Elam, Persia, Babylonia, Syria, Phoenicia, Palestine and in nearly all the countries round the Mediterranean. In Egypt many of the scarab amulets were also used as seals. Those who wish to study the scarab amulet should examine the unrivalled collection in the British Museum.

2. The ṬEṬ (or DED) was associated with the backbone, or certain of the lower vertebrae, to which it gave strength and stability in life, and renewed power to the back after death. See Chapter clv of the Book of the Dead.

3. The TJET, 𓋿 Coptic ⲧⲟⲧⲉ or ⲧⲟⲟⲧⲉ. An amulet which was commonly made of some *red* substance, *e.g.* red jasper, red glass, red wood, red porphyry, red porcelain, and carnelian, or sand, or reddish agate ; examples in solid gold are known, and in gilded stone. The Tjet is a conventional form of the genital organs of the goddess Isis (see BUDGE, *Osiris*, vol. i. p. 276 ; vol. ii. p. 280), and it was supposed to bring to the wearer, living or dead, the virtue of the blood of Isis[1]. It and the Ṭeṭ

---

[1] The Coptic makes it clear that this amulet was intended to represent the *vulva* or *matrix* of Isis. The forms ⲟⲟⲧⲉ, ⲟ⳨ and ⲧⲟⲧⲉ are the equivalent of the hieroglyphic 𓄿 𓏏 𓆑 𓂋 𓏏 *ati-t.*

are often seen in the hands of statues and on coffins, and armed with these all-powerful divine amulets, the deceased was ready to enter the Judgment Hall of Osiris. The text of Chapter clvi of the Book of the Dead is often found cut on the Tjet.

4. The URS, or head-rest or pillow, as an amulet is usually made of haematite, and is rarely inscribed; when it was intended for use as an article of funerary equipment, it was made of wood, and ivory, and stone of various kinds, and wooden and ivory examples are usually inscribed with Chapter clxvi of the Book of the Dead. The large pillows were placed under the necks of mummies to " lift up the heads " of the deceased persons in the Other World, and to prevent the " decapitation of their heads." " Their enemies shall have no power to cut off the heads of the deceased, but the deceased shall cut off the heads of their enemies," says the text.

5. The ÀB or HEART amulet was made of many kinds of red stones, red jasper, red glass, red porcelain, red paste and red wax, and it was inscribed in the breast of the mummy in place of the heart which was mummified separately. The upper part of it was sometimes made in the form of a human head. The heart was, to the Egyptians, the source of all life and thought, and it was believed to be the seat of the BA, or what may be termed the " heart soul," *i.e.* the soul of the physical body. It was connected in some way, which is, at present, not clear, with the KA, or " double," which was perhaps the sub-conscious vital power. The texts show that the heart was supposed to contain the soul of Kheperà, the self-created and self-existing god, and it was therefore immortal. The Book of the Dead

contains several spells and prayers for the preservation of the heart, viz. Chapters xxvi, xxvii, xxviii,
xxix (3 versions), xxx (2 versions). The text most
commonly found on models of the heart is Chapter
xxx*b*, which, according to one Rubric, is as old as
MEN-KAU-RĀ (MYCERINUS), a king of the IVth
Dynasty, and according to another, as old as SEMTI,
a king of the IInd Dynasty. The other spells gave

The Prayer-spell inscribed on Heart-scarabs. It was in use in Egypt for
more than three thousand years, and is perhaps the oldest complete prayer
in the world.

the deceased powers in the Other World, but Chapter
xxx*b* enabled a man to obtain the verdict of " Truth-
speaker " in the Judgment Hall of Osiris. It may
be rendered, " Heart of my mother! Heart of my
mother! Heart of my being! Oppose me not in
my evidence (or testimony). Thrust me not aside
before the Judges. Fall not away from me before
the Guardian of the Balance. Thou art my KA
in my body, Khnemu making sound my members.

Come thou forth to the place of happiness (or felicity) whither we would go. Make not my name to stink with the Assessors, who make men, during my existence. Make good a good bearing with joy of heart at the weighing of words and deeds. Utter no falsehood concerning me in the presence of the Great God. Assuredly thou shalt be distinguished rising up as a speaker of the truth."

6. The VULTURE, NER-T, made of gold, and inscribed with Chapter clvii of the Book of the Dead, when tied to the neck of the mummy, gave the deceased the strength and fierceness of the goddess ISIS, when she was wandering about in the papyrus swamps in the Delta in the form of a vulture. The use of this amulet is not older than the XXVIth Dynasty, say 650 B.C.

7. The COLLAR or PECTORAL, USEKH-T, made of gold, and inscribed with Chapter clviii of the Book of the Dead, when tied to the neck of the mummy, gave the deceased freedom from all possible fetterings about the neck. The use of this amulet is not older than the XXVIth Dynasty.

8. The PAPYRUS SCEPTRE, UADJ, was made of mother-of-emerald, and inscribed with Chapter clix of the Book of the Dead ; when laid on the neck or breast of the mummy gave the deceased renewed youth and virility, and all the qualities of the growing papyrus plant. It was worn as a pendant. Usually this amulet has the form of a budding papyrus shoot, but it is also found sculptured on a small rectangular plaque made of the *neshmet* stone. In the Papyrus of NEBSENI (early XVIIIth Dynasty) we see in the Vignette to Chapter clx of the Book of the Dead the god THOTH, ibis-headed, who is called

the " Great God," presenting to NEBSENI a plaque whereon a papyrus shoot is sculptured. The text which was supposed to be cut upon it brought to the deceased the protection of the " Words of Thoth."

9. The UDJAT, a word which means literally " Eye," was an amulet made in this form ; it typified good health, soundness, safe protection, and physical comfort and well-being generally. The twin Udjats represent the Eye of the sun and the Eye of the moon, *i.e.* the two Eyes of the very ancient Sky-god ḤER ; they are found

The Baboon, the associate of Thoth, restoring the Udjat or Eye to Àāḥ, the Moon-god, after it had been swallowed by Set, who was made to vomit it.

painted on coffins as early as the VIth Dynasty, and they were painted on articles of funerary equipment throughout the dynastic period. An ancient legend stated that the powers of evil succeeded in blinding the Eye of the Sun-god Rā during an eclipse or prolonged storm, and that THOTH came to the god and healed his Eye, and restored it to his face. Another legend stated that SET, the Devil, when prowling in the sky one evening saw the crescent moon, and swallowed it, but one of the gods, presumably THOTH, came against him quickly, and speared him, and he was obliged to vomit the crescent moon from his body.   Chapter clxvii of the Book of the Dead contains a spell the recital of which would cause THOTH to bring the Udjat to the deceased during his journey to the kingdom of OSIRIS.   The Rubric of Chapter cxl says that that chapter (which was to be recited during the longest day of the Egyptian year) was to be said over two Udjats—the one made of lapis lazuli or *mag* stone plated with gold or set in a gold frame, and the other of amethyst or carnelian.   The second Udjat, if placed on the mummy of a man, would procure for him a seat in the Boat of Rā, and make him become a god.   The Udjat amulet was made of gold, silver, copper, many kinds of semi-precious stones, wood, wax, and faïence, glazed in various colours.   The enormous numbers of Udjats which have been found in the tombs prove that this amulet possessed unusual importance in the minds of the Egyptians, and that it fulfilled a very special service.   My belief is that the Egyptians, like the Chinese, were terrified by their fear of the Evil Eye, and that the Udjat was worn or carried universally as a protection against it.

10. The COW-AMULET, AHAT, was a figure of a cow wearing the solar disk and plumes between her horns, and made of gold, which was tied to the neck of the mummy.   This was used in connection with the HYPOCEPHALUS, which was placed under the back of the head of the mummy, and was formed of a series of circular layers of linen gummed together, and covered with a thin layer of white plaster.   This

amulet was intended to represent the pupil of the Eye of Rā, and on it were drawn in outline figures of solar gods, *e.g.* Horus-Sept, Kheperà, the sons of Horus, etc. Around these figures ran the text of Chapter clxii of the Book of the Dead. The Egyptians believed that if this amulet was placed under the head of the mummy it would emit heat and keep warmth in the body of the deceased until he arrived in the Kingdom of Osiris. The chief god was PAR, but in order to obtain his assistance it was necessary to appeal to him by his secret magical names which the text supplies, viz. Haqa-haqa-ḥerḥer, Àulàuàa-qersaanqlebati, Khalseran and Khalsata. An ancient legend stated that when Rā was about to set for the first time, the Cow-goddess, fearing that he would lose all his heat during the night, caused him to be surrounded with beings of fire, which kept him warm until he rose again in the sky. The amulet AHAT was supposed to do for the deceased what the Cow-goddess did for Rā.

11. The FROG amulet is usually made of gold, hard stone, steatite and glazed faïence, but examples of it in gold are not common. It carried with it the help and protection of ḤEQIT, the goddess who presided over conception and birth, and who may be described as the " midwife goddess." She was supposed to be present at the birth of every king of Egypt, and she assisted ISIS in resuscitating OSIRIS and in making effective her union with him. The general idea associated with the frog amulet was fecundity and fertility, and among many of the tribes in Central Africa the women eat both the frog and the beetle, so that they may have large families. The little green tree frog appears in large

numbers a day or two before the rise of the Nile, and the natives regard it as a symbol of new life and prolific generation. The Copts, probably having in mind the phases of the physical development of the frog, adopted it as a symbol of the Resurrection, and it is often seen sculptured on monuments in the catacombs of Alexandria side by side with the Coptic Cross. On a bronze object in the British Museum a frog appears at the end of a phallus.

12. The NEFER amulet ♁ was frequently made of carnelian, or sand, or some semi-precious red stone, but very large numbers were made of glazed faïence, and were pierced at one end so that they might be strung with beads on necklaces and pectorals. The object represented by the amulet was, probably, in the late period a lute or some other kind of stringed musical instrument ; but originally it seems to have been the heart with the wind pipe (?). Whatever the object was it is pretty clear from the texts that the amulet was supposed to give to the wearer youth, joy, strength and happiness, and good luck generally. The word NEFER means good, to be good, beautiful, gracious, pleasant, and the like.

13. The BA amulet 🦅 was in the form of a man-headed hawk wearing a beard. It was supposed to represent the heart-soul, but it seems to be more probable that it was a symbol of the vital strength of a man, and the hawk-portion of it suggests its relationship to Horus. At all events, the root *ba* means " strength," to be powerful. After death the BA was believed to visit the body whence it came in the tomb, and in graves narrow passages were left in the pits so that the soul might

find its way there.   In the Pyramids of Meroë openings were left in the stone covering near the apex
so that the BA might enter them, and a ledge was
placed beneath each opening for it to stand on.   In
the Vignette to Chapter lxxxix of the Book of the
Dead the BA is seen visiting its body, to which it
presents the symbol *shen* ☲ , symbolic of eternal
life.   The final union of all souls with their bodies

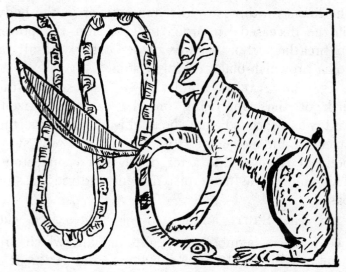

The Cat (Rā) slaughtering the Serpent of Darkness (Āpep) symbolic of the
triumph of Law, Order and Goodness over Chaos, Wrong and Evil.

was believed to take place in the heavenly ANU
HELIOPOLIS. Small figures of the BA made of
gold and inlaid with semi-precious stones, and large
figures of it, with outspread wings, were laid on the
breast of the mummy, probably with the view of
preserving the body from decay. Some think
that such figures, under the influence of the spells
in the Chapter mentioned above, flew to the place
where the gods gathered together, and represented

the person whose body lay in the tomb. And others take the view that the soul when it came to the tomb took up its abode in the BA figure. A very fine stone BA, with pendent breasts, from Nubia, is preserved in the British Museum (No. 53965). The Copts adopted the BA, and it is found sculptured on their funerary monuments (B.M., No. 1651).

14. The SMA amulet $\bar{\Upsilon}$ was buried in the folds of the linen swathings of the mummy, or in the body of the deceased, in order to give him the power to breathe ; it is usually made of dark basalt or some brownish-black coloured stone.

15. The ÁAKHU amulet $\text{\textcircled{.}}$ represented the disk of the sun rising on the eastern horizon, and was worn so that it might give a man the strength and power of HORUS or RĀ ; it was symbolic of renewed life after death and resurrection. This amulet was made of red stone and red glass or paste.

16. The SHUTI amulet $\int \,_\searrow^\frown \, [\![$ represented the two feathers, symbolic of light and air, which are seen on the heads of RĀ, OSIRIS, and ÁMEN-RĀ. The ATEF plumes $\underline{\text{\textUU}}$, which are the special characteristic of OSIRIS and PTAḤ-SEKER-ASÁR, appear to be associated with the resurrection. This amulet was made of gold and semi-precious stones of various colours.

17. The SHEN amulet Q seems to have symbolized eternity, or perhaps a very large but indefinite number of years, and the space embraced by the all-encircling power of the Sun-god. The hieroglyph is thought to represent the end of a cylindrical seal-cylinder which is either resting on,

or is being rolled over, a piece of clay to make a seal. On the other hand, it may well be a picture in outline of a ring with a long bezel attached to it.

18. The REN or name-amulet. In some inscriptions the name of the king is enclosed in what seems to be a piece of rope tied in a sort of double knot at the end of the name. As has been said elsewhere, the name of a god, or man, was regarded as his soul, and the knotted cord was intended to preserve it from evil magical influences and to maintain and prolong his life. The ordinary form of the REN is ⊂◗, and it is commonly called a " cartouche."

19. The SERPENT'S head amulet, which was made of red stone or red glass or red faïence, was regarded as a protection against the bite of the cobra and other venomous snakes. It was worn by the living and the dead, and the texts from the xxxivth and xxxvth Chapters of the Book of the Dead which are inscribed on the amulet show that it was intended to prevent the mummy from being devoured by the snakes and worms of the Ṭuat.

20. The MENÂT ⌐ 𓏤 𓂝 𓎟 amulet consisted of a necklace or collar to which was attached the curiously shaped pendant shown in the determinative of the word given above. This amulet was worn by the gods and goddesses, e.g. Hathor, Isis, Ptah and Osiris, who in the minds of the Egyptians were associated with virility and fecundity, birth and new life, and also the resurrection. It was buried with the dead with the view of preserving in them the sexual desires which they had possessed in life, and providing them with the means for giving effect to them. As an amulet for the living and the

dead it was made of lapis lazuli, and, when intended
to be attached to statues, of bronze or copper.   It
was suspended over the back of the neck, through
which it exercised its influence on the spinal column.

21. The LADDER amulet, *maq-t* ⳍ 𓅓 𓐍, provided the deceased with the means of ascending
from earth to the floor of heaven, *i.e.* the sky.   An
ancient legend says that OSIRIS wished to ascend to
heaven, but had not sufficient strength to do so.
RĀ seeing his difficulty provided the ladder, and he
and HORUS standing, one on each side of OSIRIS,
helped him to ascend.   A variant text says that the
helpers of OSIRIS during his ascent were HORUS and
SUTI, or SET.   Models of this ladder in stone and
wood have been found in the tombs, and a picture
of the Ladder is given as a Vignette in the Papyrus
of Ani (Plate xxii).   The legend is referred to in the
text in the Pyramid of Pepi I, lines 192 f, 472 and 473,
and in it we are told that it was the " two fingers
of the Lord of the Ladder " which helped OSIRIS
to ascend to the sky.   The Egyptians presumed that
the deceased might not be able to obtain the assistance of the " two fingers," and they made the amulet
described in the next paragraph to take their place.
The Hebrews also conceived the idea that a ladder
reached from heaven to earth.   See Gen. xxviii. 12.

22. The TWO-FINGERS amulet, 𓂝 𓊪 𓏤 𓏭 *dje-*
bāui, i.e. the index and medius fingers, was made of
green stone, or black basalt, or obsidian, and was
placed sometimes loose in the coffin and sometimes
among the swathings of the mummy.   It was
intended to take the place of the two fingers of the
god who helped OSIRIS to ascend the Ladder of Rā.

23. Among the primitive inhabitants of the Nile Valley models of the HEAD of HATHOR were worn as amulets by women who wished to become mothers of large families. This amulet had two forms, viz. the head of a cow and the head of a woman whose ears were large and flat like those of a cow ; both forms were cut upon plaques and scarabs which were worn as pendants of necklaces. The cult of the cow probably originated in the Sûdân, in the regions which · are inhabited by the Baḳḳâra or " Cattle-men " at the present time.

24. The KEF-PESESH amulet ☥ was used in the ceremonies connected with the Liturgy of " Opening the Mouth," and was supposed to restore to the jawbones the power of movement which had ceased owing to mummification. A couple of amulets were used in connection with the KEF-PESESH, the exact significance of which is unknown. Each has two forms, namely, ⌐ and ⌐, and is made of different kinds of iron ore. They were inserted among the linen swathings of the mummy, and brought to its protection HORUS, god of the South, and SET, god of the North.

25. The STEPS amulet *Khet*, was made of *faïence*, greenish-blue or white, and symbolized the support on which SHU stood when he separated the earth from the sky above it, and also the double steps, which resembled the Step-Pyramid of ṢAK-KÂRAH in form, on which the god KHNEMU stood, when acting as a creator god.

Among other less well-known amulets may be mentioned the ĀPER signifying " abundance," " prosperity " ; the SHUTTLE, NERT (NET), the symbol of the goddess Neith ; the SOLAR DISK on the horizon, the MASON'S MEASURE, the CARPENTER'S SQUARE, the WHITE CROWN, the RED CROWN, the HELMET, the VULTURE and URAEUS (NEBTI), the KNOT, the HAND, clenched and open ; the OFFERING-TABLET, the KA, and the FULL MOON between horns.

For drawings of about fifty of the commoner Egyptian amulets see pages 172-176.

The PECTORAL tablet as an amulet was in the form of the side of a funerary chest, and its cornice was decorated with drawings of feathers. The following are the principal scenes found on the sides : 1. The Beetle of Khepera in a boat being adored

The Vulture Goddess Mut, holding in her talons emblems of eternity and the plumes of Upper and Lower Egypt.

by Isis and Nephthys. 2. ANUBIS on a pedestal, with the deceased praying or making an offering to him. 3. The Beetle between ⸰ and ⸰. 4. RĀ and OSIRIS seated facing each other. 5. The deceased adoring the COW OF HATHOR, or OSIRIS.

The OFFERING-TABLET, or Table for offerings, as an amulet took the form of a thin rectangular plaque of stone or faïence, with a projection on one side to represent the spout or drain of the full-sized table which was placed in the chamber for sacrifices in the tomb.

Like the Sumerians and Babylonians, the Egyptians made many of their amulets in the forms of ANIMALS. Among these may be mentioned the Bull (Apis,

Mnevis, Bacchis, and the Black Bull), the Ram, the
Crocodile, the Hippopotamus, the Lion, the Lynx,
the Cat, the Dog-headed Ape and the smaller apes,
the Jackal, the animal the head of which appears
on figures of the god Set, the Pig, the Shrew-mouse,
the Hedgehog, the Ichneumon, the Hare, etc. Very
few animal amulets are found in the tombs of the
Old Kingdom. Under the New Kingdom the use
of such amulets became commoner, and it is from

The Divine Goose, or " Great Cackler," which laid the Cosmic Egg. Its
descendants flourish at Gizah at the present day.

its tombs and buildings that the large collections
of amulets which are exhibited in the great National
Museums were obtained.

The amulets in the form of BIRDS are comparatively
few. The commonest are :—The Bennu (Phoenix ?),
the Vulture, the Hawk, the Heron, the Swallow, the
Goose, the Ibis. The commonest amulets in the
form of REPTILES and INSECTS are :—The Turtle, the

Cobra, the Viper, the Scorpion, the large Snake, the Âpshait (a kind of beetle), the Abit (Mantis ?), the Grasshopper, the Frog (see p. 143), and various kinds of the dung-feeding varieties of Beetles. Amulets in the forms of FISHES are not very common. Some of them probably represent the Ȧbṭu fish and the ANT fish, which are mentioned in the Book of the Dead. They were supposed to swim one on each side of the Boat of Rā, and to drive away every evil creature that came to attack the god. A few amulets in the form of the fish with the wide, large mouth which is seen on the heads of figures of the goddess Ḥameḥit are known, but which of the fishes mentioned by Strabo (xvii. 2, 4) it represents, has not yet, I believe, been decided. The Āb or " Fighter " fish, and the Oxyrhynchus Fish, which was supposed to have swallowed the phallus of Osiris when his body was mutilated by Set, were held in great reverence. The small wooden figures in the form of worms which are found from time to time may represent the Phagrus fish, or EEL.

One of the largest classes of Egyptian amulets is formed by figures of the gods, goddesses, and lesser divine beings. Some of these were prophylactic in character and belong to the same class as the figures which the Sumerians buried under the floors of their houses and under the floors of the chambers in which men lay sick, to protect themselves and their property from the attacks of devils of every kind. Some may be compared to the Terâphîm of Laban which Rachel stole and carried away in her camel's saddle, and to the Penates of the Romans. To this class also belong the long series of wooden figures, painted black, which I saw in the great hall of the tomb of

Thothmes III in the Valley of the Tombs of the Kings in Western Thebes. In Egypt the tomb had to be protected from evil spirits and devils as well as the house, and this was effected by placing figures of the gods in the mummy chamber of the tomb, and by burying amulets in the four walls. Thus under the XVIIIth Dynasty a crude brick, with a 𓊪 facing the west mounted upon it, was inserted in the west wall ; a crude brick, with a figure of Anubis resting on a tablet of incense mounted upon it, was inserted in the east wall ; a crude brick, with a reed dipped in bitumen mounted upon it, was inserted in the south wall ; and a crude brick, with a figure like a *shabti*, seven fingers in height, set upon it, was inserted in the north wall. On this figure the ceremony of " Opening the Mouth " had to be performed. Even so, to thoroughly protect the tomb, it was necessary for a man who was cere-monially pure to perform the magical ceremony of the " four blazing torches." The torches were made of *aṭma* cloth smeared with sacred unguent ; and each torch was to be placed in the hands of man who personified one of the Four Sons of Horus. When (or before ?) the texts were recited each son of Horus was to extinguish his torch in a clay trough, over which incense had been sprinkled, which was filled with the milk of a white cow. Tradition declared that this ceremony was performed by Her-ṭaṭaf, the son of King Khufu (Cheôps). See the Rubrics to Chapter cxxxvii*a* of the Book of the Dead. A set of four crude bricks, with the amulets mounted upon them, can be seen in the British Museum (Nos. 41534–41537). The bricks are inscribed with the texts that form the Rubrics of the Chapter, and the whole set was made for a priestess of Amen-Rā at Thebes, who flourished about A.D. 1040. This set is probably unique.

Of the prophylactic figures placed in the tombs two varieties are known, viz. OSIRIS FIGURES and PTAḤ-SEKER-ASÂR (Osiris) FIGURES, and they are usually made of wood. Osiris appears in his usual mummied form and wears the Crown of the South, and his figure stands on a long, flat pedestal of wood. The figure and its pedestal are usually inscribed in hieroglyphs with a prayer to the god in which he is entreated to provide funerary offerings for the deceased whose name appears on the figure or pedestal. Many Osiris figures were made hollow, and rolls of papyri, inscribed with prayers, etc., from the Book of the Dead, were placed in them. The papyri of Hunefer and Anhai in the British Museum were found in Osiris figures.

The PTAH-SEKER-ASÂR was a modification or development of the Osiris figure. There is a painted and inscribed wooden figure fixed in a wooden pedestal, also painted and inscribed, but the figure has on its head a pair of horns, with a disk resting on them, and above these rise two plumes. The figure represents Ptaḥ-Seker-Osiris, the tri-une god of the Egyptians. In some figures there is a cavity in the pedestal, and in this a mummified portion of the body of the deceased and a little roll of inscribed papyrus were placed. In others a painted wooden model of a sarcophagus takes the place of the cavity, but in fine large examples the cavity is covered by the model of the sarcophagus. The idea underlying the use of such figures was that the body of the deceased was under the protection of Ptaḥ, one of the gods of the Creation, and Seker, a god of the tomb, and Osiris the god-man who had risen from the dead, and would effect the resurrection of the deceased, and give him unending life.

Every large collection of Egyptian antiquities contains a great number of small figures of the principal gods and goddesses made of stone, faïence, wood, etc. These are usually perforated, *i.e.* have eyelet holes, by which they can be strung on thread and so form necklaces. On the same string with the figures of the gods we often have animal amulets and bird amulets and the commoner amulets like the Ānkh, Nefer, Ṭeṭ, etc. The NECKLACE, like the PECTORAL, was an amulet, even when it consisted of beads only, and beads made of garnets, sand, carnelian, crystal, mother-of-emerald and haematite were believed to be specially protective. To describe in detail all the figures of the gods and goddesses which were worn by the living as amulets and were buried in the mummies of the dead would need more space than is here available. But the reader will gain a good idea of the forms in which they are known to us, both as actual figures and in drawings of them, and of their characteristic heads and head dresses from the series reproduced on pages 156-158. I prepared this list for my *Guide to Egypt and the Sûdân*, published by Messrs. Thos. Cook and Son, and it was reproduced with slight variations in my *Guide to the Egyptian Collections in the British Museum*, London, 1909, p. 123 f.

In the early dynastic period the Egyptians placed in each tomb with the mummy a figure of a man, or woman, which at a later period was called SHAWABTI or SHABTI or USHABTI. Usually it had the form of

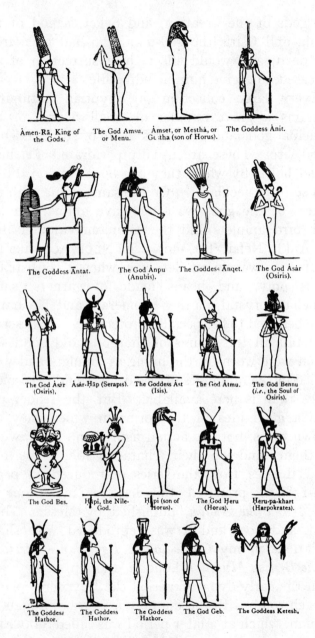

Amen-Rā, King of the Gods.

The God Amsu, or Menu.

Åmset, or Mesthá, or Gestha (son of Horus).

The Goddess Ånit.

The Goddess Āntat.

The God Ånpu (Anubis).

The Goddess Ånqet.

The God Åsår (Osiris).

The God Åsår (Osiris).

Åsår-Ḥåp (Serapis).

The Goddess Åst (Isis).

The God Åtmu.

The God Bennu (i.e., the Soul of Osiris).

The God Bes.

Ḥåpi, the Nile-God.

Ḥåpi (son of Horus).

The God Ḥeru (Horus).

Ḥeru-pa-khart (Harpokrates).

The Goddess Hathor.

The Goddess Hathor.

The Goddess Hathor.

The God Geb.

The Goddess Ketesh.

Amuletic figures of Egyptian gods and goddesses.

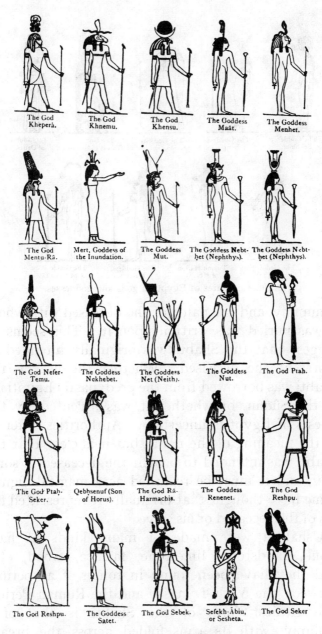

The God Khepera.

The God Khnemu.

The God Khensu.

The Goddess Maät.

The Goddess Menhet.

The God Mentu-Rā.

Mert, Goddess of the Inundation.

The Goddess Mut.

The Goddess Nebt-ḥet (Nephthys).

The Goddess Nebt-ḥet (Nephthys).

The God Nefer-Temu.

The Goddess Nekhebet.

The Goddess Net (Neith).

The Goddess Nut.

The God Ptah.

The God Ptaḥ-Seker.

Qebḥsenuf (Son of Horus).

The God Rā-Harmachis.

The Goddess Renenet.

The God Reshpu.

The God Reshpu.

The Goddess Satet.

The God Sebek.

Sefekh-Ābiu, or Sesheta.

The God Seker.

Amuletic figures of Egyptian gods and goddesses.

The Goddess Sekhmet.	The Goddess Serqet.	The God Set.	The Goddess Ta-urt (Thoueris).	Tet, a form of Osiris.

The God Tehuti (Thoth).	Tuamutef (Son of Horus).	The Goddess Uatchit.	The Goddess Upt-Hekau.

Amuletic figures of Egyptian gods and goddesses.

a mummy, and the name of the deceased with whom it was buried was written upon it. This seems to suggest that the Shabti was originally intended to represent the deceased. Whether the use of the Shabti was borrowed from the predynastic Egyptians in the Sûdân, or whether it was invented by the priests of Egypt is uncertain. Authorities differ as to the meaning of the name, but it is clear that the Shabti was intended to benefit the deceased in some way, and it must be regarded as a magical figure. Some have thought that originally it represented the KA of the deceased or his slave.

Ushabtiu were made of many kinds of hard stone, sandstone, limestone, faïence, wood, etc., and they have been found in tombs of all periods between the VIth Dynasty and the Roman Period. The earliest form of the Shabti is that of a mummy, with its arms folded across the breast, and the inscription contains nothing but the titles

and name of the deceased and that of his father
or mother.   Under the Middle Kingdom, a prayer
for funerary offerings is sometimes found inscribed
on the back of the figure.   Under the New
Kingdom, in addition to the name and titles of the
deceased, it bears a text which is identical with that
of Chapter vi of the Theban Recension of the Book
of the Dead.   The Shabti then represents a *fallah*, or
peasant servant or farm labourer, and it holds in
each hand a digging tool and, slung across its back,
it carries a loosely woven basket in which sand or

earth was carried.   The name of the deceased for
whom the Shabti was made was cut (or painted)
upon it, and also the spell which explains the use
and object of the figure under the XVIIIth Dynasty
and later.   The spell is supposed to be spoken by
the deceased himself and it reads, " In the event of
my being condemned to spread dust (*i.e.* top-
dressing) on the fields in the Ṭuat (*i.e.* the Underworld), or to fill the channels with water [by clearing
out the canals and channels and working the machine
for lifting up water on to the land or to reap during
the harvest], such work shall be performed for me by

them and no obstacle to doing so shall be put in thy way." Below this spell was written the answer with which the Shabti was supposed to reply, viz. " Wheresoever thou callest me, verily I shall be there present." The idea was that when the spell was uttered the figure would become alive and do whatsoever was necessary.

The Shabti of a king had the same form as that of the Shabti of the peasant, and the king was willing to perform the work of the Shabti in the kingdom of Osiris. Kings and nobles and priests often had large numbers of Ushabtin buried with them. Belzoni found over seven hundred in the tomb of Seti I, and it is probable that the full number buried with the king was seven hundred and thirty, *i.e.* two figures for every day in the year. One-half of these would be expected to work by day and the other half by night. A few examples of the Shabti are known (see British Museum *Guide to the IVth, Vth and VIth Egyptian Rooms*, p. 6), on which the spell written on the figure is a prayer for funerary offerings, and Chapter xxx*b* of the Book of the Dead, instead of Chapter vi. A rare example (B.M., No. 29403) holds ⚏, the symbol of Osiris, in one hand and ⚏, the symbol of Isis, in the other, and the soul of the deceased ⚏ is seen nestling on the breast of the deceased.

Among the amulets which were held to be of special importance by the Egyptians were the Vignettes which are found in the Book of the Dead. It is possible that they may have been added merely as illustrations of the various texts in that work, but I believe that, like the drawings of the Bushmen which are found in caves in South Africa, they were drawn and painted with an object which had nothing to do with artistic ideas or development. That object was to benefit the dead by magical means. When the priest ordered the scribes of the temple to draw or paint Vignettes in which the deceased is represented as acquitted of the charges brought against him at the judgment of the dead, and declared to be a "truth speaker," and received by Osiris, and rewarded by him with a homestead in the kingdom of Osiris, and eating celestial food, and drinking celestial waters, and consorting with the righteous, and adopted by the gods, assuredly he believed that these Vignettes would operate in such a way that the deceased would attain to the freedom of beatified souls, and an unending life of everlasting joy and happiness in the company of Osiris. And it was the same with the Vignettes which represented the deceased as seated in the " Boat of Millions of Years " of the Sun-god, living upon the light of the god and arrayed therein.

Of all the inscribed Egyptian amulets known to us the large collection of funerary texts which is commonly known as the " Book of the Dead " is the greatest. Under the Old Kingdom a Recension of these texts was cut in hieroglyphs on the walls of the corridors and halls of the pyramids of Unas, Teta and other kings. The funerary ceremonies connected with the " Opening of the Mouth " and the presentation of the canonical offerings on which the KAU of the deceased kings were supposed to live, were, even in the third millennium, very old. The dominant god in the earlier copies of this Recension was the Heliopolitan god Rā, but in the

later copies he was superseded by the indigenous
god Osiris of Ṭeṭu. Under the XIth and XIIth
Dynasties another Recension of funerary texts was
inscribed on the sides of sarcophagi and tomb
chambers. Texts unknown in the earlier Recension
appear, and a group of them formed the " Book of
the Two Ways [to the Kingdom of Osiris]."

The great collection of texts adopted by the Theban
theologians was called by them " PER-T EM HRU,'' a
title which means something like " Appearance in
the day " or " Coming out into (or by) day." It
contained a large number of ancient spells and incantations, and some beautiful prayers to Osiris and
Rā ; and one section of Chapter cxxv (which is
generally known as the " Negative Confession "
because each of the forty-two declarations made
by the deceased before the forty-two Assessors of the
Judgment Hall of Osiris begins with the words
" I have not ") contains what we may regard as the
religious and moral CODE of OSIRIS. Though a few
of the sections which are found in the texts of the
Old Empire are retained, the Theban Recension is
practically a new edition of the principal texts
which deal with the life and conditions under which
the souls of the dead exist in Amenti and the Ṭuat.
Two great and important features of it are the
Vignettes, which are sometimes drawn in outline
and sometimes coloured, and the Rubrics, which
describe the magical ceremonies which have to be
performed by the priest or the son of the deceased
during the recital of the texts.

The Saïte Recension is based on the Theban,
and it contains texts which illustrate beliefs which
are probably of Sûdânî origin. The Books of

the Dead of the Graeco-Roman Period contain
a hymn or two and one or more of the sections
of Chapter cxxv. which deals with the Judgment. All the spells which we find in the
Theban and Saïte Recensions are omitted, probably because the Egyptians had, under the
influence of Greek thought and influence, ceased
to believe in their efficacy. The Theban Recension
is found written in hieroglyphs on roll of papyrus
which are sometimes 70 or 80 feet long ; the Papyrus
of Nesi-ta-nebt-Ashru, which is written in hieratic,
is about 130 feet long. The roll was placed in the
coffin or in a separate box in the tomb, or between
the legs of the deceased, or in a niche in the wall of
the tomb. The Papyrus of Nu and the Papyrus
of Ani were tied round with papyrus cord and
sealed with mud seals. Other funerary works which
were used as amulets were : " The Lamentations of
Isis " ; " The Festival Songs of Isis and Nephthys " ;
" The Litanies of Seker " ; the book, "May My Name
Flourish" ; " The Book of Traversing Eternity " ;
" The Book of Respirations " (or, Breathings), i.e. the
Shai-en-Sinsinu.

The Egyptians made amulets of a colossal size,
probably with the view of protecting a whole com-
munity. On February 22, 1908, Mr. Legrain excavated a colossal stone beetle (scarabaeus sacer) at
Karnak. It was mounted on a pedestal which had the
shape of an ordinary Egyptian altar and stood at the
north-west corner of the Sacred Lake. A still
larger beetle in green granite was acquired by Lord
Elgin at Constantinople, and is now in the British
Museum [No. 865 (74)]. It is 5 feet long, 3 feet
wide, and weighs over two tons. The greenstone

models of the TURTLE which have been found in predynastic graves were undoubtedly amulets in the
ordinary sense of the word, but not the large stone
turtle (now in the British Museum), which was too
large to wear and could not be easily carried about.
It was probably set upon a pedestal which stood
within the precincts of some temple. Another
colossal amulet was the UMBILICUS which Legrain
found at Karnak and is now in the Egyptian Museum,
Cairo. Whether we should include among amulets the
great granite obelisks of Heliopolis and Karnak and
Tanis and the smaller stone obelisks which are found
in tombs of the Old Empire is doubtful. But small
stone obelisks, which are small enough to be strung
on necklaces, have been found together with other
amulets and beads in the tombs of the New Kingdom,
and they were laid among the swathings of mummies
of this period. As the obelisk was at that time a
symbol of the god Amen, and the name of that god
was written with the hieroglyph of an obelisk, it is
possible that the little models had no magical
significance.

The spells which are found in the religious texts
of periods of Egyptian history show that the fear of
serpents, scorpions and reptiles of all kinds was
universal among the Egyptians. These noxious
creatures were believed to be forms or incarnations
of evil spirits which, whenever possible, attacked the
dead as well as the living. The gods were, generally
speaking, held to be immune from these attacks
because they possessed the " fluid of life "
sa en ānkh, which was the peculiar attribute of
divine beings. But it must not be forgotten that
the mighty Sun-god Rā very nearly died from the

bite of a reptile which had been fashioned by Isis, and that Horus, the son of Isis, did actually die through the sting of a scorpion. But Horus was restored to life by means of certain magical formulas which Thoth imparted to Isis, and the Egyptians had these formulas engraved on stone stelae and wooden tablets, which they placed in their houses and tombs to protect them against the attacks of evil spirits in the form of deadly reptiles. These stelae are called " Cippi of Horus " and are usually made of hard, black stone, and have rounded tops, and they may be described briefly thus : On the front of the stele is a sculptured figure of Horus the Child (Harpocrates) in relief. He stands on two crocodiles, and he grasps in his hands serpents, scorpions, a lion and a horned animal (ibex ?), all of which represented associates of Set the god of Evil. Resting on the head of Horus is the head of "the Aged" god, which is somewhat like that of Bes, and the figure of Horus and the head together symbolize the old god who renews his youth and strength perpetually. By the side of Horus the Eyes of Rā, *i.e.* the Sun and figures of solar gods, are placed. The base of the stele and the reverse are covered with magical texts and spells which averted evil from the house or tomb in which the stele was placed. Many good examples of this amulet are to be seen in the British Museum.

The largest and most important of such amulets is that which is commonly known as the " Metternich Stele," and it was given to Prince Metternich by Muḥammad 'Alî Pâshâ. It was found in 1828 by workmen who were digging out the site for a reservoir in a Franciscan Monastery in Alexandria.

The colossal Cippus of Horus, which is commonly known as the
" Metternich stele " (Obverse).

The colossal Cippus of Horus, which is commonly known as the
" Metternich stele " (Reverse).

According to a statement in the text (l. 87) it was made for Ānkh-Psemtik, son of the lady Tent-Ḥet-nub, prophet of Nebun, overseer of Temt and scribe of Ḥet, who flourished in the reign of Nekht-neb-f, who reigned from 378 B.C. to 360 B.C. Drawings of the obverse and reverse of the monument are given on pages 166 and 167. The texts make it clear that the monument was intended to protect the inmates of some building, perhaps a temple, from the attacks of scorpions. On the obverse, reverse and sides the figures of nearly three hundred gods, and celestial beings, and sacred animals, and atropaic symbols are cut. As some of the gods had several forms, we may assume that there were on the stele a sufficient number of gods to provide a special protector of the building in which it stood for each of the 365 (or 366) days of the year. These protectors included the Companies of the Gods of Heaven, Earth, and the Ṭuat ; the Year-god and the seasons of the year, and the gods of the months and days and hours of the day and night ; the gods of the Planets and stars, and the Signs of the Zodiac and the Dekans ; the gods of the nomes and great cities and towns ; and many local polytheistic deities. On the rounded portion of the obverse is a solar disk in which appears Khnemu, with four rams' heads. The eight spirits of the dawn acclaim him ; and below them are five rows of gods. In the relief below them stands Harpocrates with his feet on crocodiles. In each hand he grasps a serpent, a scorpion and a Typhonic animal. Thoth and Rā, each standing on a serpent of many coils, adore him. Behind Rā stands Isis. On the reverse we have a polytheistic winged figure which stands on an oval containing figures of the incarnations of the Seven Powers of Evil. And below these are five rows of gods. The hieroglyphic texts contain the following :—

1. Spell to destroy Āpep, a huge serpent, which "resembled the intestines" (compare the Sumerian Khumbaba). Horus recited the spell over Āpep, and the monster vomited forthwith. Said over a man who was bitten or stung by any reptile, it would make him vomit the poison and save his life.

2. Spell to destroy the work of the CAT, *i.e.* a baleful form of Isis, daughter of Rā. Every member of her body contained a god or goddess ; she could destroy the poison of any and every reptile, and could also through her immense magical powers poison whom she pleased.

3. This spell is full of difficulties. It refers to some mythological event in which Rā was invoked to make Thoth turn back Set, the god of the " Stinking Face." Horus is summoned to the help of his father Osiris, and there is an allusion to the cries of grief which Isis uttered when she came to the quay at Neṭit, near Abydos, and saw her husband's dead body lying there. Osiris was slain by the machinations of Set, who seized Isis and shut her up in a strong tower intending to make her marry him and so legalize his position as king of Egypt which he had usurped.

4. The narrative of Isis, who was with child by her dead husband, and who, with the help of Thoth, succeeded in escaping from her captivity. Accompanied by Seven Scorpion goddesses, she set out on a journey to the Reed Swamps, where she intended to hide herself until her child was born. She applied at a house for lodgings for the night, but the

landlady shut the door in her face. One of the Seven Scorpion goddesses forced her way into the woman's house and stung her child to death. The mother's grief was so bitter that Isis uttered a spell over the dead child, and the poison of the scorpion ran out of his body, and he came to life again. The words of the spell are cut on the stele, and were treasured by the Egyptians as an infallible cure for the stings of scorpions.

Soon after this Isis was obliged to leave her hiding place for a few hours, and to leave her son Horus alone. The terrible scorpion Uḥât, seeing that the child was unprotected, attacked him and stung him, and when Isis returned she found Horus lying dead on the reeds. She examined the body of the child and found the mark of the sting of the scorpion which had been sent by Set, and then she burst forth in such heartrending laments that men and gods were compelled to sympathize with her. Her sister Nephthys came with Serqit, the Scorpion-goddess, and advised her to appeal to heaven for help. Then Isis cried out to heaven, and the sailors in the Boat of Millions of Years ceased to row and the boat of the Sun-god stood still. From it Thoth, the author of spells and words of power, descended, and he had with him the WORD which all heaven and earth and hell had to obey. After some talk with Isis he uttered the mighty spell which transferred a portion of the " fluid of life " from Rā to the body of Horus, and the poison left the child's body forthwith and he breathed again and lived. Thoth promised that he would protect Horus, and he would defend him in the Hall of Judgment in Anu, and would give him power to repel every attack which might be made upon him and ensure his succession to the throne of Egypt. At the same time he declared that it was the spells pronounced by Isis which had brought about this happy result, for it was she who had caused the Boat of Rā to stand still, and it was her magical power which had forced him to descend to earth and to do her will.

Such is a summary of the contents of the magical texts which are inscribed on the Metternich Stele. The text is in places manifestly corrupt, and many of the allusions in it are obscure, and at present inexplicable, because we have no knowledge of the details of the system of magic which was in the IVth century B.C. an integral part of the Egyptian Religion. The compositions on this Stele prove that, notwithstanding the whole-hearted belief of the Egyptians in the power of Osiris, whenever they were in serious difficulties they turned to the ancient magic of their country to help them.

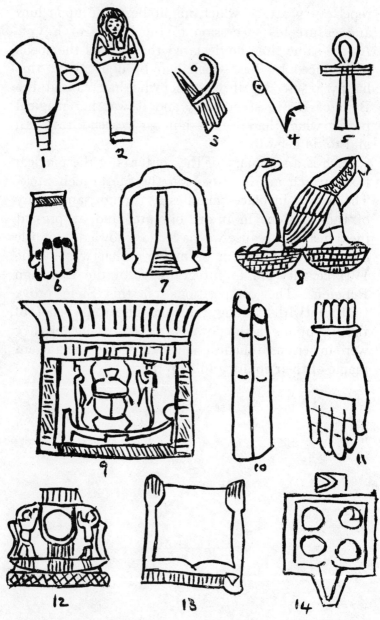

EGYPTIAN AMULETS.

EGYPTIAN AMULETS.

1. A helmet and part of the head-gear of a soldier.

2. The SHABTI figure (plur. Shawabtiu) holding implements used in agricultural work, digging, planting, etc.

3. The Crown of the North (Net or Ṭeshert), the Red Crown.

4. The Crown of the South (Ḥedjt), the White Crown. The two crowns were united thus ⚑ and the sign was read SEKHEMTI.

5. The Ānkh, the symbol of life everlasting. It is perhaps an old form of the Tjet, or symbol of Isis.

6. The right hand with the fingers closed over the palm.

7. A knot (?)

8. The Vulture-goddess and the Uraeus-goddess, the divine protectresses of Upper and Lower Egypt respectively; the phonetic value is " NEBTA," and must not be confounded with " NEBUI," the phonetic value of ⚬ ⚬ , the Two Lords being Horus and Anubis.

9. Common form of the pectoral, viz. that of a pylon. The scene represents Isis and Nephthys adoring Kheperà the Creator and Generator in his boat.

10. The two fingers (djebāui) of Horus, who by means of them assisted Osiris to mount the Ladder when he ascended into heaven.

11. The open hand, symbol of liberality and generosity; the hand of Fâtma is probably a development of this amulet.

12. The full moon on the 16th day with horns.

13. The breast and two arms and hands, symbolic of the vital power of a being, the KA. Later the word was symbolic of what maintained the vital power, i.e. food, victuals.

14. The tablet for offerings which was placed in a tomb.

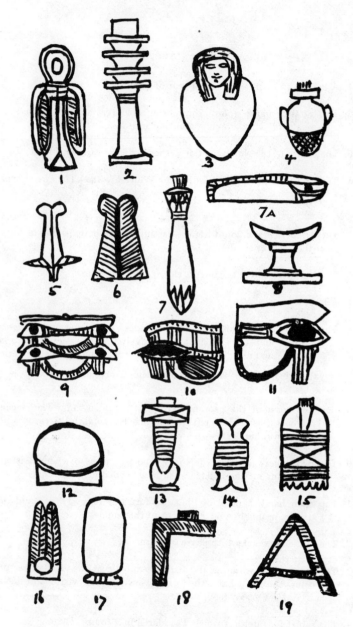

EGYPTIAN AMULETS.

EGYPTIAN AMULETS.

1. The Tjet, a conventional representation of the genital organs of Isis.

2. The Ṭeṭ, a portion of the backbone of Osiris.

3. The Heart, with a portrait head of the owner of the amulet.

4. The Heart ; commonest form.

5. Two plumes resting on a pair of horns of the Kudu (?) ; a special crown.

6. The two plumes of Åmen ; later the Atef Crown.

7. The Papyrus Sceptre.

7A. The Eye and eyebrow of Horus, specially symbolic of strength.

8. The Pillow or head-rest which was used by the living and was placed under the necks of mummies.

9. The quadruple Eye of Rā in the four quarters of the world.

10. The Udjat or Eye of Rā.

11. The Udjat or Eye of Aāḥ, the Moon-god. As the two Eyes of Heaven they appear thus

12. The solar disk on the horizon ; an amulet for both morning and evening.

13. The Sma, *i.e.* the lungs ; it was supposed to assist the breathing.

14. The Nert, shuttle or an instrument used in weaving ; symbol of the goddess Neith ; or two bones of the spine (?).

15. The Āper or tassel ; perhaps a decorated pendant symbolic of happiness.

16. The solar disk on the horizon with plumes rising from it.

17. The Name-amulet (Ren) commonly known as the Cartouche. It was originally made of rope or cord.

18. The Mason's angle measure.

19. The Carpenter's square.

EGYPTIAN AMULETS.

1, 2. Hare. 3. Baboon. 4. Ape. 5. Sow with young. 6. Lions united.
7. Ram of Amen. 8. Apis Bull. 9. Lion. 10. Singing Ape. 11. Frog.
12. Hedgehog. 13. Jackal. 14. Crocodile. 15. Cat.

CHAPTER VI.

ETHIOPIAN (ABYSSINIAN) AMULETS.

The early history of that section of the " black-visaged " peoples whose home was the country in north-east Africa now known as Abyssinia is lost, if it ever existed, and of the superstitions and religion of the primitive Ethiopians there is nothing to be said. A black stone Cippus of Horus, which was imported into Ethiopia from Egypt, and was discovered by the great traveller Bruce, proves that there lived in the country during the IVth or IIIrd century B.C. people who were acquainted with, and who probably practised, the " Black Magic " of Egypt. The Arabs who invaded Ethiopia in the Xth century B.C. introduced Sabaeism, or the cult of the sun, and moon, and stars, and sky, and earth, into the country, and the Hebrew traders who settled in Ethiopia several centuries before Christ, of course took with them their religion of Yahweh or Jâh. One thing is quite clear ; up to the beginning of the IVth century A.D. the Ethiopians were pagans, magicians were their priests, and every branch of magic flourished. The conquests of the Egyptians in Upper Nubia in the second millennium before Christ were known to the peoples of Northern Ethiopia, and they learned from the Egyptians many kinds of magic, and the use of Egyptian amulets. But of the native amulets of that period we know nothing. Whilst king 'Êzânâ, king of Aksûm, was fighting on the Island of Meroë his soldiers captured a priest who was wounded in the fight.   They took from the priest a *ḳedâda* of silver, and a *ḥeḳat* of gold.   The *ḥeḳat* of gold was, undoubtedly, a magical box or case in which was placed the *ḳedâda* of silver, which was probably a figure of some object which the priest carried about with him to give him magical power over the enemy against whom his lord was fighting.   (See my *History of Ethiopia*, vol. i. p. 256, l. 26.)

In the first half of the IVth century of our Era Ethiopia was ruled by the mighty king 'Êzânâ, the Aizanes of the Greeks, and before the close of his reign he renounced paganism and made Christianity the official religion of his empire.   The crescent and the star, the symbols of SABAEISM, which was brought into Ethiopia by the Arabs, were replaced by the Christian Cross at the beginning of his inscriptions. It does not by any means follow that his subjects throughout the country abandoned their pagan cults and amulets, but there is no doubt that among such of them as embraced Christianity the Cross became the first and greatest of all amulets and protective symbols.   Pictures of the Cross are nailed to the walls of houses to protect them from evil spirits, and they are often laid on the bodies of sick persons, old and young, to annul the evil influences which are causing the sicknesses.   The

commonest form of the Cross is , but several

other forms are known, and the group of six crosses figured on p. 179 are characteristic examples.   These are taken from a magical Book of the Dead in the

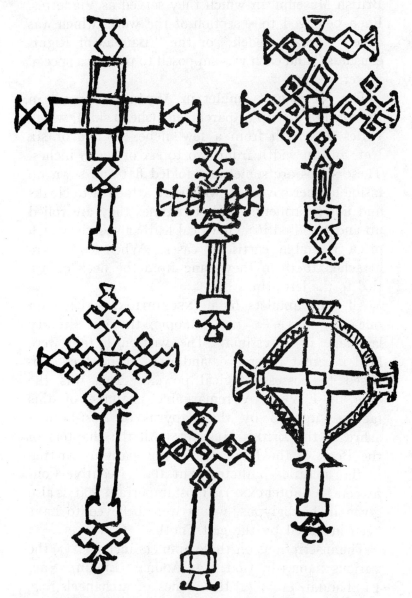

Tracings of the magical forms of the Cross found in an Ethiopian Book of the Dead called " Lefâfâ Ṣedeḳ " (Brit. Mus. MS. Add. 16204).

British Museum, in which they served as Vignettes. Each belonged to a section of the work, which was called " Lefâfâ Ṣedeḳ," or the " Bandlet of Righteousness," and each was supposed to possess a special power. The commonest amulet in Abyssinia appears in the form of a strip of parchment (sheep skin), which varies in length from a few inches to five or six feet, and in width from two to six or seven inches. These strips are sometimes folded flat and sewn up inside leather coverings which are attached to cloaks and inner garments, and sometimes they are rolled up and enclosed in cylindrical leather sheaths which often resemble cartridge cases. When cords are attached to them they hang from the neck or are tied to the left arm.

All such amulets have INSCRIPTIONS written on one side in Gĕ'ĕz, i.e. Ethiopic, the old literary language of Abyssinia. The written letters were held in great reverence, and were themselves supposed to possess magical powers. This was the case in EGYPT. A remarkable example of this fact is supplied by the Papyrus of Nesi-ta-neb-ashru in the British Museum. All the chapters of the Book of the Dead are in this papyrus written in the hieratic characters, but the " Negative Confession" (Chapter cxxv), a most important text, is also given in hieroglyphs, which were believed to have been invented by the god Thoth.

The inscriptions on these amulets include : (1) the various names of God, e.g. Adônai, Elohîm, Yâh, Él-Shaddai, etc. ; (2) the names of archangels, e.g. Michael and Gabriel ; (3) the magical names of Christ ; (4) the names of the fiends and devils which produce sicknesses and diseases in the human body ; (5) strings of letters arranged singly or in groups of three—spells which cannot be translated, *e.g.* the ancient palindrome, SATOR AREPO TENET OPERA ROTAS ; (6) traditional " words of power," *e.g.* those used by Christ, " Asparaspes ! " and 'Askorâskîs ! " and those used by SOLOMON, " Lôfham ! " and " Maḥfelôn ! " (7) Legends of our Lord and St. Sûsenyôs the martyr.

On many of the longer amulets there are drawn or painted FIGURES of some of the Seven Archangels, *e.g.* Michael and Gabriel, who are usually represented in the form of knights of the Byzantine period, and figures of saints, *e.g.* Sûsenyôs, the martyr, and St. George of Lydda.   The saints sometimes appear on horseback, and they are generally provided with a long spear with which they are spearing either the " dragon," or some prostrate fiend.   Side by side with these we find series of MAGICAL DRAWINGS which were supposed to protect the wearer of the amulet.   These are as important as the figures of angels and saints and the actual texts.   The Ethiopians and their descendants the Abyssinians wore their amulets for the material benefits which they believed would accrue to them through them. Women believed that they would give them fecundity and conception, and immunity from miscarriage, and safety during the period of gestation, and a safe delivery and healthy children ; and they expected them to protect their children from the Evil Eye. Men wore them to give them virility and strength, and both men and women expected them to preserve them from the attacks of the devils which cause sickness and disease.

The greater part of a good typical amulet is reproduced on Plate XVII. It was written about the end of the XVIIth century for a woman called " 'Absarâ Dengel," *i.e.* the Virgin hath sent her as a " glad tiding." At the top is the figure of an archangel or angel, with a halo from which emerge rays of light. He is arrayed in voluminous flowered garment, and holds a sword in his right hand. The inscription begins with the usual formula, " In the Name of the Father, and the Son, and the Holy Ghost, One God." Then follows a prayer that 'Absarâ Dengel may be saved from miscarriage and a series of sicknesses of various kinds, and from the demon who attacks children when they are suckling at their mothers' breasts. Next we have the Legend of Sûsenyôs, who was martyred in the reign of Diocletian. According to this, Werzelyâ, the sister of the saint, had union with the Devil, and the saint slew her. Sûsenyôs married, and his wife bore him a man child, who was killed by Werzelyâ. Sûsenyôs then mounted his horse and, taking his spear in his right hand, went forth to slay Werzelyâ. An old woman told him where she was, and he went into a garden and found her sitting under a tree, with a company of devils grouped about her. The saint dismounted and knelt down with his face to the earth and prayed for strength to kill Werzelyâ, the murderer of children, and the closer of the wombs of women. Then he remounted his horse, and took his spear in his right hand and drove it through the right side of Werzelyâ. As she was dying she swore by the Seven Ranks of the Archangels that she would never again go to any place [or person] where the name of Sûsenyôs was found. Therefore the

PLATE XVII

Portion of the amulet of 'Absarâ Dengel.   Vignette : St. Michael the Arch-angel.   Text : The legend of Sûsenyôs, who slew the devil-woman Werzelyâ, his sister.

woman who has hung on her person an amulet
on which the name of Sûsenyôs and the story of his
life are written was held to be safe from the attacks
of Werzelyâ, and her child also, when suckling at
her breast. After Sûsenyôs had slain Werzelyâ he
became a martyr, and the prayer which he prayed
in the garden before he speared her was regarded
as a spell of very great power.

The fear of the Evil Eye always has been, and still
is, common in Abyssinia. The pagan Ethiopians,
like the Egyptians, wore stones, beads and other
objects to attract the Evil Eye away from their
persons, but the Christians used other means, and
tried to avert it by the use of a spell. This spell
took the form of a legend, which we find written on
many parchment amulets, and which may be thus
summarized : Our Lord and His disciples were
walking by the Sea of Tiberias and they saw an old
woman of most foul appearance and terrifying aspect
sitting upon a seat of filth. Her eyes shot out rays
of yellow light like the glitter of gold, her hands and
her feet seemed to be like wheels, or to move about
like wheels, and flashes of fire sixty-eight cubits
(*i.e.* over one hundred feet) came forth from her
mouth. The disciples said to Our Lord, " What
is this thing, O Lord ? " And He replied, " This
is the Eye of Earth, evil and accursed. If a glance
of it falls on a ship at sea, straightway that ship
sinketh. If its glance followeth a horse, both horse
and rider are cast down. If its glance falleth on a
cow which is being milked, the milk goeth sour
and is turned into blood. When this Eye looketh
upon a woman with child, a miscarriage taketh
place, and both child and mother are destroyed."

Then our Lord pronounced the two words of power " 'Asparaspes " and " 'Askôrâskîs," and the disciples took the Eye of Earth, which was called " 'Aynat," and they burned the old woman and scattered the ashes of her to the east and the west, and to the south and the north. An amulet with this legend written upon it was supposed to keep away any trouble from the eyes of its wearer.

Some of the best-written and oldest amulets contain prescriptions which are sheer nonsense· Thus in the amulet of Walatta Kîdân the wearer is told to recite seven times the sounds—

Shar	Shar	Shar	Shar	Shar	Shar	Shar
Djar	Djar	Djar	Djar	Djar	Djar	Djar
Tjê	Tjê	Tjê	Tjê	Tjê	Tjê	Tjê

This formula is said to have been given by God to 'Adernâhâ'êl, who was instructed to make it known to men who suffered from colic and stomach ache. And in another amulet we are told that evil spirits and diseases of all kinds may be kept away from a man by reciting the formula—

Yâlbed	Yâlbed	Yâlbed	Yâlbed	Yâlbed	Yâlbed	Yâlbed
Nôr	Nôr	Nôr	Nôr	Nôr	Nôr	Nôr
Ha	Ha	Ha	Ha	Ha	Ha	Ha
Kâ	Kâ	Kâ	Kâ	Kâ	Kâ	Kâ
Ae	Ae	Ae	Ae	Ae	Ae	Ae
Aô	Aô	Aô	Aô	Aô	Aô	Aô

A most curious and interesting example of the Ethiopian amulet folded and in book form was brought to me in the British Museum several years ago for description by the late Father Pollen, S.J. After his death I asked Father Thurston, S.J., if he knew what had become of it, and he informed me that it belonged to the Convent of the Sacred Heart at

Hammersmith, and advised me to make further enquiries of the Lady Superior. I did so, and the Abbess very kindly sent it to me for further examination. How the amulet got to England is not known, but it was probably brought home by one of the Roman Catholic missionaries a generation or two ago, and either given by him or a brother missionary to the Convent. After a further examination of the amulet I told the Abbess that I should like to write about it, and after a short correspondence I made a modest offer to buy it, and my offer being accepted I became the possessor of the amulet and am now able to describe it. The amulet is in the form of a book and measures $4\frac{1}{4}$ inches by $3\frac{1}{4}$ inches. It consists of one long strip of parchment 14 feet 4 inches in length, which is formed of several short strips neatly sewn together. This strip is covered on both sides with columns of Ethiopic text written in black ink and arranged in page form, the titles of the various compositions, and the names of saints and the Virgin Mary, and the name of the owner of the amulet being in red ink. Many pages are water stained, and in a few places, where the text has been rubbed away or otherwise destroyed, patches of vellum inscribed with the missing portions of lines have been added. The little book can be drawn out like a concertina. The oldest parts of the text were probably written in the XVIIth century. The name of the first owner of the book was BATRA GÎWÂRGÎS, *i.e.* " staff of George," but in two places at least we find the name WALDA MARYÂM.

Perhaps the most interesting feature of this amulet is due to the fact that it throws considerable light on

the Ethiopian's views about religion. If we begin at
one end and turn over folio after folio we find that the
texts written on one side of the long strip of parchment
(which we have already said is over 14 feet long) are
taken from the Homilies of Severus of Antioch on
St. Michael the Archangel, and the Miracles of the

The Divine Face surrounded with the Eight Aeons or Emanations, and
the Seven Astrological Stars.
(From the amulet of Batra Gîwârgîs.)

Virgin Mary. All very right and proper for an
orthodox Ethiopian Christian. But when we turn
the book over and from the other end of it read the
texts on the other side of the strip of parchment,
we find series of spells and charms, and magical
prayers and drawings which were beloved by the

pagan Ethiopian. The one strip of parchment was
thus able to supply both of the spiritual wants of
BATRA GîWÂRGÎS, and illustrates the character of the
product of the religious views produced by fusing
Christianity with paganism and its religious magic.

The magical drawings in the book are of considerable interest.   The first of them is painted in crude

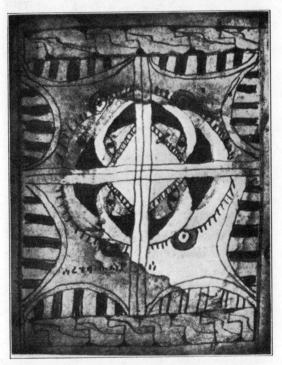

Magical Drawing representing the Chariot of Elijah.
(From the amulet of Batra Gîwârgîs.)

colours and purports to represent the Divine Face
(see page 188). A human face, with large prominent
eyes, is seen set in a rectangle, from each side of
which two right-angled triangles (?) project. Above
and below the square are three "heavens," or aeons,
or aspects of the Deity, and on each side of it is one

heaven. The seven symbols, each formed of two interlaced crescents, the horns of which terminate in small circles, represent the Seven Planets. These last are found in Greek and Coptic magical papyri. The whole scene probably represents the heavens by day, for immediately following this vignette is a

Magical Drawing representing the Net in which Solomon caught the fiends and devils.
(From the amulet of Batra Gîwârgîs.)

somewhat similar central face and figure which symbolizes the heavens by night ; a star is attached to the ends of the light projections from the rectangle containing the features of a man. Several pages in the little book are filled with drawings of various forms of the Cross, groups of four eyes, and human

heads which probably represent Christ and the Four
Evangelists.   No explanations are given of the
linear designs which appear in large numbers,
but their significations must have been well
known of the owner of the amulet, for the name
of BATRA GÎWÂRGÎS is found on nearly all of them.

Solomon with his wife.
(From the amulet of Batra Gîwârgîs.)

Some of the drawings are of special interest, for I
have found them in no other Ethiopic manuscript.
Among these may be mentioned the SARGALÂ 'ÊLYÂS
or " Chariot of Elijah " (page 189), the object
of which was to give BATRA GÎWÂRGÎS the means
of ascending into heaven when his soul left the
earth.

Traditions extant in Hebrew, Syriac, Arabic and Ethiopic all agree in stating that King Solomon was a master magician, and that he had authority over all the fiends of Hell, which he caught in a net like fishes, as he had over all beasts and birds. The Ethiopian Christian wished to possess this

Adam and Eve, who holds up a serpent, sitting in the Garden of Eden.
(From the amulet of Batra Gîwârgîs.)

authority, and we find in the amulet of BATRA GÎWÂRGÎS a picture of the MARBABETA SALÔMÔN or "Net of Solomon" (page 190). Many Ethiopian historians, accepting the legend of Solomon's union with MÂKĔDÂ, the Queen of Sheba, have regarded Solomon a the true founder of their kingdom. As

BATRA GÎWÂRGÎS wished to obtain the benefit of
his protecting magic, and this could be best secured
by drawing a picture of him, together with his potent
spells, on his amulet, we find there the scene reproduced on page 191.   Here we see King Solomon seated in a sort of shrine, with his long hair

The Cross with the Divine Face.
(From the amulet of Batra Gîwârgîs.)

falling on each side of his head.   By his side is seated
a woman who is covering her mouth, in the well-
known Oriental fashion, with a portion of her outer
garment.   She is wearing shoes with pointed turned
up toes.   A little above the king's head on his
right is the crescent moon, and a little above the
woman's head, on her left, is the sun.   This scene

is described as " Salômôn mesla bê'esîtû," " Solomon with his wife," the wife here represented being the Queen of Sheba.

Another drawing, which is very rarely found in magical texts, is that which is reproduced on

The Cross of 'Abû Fara.
(From the amulet of Batra Gîwârgîs.)

page 192. Here we see Adam and Eve, who are both naked, seated in the Garden of Eden. Eve is holding up with her right hand a long serpent, which appears to be speaking to her. The Ethiopic description of the scene is " Za kama 'ashatâ kaysî la-Hêwân," i.e. " How the serpent

seduced Eve." The tree with the forbidden fruit
is on the left of Eve, and the object on the right
of Adam is perhaps the mandragora. The object of
including this picture among the Vignettes in the
amulet is not clear. Another remarkable drawing is reproduced on
page 193. Here we have on the right a variant
form of the Divine Face which forms the centre
of a cross. To the left of it is a cross drawn on a
cross-shaped background, and on each of the four
arms is an eye. Below are fifteen small panels on
which are drawn groups of four eyes, pairs of eyes,
and X-shaped crosses. This drawing was regarded
as a very special protection against the attacks of
fiends and devils and the EVIL EYE, and it was
intended to show that the Face of God dwelt in
the cross and in figures and drawings of it. Finally we
may note the very elaborately decorated cross which
is reproduced on page 194. Above it is written in
Ethiopic " Deliver thy servant Batra Gîwârgîs,"
and below are the words " ṭebab za 'Abûfara Selṭâna,"
which may be rendered the " wisdom (or, medicine)
of Abû Fara (?) our Sulṭân."

The inscriptions which are found on parchment
amulets, *i.e.* prayers, spells, magical names and
names of the Deity and angels are generally derived
from Jewish, Christian (*i.e.* Gnostic and Coptic)
sources, and these are comparatively easy to identify.
There are however some which are of pagan origin,
and words, names and formulas are found in them
which are inexplicable. Occasionally we meet with
a mixture of paganism and Christianity in the
inscriptions, and among magical writings of this
class special mention must be made of a little work

entitled " LEFÂFA ṢEDEḲ " or the " Bandlet of
Righteousness." The rubrics in it claim that if a
man carries a copy of it on his person it will make
his business in this world to prosper, and give him
health and strength and preserve him from attacks
of sickness caused by demons, and help him to come
forth uncondemned by the Great Judge in the Hall
of Judgment, and to escape punishment in the River
of Fire in Hell. The preliminary narrative states
that the author of the book was God, who dictated
it to our Lord, who wrote it down and gave it first
to MARY, His Mother, and subsequently to the Archangel MICHAEL, who made its contents known in
due course to the Apostles and others. It is further
stated that when God heard from His Son of the
tears and distress of the Virgin Mary when she
thought of her parents and kinsfolk being punished
in the River of Fire, He dictated the book to His
Son so that the happiness of the Virgin in heaven
might not be destroyed. The Lefâfa Ṣedeḳ is
constructed on the same plan as the Egyptian
Book of the Dead, and is a veritable Ethiopian
Book of the Dead. But the author, who was a
Christian, substitutes God for Rā, Christ for Thoth,
and the Virgin Mary for Isis. The magical names of
the Persons of the Trinity, and the names of the
Archangels and other celestial beings take the places
of the names of Egyptian fiends in the spells which
were believed to preserve the dead body intact,
and to ensure its remaining in its grave, and to
enable the soul of the dead man to find its way
through the earth to the dread Hall of Judgment,
and to save it from the River of Fire. The texts
in the Lefâfa Ṣedeḳ were written on a strip or sheet

of linen which was wrapped round the body of the dead, just as a sheet of papyrus inscribed with copies of Chapters of the Book of the Dead was often wrapped round the body of the dead Egyptian. The belief in the existence of a Hall of Judgment and a River of Fire was borrowed from the Egyptians, and it is possible that some of the magical names given in the Lefâfa Ṣedek are transcriptions of the names of Egyptian devils. The Ethiopic text with an English translation and a commentary are published in my *Bandlet of Righteousness*, London, 1929 (Luzac's Series).

The Ethiopians believed that Moses, Solomon, Christ and His Apostles and Disciples were all magicians, and therefore the Books of the Old and New Testaments and copies of them were often regarded as amulets. The " BOOK OF THE MIRACLES OF THE VIRGIN MARY " and the " WEDDÂSÊ MARYÂM " or " Praises of Mary " were also considered to be sources of magical protection. The Book of Psalms formed a very favourite amulet among those who could afford to pay for a copy of it to be made. And certain native Ethiopian books are regarded with very great veneration throughout Abyssinia, and upon the possession of the most famous of these, the KEBRA NAGAST, or " Glory of Kings," the stability of the kingdom was at one time supposed to rest. It will be remembered that when the British Army captured Makdalâ, the strong fortress in which Theodore, the mighty Abyssinian king, had established himself with his army, the great collection of about 900 Ethiopic manuscripts which Theodore had collected fell into the hands of the British. These were brought to the British

Museum in 1868, and the late Professor William Wright, who catalogued the collection, found among them two fine copies of the KEBRA NAGAST. He printed full descriptions of them in his *Catalogue of the Ethiopic MSS.*, London, 1877, No. CCCXCI, p. 297, and in the *Zeitschrift der Deutschen Morgenländischen Gesellschaft*, Bd. XXIV, pp. 614, 615. On August 10, 1872, Prince Kasa, who was subsequently crowned as King John IV (December 14, 1872), wrote to Earl Granville thus :—

" Again, there is a book called KIVERA NEGUST (*i.e.* KEBRA NAGAST), which contains the LAW of the whole of Ethiopia, and the names of the Shûms (*i.e.* Chiefs), Churches, and Provinces are in this book. I pray you will find out who has got this book, and send it to me, for in my Country my people will not obey my orders without it." In short, King John IV says that without this book he cannot rule Ethiopia. A copy of this letter was sent to the British Museum, and the Trustees decided to grant King John's request, and the manuscript was restored to him on December 14, 1872. M. Hugues Le Roux, a French envoy from the President of the French Republic to Menyelek II, King of Ethiopia, applied personally to the king for permission to make a translation of the KEBRA NAGAST. The king was most willing for the book to be translated, and he replied in words which M. Le Roux translates thus : " Je suis d'avis qu'un peuple ne se défend pas seulement avec ses armes, mais avec ses livres. *Celui dont vous parlez est la fierte de ce Royaume.* [The italics are mine.] Depuis moi, l'Empereur, jusqu'au plus pauvre soldat qui marche sur les chemins, tous les Ethiopiens seront heureux que ce livre soit traduit dans la langue française et porté à la connaissance des amis que nous avons dans le monde. Ainsi l'on verra clairement quels liens nous unissent avec le peuple de Dieu, quels trésors ont été confiès à notre garde. On comprendra mieux pourquoi le secours de Dieu ne nous a jamais manqué contre les enemis qui nous attaquaient." The manuscript was fetched from Adis Ababa for M. Le Roux to use, and he found written on the last folio the words, " This volume was returned to the King of Ethiopia by order of the Trustees of the British Museum, December 14, 1872. J. Winter Jones, Principal Librarian." M. Le Roux adds the following most interesting facts :— " C'était le livre que Théodoros avant caché sous son oreiller, la nuit où il se suicida, celui que les soldats anglais avaient emporte à Londres, qu'un ambassadeur rendit à l'Empereur Jean, que ce même Jean feuilleta dans so tente, le matin du jour où il tomba sous cimeterres des Mahdistes, celui que les moines avaient dérobé " (*Chez la Reine de Saba*, Paris, 1914, pp. 120–121).

CHAPTER VII.

GNOSTIC AMULETS.

"Gnostics" is the name usually given to a group of religious sects which flourished in WESTERN ASIA and EGYPT between 250 B.C. and A.D. 400. One and all claimed that they possessed γνῶσις, *i.e.* "knowledge," but that "knowledge" was of a highly spiritual nature, and was transcendental, supernal and celestial in character. According to some of the Gnostics, that knowledge was obtained by a series of revelations which were made by the One great God, Who was the Creator and Sustainer of the universe, to men who had fitted themselves to receive them by self-abnegation, fasting and prayer. The oldest history of the Gnôsis and the tenets of its followers will be found in the work of HIPPOLYTUS (died or was martyred in the first half of the IIIrd century A.D.), *Refutation of all Heresies.* Another history written a couple of centuries later is the "Panarion" of EPIPHANIUS. The Coptic works, "Pistis Sophia" (*i.e.* Faith-Wisdom) and books of IEÛ provide us with a great deal of original first-hand information. The tenets of some of the Gnostic sects were derived primarily from INDIA, and they travelled westwards through PERSIA to SYRIA, PALESTINE, EGYPT and GREECE with the Buddhist envoys to the SELEUCIDAE and the

PTOLEMIES who were sent thither by the kings of India in the IIIrd and IInd centuries B.C. Modern research has shown that the pictographic writings of the Indians and Sumerians were almost identical in character, and it may be that there is Sumerian influence in Gnosticism. The astrological element in Gnosticism, of which so many examples are found on Gnostic amulets, certainly came from Babylonia, the home of astrology. (See the Section on the *Signs of the Zodiac*.) And it is tolerably certain that many of the curious linear signs which represent the sun, moon, planets and other stars, are garbled copies of early Sumerian pictographs.

The remains of the Gnostics now available for study show that, viewed as a whole, their Gnôsis or " knowledge " was influenced by the teachings of the ZEND-AVESTA, the cult of MITHRAS, Manichaeism, the popular form of religion current in Egypt during the Graeco-Roman period, Hebrew books like the Book of Enoch, the Jewish Ḳâbbâlah, and early Christian Literature. The Church during the Ist and IInd centuries condemned Gnosticism unsparingly, but in the end it was recognized that a Gnostic might also be a good Christian. For the noblest part of the Gnostic's religion proclaimed the conquest of Darkness by Light, and of Evil by Good, and it was taught esoterically; but many of those who proclaimed themselves to be Gnostics never plumbed the depths of its fundamental truths. A work like the present is no place to describe the Gnostic system and the tenets of the various sects who taught it ; those who wish to study it will find much information on the subject in MATTER, HISTOIRE,

Critique du Gnosticisme, 2 vols: and plates, Paris, 1828 ; C. W. KING, *The Gnostics and their Remains*, London, 1864 ; LIPSIUS, *Der Gnosticismus*, Leipzig, 1860 ; and MANSEL, *The Gnostic Heresies*, London, 1875.

The Gnostics, in common with the peoples among whom they lived, adopted the use of amulets, and as far as the inscriptions and figures on them can be understood, aimed at securing by their means knowledge of a celestial character, and the protection of the Great God Who was ONE and Who embraced ALL within himself, both in this world and in the next. The amulets are made of various kinds of semi-precious stones, *e.g.* blood stone, iron ore or haematite, green jasper, nefrite, agates of various kinds, sard, carnelian, crystal, chrysoprase, beryl, chalcedony, obsidian, lapis lazuli, nicolo, onyx, plasma, granite, etc. Some of these stones were believed to possess the powers and influences of the planets, and to confer upon the wearer wisdom, health, strength, shrewdness, and the ability to absorb transcendental knowledge. They have various shapes—triangular, square, oval, etc.—and vary in size from half an inch to three inches in length. The most popular stones are black and green in colour, and it is probable that these were supposed to possess medicinal properties. The inscriptions on nearly all Gnostic amulets are in Greek uncials, but a few are known which are inscribed in a sort of pictographic script. Quite nine-tenths of the Gnostic amulets now known were found in Egypt, and it is therefore not surprising that they bear on them figures of Egyptian gods and goddesses, and Nilotic

creatures and symbols. The Egyptian Gnostics
rejected many of the pagan cults of the early
dynastic Egyptians, but they regarded Rā, Horus
and Harpokrates as forms of their "One God of
heaven," and they connected Isis with the Virgin
Mary, Osiris and Serapis with Christ, and Hathor
with the naked woman who was the symbol of
wisdom according to the latest form of Gnosticism
in the IVth or Vth century.

The Gnostics attached great importance to the
NAMES of God and of the archangels. The name of
God appears as IAⱲ, which represents the Hebrew
Y[A]H or Yâh (Jâh), but sometimes the god referred
to seems to be MITHRAS or even ORMAZD. Other
names of God are ΣΑΒΑⱲΘ SABAÔTH (from the
Hebrew word meaning "hosts") and AΔONAEI
(from the Hebrew ADÔNÂY). IAÔ is described as
Ⱳ ⱲN "the Existing," and the ΤΡΙΜΟΡΦΕ ΘΕΟ
"three-form God," and the name is often written
between Alpha A and Ômega ΩΜΕΓΑ. The names
of many of the archangels appear on these amulets,
e.g. MICHAEL, GABRIEL, PANIEL, RAGUEL, URIEL,
SURIEL, and RAPHAEL. Of the Patriarchs MOSES
and SOLOMON are mentioned, but the pentacle
which contained the ineffable name YHWH is rarely
represented. The name of MOSES appears because
he was connected with the setting up of the brazen
serpent (Num. xxi. 9), and SOLOMON because his
seal worked miracles ; it is possible that the OPHITES,
the object of whose cult was a serpent, regarded
MOSES as the founder of their sect. Considerable
importance was attached to the Seven Vowels,
and they are found in various forms of combination on many Gnostic amulets. Thus we

have **AEHIOYW**, **AIOY HEWI**, **YOIYHIYHIYHI**, and sometimes they are grouped so as to form a triangle, thus—

A
E E
HHH
I I I I
O O O O O
Y Y Y Y Y Y
W W W W W W W

Though all the Gnostic amulets known to us are post-Christian in point of age, the figures and symbols cut upon them are far older, being chiefly of Egyptian origin. And originally such figures and symbols were believed to give the wearer of them health, strength, virility and prosperity, and had a much closer relation to magic and medicine than to religion. It was the Gnostics who by adopting them gave them their religious significance. All the animal figures found on the amulets represent strong virile beasts, and the birds and reptiles and insects represent those which are notorious for their swiftness and strength, and fecundity. And it is the rising and not the setting sun, and the crescent and not the full moon, which are depicted. One of the most important creatures is the AGATHODEMON or " Good Genius," a type of the Sun-god. He appears in the form of a huge serpent with the head of a lion on which is a crown with 7 or 12 rays. He is usually called CHNOUBIS, or CHNOUPHIS, or CHNOUMIS, but the form CHOLCHNOUBIS also appears. One of his titles is SEMES EILAM (Heb. *Shemesh 'ôlâm*), *i.e.* the SUN of the Universe, when his crown has seven rays which represent the Seven Heavens ; to each is attached one of the vowels of the Greek alphabet **ΑΕΗΙΟΥΩ**. The serpent CHNOUBIS, like the brazen serpent of MOSES (Num. xxi. 9), was regarded as a god of healing, and the renewer of life, for the serpent renews its life by sloughing its skin. The magical sign ~~ΩΩΩ~~, which is often found on the back of Chnoubis amulets, is probably a garbled

Chnoumis above a Bacchic altar. The inscription on the right contains the opening words of " I, even I, am the Good Spirit." (From KING, Plate D, No. 2.)

form of the serpent and staff which AESCULAPIUS carried, and which in their turn were borrowed from the SUMERIANS (see BUDGE, *Divine Origin of the Craft of the Herbalist*, p. 14). According to the writer HEPHAESTION and others Chnoubis was the name of one of the three Dekans in the Sign of the Zodiac CANCER, and it was set in the breast of LEO, and therefore was believed to be efficacious for the cure of all diseases in the chest and stomach. The two following inscriptions on Chnoubis amulets confirm these statements :—In the one is the prayer, " Protect the stomach of Proclus " (KING, *Gnostics*, p. 223), and in the other, " Place the womb of such-and-such a one in its proper place, O circle of the sun " (MATTER, *Gnosticisme*, Plate ii C, No. 4).

Another group of Gnostic amulets, which is called by KING " Abraxaster," reproduces a number of figures of gods, goddesses and symbols which, though

derived from Egypt, are not as old as CHNOUBIS.
The chief god among these is the jackal-headed god
ANUBIS, who, in addition to his own head, also has
the head of a man.   In ancient Egyptian theology
Anubis led the souls of the dead to the kingdom of
OSIRIS ; but in the Gnostic System he was supposed
to lead them along the paths of the planets to the
Pleroma.   He possessed the words of power which

1. Anubis, holding a sceptre and standing on an open left hand, the
symbol of justice.   The inscription behind him is the palindrome
" Ablanathan," of doubtful meaning.
2. The goddess of Truth (the Egyptian Maāt), standing on a figure of an
internal organ of Isis.   The inscription behind her means " the Sun Everlasting " or the Sun of the World.   (From KING, Plate F, No. 5.)

enabled him to pass through all the gates of heaven,
and to overcome the resistance of any and every
god who would oppose him.   He presided over the
weighing of the hearts of the dead like THOTH, but
the Gnostics identified him with CHRIST.

Another old Egyptian god figured frequently on
Gnostic amulets is Ḥer-pa-Khart or HARPOKRATES,
i.e. Horus the Child, a form of the newly risen
Sun-god.   He is represented in the form of a child,

with a lock of hair on the right side of his head ; a finger of his right hand is in his mouth, and he holds a flail in his left hand. He is seated on a lotus flower, in a boat, one end of which ends in the head of an ass and the other in the head of a bird. He is called IAΩ, as is ABRAXAS himself. With him are seen two hawks and the sun and moon. The goddesses ISIS and HATHOR appear either as figures or symbols, a circle often typifies the Sun-god, as

Horus the Child (Harpokrates) seated on a lotus in the magical boat of Iaô, one end of which terminates in an ass's head (Anubis) and the other in the head of a hawk (Horus). In the field are the morning star and a crescent moon. (From KING, Plate C, No. 3.)

in Egyptian hieroglyphs, and THOTH symbolises CHRIST.

OSIRIS appears sometimes in the form of an aged man, with his hands crossed on his breast like those of a mummy.

On gems of this class we find figures of PRIAPUS. He is represented as an ithyphallic man, four-headed, four-winged, and four-handed, holding four sceptres, and he has the tail of a bird of prey ; an inscription found on the reverse of such figures is the palindrome ABΛANAΘANAΛBA.

We now come to the ABRAXAS or ABRASAX amulets, none of which is older than the second century A.D. ; in fact, it is commonly believed that they were invented by Basilides himself. According to some the name of ABRASAX represents the Hebrew words "Habběrâkâh," literally "the blessing," but it is far more likely to be a garbled form of the name

1.   2.

1. The god Abrasax, with the head of a cock, and a human body with a bird's head and legs, formed by two serpents. He bears a shield on his left arm and brandishes a mace with his right hand. In the field are five stars representing the Five Planets, and below him is the thunderbolt. The above figure is found cut on the obverse of a copper disk found in France. (From KING, Plate A, No. 3, obverse.)

2. The three-headed Hecate, the Queen of Hell, but only four feet are represented. In the hands of the lower pair of arms she grasps two serpents, the thunderbolt and a club ; in the hands of the upper pair of arms are knives. This figure is cut on the reverse of the copper disk which has Abrasax on the obverse. (From KING, Plate A, No. 3, reverse.)

of some god, Egyptian or Indian. The total of the numerical values of the letters of his name is 365, thus :—A = 1, B = 2, P = 100, A = 1, C = 200, A = 1, and Z = 60. And the total of the numerical values of the letters in the name of MITHRAS (Meithras)—M = 40, E = 5, I = 10, Θ = 9, P = 100, A = 1 and C = 200—is also 365 ; and, according to some, ABRASAX and MITHRAS were one and the same person. The Gnostic MARCUS, who founded his whole system, which was borrowed from the Hebrew Ḳabbâlâk, upon these numerical deductions, discovered that the numerical values of the 24 letters of the Greek alphabet added together form a total of 888, which is the same as that of the letters in the name of JESUS, IHᴄOYᴄ—I = 40, E = 8, ᴄ = 200, O = 70, Y = 400, ᴄ = 200. ABRASAX represented

the 365 Aeons or emanations from the First Cause, and as a Pantheus, *i.e.* All-God, he appears on the amulets with the head of a cock (PHŒBUS) or of a lion (Rā or MITHRAS), the body of a man, and his legs are serpents which terminate in scorpions, types of the Agathodaimon. In his right hand he grasps a club, or a flail, and in his left is a round or oval shield. He is called by all the names of the God of the Hebrew, namely YÂH, ADÔNÂI,

A god in the form of Osiris as a mummy, with the Seven Stars, the Pentagram of Solomon, and the celestial orb. (From KING, Plate H, No. 5.)

and ṢABAÔTH. The palindrome ABLANATHANALBA is said to mean "Thou art our father," but this can hardly be a correct translation.

Many of the Gnostic amulets which were cut in the IInd century have long inscriptions on their edges and backs, and nearly all of them are untranslatable. This is due to the fact that each letter is the initial of a word, and no keys to these lengthy formulas have been found. Such inscriptions are due to Jewish influence, and are of Ḳabbalistic character. An interesting example of this influence is given on page 209. Here we have a figure of an old man with his hands crossed on his breast. Around him are seven stars symbolising the planets, the celestial globe, the Pentacle or Solomon's seal, and some undecipherable signs. He represents the 365 Aeons, all of which were supposed to be contained within him. He is a form of the Adam Ḳadmôn of the Ḳabbalists and the Primal Man whom God made in His own image. The second Adam of the OPHITES was conceived to have the same form. A drawing of the Primal Man according to the Ḳabbalists, reproduced from Ginsburg's work on the Ḳabbâlâh, will be found in the section on the Ḳabbâlâh.

The Arch-demon Set or Typhon-ass-headed. He has four wings, and he holds by its tail a scorpion in each hand. Above his head is a beetle with outstretched wings. Close to his neck are the crescent moon and the morning star. This was an amulet against scorpions and other reptiles. (From KING, Plate G, No. 2.)

Many of the amulets which are commonly called "Gnostic" have nothing to do with the doctrines of the true Gnôsis, and are merely charms which were intended to protect the wearer from ailments of the body, and to procure them material prosperity. A typical example of such charms, which is a charm against the bites of scorpions, is given above. And the amulets made of iron ore or haematite were probably worn with the view of giving virility to men and fecundity in women. Dr. Campbell Thompson has shown that this substance was used with a similar purpose in Babylonia and Assyria ; see his article in *Man* for January, 1928, p. 13. The following is an example of the drawings of amulets which are found in Greek magical papyri.

Amulet in a magical papyrus of the IVth or Vth century. In the upper part of the border is the well-known palindrome Ablanathanalba ; in the lower part is the spell *ai aη λαι λεμ τασω*. On the right and left are two series of Greek vowels, and in the centre is the word of power Akrammachamarei. Some of the magical signs are symbols of the heavens and the sun, moon and stars. (From KENYON, *Greek Papyri in the British Museum*, London, 1893, Papyrus CXXIV, p. 122.)

CHAPTER VIII.

The prehistoric Hebrews, like the nations round about them, made use of uninscribed amulets to protect them from the Evil Eye, and from hostile influences of every kind. Such amulets were made of semi-precious and precious stones, stones which possessed peculiar shapes or forms or were marked in some way naturally, berries of trees and plants, and grain of various kinds. According to Bischoff (*Die Elemente der Kabbalah*, ii. 190) animals could be protected from the assaults of devils and the Evil Eye by a fox's tail or by patches of some white substance placed between the eyes. A special stone was attached to the body of a pregnant woman to prevent miscarriage, and knotted cords or bands were tied to the new-born babe to preserve it from all evil. The prehistoric Hebrews probably possessed a far-reaching system of magic, but we do not know much about it. It is, however, quite clear that many of the magical practices which are made known to us by the Hebrew Bible were of very great antiquity, and were winked at by the lawgivers and prophets because it was impossible to put an end to them. Moses himself was so great a magician that he defeated Pharaoh's magicians in their own arts, and when necessity demanded it he set up the brazen serpent, the belief in the power of which was undoubtedly of pagan origin. The Hebrews inherited

much of their magic from the Sumerians and Babylonians, and many details of it survived among the
Jews and others even after the Middle Ages. We
read in the famous Epic that Gilgamish succeeded in
obtaining speech with the spirit of his dead friend
Enkidu through the good offices of Ea and Nergal,
and Saul, the Lord's anointed, had recourse to the
witch of Endor, who must have enjoyed a great
reputation as a raiser of the spirits of the dead to
obtain speech with the spirit of Samuel.

Among the different kinds of Hebrew amulets
which are made known to us by the Bible may be
mentioned :—

1. The SAHARÔN, which was probably made of
metal and had the form of a crescent, *i.e.* the
crescent moon. It was worn by women (Isa. iii. 18),
and by kings (Judges viii. 26), and was tied to the
necks of camels (*ibid.*, verse 21) to protect them
from the Evil Eye. The crescent was a favourite
amulet among many peoples of Western Asia, and
it represented to them the strength and protection
of the *waxing* and not the waning moon. The Himyarites and other peoples of Arabia added a star
to the crescent, and the Abyssinians adopted both
as sacred emblems, as at a later period the Turks
did also.

2. The TERÂPHÎM. These were small figures of
men or of gods in the forms of men, presumably
made of clay generally, but some were probably
made of semi-precious stones if they were intended
to be worn on the body. They seem to have been
of the same character as the so-called " Papsukkal "
figures which have been described in the section on
Babylonian amulets. We first hear of them in

Gen. xxxi. 19, 30, where we read that Rachel, the daughter of Laban, stole the *terâphîm* of her father and went away with them when she accompanied her husband Jacob when he fled from Laban's house. The respect in which Laban regarded these figures is evident from the fact that he calls them " my gods " ; and they must have been easily portable, for Rachel hid them in her camel's saddle. See also Judges xviii. 24. It is clear that although many men kept *terâphîm* in their houses, *e.g.* David (1 Sam. xix. 13), and Micah, who had a "house of gods" and made an ephod and *terâphîm* (Judges xvii. 5), they were regarded as profane things and were associated with the heathen practice of divination. Before Jacob went to Bethel to present himself before Yahweh he made all his people to hand over to him their "strange gods" and ear-rings (*i.e.* crescent-shaped amulets), and he hid them under the oak which was in Shechem (Gen. xxxv. 4). There were apparently several kinds of *terâphîm*, *i.e.* some were kept in the house or tent and were regarded as household gods, like the penates, some were hung on the bodies of animals, and some were used for purposes of divination. The last-named class was condemned by the prophets (1 Sam. xv. 23), and Josiah put them away with familiar spirits, and wizards and idols (2 Kings xxiii. 24). Ezek. xxi. 21 describes the king of Babylon using *terâphîm* for divining purposes, and in connection with the shuffling of arrows and inspection of the liver of the slaughtered animal. There is no doubt that the Hebrews derived the use of the *terâphîm* from the inhabitants of Lower Mesopotamia, where, according to a tablet translated by Sidney Smith, the prophylactic and atropaeic figures in a house were regarded as house property, and were sold with the house.

3. LEHÂSHÎM. The singular of this word *laḥash* was applied to any object or ornament which was associated with the whispering of incantations, spells charms, prayers, etc., and which was used as an amulet. The plural is found in Isa. iii. 20 f, when the jewellery and ornaments and attire of the daughters of Jerusalem is criticized and condemned. Among the objects enumerated are ear-rings, arm-chains, stepping-chains, girdles, finger-rings, bracelets, armlets, scent tubes, mirrors, etc. To describe these is impossible, for no pictures of the luxurious garments and ornaments worn by rich women of the time of Isaiah are extant. Among them were certainly many *leḥâshîm* or " amulets," and it is very probable that every article of apparel possessed an amuletic character.

4. BELLS. These were attached to the skirts of the vestments of Aaron the high priest (Exod. xxviii. 33), and their tinkling sounds were intended to drive away evil spirits. Isaiah (iii. 16) suggests that women attached bells to their skirts " making a tinkling with their feet." The ancient Egyptians wore bells as amulets, and their descendants, the early Copts, followed their example, and used them to drive away evil spirits during the celebration of the Eucharist. A bell of the Assyrian period decorated with figures of animal-headed deities is preserved in the Berlin Museum (figured by MEISSNER, *Bab. und Assyr.*, No. 142). And in modern caravans, horses, asses and camels frequently have bells tied to their necks to drive away evil spirits.

5. FIGURES OF GODS. The Babylonians, Assyrians and Egyptians all wore figures of gods as amulets. Now the Hebrews, being monotheists and worshippers of Yahweh, of whom no figure could be made, when they wished to do as the heathen did, and wear or carry into battle figures of gods as amulets, they were obliged to have recourse to heathen deities. Thus when Judas Maccabaeus and his company went out to bury the bodies of the dead with their kinsmen in their fathers' graves, they found under the coats of every one that was slain " things consecrated to the idols of the Jamnites, which was forbidden to the Jews by the Law." Judas decided that " this was the cause wherefore they were slain " (2 Macc. xii. 39, 40). The Philistines apparently carried figures of their gods with their army when they went forth to fight, but when David defeated them at Baal-perazim they dropped them and fled, and David ordered them to be burned with fire (1 Chron. xiv. 12).

6. ṬÔṬÂPHÔTH, or Phylacteries, *i.e.* frontlet bands which were worn between the eyes ; see Exod. xiii. 9, 16 ; Deut. vi. 8 ; xi. 18. They were made of skin of some sort and were inscribed with special formulas, *e.g.* " Hear, O Israel : The LORD our God [is] one Lord : And thou shalt love the Lord thy God with all thine heart, and with all thy soul, and with all thy might " (Deut. vi. 4, 5). Fillets or bandlets thus inscribed were to be worn either between the eyes or on the hand.

7. MEZÛZÂH. This word means a " gate-post " or a " door-post " and was given to a strip of leather which was inscribed with the verses from Deuteronomy quoted above, and then attached to the door-post of the house. See Deut. vi. 9 ; xi. 20,

8. The ṢîṣîTH or " tassel," or " lock " [of hair],
or " fringe." This was made like the phylactery
and mezûzâh by Divine Command :—And the Lord
spake unto Moses, saying, " Speak unto the children
of Israel, and bid them that they make them fringes
in the borders of their garments throughout their
generations, and that they put upon the fringe of
the borders a ribband of blue " (Num. xv. 38).
" Thou shalt make three fringes upon the four
quarters (or wings) of thy vesture wherewith thou
coverest *thyself* " (Deut. xxii. 12). There is no doubt
that the Ṭôṭâphôth, Mezûzâh and the Ṣîṣîth were
amulets, and that the use of them goes back into
prehistoric times. Originally the Ṭôṭâphôth were
precious stones which invariably possessed the
power of driving away evil spirits, and therefore
had no need of inscriptions.

Though there is no proof that the Hebrews in
general under the Mosaic dispensation used amulets,
it is tolerably certain that the pagan belief in their
efficacy was tacitly and unofficially adopted by them,
especially when after they had learned to write, they
could inscribe the Great Name of God, and the names
of His angels, and passages from their sacred books
on them. The pagan amulet was made efficacious by
the words (*i.e.* the charm or incantation) which were
pronounced over it by the magician, or priest, or
physician of the time, but the words were profane,
and represented a belief in the power of the devils
which the monotheistic Hebrew could not accept. But
the object itself, whether it was a strip of leather,
or a stone or metal plaque, might be used by him
provided the words pronounced over it or written
upon it were derived from the Hebrew Scriptures,

The true history of the use of Hebrew amulets is, I believe, only to be derived from the Ḳabbâlâh, a very ancient work which deals with Jewish mysticism in theory and practice. Assuredly those who assert that the Ḳabbâlâh is not older than the Xth century of our Era are in error. For internal evidence contains proofs that its authors borrowed many of their beliefs from Babylonian and Egyptian sources which became available to them through the works of writers in Greek in the Ist and IInd centuries. The early compilers of the Ḳabbâlâh tried, as Dr. Gaster says (Hastings' *Encyc.*, vol. iii. p. 454) to adopt and to adapt many elements from other sources and to mould them in accordance with the fundamental principle of the Unity of God and of the limited power of evil spirits. Popular beliefs know no rigid dogma, and much of that which is held to be strong and efficacious among other peoples is taken over in the belief that it would be beneficial. Many popular books have been written on Ḳabbâlâh, but they are untrustworthy because the writers make it evident that they have never read the literature of practical Ḳabbâlâh, which, as Dr. Gaster rightly points out, is still mostly in MSS. He goes on : " It is found among the medical recipes as a recognized part of the medical practitioner, who would use drugs and amulets indiscriminately or conjointly, for the use of the amulet is as widespread as that of any other medicine. There is nothing for which one or more amulets could not be prescribed, and the practice goes even further, for by means of amulets such results could be obtained as the drug alone could not effect . . . . The subduing of evil demons through the invocation of the aid of good spirits is only a materialization of higher spiritual truths. Faith is the underlying principle."

The principal classes of INSCRIBED AMULETS sanctioned by Ḳabbâlâh have been grouped by Bischoff in his *Elemente der Kabbalah* (p. 191 f.) and may be briefly described. The simplest of them contained merely extracts from the Bible, *e.g.* " I will put none of these diseases upon thee, which I have brought upon the Egyptians : for I am the LORD that healeth thee " (Exod. xv. 26). Another favourite extract was " Thou shalt not be afraid for the terror by night ; nor for the arrow that flieth by day ; nor for the pestilence that walketh in darkness ; nor for the destruction that wasteth at noonday " (Ps. xci. 5, 6). The ḲEṬEB or " noonday devil " was greatly feared, and the words rendered by " terror by night " and " pestilence " were the names of terrifying devils that caused sickness. The text of Psalm xcvii was often written on leather in the form of a seven-branched candlestick, and worn as an amulet, and the beautiful Psalm cxxi was often copied for amuletic purposes. Sometimes the text on an amulet contained a play on words, *e.g.* " Joseph is a fruitful bough by a well " (Gen. xlix. 22). The word *'ayin* means both " eye " and " well," and the verse is intended to say that Joseph was victorious over the Evil Eye, and that every descendant of his shall be also. Other very favourite texts for amulets were " Hear, O Israel : The LORD our God is one Lord " (Deut. vi. 4), and Aaron's Blessing, " The LORD bless thee, and keep thee ; the LORD make his face shine upon thee, and be gracious unto thee : the LORD lift

up his countenance upon thee, and give thee peace "
(Num. vi. 24–26).

The inscriptions on amulets were sometimes
intended to cure one particular sickness or disease.
Thus the formula SHEBRÎRÎ was used to heal any
disease of the eye, and also to counteract the effects
of the Evil Eye. It was written in this form :—

The patient began by pronouncing the whole
formula : the next time he dropped a letter, and
the following time another letter, and so on till
there was no letter left to pronounce. As the
formula diminished so the sickness would diminish,
for the patient said " Shebrîrî, Brîrî, Rîrî, Îrî, Rî, Î."

The formula ABRACADABRA, which was intended
to heal a man suffering from fever, belongs to the
same class. This formula is said to have been
invented by Serenus Sammonicus, the physician of
the Emperor Caracalla, but it seems to me that the
formula is based upon something which is much
older, and that in any case the idea of it is derived
from an older source. Many attempts have been
made to find a meaning for the formula, but the
explanation put forward by Bischoff in his " Kabbalah " (1903) is the most likely to be correct. He
derives the formula from the Chaldee words אַבְדָא,
כְדָבְרָא i.e. ABBÂDÂ KĖ DÂBRÂ, which seem to be

addressed to the fever and to mean something like " perish like the word." This cryptic utterance becomes clear when we see the form in which the formula had to be written on the amulet in Hebrew letters, viz. :—

א ר ב ד כ א ר ב א
ר ב ד כ א ר ב א
ב ד כ א ר ב א
ד כ א ר ב א
כ א ר ב א
א ר ב א
ר ב א
ב א
א

The patient, or some one on his behalf, recited the formula thus :—

Abracadabra, Abracadabr, Abracadab, Abracad, Abrac, Abra, Abr, Ab, A ; in other words he dropped one letter of the formula each time he repeated it, and as the formula diminished the fever became less. One point, however, needs elucidation ; why is the third letter of the formula R and not D ? We may note that the letters are nine in number, *i.e.* 3 × 3, and that both 9 and 3 had a mystic and magical significance ; also that the formula is repeated when reading the terminal letters diagonally from the bottom of the triangle to the top on the left-hand side. The repetition of the *Aleph*, the first letter of the Hebrew alphabet, nine times may have had a magical significance.

Here too must be mentioned the formula against fever which Dr. Gaster has translated from one of his own manuscripts. It is of special importance because it is accompanied with careful directions as to the manner of writing it, and these illustrate the implicit faith in the efficacy of the amulet of those who used them. The formula reads :—

Ab Abr Abra Abrak Abraka
Abrakal Abrakala Abrakal
Abraka Abrak Abra Abr Ab.

" And the people called unto Moses and Moses prayed to God, and the fire abated " (Num. xi. 2). "May healing come from heaven from all kinds of fever and consumption-heat to N son of N. Amen. Amen. Amen. Selah. Selah. Selah." Here is the perfect Hebrew amulet which contains (1) The magical NAME Abrakala ; (2) The TEXT from the Bible ; (3) The PRAYER, which is the equivalent of the pagan incantation ; (4) The THREEFOLD AMEN and the THREEFOLD SELAH. Dr. Gaster (Hastings' *Encyc.*, vol. iii. p. 455) has translated the directions for writing this amulet. The Name must be written exactly as it is written in the scroll of the Law on specially prepared parchment. It must be written with square or " Ashûrî " letters so that no letter shall touch the next, *i.e.* there must be a free margin round each letter. It must be written in purity and whilst fasting. It must be wrapped in leather or in some soft rag, and be wrapped round with a piece of clean leather. It is to be hung on the neck of the patient without his knowing it or when he is asleep, and he is not to look at it for the next twenty-four hours. The lines for the writing must be drawn on the hairy side of the parchment and the writing is to be done on the flesh side, and in the name of the

patient. The parchment must be cut and the lines
drawn on it in the patient's name. When the writer
dips his pen into properly prepared ink he must say :
" In the Name of Shaddai who created heaven and
earth. I, N, the son of N, write this *Kemi'a* for X,
son of X, to heal him of every kind of fever." And
then he must say the blessing of the *Kemi'a* as follows :
" Blessed art Thou, O Lord our God, Who hast
sanctified Thy great Name and hast revealed it to
Thy pious ones, to show its great power and might
in the language [in which it is expressed] in the
writing of it, and in the utterance of the mouth.
Blessed art Thou O Lord, holy King, whose great
Name be exalted [Codex Gaster, xxxviii. fol. 11.
' The Etshada'ath of Elisha of Ancona ' of 1536."

Another formula, which is directed against fire,
is written in connection with the so-called " shield
of Solomon," *i.e.* the well-known hexagram

In the centre of this are written the four letters
אגלא, that is to say, the initial letters of four
Hebrew words which are translated, " Thou art
mighty for ever Adonai." By the six sides of the
two triangles are written in magical order the names
of God, YH and YHWH. On the front and back
of the parchment on which the " shield " is written,
we have

ו ת שׁ ק ע
ת שׁ ק ע
שׁ ק ע
ק ע
ע

This formula WATTISHḲ'A, literally " and it (*i.e.* the fire) dwindled " is found in Num. xi. 2, where the story is told of the fire which broke out in the camp of the Israelites, at the place which Moses subsequently called "Tab'êrâh." This amulet was believed to possess very special powers because the formula was associated with the " shield " of David.

Amulets to protect pregnant women and women in child-bed were as common among the Hebrews as among pagan nations. They were written upon parchment, and also upon the door and walls of the chamber wherein the woman lay. And if they were to be really effective, the texts had to be written in ink in which holy incense had been mixed, and even the copyist had to be a man ceremonially pure and a believer. One of the most important and powerful child-bed amulets is reproduced on the opposite page from the British Museum copy of the rare Hebrew work generally known as the " BOOK of RâzîÊL." In the section to the right we have three figures, inexplicable to me, but according to the inscription above the first two represent Adam and Eve, and the third the Night-devil Lîlîth, who was a spirit wife of Adam before God gave him a wife of flesh. Above are the names of the angels Senoi, Sansenoi, and Samangeloph. In the section to the left are the three seals of these three angels, the first protecting Adam, the second Eve, and the third Lîlîth. The Hebrew text below the drawing says that the woman will be protected by the Name EHYH (*i.e.* God) from all the evils and calamities which are enumerated therein. This amulet had a double purpose. The three figures of the angels

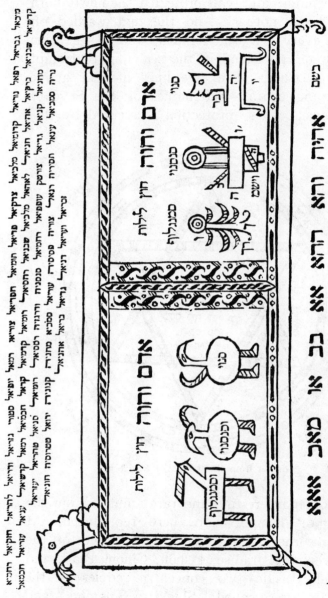

Amulet from the "Book of Râziêl."

and their names and seals protected the newly born babe and its mother. And the text warded off any and every evil which Lîlîth, who was kept in captivity on an island in the sea, might attempt to do to either. The five lines of text above the drawing contain the names of the Seventy Great Angels whose protection is secured by this amulet.

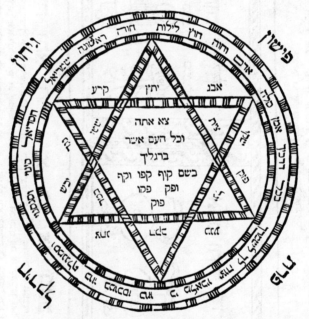

Amulet from the "Book of Râzîêl."

Two other interesting and rare amulets from the " BOOK OF RÂZÎÊL " are here reproduced. At the four corners of the first are the names of the four rivers of Paradise, Pîshôn, Gîḥon, Prâth and Hiddekel. Inside two concentric circles is the Hexagram, or so-called " Shield of Solomon " and fourteen groups of three letters and the words, " Go

forth thou and all the people who are in thy train,"
and permutations of the initial letters of the Hebrew
words for " holiness and deliverance." Between the
circles are the names of Adam, Eve, and Lîlîth,
Khasdiel, Senoi, Sansenoi, and Samangeloph, and
the words " He hath given his angels charge
concerning thee, that they may keep thee in all thy
ways. Amen. Selah."

Amulet from the "Book of Râzîêl."

At the four corners of the second amulet are the
names of the rivers of Paradise. In the centre are
the two triangles of the Hexagram arranged base to
base, and the words which occur in the centre of the
first amulet. The magical letters are " K and P,"
i.e. " holiness and deliverance." In the outer
circle are the words " He shall give his angels," etc.,
and in the inner circle are fourteen groups of three
letters which have esoteric significations.

A third amulet here reproduced from the Bcok of Râzîêl was intended to give the wearer success in business. It was written on parchment and was worn on the left arm. Here we have the word ṢLḤ " make to prosper " in four permutations and the Name of God YH (= YHWH).

Sometimes the inscriptions for the amulets were written in the Ḳabbalistic forms of the letters of the Hebrew alphabet, and specimens of three of these are reproduced below. The first is intended to secure for the wearer the favour of both God and

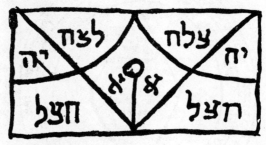

An amulet to give the wearer success in business.

man. It was written on a strip of clean hart's skin, and the text reads : " May thy favour, O YHWH, be with so-and-so, the son of so-and-so, even as it was with Joseph the righteous man," even as it is written, " And the LORD was with Joseph, and covered him with grace, and made him to obtain favour in the sight of all those who saw him," in the name of Michael, Raphael, Uriel, and the other angels.

The second was intended to secure for the wearer love and friendship. It was written with a copper pen upon a strip of parchment, with ink made from lilies and crocuses. The text was Psalm civ in its entirety.

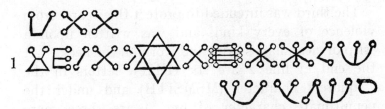

Amulet to give the wearer favour with God and man.

Amulet to procure for the wearer love and friendship.

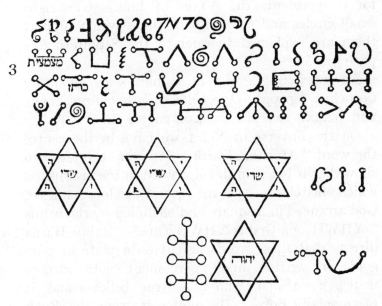

Amulet to protect the wearer against the attacks of foes and injury from
lethal weapons.

The third was intended to protect the wearer from violence of every kind, and was written upon a strip of clean hart's skin, and worn on the neck. At the end of line 2 are six Hebrew letters in the "square" character (MṢMṢITH) and under the penultimate character of line 3 are three more (KTZ) ; I can find no explanation of these. Below the four lines are three hexagrams, or "shields of Solomon." In the centre of each is SHADDAI, a name of God, and in four of the angles are the letters of the ineffable Name YHWH. Below these is a third hexagram in which is written YHWH. The three signs to the right of it are the Hebrew letters Shin, Daleth and Yud, *i.e.* Shaddai. The character to the left of the lowermost hexagram has nothing whatever to do with the Cross of the Christians, for it represents the "Tree of Life." The eight small circles and the ten short lines which support them are explained to refer to the Sephîrôth (see page 370).

An interesting group of amulet seals given by Cornelius Agrippa (*De occulta philosophia* pp. ccxxx and ccxxxi) is reproduced on page 232.

On the obverse of No. 1 we have in the centre the word "Araritha," with a dot over each letter to show that it is the initial of a word in the inscription which encircles it. On the reverse are four names of God arranged in a square and encircled by the words "YHWH our God is YHWH One." Rabbi Harna directs that these words be cut on a plate of pure gold, or written upon parchment with incense water, by a man who is a true believer and [is ceremonially pure]. He quotes it from the Book of Speculation.

In No. 2 was an amulet which was intended
to protect the wearer from earthquakes, and
from baleful devils and wicked men. On the

CORNEL. AGRIPPA a Nettesheim.

Henry Cornelius Agrippa von Nettesheim, physician and magician,
Secretary to the Emperor Maximilian I, and the author of the famous work
De occulta philosophia.   He was born at Cologne on the 14th of September,
1486, and died on the 18th of February, 1535.

one side we have the letters BWWWW and on the
other SMDBH (read SMRKD), that is to say the
initial and final letters of the first five verses of the
Book of Genesis.

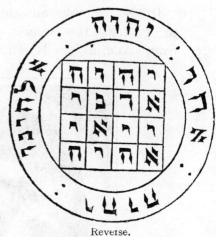

Obverse.

1

Reverse.

Obverse.

2

Reverse.

3

4

5

No. 3 is, of course, a Christian amulet, the general style of which was copied by Hebrew amulet writers.

No. 4 gives the pentagram, not the hexagram, or so-called "shield of Solomon." The inscription round it consists of five Greek letters, viz. *ιγίρα* meaning something like "wholesome," "good for the health." The pentagram is found

Three forms of the Pentagram with circles at the angles. By the angles of the first are the names of archangels, Michael, Gabriel, Ḥananîêl, etc. in the centre of the second are the words "Sheehimah of YHWH." From a manuscript of the Ḳabbâlâh in the British Museum (Oriental 4596).

on early Sumerian pottery, and it is possible that the hexagram is a later modification of it.

In the centre of No. 5 are four Hebrew letters, MKBY, each with a dot over it; these are perhaps intended to represent the name Maccabaeus. But the dotted letters are the initial letters of the

Hebrew words which we translate by " Who is like unto Thee among the gods ? "

Another very popular form of amulet was a stone, or metal plaque, or piece of parchment inscribed with a magical square of numbers, that is to say with Hebrew letters in the "square" character. The numbers were so arranged that whether added up horizontally, or perpendicularly or diagonally, the total was the same. The magical squares which refer to the Seven Planets are given on pages 394 ff. Magical squares were also constructed with the letters which give the name of God in whichever direction they are read. A good typical example is given by Dr. Bischoff (*Die Elemente*, vol. ii. p. 126), which is here reproduced. A magical square containing the Name ELOHÎM is written thus :—

ס	י	ה	י	ס
י	ה	ל	ה	י
ה	ל	א	ל	ה
י	ה	ל	ה	י
ס	י	ה	י	ס

In this case the initial letter or " key " is the *aleph* in the middle of the third line. The name Elohîm is obtained by reading upwards or downwards and sideways, but not horizontally. In the same work Dr. Bischoff gives a square of seventeen lines containing the German rendering of the Hebrew words meaning " the Lord watch over thee," DER

HERR BEHÜTE DICH. The "key" is the letter D
in the middle of line 9 :—

H	C	I	D	E	T	Ü	H	E	H	Ü	T	E	D	I	C	H
C	I	D	E	T	Ü	H	E	B	E	H	Ü	T	E	D	I	C
I	D	E	T	Ü	H	E	B	R	B	E	H	Ü	T	E	D	I
D	E	T	Ü	H	E	B	R	R	R	B	E	H	Ü	T	E	D
E	T	Ü	H	E	B	R	R	E	R	R	B	E	H	Ü	T	E
T	Ü	H	E	B	R	R	E	H	E	R	R	B	E	H	Ü	T
Ü	H	E	B	R	R	E	H	R	H	E	R	R	B	E	H	Ü
H	E	B	R	R	E	H	R	E	R	H	E	R	R	B	E	H
E	B	R	R	E	H	R	E	D	E	R	H	E	R	R	B	E
H	E	B	R	R	E	H	R	E	R	H	E	R	R	B	E	H
Ü	H	E	B	R	R	E	H	R	H	E	R	R	B	E	H	Ü
T	Ü	H	E	B	R	R	E	H	E	R	R	B	E	H	Ü	T
E	T	Ü	H	E	B	R	R	E	R	R	B	E	H	Ü	T	E
D	E	T	Ü	H	E	B	R	R	R	B	E	H	Ü	T	E	D
I	D	E	T	Ü	H	E	B	R	B	E	H	Ü	T	E	D	I
C	I	D	E	T	Ü	H	E	B	E	H	Ü	T	E	D	I	C
H	C	I	D	E	T	Ü	H	E	H	Ü	T	E	D	I	C	H

The greatest of all the amulets known to the
Hebrews was, and is, the Book of the Law, the
TÔRÂH or Roll inscribed with the Five Books of
Moses, or the Pentateuch. It is to them what the
PERT-EM-HRU was to the Egyptians, and the papyrus
volumes of the Scriptures to the Copts, and the
ḲUR'ÂN to the Arabs, and the KEBRA NAGAST to the
Ethiopians or Abyssinians. Its power and might were
invincible, both in the synagogue and the house.
It was the greatest of all the child-bed amulets. A
remarkable proof of this is given by Dr. Bischoff
(*Die Elemente*, vol. iii. p. 123), who has reproduced
from an old print a scene in the birth-chamber.

On a wall are written the names of Adam, Eve and
Lîlîth, and it was absolutely necessary to protect
the woman who was about to bring forth from the
last named, who was the she-devil wife of Adam
before God gave him Eve. On a table stands a
shrouded Roll of the Law, and on this the woman,
who is on the birth-stool, fixes her eyes and prays
for help in her hour of need. Many a wealthy Jew
keeps a Tôrâh in his house as a priceless treasure.
In Eastern Europe the Jews have had the Hebrew
text of their Scriptures reproduced by photography
in the form of an ordinary book from one of their
famous Rolls, and this miniature copy of the Book
of the Law measures only one inch in height and
three-quarters of an inch in width. It is provided
with a white metal case, with a ring for hanging
it round the neck, on one side of which is a small
magnifying glass which enables the wearer to read
the text with comparative ease. The general appearance of the amulet is that of the Ḳur'ân which is
shown on page 53.

The silver Hebrew amulet here reproduced was
formerly in the possession of the late W. H. Rylands,
F.S.A., who obtained it from a friend who brought
it from Palestine. Mr. E. T. Pilcher published a
copy of the obverse and a transcript of the text, with
an English translation, in the *Proceedings of the
Society of Biblical Archaeology*, Vol. xxxii. (1910),
p. 125. But he did not recognize that the text
consisted of a series of abbreviations which needed
completions, and contained a number of allusions
to Ḳabbâlâh, and the result was that his translation was incorrect in nearly every particular. In
the number of the *Proceedings* for May, 1910, Dr.

Gaster published the text on both sides of the amulet and gave a correct transcript of it, after completing the abbreviated words and adding the words which were wanting, and an English translation which reads :—

Obverse.   Reverse.

Silver Kabbalistic amulet.

OBVERSE.

1. In the Name of the Lord God of Israel we shall do and prosper.

2. " I beseech thee by the power of the greatness " of God, the Lord of Hosts, the God of Israel.

3. In the names of the angels of the God (of Israel) I conjure you all

4. kinds of Lilin (*i.e.* night-devils), male and female,

5. and Demons, male and female,

6. by the power of the holy Name,

7. " Accept the prayer of thy people, exalt them, purify them, O Thou Who art tremendous," combined with

8. its root (*i.e.* source) YHWH, that they do not

REVERSE.

1. enter to any

2. place where there be

3. in it " O mighty one, those who beseech thee," nor shall touch

4. it at all, nor hurt by the power of

5. the holy Name " thy right hand shall loosen the bondage."

6. " Thy single ones, like the apple of thine eye, guard them, combined with

7. its root (*i.e.* source) ADNI, and with

8. the name of 26 (letters) (the Tetragrammaton) " Accept our entreaty, and hear our cry, Lord who knowest the hidden things."

9. " May the Lord preserve thy going out and thy coming in from now and evermore." Amen. Selah.

CHAPTER IX.

MANDAEAN (MANDAÎTIC) AMULETS.

The MANDAEANS (MANDÂŶÊ), who are also known as ṢÂBÆANS (*i.e.* worshippers of the host of heaven), and MUGHTASILS (*i.e.* " the washers," because of the frequency of their ablutions), and " Christians of St. John " (because of their tradition that they are descended from the disciples of St. John the Baptist), are a Semitic people who live in Lower Babylonia and on the banks of the Shaṭṭ al-'Arab, and who speak a dialect similar to that found in the *Talmudh Babhlî*. Their ancestors before the Christian Era were pagans, and practised magic, and believed in a form of astrology which seems to have been of Babylonian origin. The Christian Mandaeans clung to the belief in the magic practices of their ancestors, and on it they welded many elements of belief which they derived from the Gnostics, the Jews, the Iranians or Persians, and Christians. They had no Sabbaths and did not practise circumcision. When they pray they do not turn towards Jerusalem, but towards the north, where are the great mountains from which flow the rivers Tigris and Euphrates. The sources of these rivers is the world of light where the SUPREME LIFE, *i.e.* God, lives and reigns. In the waters of these they bathe morning and evening, especially on Sundays and days of fasting. They also observe a bathing festival in which whole communities go to the river and bathe ceremonially

under the direction of their priests, or according to
their private rules. They believe that through these
immersions in the " waters of light " they receive
a renewal of life from the Great Life, the Master of
the Universe, and all virtues. It would be impossible
for them to practise their religion in a region where
there were no rivers and streams, and it is due to this
fact that they have always lived in the district
round about Ḳurnah, where the Tigris and Euphrates
unite to form the Shaṭṭ al-'Arab. One of the names
by which they are known, viz. " Mughtasilin " may
be rendered " Baptists." Their term for " baptism "
is *maṣbutâ*, because with them the ceremony takes
place in " living," *i.e.* flowing water. They despise
the Christian ceremony because they say that it is
performed in " dead," *i.e.* still water. Their God,
" Life," is the King of Light, and dwells with His
angels in a heaven which is high above the heavens
or spheres of the stars and planets and Signs of the
Zodiac. Below the starry spheres is our earth,
which is formed of matter derived from some of the
solidified water of the primeval World-Ocean. In
some portion of this Black Water dwells a great
she-devil called RÛHÂ, and her husband 'UR, who
is also her son, and great armies of evil spirits. 'Ur is
the god of Darkness, and is the great antagonist of
the god of Light. Here we have a cosmogony
derived from the ancient Sumerians, and Tiâmat,
Kingu and Marduk under other names, and we may
regard the Mandaeans as the representatives of the
ancient worshippers of Ea, the great Water-god of
Eridu.

One of the books of the Mandaeans, the ḲOLÂSTÂ,
contains a series of ill-drawn pictures which are

supposed to represent the places at which the souls
of the dead alight on their way to heaven, and in
one part of it are drawings of the scales in which
presumably souls were weighed and the throne of
ABATÛR. These facts seem to suggest that the
writer of the work had seen a copy of the Saïte Recension of the Book of the Dead, and that he copied
some of the Vignettes of Chapter cli, and a part of
the introductory scene of the Psychostasia. On the
other hand, the Book ASFAR MALWÂSHÂ, which deals
with a system of astrology based on the Signs of the
Zodiac, seems to have been derived from the works
of the later Persian astronomers, though these in
turn were based on the astrological literature of the
Babylonians.

The LANGUAGE of the Mandaeans is written in an
unusual script, one of the great advantages of which
is the fact that the vowels are represented by letters,
and the reading is not therefore confused by dia-
critical points. The LITERATURE is relatively small,
and the three principal works are the SIDRÂ RABBÂ,
or GINZÂ, and the SIDRÂ D' YAHYÂ or Book of John
the Baptist, and the DRÂSHÊ D' MALKÊ or DIS-
COURSES OF KINGS, and the ḴOLÂSTÂ, which contains
Hymns and Discourses regarding Baptism and the
Departure of the soul from the body. Some sections
of these works are as old as the Ist century A.D.,
and much of the rest was written before the rise of the
Arab kingdom in Mesopotamia in the VIIth century.
The Mandaeans, like the Babylonians, lived lives
of fear because they believed in the existence of
myriads of fiends and devils which caused sicknesses
and death to themselves and damage to their
material property. The priests of the Mandaeans

condemned all magical practices, but in spite of this the people clung to the use of amulets. Examples of these are rare, and the two best known are in the British Museum (Add. 23602, B, fol. 26, and foll. 26–28). Portions of these are reproduced on Plates XVIII and XIX. A transcript into Hebrew letters of the left-hand column fol. 25 is given by WRIGHT, *Catalogue of the Syriac Manuscripts in the British Museum*, vol. iii. p. 1219. But the Mandaeans. like the Syrians and Arabs, possessed a large collection of charms and magical prescriptions, and when written down they formed a real " Book of Magic." Two leaves of such a codex are preserved in the British Museum (Add. 23602, B, foll. 23, 24), and a note on one of them says that the volume belonged to Yahyâ bar Ḥavvâ Sîmath (Wright, *op. cit.*, p. 1218).

The texts on the amulets contain prayers, which are to all intents and purposes incantations, and it is clear that they were intended to produce magical effects. The text on fol. 25 is accompanied with a magical figure, part of which is still visible. This proves that the Mandaeans copied the amuletic scrolls of Western people, Egyptians, Gnostics, Greeks, Syrians and others. For the history and religion of the Mandaeans, see Petermann, *Reisen im Orient*, Leipzig, 1860–61 ; N. Souffi, *Études*, Paris, 1880 ; Nöldeke, *Mandäische Grammatik*, Halle, 1875 ; and Brandt, *Die mandäische Religion*, Leipzig, 1889.

The two amulets mentioned above were worn on the body or carried about by their owners, but besides scrolls like these the Mandaeans had amulets which they intended to protect their houses and lands from the attacks of evil spirits. These were in the form of terra-cotta bowls which were placed

PLATE XVIII

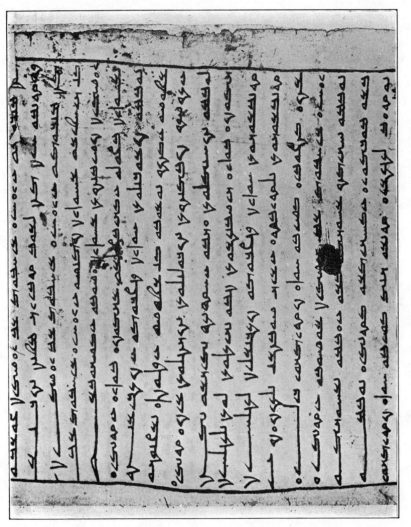

Extract from a Mandaean amulet in the British Museum

PLATE XIX

Extract from a Mandaean amulet with magical drawings
in the British Museum.

by or under the foundations of their houses, and
were inscribed with magical texts. See what is
said in the section on divination by water and
Babylonian bowls, page 445 f. During the American
excavations at Nippur a great many such bowls were
found, and a good monograph on them has been
written by Prof. J. A. Montgomery, entitled *Aramaic
Incantation Texts from Nippur*, Philadelphia, 1913.
In the introductory chapters of this work will be
found (1) a summary of the work done on the bowls
by the older scholars, Chwohlson, Wohlstein-Stūbe,
Hyvernat, Ellis, Lidzbarski and others, and (2) a
discussion on the use and object of the bowls, demons
and evil spirits and kindred matters. These are
followed by a series of translations of the Mandāitic
and other texts on the bowls, with grammatical
and other notes, and complete transcripts of the
texts are given at the end of the volume. The general
character and contents of the inscriptions on the
Nippur bowls is illustrated by the two following
translations made by Prof. J. A. Montgomery.

THE AMULET OF EPHRÂ BAR SABÔRDÛCH.

(MONTGOMERY, No. 1, p. 117.)

(1) This the amulet of Ephrâ (2) bar Sabôrdûch,
wherein shall be (3) salvation for this Ephrâ bar
Sabôrdûch and also (4) for this Bahmandûch bath
Samâ, that there be for them (5) salvation, namely
for this Ephrâ bar Sabôrdûch, and for this Bahmandûch bath Samâ (6). Amen. Amen. Selah.
    This is an amulet against the Lîlîths that haunt
the house of (7) this Ephrâ bar Sabôrdûch, and this
Bahmandûch bath Samâ (8) I adjure you, all species

of Lîlîths in respect to your posterity which is begotten by Demons (9) and Lîlîths to the children of light who go astray ; WOE, who rebel and transgress against the proscriptions of their Lord; Woe, from the blast (10) fast flying ; Woe, destroying ; Woe, oppressing with your foul wounds . . . who do violence and trample and scourge and mutilate (11) and break and confuse and hobble and dissolve (the body) like water ; Woe, . . . ; and where you stand, (12) and where you stand (*sic*) fearful and affrighted are ye bound to my ban,—who appear to mankind, to men in the likeness of women, (13) and to women in the likeness of men, and with men they lie by night and by day.

With the formula TWM (14) SH·SH GSH GSHK, have I written against thee, evil Lîlîth, whatsoever name be thine. We (15) have written. And his name shall save thee, Ephrâ, for ever and ever.

AMULET OF ADAḲ BAR ḤÂTHÔI AND AḤATH BATH ḤÂTHÔI.

(MONTGOMERY, No. 6, p. 141.)

(1) A *press* which is *pressed* down upon Demons and Devils and Satans and impious (2) Amulet spirits and Familiars and Counter-charms and Lîlîths male (3) and female, that attach themselves to Adaḳ bar Ḥâthôi and Aḥath bath Ḥâthôi—that attach themselves to them, and dwell (4) in their archways and lurk in their thresholds, and appear to them in one form and another, and that strike and cast down and kill. And this *press* (5) I *press* down upon them in days and in months and in all years, and this day out of all days,

and this month out of all months, and this year (6) out of all years, and this season out of all seasons. And I come and put a spell for them in the thresholds of this their houses, and I seal and bind them. Fastened up are their doors (7), and all their roofs.

And this *press* I *press* down upon them by means of these seven words, (8) by which heaven and earth are charmed ; in the name of the first *Gishmîn* and *Marbîl ;* of the second, *Gishmîn* and *Marbîl ;* of the third, *Marbîl ;* of the fourth, *Mashbar ;* of the fifth, *Morah ;* of the sixth, *Ardibal ;* of the seventh, *Kibshin* (presses) with which is repressed (9) . . . with them are *repressed* all evil Spirits and impious Amulet spirits and Lîlîths male and female and Familiars and Counter-charms and Words, that they appear not to Adak̲ bar Ḥâthôi and to [Aḥath bath Ḥâthôi] (10) neither in dream by night nor in sleep by day, and that they approach neither their right side nor their left, and that they kill not their children, and that they have no power over their property, what they have (11) and what they shall have, from this day and for ever.

And whosoever will transgress against this *press* and doth nor accept these rites, shall split asunder violently and burst in the midst. And the sound of him shall resound with the resonance of brass in the spheres of heaven, (12) and his abode shall be in the seventh (?) hell of the sea, from this day and for ever. Amen. Amen. Selâh.

CHAPTER X.

PHOENICIAN AMULETS.

Speaking generally the country of Phoenicia is that part of Syria which extends from the Nahr al-Kabîr, *i.e.* the "Great River" (Eleutherus) in the north to Mount Carmel on the south, but Joppa was sometimes considered to be Phoenician territory. The Phoenicians were Semites and belonged to the Canaanite peoples, though they and the neighbouring peoples called them "Sidonians." The Greeks called them "Phoenicians," Φοίνικες, and their land "Phoinike," Φοινίκη. Some derive "Phoenician" from the Greek φοινός, "blood red," and not from φοῖνιξ, the "date palm," which does not grow readily in the country, so the Phoenicians were the "red men." Unlike the Semites generally, the Phoenicians loved the sea, and their ships on the sea and their caravans by land carried the produce of Egypt and Babylonia to the ends of the known world. The language of the Phoenicians, like the Hebrew and the dialect of Moab, was descended from the old Canaanite language, and belonged to the Northern Semitic Group of languages.

The Phoenicians were not a literary people, and it is very doubtful if they invented the alphabet as Pliny (v. 13, vii. 57) believed, for the letters which they used are identical with those of the Siloam Inscription

and those found on the Stele of Mesha, king of Moab
(Moabite Stone, casts of both inscriptions can be
seen in the British Museum), and the Zingirlî
inscriptions. The Phoenician alphabet underwent
many changes in the countries where it was adopted,
but it became the mother-alphabet of the Greek and
Latin, and eventually of the modern European
alphabets. It is possible that the Phoenicians
possessed a native religion, but very little is known
of their theology. Their cosmogonies and many of
their legends and myths were borrowed from the
Babylonians, the Egyptians and the Greeks. They
were well acquainted with the names of many of the
gods of these peoples, and their names often contained the names of foreign gods, e.g. Bêl and Bêltis,
Ishtar Tammûz, Isis, Osiris, Hathor, Horus, Thoth,
etc.

Their views about the survival of the soul
after death were similar to those of the Hebrews,
but they buried their dead with great care. One
of their chief native gods was *Eshmûn*, the god of
medicine, who was identified with the Greek god
Asklepios. In times of trouble they did not hesitate
to sacrifice their first-born children, and they slew
their prisoners of war on the altar before their
tabernacles (Diodorus, xx. 14). And women sacrificed their virginity in the sanctuaries of Astarte
(see 1 Kings xiv. 24). A large proportion of
the Phoenician population devoted themselves to
making the purple and fine linen which were so
much admired by the ancients, and to working
in metal. The gold came from Egypt and the
Sûdân, and iron and copper came from Cyprus.
Thus some members of a family produced the

vases, bowls, and pots which the other members
of it carried off in their ships and sold in Europe,
or Asia, or Africa, or India. In this way the
commission of the middle man was saved. The art
of dyeing was derived by them from Babylon and
glass blowing from Egypt, and it seems that the
Phoenician invented very little in literature or in
the arts and crafts, but his work was careful,
accurate and refined. Witness the inscribed and
embossed copper bowls from Nimrûd which are now
in the British Museum. And the bronze lion
weights in the British Museum prove that he introduced into his own country, and also into the
neighbouring countries, a system of weighing with
accurate weights.

The small collection of PHOENICIAN AMULETS in
the British Museum is of considerable interest.
It shows that the Phoenicians adopted the seal-
cylinder of the Babylonians and Assyrians, and the
cone-seal of the Persians, and the scarab of the
Egyptians. The devices engraved upon these
objects are Assyrian and Egyptian in origin, but
they are treated in a manner which is characteristic
of Phoenician work in metal and stone. The line
engravings are carefully executed, and the work
is of a more delicate character than that found on
purely Babylonian or Assyrian and Egyptian seals
and scarabs. On the oldest of them, which probably date from about 500–400 B.C., the influence of
Persian Art is very marked. The scarabs made of
hard stone were undoubtedly used as seals, but there
is no evidence that the Phoenicians held the same
religious views about the *scarabaeus sacer* as the
Egyptians. The group of scarabs in steatite and

paste from Umrît, which were exhibited in the
same case as the Phoenician scarabs in the British
Museum, are native imitations of Egyptian scarabs
and were made in Phoenicia about 300–200 B.C.
The Phoenicians believed that they could hold intercourse with the dead by dropping little rolls made
of thin sheets of lead with inscriptions upon them
into the tombs, but it is doubtful if these are to be
regarded as amulets.

The following reproductions of cylinder-seals with
Phoenician inscriptions on them have been made
from casts supplied by Mr. Augustus Ready of the

1

British Museum ; all the originals are in the British
Museum (Department of Egyptian and Assyrian
Antiquities) :—

1. Cylinder-seal engraved with the figure of a
king or hero who is grasping with each hand a fore
leg of a mythological beast. Each beast is winged
and the head of the beast on the right is provided
with a pair of horns. Above the male figure is the

symbol of a god (Ahuramazda or some Assyrian god), the lower part of whose body is the winged circle with projecting claws and a tail. The inscription reads, " SEAL OF PRSHNDT, SON OF ARTDTN " ‎חתם פרשנדת בר ארתדתן.‎ Height of seal 1⅜ inches.

2. Cylinder-seal engraved with a bearded figure of a king with two pairs of wings, who is grasping in each hand a foreleg of a beast with the head and

2

wings and claws of a bird, and the body of a rampant striped animal. The inscription reads " HRTKL " (?) ‎הרתכל.‎ Height of seal 1⅛ inches.

3. Cylinder-seal inscribed with : (1) The sacred Tree. (2) Two Scorpion-men supporting a winged disk from which two divine figures emerge. (3) A worshipper (royal ?). (4) A priest carrying a small horned animal to offer up as a sacrifice. In front

of him is the sign  which some have identified
with the pudenda muliebris, and behind his head
is a star. The inscription reads " Belonging to
PLTḤAN " לפלתחאן. Height of seal ⅞ inch.

3

4

4. Cylinder-seal inscribed with a figure of a man
who is standing in worship before a symbol (lightning
or thunder-bolt ?), above which is a winged disk
with a lion's head. On each side of the symbol
is a priest wearing a winged garment. The

inscription reads " YRPAL, the son of HR'DD "
ירפאל בר הרעדד. The name Yrpel is written
twice.   Height of seal 1⅜ inches.

5. Cylinder-seal inscribed with a figure of the
sacred tree under a winged disk.   On one side of the
tree is a sphinx with the lunar crescent above it,
and on the other is a goat.   Two men are performing

5

6

a religious ceremony.   The inscription reads "Belonging to SRGD " לסרגד.   Height of seal ⅞ inch.

6. Cylinder-seal inscribed with figures of two
scorpion-men standing, one on each side of sacred

tree (?), and supporting a winged disk from which project the heads of three divine beings. A priest and a worshipper are performing a religious ceremony. On the left is the figure of a god holding a gazelle, or goat, under each arm. The inscription reads " Belonging to MDBRG " למדברג. Height of cylinder $\frac{15}{16}$ inch.

7

7. Cylinder-seal inscribed with three human figures, which was dedicated to the god Hadad. The inscription reads " Belonging to AKDBN, the son of GBRD, the eunuch, which he offered to HDD " לאכדבן בר גברד סרס אשר הקרב להדד. Height of seal $1\frac{1}{2}$ inches.

CHAPTER XI.

SAMARITAN AMULETS.

Less than twenty years ago had I been asked, "Have the Samaritans amulets, and, if so, what are they like?" my answer would have been, "There are no Samaritan amulets, and if there are I have never seen any." But thanks to Dr. M. Gaster, that lacuna is filled up now, and it is possible as the result of his researches to tell the reader a great deal about Samaritan amulets. This gentleman discovered that the Samaritans of Nablûs possessed, among other literary treasures, a number of Samaritan amulets, or, as he calls them, "phylacteries," and he took steps to open up intercourse with them with the object of acquiring some information about them. At first, like all other Orientals, who possess ancient manuscripts, they pretended to know nothing about such things, but after some years of friendly relations with Dr. Gaster they admitted that they had among them a number of phylacteries. After from twelve to fifteen years of constant communication and patient negotiation, he succeeded in obtaining from them all the phylacteries they had, some fourteen in number. Besides these he obtained photographs of two others, one in the British Museum (Add. 27456) and the other in the possession of Mr. D. S. Sassoon. Having worked for some years on this entirely new branch of Semitic literature, he published the results of his labours in several articles in the *Proceedings of the Society of Biblical Archaeology* (March, May and June, 1915, Feb., 1916, and Feb., 1917). These he has reprinted in his *Studies and Texts*, in three volumes, London, 1925–1928 (vol. i. p. 387 f). The main facts about Samaritan phylacteries which are given below I owe to his invaluable work.

Of the early history of the Samaritans nothing is known. One tradition says that their great ancestor was SHEMER, who sold the site of his city, which was called Samaria after his name, to Omri (1 Kings xvi. 24) ; the dwellers in the city were called " SHOMRONÎM," a name which is once mentioned in the Bible (2 Kings xvii. 29). Originally a Samaritan was a dweller in the city of Samaria or in the country of which it was the capital, but after the King of Assyria (Shalmaneser IV or Sargon II) transferred there natives of Babylon, Cuthah, Arva, Hamath and Sepharvaim (2 Kings xvii–xviii), any one of them might describe himself or be described as a Samaritan. The original Samaritans were pagans, but between the time of the settlement of foreigners on a large scale in their city by the king of Assyria, and the birth of Christ, they adopted in a great measure the Jewish religion, although they clung to their idols and magical practices. And they held that Mount Gerizim (see John iv. 20), and not Jerusalem, was the true seat of God's worship. About the great schism which converted the Jews and the Samaritans into bitter enemies of each other this is not the place to speak, and it is sufficient to say that the Samaritans were regarded as an independent sect in the time of our Lord. They accepted the monotheism of the

Jews, and the Law, and believed that a Messiah whom they called " Taheb " was to come. Their phylacteries show that on a very large number of points their beliefs were identical with those of the Hebrews.

The first thing to note about the Samaritan phylacteries is that they were not the equivalents of the TEPHILLÎN, or prayer scrolls, or " frontlets," but real AMULETS which, as Dr. Gaster says, " would be worn constantly, and they were also looked upon as superstitious practices, used not only by the Jews, but by almost every other nation of antiquity " (p. 387). They were in their oldest and simplest forms the outcome of pagan magic, and they were made and worn notwithstanding the fact that the use of them was forbidden under the penalty of death. The Samaritans added Hebrew beliefs to their own native beliefs, and then tried to observe both, and they neither rejected nor abolished any of their own indigenous views or practices. The phylacteries came into being probably during the Ist or IInd century of our Era, but none in the possession of Dr. Gaster is older than the Xth or XIth century. The Samaritans who lived in Egypt borrowed ideas from the worshippers of Rā and Osiris, and from the various sects of Gnostics, and probably also from the Babylonians, whose magic and religion were being made known by the Greeks who had lived in Babylon and had studied the ancient cuneiform records in the Libraries of Babylon.

The Samaritans regarded the ineffable names of God as " words of power," and held them to be the foundation of all the virtue which their phylacteries possessed. They thought that the Tetragrammaton

could not be pronounced, and some of them substituted for it " Elohim." The letters of the names
of God are treated as mathematical figures, and thus
mathematical calculations are derived from the names
of God and from the various permutations and sub-
stitutions to which that name has been subjected,
and the Samaritans seem to have known the very
name by which these manifold operations was known
among the Jews, *i.e.* " Gematria." Dr. Gaster
thinks that Gematria is a mistake for " Grammata,"
i.e. " writings," and that for the " Ephesia Gram-
meta " of Greek mystical literature we should read
Aphasia Grammata, *i.e.* " ineffable writings." In
the phylacteries we find every one of these mysterious
names, forms, symbols, changes, and permutations
fully represented. And the two names of God
EHYH and YHWH are intertwined.

The Jews were commanded by Deut. vi. 9 to write
certain " words " on the lintels and door-posts of
their houses, but they did not carry out the command
literally. They wrote the words of Deut. vi. 4–9
and xi. 13–21 on strips of parchment and fastened
them to the door-posts. These are called *mezzuzôth*.
The Samaritans acted differently, for they cut the
" words " on the stones of their houses. Moreover,
by the "words" they understood the " ten words,"
i.e. the Ten Commandments, and these, as well as
other verses from the Bible, are cut on their monuments. (See Dr. Gaster's list on p. 400.) There is
in the British Museum (Semitic Room No. 556) a
stone inscribed in Samaritan with two verses from
Deuteronomy, and though it formed part of a wall,
it is in truth a phylactery. On some stones the Ten
Words of Creation are given instead of the Ten

Commandments. These are the fundamental "words of power," the real Logos. Among the characteristics of Samaritan phylacteries is one which is of considerable interest, for it is a testimony to their great antiquity—I mean that of the Palindrome. "Certain verses of the Bible, expecially Exod. xv. 15, 16, are written backwards, starting, as it were, with the last word of verse 16 and going backwards, the order of the words, not of the letters, being reversed. Similarly Exod. xiv. 19 ff ; xvii. 13 are written in the form of Palindrome" (Gaster, p. 405).

The Samaritan name for the phylactery is Akhtaba, but in Codex, Gaster B, the variant FLKTRA is given, which, of course, represents the Greek φυλακτήρια. The phylactery is not to be confused with the prayer scrolls (Tephillîn) which were only put on during times of prayer, for it was an amulet in the true sense of the word, like the kâmi' of the Jews, and is, probably, equally as old.

The Samaritan phylactery appears in several forms :—1. As a square sheet of parchment, which practically represents a whole skin of a goat. One in the possession of Dr. Gaster is between 17 and 22 inches in height, and another is 27 inches wide. 2. As a scroll which varies in length and width. 3. As a booklet, which was probably carried in a case. 4. As scraps of paper. 5. As a metal disk, like a coin or medal. 6. As inscribed stones. The one Samaritan phylactery in the British Museum (Add. 27456) is a large sheet of parchment which was folded several times and carried in a metal case. A section of the text is reproduced on Plate XX

PLATE XX

Extract from a Samaritan phylactery in the British Museum (Add. 27456).

PLATE XXI

The metal case which held the phylactery in the British Museum.

and a full-sized view of the case on Plate XXI. The case has a tightly fitting cover with flanges, and on the edges are a series of rings through which a cord was passed, and it probably hung as a pendant on the breast of the wearer. Each side is embossed with a rectangular geometrical design. Around these designs run lines of Samaritan text, and one begins " In the Name of El-Shaddai YHWH." Then follows a passage from Exod. xiv. 14, " The LORD shall fight for you, and ye shall hold your peace." The official *Catalogue* assigns this phylactery to the XVth century. The parchment is much damaged through folding it, and all the phylacteries known have suffered in this way ; with one exception there is only one *complete* phylactery known.

Two kinds of ink were used, both presumably made from lamp-black ; the one when dry is pale and the other is very black and shiny, as if gum had been mixed with it. But the pale ink has " bitten " deeper into the parchment than the very black ink. The writing is apparently on the fleshy side of the skin. " The skin is divided into seven columns of equal width (3 inches). These are separated one from the other by a space of $\frac{3}{4}$ inch, which has not been left blank. These seven columns are surrounded on all four sides by two lines of writing, of which one is a Palindrome of verses from Exod. xiv. 16 ff and xvii. 8 ff. This writing is then continued in single lines filling up the blanks between the columns. In order to insert these lines, the scribe has turned the skin to the left, and starting from the bottom he wrote parallel to the side line. In the same manner are the other lines written. . . .

In these lines round and between the columns one may detect the oldest form of illumination, the verses and the letters preceding floral and other architectural illustrations " (Gaster, p. 411). Cursive writing is never found on the phylacteries. Neither the name of the writer nor that of the owner of any phylactery is given upon it, and therefore it could be worn by any one. The text on the scroll is written vertically, not from right to left, but from top to bottom, the whole text forming one single column.

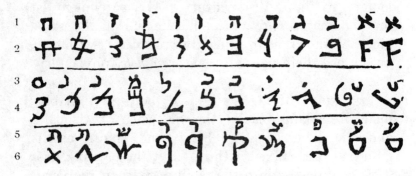

THE HEBREW AND SAMARITAN ALPHABETS.
The Hebrew letters are given in lines 1, 3, 5, and their Samaritan equivalents in lines 2, 4, 6 below them. (Reproduced by permission from GASTER, *Studies and Texts*, Vol. i. p. 611.)

The phylacteries in the form of strips of paper contain short formulae, accompanied sometimes by mystical diagrams, which are taken from the old, large phylacteries. The smallest formulae are found on the silver-gilt medals which are worn by children at the present day to protect them from the Evil Eye. All these manifold phylacteries " have an ancient mystical tradition, which in its essence and fundamental principles is undistinguishable from the Jewish cabbalistic tradition."

By the help of the Samaritan phylactery "some hitherto inexplicable features in Greek magical texts find a satisfactory explanation ; and, finally, that one of the oldest forms of the real phylacteries has been preserved by the Samaritans in their SHEM HAMITFARESH" (Gaster, p. 420).

In his *Studies and Texts* (vol. i. p. 425 f) Dr. Gaster gives a complete translation of a phylactery (Codex D 1105), from which the reader will see how Bible history, prayers, lists of magical names, the letters of the alphabet, etc., are welded together to form a most powerful amulet. From it the following extracts are taken :—

This writing is good for every man who is clothed with it. Amen. . . . And the magicians could not stand before Moses, and so may they also not stand before those who are clothed with Thy name, O Lord, be it male or female . . . . May it not be exterminated, and pray thee it may not turn back, may every man who is clothed with this good phylactery (*phiḳlṭra = philḳṭra*) be free from every demon and every spirit, and every wicked one, and from every harm and from every beast. Amen (3 times). Rise, O Lord. Return, O Lord, to him who is clothed with these writings. Save him from every bad thing. Pishon, Gihon, Dkl and Perat [the four rivers of Paradise] For I am the Lord that healeth thee. Keep me, O God of the holy Tabernacle. Keep me, O God of the sanctuary. Keep me, O god of the Prophet. Keep me, O God of Mount Garizim. Keep me, O god of the priests. Keep me, O God of the holy ones. Keep me on the way upon which I walk and do not pass over my prayers, for this reward me and save me from all

evil. [Then comes the name] YHWH ten times. . .
Whosoever wears this writing, may the fear of You
and the trembling before You be upon all the beasts
of the land and all the birds of heaven. . . He who
rideth the heavens, my Master, the holy God, save
me from all evil, YHWH (5 times) God of gods,
enlarge me from all stress and anguish and remove
from us the snake . . . YHWH (10 times), YHWH
Elohim, YHWH (3 times), Elohim YHWH Elohim
YHWH Elohim, Adam, Noah, Abraham, Isaac,
Jacob, Joseph, Levi, a Kehath, Amram, Moses,
Aaron, Eleazar, Ithamar, Pinehas, Joshua, Kaleb,
the Seventy Elders [Mystical letters] ANGDKNH.
Master, be good unto me, Master by these
names.

Thou art the Lord, our God, the honoured one
A.a.A.[1] Found in all places Thou seest, but art
not seen : Thou hast made the luminaries and stars
that they may shine through Thy goodness upon the
whole earth. Mayest Thou be praised for ever ! In
the name of the Lord, the Lord, the Lord. Every
day and night we bow down to Thee, O high God,
and we bow down and we pray to Thee, and we
exalt Thee for there is none like Thee, our God and
the God of our fathers. Grant us help from thee
and send an angel by Thy goodness, and bless us in
everything and keep us from our enemies and our
adversaries by Thy goodness, the mighty God of
spirits of all flesh. Master of Masters, do not forsake
us AHYH (twice 10 times), high God, King, merciful,
awful.

---

[1] *I.e.* AHYH ASHR AHYH (Exod. iii. 14).   Rendered in our
Bible I AM THAT I AM.

Lines 569–578 form a square composed of the
Hebrew words, " The Lord, great God," in ten lines
of eleven letters each, so arranged that the top line
and the two vertical lines contain exactly the same
words. Moreover, the first and last letters of each
line are identical, and each line, vertical and hori-
zontal, contain the same letters. The square is also
divided like the preceding alphabet (lines 539–560)

Magical square from a Samaritan phylactery. (Gaster, Codex D 1105.)
(Reproduced by permission from GASTER, *Studies and Texts*, Vol. iii. p. 128,
and see Vol. i. p. 441.)

into two triangles by the letter L. Each letter is
enclosed in a square. The square is flanked right
and left by two lines written vertically :—

May be exalted this great Name !
May it be hallowed and uplifted !
May it be beautified and honoured !
May it be praised and declared mighty !

CHAPTER XII.

SYRIAC AMULETS.

We owe our knowledge of the existence of Syriac amulets almost entirely to a small volume entitled "The Little Book of Protection," which is written in Syriac and has been edited from four manuscripts and translated by Sir Hermann Gollancz (*The Book of Protection*, London, 1912). Two of the manuscripts are in the possession of Sir Hermann ; the third is in the University Library, Cambridge (see Wright, *Catalogue of the Syriac Manuscripts preserved in the Library of the University of Cambridge*, 1901), and the fourth is in the British Museum (Oriental, No. 6673). In this little work we have "a collection of charms," which was probably written for or compiled by a native of the country which lies to the north of Môṣul. The owner of the book was a Christian and it was possible that he was priest or some kind of officer of the Nestorian Church to whom men made application for bans or spells, and incantatory prayers, and formulae of blessing to help them spiritually and physically and to protect their flocks and herds and possessions generally. The source of the power which underlies all these amuletic texts or "charms" is the ineffable Name of God YHWH and His other Names AHYH (Asher) AHYH, El-Shaddai, Adonai, and El-Ṣabâôth (Lord of Hosts), and the Ten Words of God the utterance

of which produced the universe. In this matter
the Syriac " charms " are identical with those of
Hebrews in their Ḳabbâlâh, the Egyptian Christians,
the Abyssinians, the Samaritans and the Arabs.

Facsimile of a page of the Syriac MS. of the " Book of Protection " in the
British Museum (Orient., No. 6673.)

The written Name of God was God Himself, and so
were all the Names formed by the changes and
permutations of the letters of His Name.

As to spells or bans the mightiest of all spells was
the Lord's Prayer(1), and after this come the Prayers

of Adam and the Holy Angels (2 and 3), and the
Gospel (4).   In the spell against fear and trembling
comes the name of St. George the Martyr (of Lydda),
whose prayer is quoted (5).   The spell of Jesus
(16) destroyed the power of engines of war, guns,
catapults, etc., used by any enemy.   The spell of
Solomon cured lumbago (10) ;   the spell of St. Thomas

The angel Gabriel mounted on a white horse driving his spear into the
body of the devil-woman of the Evil Eye   (From Brit. Mus. MS., Orient.,
No. 6673.)

expelled the Spirit of Lunacy from a man, and freed
the 366 members of his body from it (12) ; the spell
of the Crucifixion destroyed the power of swords,
daggers, arrows, etc. (9).   Then we have spells against
sickness of every kind (11) ; ˙ headache and the 72
aches in ears, eyes, etc. [in this spell Gannus and
Sloonus are mentioned] (13) ; chattering teeth (17) ;

cramp [mention of Mâr Awgîn], 20 ; spiders ? (19) ;
dogs (21) ; apparitions (22) ; the Evil Eye on men
(23) ; colic and chill (25) ; cattle disease (26) ; mad
dogs and wild beasts (27) ; fevers (28) ; distracting
noises and sounds (33) ; wolves (35) ; lying dreams
(36) ; serpents (37) ; scorpions (38) ; Evil Eye on
cattle (39) ; sorcerers ˙(42) ; the Evil Spirit (46) ;

Mâr George (of Lydda) spearing the Great Dragon.   (From Brit. Mus.
MS., Orient., No. 6673.)

sparrows and insects which devour crops (47) ; crops
catching fire (48) ; bleeding of the nose (49) ; crying
children (50) ; bewitchment (51) ; the wiles of
devils (52) ; boils (Aleppo " button," Baghdâd boil,
etc.), and the itch (53).

Interspersed with the spells we have incantatory
prayers for the huntsmen and fishermen who wish

for success (14) ; for those who wish for the possessions of this world and riches (15) ; for peace in
general (19) ; for peace in the household (30) ; for
those who travel by night (32) ; for those who are
travelling on business (31) ; for favour with all
men (40) ; for women in travail (43) ; and formulae
for making the cow docile (24) and for keeping her

King Solomon spearing a devil. (From Brit. Mus. MS., Orient., No. 6673.)

milk sweet (44) ; and formulae for blessing crops
and vineyards (29), and blessing the house (34).

Two sections (6 and 7) contain prayers which a
man is to use when he is compelled to appear before
kings, governors, judges, and other dignitaries, for
they will cause him to have an " open and winning
countenance " before them, and impress them favour-
ably on his behalf.   In No. 6 mention is made of

Alexander the Great and the garment in which he was arrayed and with which he subdued the whole earth. Tradition says that Alexander built a gate or door behind which he imprisoned Gog and Magog and a large number of filthy nations. The name of Alexander also appears as a word of power in Ethiopic spells.

Elijah (right) and Enoch (left) eating the fruit of the Tree of Life in Paradise.
(From Brit. Mus. MS., Orient., No. 6673.)

Codex C (section 3) shows that the compiler of the *Little Book of Protection*, like the Hebrews in Ḳabbâlâh, Samaritans, and Ethiopians, believed firmly in the power of a spell cast in the names of the Archangels and Angels, and the list he gives of them is instructive. For we find grouped Gabriel, Michael, Ariel ; Michael, Azriel, Shamshiel, Ḥarshiel, Sarphiel, Nuriel ; and following the ineffable Name of God, we have Shamshiel, Ṣuṣniel, Shamiel, Hiniel,

Zadikiel, Prukiel, Sahariel, Zakiel, Diniel, Eshiniel,
Takifiel, Gabriel, the mighty one, Shamshiel, Sahariel,
Makiel, Yomiel, Cukbiel, Shufiel, Mariel, Mehalalel,
Zatriel, Umiel, Ḥshaḥshiel, Tariel, Aziziel, Maniel,
Samiel. " By these holy names I bind, ban, stop the
mouth and tongues of evil men, jealous and wicked
judges, emirs, satraps, governors, men in authority,

Mâr Daniel, the prophet, as an equestrian knight, spearing the " wolf
which lieth in wait for the sheep." (From Brit. Mus. MS., Orient., No. 6673.)

rulers and chiefs, executioners, prefects, the foreigner,
the gentile, the infidel." A spell or ban formed of the
names of Christian saints is given in section 52 of
Codex A.

The Legend of the Evil Eye and Mâr 'Abhd-
Îshô' is of great interest, for it is different from the
version usually given in Ethiopic amulets (see
Budge, *History of Ethiopia*, vol. ii. p. 592). The

Evil Eye appeared to the saint, and called him and
wished to consort with him ; thereupon he bound
her and cursed her and tied her up, and made her
tell him her names.   She mentioned six, *i.e.* Miduch,
Edîlta, Monelta, Lilita, Malvita, and Mother, strangler
of boys.   Later she declared that she had twelve (*sic*)
other names, viz. Gĕos, Edilta, Lâmbros, Martlos,
Yamnôs, Sâmgos, Domos, Dirba, Apiton, Pegogha,

Thaumasius, the martyr, as an equestrian knight, spearing the " spirit of
the daughter of the moon."   (From Brit. Mus. MS., Orient., No. 6673.)

Zarduch, Lilita, Malvita, and Mother, strangler of
boys.   Section 19 of Codex C enumerates the various
kinds of the Evil Eye and of the men who possess
it.   Here we have mentioned the eye of the seven
evil and envious neighbours, the eye of all kinds,
the eye that woundeth and pitieth not, the eye of
the father, mother, foreigners, gentile, man, woman,
old man, old woman, and infidel, and the dark-grey

eye, and the jealous eye, and the caerulean eye
are grouped together. In connection with the
caerulean or blue eye we may note the Arab description of the Frank : " Yellow of hair, blue of eye,
and black of heart." Some of the " charms " are
very homely in character. Thus we have a " charm "
to keep the ox from falling asleep whilst ploughing

Rabban Hôrmîzd as an equestrian knight spearing " a lion or a mad
dog." (From Brit. Mus. MS., Orient., No. 6673.)

(C. 5), and one to prevent boys from crying (A. 50),
with an allusion to the Seven Sleepers of Ephesus
who slept in a cave for 377 years without waking.

Legends about the powers of King Solomon as a
magician are numerous, and thanks to various
passages in the Bible, the Talmûdh, the History of
Josephus and the Ḳur'ân are tolerably well known.

The ring with which he worked miracles is said to
have been made of pure gold, and in it was set a
single beautiful *shamîr* stone (diamond ?) on which
was engraved the four letters of the ineffable name
of God, or the pentacle to which the names " shield
of David " or " shield of Solomon " have been given.
The vignette given in Codex A, p. 54, suggests that

Portraits of the Four Evangelists—Matthew, Mark, Luke and John.
(From Brit. Mus. MS., Orient., No. 6673.)

the stone was in the form of an eight-rayed star,
with a smaller four-rayed star cut on the face of it.
Between two double concentric circles are written
the following seven names :—

SLYT SPYLT TRYḴT PPMRYT ḤLPT AYLPT ḤLYPT

The text, however (section 41, ed. Gollancz, p. 26),
says that there were other names [twenty-nine in
number] on the ring, and we can only assume that

these were engraved on the gold ring itself. These names are :—

HKKPS	PTPNT	LMPS	DKST	PSDMST
SHHLT	RHMT	WHLYPT	LMSTMPS	SHKLLT
TWRSP	KPYDT	DMPST	MRYPT	PSYT
HSPT	SHPLT	KTYBT	PSYT	DMPS
BRWLHT	HKYKT	TRKLT	PPT	PRYSHT
ALYLT	PPAYSHNT	YSHRYET		PLISHT

I can no more explain these names than Sir H. Gollancz can. They may be names formed by a sort of cypher arrangement of the letters which compose the names of God, YH, YHWH, AHYH and ADONAI, or of some words or verses of the Hebrew Bible, or permutations of the names of the attributes of God. But on the other hand they may be a string of quite meaningless names such as we find in Egyptian and Greek papyri, and Coptic magical texts. The repetition of them in the Names of the Persons of the Trinity formed a charm against pains and sicknesses, and gave him that carried them a " frank countenance " before kings and judges.

All four of the Codices used by Sir Hermann contain Vignettes, and he has published several of those found in A and B. All the Vignettes seem to be the work of one man or one school of illustrators, and for comparative purposes I have reproduced the several Vignettes from the Codex in the British Museum. These are given in the preceding pages and have not been published before.

CHAPTER XIII.

BABYLONIAN TERRA-COTTA DEVIL-TRAPS.

The Hebrews who lived in the various quarters of the eastern half of Babylon, and in the western suburbs of the city where the town of Ḥillah now stands, buried under the four corners of the foundations of their houses and other buildings inverted terra-cotta bowls inscribed with magical texts. The Hebrews who lived at Cuthah and Niffar and other places did the same thing, and they all did so with the idea of shielding their houses and homes and themselves from the attacks of all kinds of evil spirits, and from the baleful influences of earth-inhabiting demons. These bowls were to the Hebrews what the prophylactic clay figures which have been described above were to the Sumerians and Babylonians (see page 97 f). The British Museum possesses a very large collection of such bowls, which have been obtained from excavations made in Babylonia and Assyria by Layard and several officers of the British Museum between 1850 and 1906, and from native dealers. Some of these are inscribed in the Hebrew language with the " square " Hebrew characters, and others in the dialect of the Targûms in a species of cursive Syriac characters, and others in Mandaïtic (*i.e.* a Semitic dialect similar to that found in the *Talmûdh Babhlî*) in its own special character. The oldest of these bowls, those with Hebrew inscriptions inside them, date

from the Ist or IInd century B.C., and the most
modern are not older than the VIth century A.D.
The reproductions of four of the bowls in the British
Museum Collection which are given in this Chapter
illustrate the palaeography, and the following

I.—Terra-cotta Devil-trap, with a magical spiral inscription in Hebrew
letters, written for the protection of the house and estate of Bahran
and Bathniun against the power of Lilith, Yṣpandarmid, Bahr of the
desert and other devils. The inscription begins in the centre and
ends at †. (British Museum, 51–10–9, 96.)

paragraphs will give an idea of the contents of the
inscriptions.

The text on the first bowl (No. I) begins with a
statement that the spell or incantation written
below is intended to drive away the Devil, the

Spirits, Satan, Niriek, Zariah, Abtûr-Tura, Dân and Lîlîth from the ground of Bahran, and Bahr of the desert and Yṣpandarmid from the ground of Bathniun, and from all the house. O Thou eternal Good God, crush the power of the Devils and the spirits of the Fiends, the great power of Lîlîth . . . I drive you away from the neighbourhood of Bahran's house, and from the house of Bathniun, and from all the regions round about them. As the devils write bill of divorce and cast away their women who never again approach them, so do ye accept [this] your bill of divorce, and receive your dowry which is [here] written, and get ye gone, betake yourselves to flight, make haste to depart, and forsake the house of Bahran and the house of Bathniun in the Name of the Eternal God. Get ye forth into the darkness, away from the man of power, and sealed with his ring, in such wise that every man may know that ye are no longer there. And then shall be there a good light. Amen. Amen. Amen. Selah. For a discussion on the text see the literature quoted by Schwab in *Proc. Soc. Bibl. Arch.* for April, 1890.

The text on the second bowl (No. II) is a long cursing formula which is directed against spirits, and demons, and devils of every description, both male and female, which bring diseases and sicknesses upon men and women, and against magicians of every kind, both male and female, who by word, or curse, or ban, or act do harm to men. This formula will make the curses and incantations of evil spirits and demons to have no effect, and it will make the magical ceremonies of the sorcerer to be innocuous.

It will make even the stars and the planets to turn back in their courses if their powers have been invoked and employed by the magician in his nefarious work. And it will make the " curse of the woman to end in smoke." Moreover, this

II.—Terra-cotta Devil-trap, with a magical spiral inscription in Hebrew letters containing a comprehensive curse on all devils and magicians, male and female. The recital of it secured for a man the help of the stars of heaven. (British Museum, 51–10–9, 100.)

formula carries with it the protection of the good angel who has eleven names. This text is very involved and is most difficult to translate, and Zenker, Halévy and Schwab, who have studied it and published it, differ very considerably in their renderings and translations of it. And though the general meaning of most of the text is clear, there are in it certain passages which have not as yet been satisfactorily explained.

The text of the third bowl (No. III), which begins

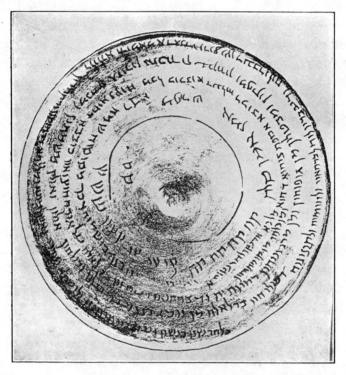

III.—Terra-cotta Devil-trap, with a magical spiral inscription in Hebrew letters containing a spell which was intended to protect Bar-Hayy, the son of Lâlâ, and his property from all evil. (From Halèvy, *Melanges*, p. 229.)

on the edge and ends in the centre, was first published by Halévy, and republished by Schwab (*Proc. Soc. Bibl. Arch.* for April, 1890, p. 310). It shows that the bowl was regarded as an amulet, and that it was written for BAR-HAYY (?), the son of LÂLÂ. The following rendering will give an idea of the inscription : " Let all the evil sorcerers, and violent attacks and cursings, and vows, and undertakings, and speech (hasty words or threats ?), whether near or far, by night or by day, by men or by women, which it is possible to be directed against BAR-HAYY (?), the son of LÂLÂ, or his son or his property, let all these things, without any exception, be cursed, and banned, and driven away, and rent asunder, and expelled, and utterly destroyed away from the bodies of the children of BAR-HAYY (?), the son of LÂLÂ, and the bodies of their sheep and cattle, and from the habitations of each of them on the road of Ḥoṣî. O thou star, who art the mightiest of all the stars in the world, from thee cometh health, O thou who art the queen of all those who work sorceries, in the name of KARMESÎSÎH, that great and ineffable name. Amen. Amen. Selah."

The text of the fourth bowl (No. IV) has been published by Layard and Halévy and studied by Schwab (*op. cit.*, p. 314). In the opening words it is distinctly stated to be an amulet (*Ḳâmî'h*) of divine origin inasmuch as it came from the water of heaven, wherein it was sealed and hidden. It was specially prepared by means of the water to protect its owner and his kinsfolk who live with him, and to deliver him from banning, and baleful visions, and sorceries, and cursings, and water which is stagnant, and water which is impure, from fouled wells (?), from every kind of evil worker, active or passive, from evil spirits, whether male or female, from the Evil Eye, and from sorceries practised by men or women. The names of the two mighty angels who are invoked to make the amulet operative are BABHNĔ'Â and MAMBE'Â. After a mutilated passage in which

" darkness, fog and mist " are mentioned come the
words, Amen. Amen. Selah.

On another bowl in the British Museum is a Hebrew
inscription written not in spiral form but in con-

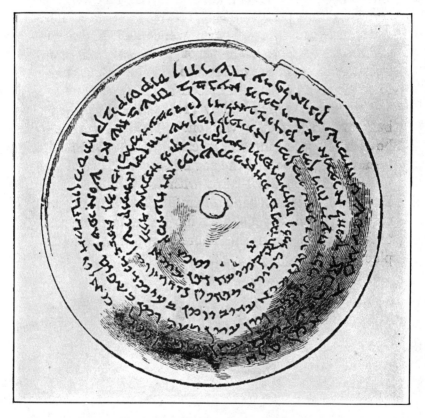

IV.—Terra-cotta Devil-trap, with a magical spiral inscription in Hebrew
letters containing a spell which was intended to protect its owner
from all evil spirits and the Evil Eye. (British Museum.)

centric lines. It reads : The health of the heavens
to set life on the threshold of Ashîr Meḥadiud, and
to him that is under the sight of it in the Name of the
Eternal, the Holy One, the great God of Israel,
Whose word as soon as it is uttered is fulfilled.

Behold the bed of Solomon is surrounded with sixty of the mightiest of the mighty men of Israel.

May God bless thee and keep thee; may He make His face to shine upon thee and be gracious unto thee; may He make bright His face on thee and give thee peace. Amen. Amen. Selah. This is the famous blessing with which Aaron, by the command of God given through Moses, was commanded to bless the children of Israel. I have not found it on any other inscribed bowl.

The words which follow are from Isa. xliv. 25, but are incorrectly written. The text on this bowl is of special interest because there is visible in it an attempt to unite the paganism which permitted the use of such devil-traps with the religion of the Hebrews, which forbade all trafficking with magical ceremonies and spells and incantations. In this text passages from the Hebrew scriptures take the place of native pagan spells.

CHAPTER XIV.

THE RING AMULET.

When and where and why men first began to wear rings cannot be said, and the fundamental ideas which they held about them can only be guessed at. They probably associated the ring with the solar disk and believed that it therefore possessed strength and power and continuity and wore it as an AMULET. Whether made of metal or stone matters little, but if made of gold or some semi-precious stone, which was credited by them with the possession of some magical property, its invisible power would be increased. The Sun-god Shamash represented on the famous " Sun-god Tablet " in the British Museum holds a ring and a staff, and in the well-known relief on which Marduk is seen in royal attire and armed as a warrior, he holds a ring and a staff in his left hand. We thus see that the ideas of divinity, sovereignty, strength, power, and protection were associated with the ring in very early times, and long before it was turned into a signet of seal or had a bezel attached to it. The gods themselves may have needed a ring as an amulet, and in any case it represented their authority and dignity, and was a part of their regalia. The Greek mythologists invented a fable to account for the origin of the finger-ring. Jove, upon loosing the Titan Prometheus from the bonds to which he had been condemned to eternity, obliged him as a perpetual penance, as an equivalent to his original sentence, to wear for ever upon his finger a link of the chain enchased with a fragment of the Caucasian rock of torture.   Thus ornamented, Catullus introduces him at the Wedding of Peleus (l. 295).

" Came wise Prometheus ; on his hand he wore
   The slender symbol of his doom of yore."
                              (See C. W. King, *Engraved Gems*, p. 12.)

The goddess Nekhebit presenting the two Egypts united and the sovereignty
of the whole earth to the King of Egypt.

At an early period men began to have their names cut upon their rings, but they soon found that it was necessary to widen and thicken that part of the ring which was intended to bear the name.   This resulted in the formation of the SIGNET RING, which was well known in Egypt in the Archaic Period, and is seen in the annexed illustration.   Here we see the Vulture-goddess Nekhebit holding in one claw the symbol of the union of Upper and Lower Egypt, and in the other the symbol of the circuit of the earth ruled by the sun in the form of a signet ring. Within this are written the hieroglyphs B and SH, *i.e.* the consonants of the name of Besh or Bash, a king who is now generally known as KHA-SEKHEMUI. This inscription is found on a stone vase which Mr. Quibbell excavated at Hierakonpolis, a very ancient city of Upper Egypt.

Two forms of the signet ring are here shown. In A the bezel and ring form one whole, and in B we have an example of the splayed bezel.

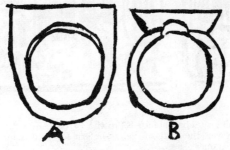

We should naturally expect the oldest form of the signet to be found in Babylonia, but such is not the case, for, as already said, the Babylonians and Assyrians had their names cut upon cylinders of stone which are commonly known as " cylinder-seals." These were perforated through their length and were threaded on a string, by which they were suspended from the neck or tied to the arm or wrist. Impressions of them were made by rolling them on the clay tablets, and some think that the hieroglyph ◯ represents a cylinder-seal being rolled on a tablet of moist clay. The cylinder-seal was adopted by the Egyptians at a very early period, and many examples which were made under the old kingdom are to be seen in the British

Museum.   One of the most recent cylinder-seals known is here represented.   It is made of white *faïence* and is inscribed with names and titles of Sebek-neferu-Rā, a king of the XIIIth dynasty. To the same period may be ascribed the blue glass cylinder-seal, mounted in gold, which forms the

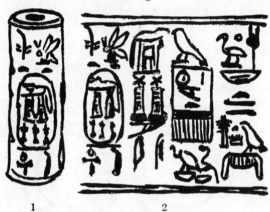

1   2

1. Cylinder-seal of Sebak-neferu-Rā in the British Museum.
2. Inscription on the seal of Sebak-neferu-Rā containing the King's official names.

bezel of the ring here shown (A) ; in B a scarab forms the bezel, and both it and the cylinder are attached by wire to the rings.   See Hall, H. R., *Catalogue of Egyptian Scarabs [Cylinder-Seals], etc., in the British Museum*, London, 1913.

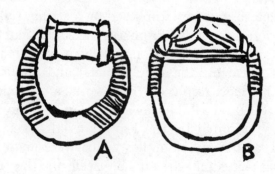

A considerable number of rings made of red jasper, red *faïence*, and red glass have been found in the tombs of Egypt ; all are uninscribed and all have a gap in them. How and why they were used is not known, but a recent view about them is that they were worn as amulets by soldiers and by men whose work or duties brought them into conflict with their enemies, to prevent them from being wounded, or if wounded, to stop the flow of blood. It is possible that they were worn by women to prevent bleeding.

The Hebrews, like the Egyptians, used the signet ring. Thus when Judah asked Tamar what he should give her as a pledge she replied, " Thy signet ring (*khôthâm*) and thy cord [to which it is attached] and thy staff " (Gen. xxxviii. 18). From this it is clear that Judah's signet ring was attached to a cord, and that it hung suspended from his neck or tied to his wrist. And in Gen. xli. 42, it is said that Pharaoh removed his signet ring (*tabba'ath*) or seal from his hand and placed it on Joseph's hand, and so transferred his authority to him and the right to affix the king's seal on all documents. The bezel of that Pharaoh's ring was undoubtedly inscribed with the pre-nomen or nomen, perhaps both, and his principal titles, and the Egyptian royal rings in the British Museum indicate the general appearance of the ring. Ahasuerus, too, used a signet ring which he first entrusted to Hâmân and, having withdrawn it from him, gave it to Mordecai (Esther iii. 10 ; viii. 8, 10). So much has already been said about Solomon's famous magical ring that no further description of it here is necessary.

The finest collection of rings known, viz. those of
the British Museum (which includes the Franks'
Collection) and the Victoria and Albert Museum
(Lord Londesborough's collection) show that the
ancients made rings of many kinds of materials—
gold, silver, bronze, iron, lead, glass, alabaster,
steatite, limestone, terra-cotta, carnelian, sand,
chalcedony, agate, ivory, bone, amber, jet, crystal,
glass, etc. And in some rings both gold and silver
are used, probably with a view of increasing their
amuletic powers. The RING-AMULET was made more
efficacious if the bezel was made of a certain kind of
stone, or in a certain form, on which some magical
symbol was engraved. The gold ring with a frog
bezel, described by Mr. F. H. Marshall (*Catalogue
of the Finger Rings*, p. xxiii), and the rings with
phalli engraved upon them were undoubtedly fertility amulets, and the silver rings with gold studs
inserted in them were intended to protect the
wearer against the Evil Eye. The rings on bronze
models of hands were doubly powerful amulets.
The early Christians attached great importance to
amulet-rings or charm-rings, and they adopted the
views of the pagans and Gnostics as to their value
as protections against the Evil Eye. Provided that
the ring and its bezel were made of materials possessing the magical qualities desired, and the symbol,
or figure, or inscription, *i.e.* word of power, engraved
upon the bezel was correct, the wearer of the ring
believed that he was protected from every calamity,
accident and harm which the Evil Eye and its
baleful influences could bring upon him.

Among the RELIGIOUS AND ECCLESIASTICAL RINGS
described by Mr. O. M. Dalton (*Franks' Bequest,*

Catalogue of the Finger-Rings, London, 1912) may
be mentioned those which are inscribed "Ave
Maria gratia plena Dn (= Dominus tecum) ;
Mater Dei mamanto (No. 696) ; Qui p[ro] aliis
ring with an inlaborat " (No. 205) ; the nun's
orat p[ro] se inscription which is translated, "This
is the ring of chastity. I am the spouse of
Jesus Christ " (No. 712) ; the massive gold band
engraved with the figure of Christ in the tomb,
the Cross and Instruments of the Passion, with
the Five Wounds at intervals, which are described as the well of pity, the well of mercy,
the well of comfort, the well of grace, and the
well of everlasting life. Inside is engraved :
"Wulnera quinq̄ dei sunt medicina mei pia crux
et passio Xti sunt medicina michi jaspar melchior
baltasar ananyzarta tetragrammaton " (" jaspar
melchior baltasar " are the Three Kings of
Cologne) (No. 718) ; the silver hoop inscribed
" S.M. Magdalena ✚ ora pro m[e] " (No. 773) ; the
ivory signet inscribed " In hoc signo vinces " (No.
778) ; the gold ring inscribed " Dignare me Laudare
te Virgo Sacrata " (No. 778) ; and the DEATH RINGS
inscribed " ✚ Mors bonis grata " (No. 813) ; " Death·
sy · myn ✚ Eritag " (No. 814), and " dye to live "
(No. 815).

Mediaeval and modern AMULET-RINGS.—Many of
the rings described by Mr. Dalton have inscriptions,
but some of them are untranslatable and are clearly
magical formulae, *e.g.* GA|GNO|OIT|OIP|AN etc.
(No. 864) and ΛAELA · AEΛA · GELA · GHOTIS
(No. 865) ; +AGLA+AD░OS+VDROS+IDROS+TEBAL
+GVT+G░░░ (No. 866). These are probably charms
against sickness. The first word of the last formula

AGΛA is said to be formed of the initials of four Hebrew words, and to stand for—

אתה גבור לעולם אדני

" Thou art the mighty one for ever, Adônây." The ring No. 870 was an amulet which protected a man from epilepsy or the " falling sickness " (Ananizarta). The ring-amulet inscribed *Jesus autem transiens* was believed to protect travellers by land and sea from the attacks of thieves and robbers. Many ring-amulets are inscribed with the name of JESUS, or *Ihesus Nazarenus Rex-Jude[orum]*, and many with *Jaspar, Baltasar and Melchior*, the names of the Three Kings of Cologne, who were three of the Magi who went to Bethlehem to worship the Infant Christ. The first brought myrrh, the second gold, and the third frankincense. On some we find the pentagram, on others words from the Service of the Mass (*e.g.* AGIOS+OΘEOS+ATANATO, " Holy [is] God Immortal " (No. 892), or the names of archangels, *e.g.* Sadayel, Raphael and Tiriel (No. 894). Gold and silver rings set with a TOADSTONE (*crapaudina, bufonius lapis, batrachites*) were supposed to guard their wearers against diseases of the kidneys, and the stone itself was regarded as a special protection of newly-born children. Prof. Ray Lankester has shown that the " toadstones " are not stones at all, but the palatal teeth of a small ganoid fish called *Lepidotus*, and that they derive their coloration from the iron salts present in the rock. Rings set with pieces of horn or of an ass's hoof were supposed to save the wearers from attacks of epilepsy. The ring No. 919 is inscribed with a formula which is probably of Gnostic origin and reads—

ARXENTEX NOC CONN
OYXEPICΔPXΔMNEP
XMΔNOCOPNⲰΦPIOC

Posy-Rings and Fede-Rings.—Any ring which bears a motto or verse of an amatory nature is a posy (" poesy ") ring. The " Fede "-Rings or Betrothal Rings are in origin Roman, and they received this name from the two hands clasped in truth, which they always have in a conspicuous position. The following typical inscriptions on Fede-Rings are taken from Dalton, *Catalogue* (p. 161 f) :— *Ave Maria gratia plena ; Jesus Nazarenus Rex ;* Dulce·domum·fides, p·n·Sola·f·a·ama ; *Je suis ici en lieu d'ami ;* God help ; Be true in heart Tho farr apart.

On Posy-Rings we have :—

1. A + frind + to + the + end +
2. A vertuous wife preferveth life
3. All I refufe and thee I chufe
4. As dear to me   As Life can be.
5. As God hath knit to hartes in one
6. So none shall part but death alone.
7. As this Ring tells twas Bedwin Bells.
8. Afke + and + Haue
9. By god alone wee two are one
10. + BY·TREVTH·YE·SHALL·TRYE·ME
    + BY·TYME·YE·SHALL·SPYE·ME
    + SO·FYND·SO·SET·BY·ME
11. ERAM * NON * SVM

12. GOD CONTINV LOVE IN US.

13. God did forefee wee fshould agree

14. God did forefee whats beft for me.

15. I dare not fshow the love I owe.

16. I loue you

17. If loue you bare thif forr me ware.

18. IN LOVE LINKT FAST WHILE LIFE DOTH LAST.

19. Many are thee stars I see
Yet in my eye no starr like thee.

20. NOT · THE · GYFT · BVT · THE · GEVER

21. Our [hands] and [hearts] with one consent
Hath tied this [knot] till [death] preuent.

22. Since god hath joynd us two together
Let us liue in love and serue him ever.

23. Y · AM · YOYRS · FOR · EVER.

There is a good collection of Jewish Marriage-rings in the British Museum (see Dalton, *op. cit.*, p. 189 f.) and many bear the inscription *Mazzāl ṭôbh* מזל טב "Good luck." They were never worn in daily life and were only placed by bridegrooms upon the fingers of wives during the ceremony ; they were therefore only symbolical.

Rings were also worn as MEMORIALS, and those which are inscribed "*Memento Mori*" must be classed as such.

As the ring has been from a very early period the symbol of sovereignty and authority we have Royal-Rings, Coronation-Rings, Papal-Rings, Archiepiscopal- and Episcopal-Rings, Investiture-Rings, Serjeants-Rings, etc. Among FANCY RINGS must be grouped rings set with diamonds which their wearers used for writing on glass; the DIAL-RINGS which were used for making astronomical observations; the Sphere-Ring with the Signs of the Zodiac, Planets, etc.; the Puzzle-Ring, the Trinity-Ring (made of three interlacing hoops turned from the solid, by Stephen Zick); Carnival-Rings, Key-Rings, Poison-Rings, in which the poison was placed in the bezel of the ring under the inset gem; Perfume-Rings, in which choice perfume was placed in the bezel, and escaped when the gem above it was pressed; Cramp-Rings, Gift-Rings, given to beloved persons and friends; Bow-Rings, Votive-Rings, laid up in temples; Funerary-Rings, which were offered to the dead and are found in graves; Reliquary-Rings, Medical-Rings, *i.e.* those which were worn to cure the " falling sickness " or epilepsy, or applied to the eyes to cure ophthalmia or to the body generally to cure the bites of vipers, scorpions, serpents, etc.; and Holy-Rings—viz. those which had been blessed by saints or martyrs.

The MIZPAH RING.—This was made of a tolerably deep plain band of gold with flanges. Between the flanges the word MIZPAH appeared, either engraved on the ring itself or on a band of enamel. The word MIZPAH is derived from the Hebrew MIṢPÂH מִצְפָּה and means " watch-tower " or " place for keeping a look-out " and was given as a name to many hills in Palestine. The giver and the receiver of the MIZPAH Ring cared nothing for the meaning of the name, but regarded it as a witness between them remembering only Laban's words in Gen. xxxi. 49, " The LORD watch between me and thee when we are absent from one another."

Among Orientals when the ring is not used as a seal, the name of the owner being cut on the bezel, it is worn as an amulet. The metals gold and silver carry in them the influences and powers of their planets, and the stones of which the bezels are made add to these their prophylactic, atropaeic and medicinal powers. On the bezels of Arabic rings we find the name of Allâh and Muḥammad His Prophet, and the Declaration of the Unity of God ; Persian rings often bear the name of 'Alî and Ḥasan and Ḥusain. We find on the bezels of some Arabic rings squares containing numbers, e.g. No. 2298 in the British Museum. On the octagonal bezel of this ring is cut the following :—

9	8	18	1
8	18	1	9
1	9	8	18
18	1	9	8

The total of each row of figures whether added up horizontally or perpendicularly is 36. Now, the letters of the Arabic alphabet have numerical values, and sometimes these magical squares contain nothing but letters, and the numbers in the squares above probably have a direct connection with the letters which have their numerical values. Taken together these letters will represent some words from the Ḳur'ân or some sacred name, which is regarded as a word of power. Here is an example. One of the great names of God is MUSAWWIR, " He who fashioneth." Now the numerical values of the consonants in this name are M = 40, Ṣ = 90, W = 6, and R = 200, total 336. These are taken and made

into the first line of a four-lined magical square,
and to these are added a series of numbers which,
when added up horizontally or vertically or diagonally, make 336, thus :—

200	6	90	40
89	41	199	7
32	92	4	198
5	197	33	91

[But it is clear that misprints have crept into
Doutté's copy.]

Doutté says (*op. cit.*, p. 194) that this square was
used as a amulet and was believed to make a barren
woman become a mother. It owed its efficacy to
the Name of God represented by figures.

On another ring described by Dalton (No. 2304)
is the following magical diamond of figures—

The ZODIAC-RING.—This consists usually of a
flat hoop, plain or ribbed, of gold on which the Signs
of the Zodiac, made of gold wire, are soldered ; above
and below are soldered plain or scrolled flanges.
Few, if any, of them are older than the XIXth
century. The metal workers of the Gold Coast
used to come to travellers and make these rings
in their presence. Having obtained two or three
sovereigns from the traveller they melted them
with a blow pipe and fashioned a ring from them.
In the 'fifties and 'sixties of the last century several
were brought to Liverpool where they found a ready

market. The forms of the signs were taken from Arabic manuscripts and appear thus :—

♈ ♉ ♊ ♋ ♌ ♍ ♎ ♏ ♐ ♑ ♒ ♓

There is no doubt that the custom of wearing finger-rings has been continuous. Both Mr. F. H. Marshall and Mr. O. M. Dalton have in their Catalogues of the Finger-Rings in the British Museum devoted several paragraphs to discussing how they were worn. In ancient times they were usually worn on the fourth finger, next the first finger. Rings were not generally worn on the middle finger —the *digitum infamis*. The fourth finger was usually chosen first for reasons of convenience, and next because there was a popular belief that a nerve ran straight to it from the heart. Betrothal and marriage rings were usually worn on the third finger, which was perhaps the most favoured for the wearing of rings generally. Down to the XVIth century a ring was commonly worn by both men and women on the thumb. The signet-ring was often worn on the first finger, and episcopal-rings on the first or third. Rings were also strung round the neck and threaded on the cords of hats. Mr. Dalton points out (p. xxiv) that ladies sometimes wore as many as ten rings on the fingers, and men six.

The reader who wishes to study the history of the origin and development of rings, especially the ornamental varieties, should examine the collection of 4,183 rings in the British Museum, all of which are described, and some hundreds of them illustrated, in the Catalogues written by Messrs. Marshall and Dalton. And he should consult the following works : —Dalton, O. M. *Catalogue of Early Christian*

Antiquities, London, 1901 ; King, C. W., *Antique Gems and Rings*, 2 vols., London, 1872 ; and his *Handbook of Engraved Gems*, London, 1866 ; Middleton, J. H., *The Lewis Collection of Gems and Rings*, London, 1892 ; and the article *Annulus* in Smith, W., *Dict. of Greek and Roman Antiquities*, London, 1890. A great amount of information concerning rings is given by Kirchmann, J. (*De Annulis liber singularis*, Lubecae, 1623), and Fortunius Licetus (*De annulis antiquis*, Utiari, 1645), who collected and printed a large number of references and allusions to rings from the works of classical writers.

CHAPTER XV.

STONES AND THEIR PROPHYLACTIC AND THERA-PEUTIC QUALITIES.[1]

AGATE.—Several kinds of agate are known, and all of them are used extensively in the East. The " red agate," which is mentioned by PLINY (*Hist. Nat.*, xxxvii. 54) and known as " blood agate," was a protection against the large spiders and scorpions. The so-called " green agate " is potent in quelling disease of any kind in the eyes. The brown agate, or " tawny agate," is the most powerful of all and the most popular, for it makes the warrior victorious, protects a man against every kind of poisonous reptile, gives a lover favour in the sight of his lady, the sick man who holds it in his hand recovers, and gives a man riches, happiness, health, and long life. It also increases a man's intelligence. It drives away fevers, epilepsy, and madness; stops the flow of rheum in the eye, reduces menstruation, disperses the water in dropsy. In ITALY and PERSIA it protects the wearer against the " Evil Eye." The triangular agate amulets worn in SYRIA on the neck

[1] The best authorities on this subject are :—Groth, *Grundriss der Edelsteinkunde*, Leipzig, 1887 ; Lorenz, *Die okkulte Bedeutung der Edelsteine*, Leipzig, 1915 ; Pachinger, *Glaube und Oberglaube im Steinreich*, and of course many of the sections in the works of Dr. S. Seligmann on the Evil Eye (*Der böse Blick*, Berlin, 1910 ; and *Die Zauberkraft des Auges und das Berufen*, Hamburg, 1922).

keep away intestinal troubles. Black agate, with white stripes, is greatly prized, but green agate is also greatly treasured ; for if a woman drinks the water in which a green agate ring has been washed she will never be sterile. The amulets of grey agate which are common in Egypt, and are worn on the neck, prevent stiff-neck and ward off colic and diarrhoea.

MOSS-AGATE.—This beautiful stone with markings in it resembling trees and vegetation is much prized by the husbandman, who wears a moss-agate on his right upper arm, and places one in the right horn of each of his oxen, so that he may have an abundant harvest.

ALUM.—In PERSIA, SYRIA, PALESTINE, EGYPT, and westwards along the whole of the northern coast of AFRICA alum is the favourite means of protection against the Evil Eye ; its therapeutic powers were well known to PLINY (*Hist. Nat.*, xxxv. 52). In MOROCCO both Jewish and Arab magicians use it, mixed with salt, on their patients, the former calling upon the names of ABRAHAM, ISAAC, JACOB, and ELISHA, and the latter reciting the CXIIth Sûrah of the Ḳur'ân, which declares the absolute unity of GOD. Pieces of alum, or sticks of alum, are used as house amulets, and in PERSIA, TURKEY, PALESTINE, and EGYPT mothers place bits of alum in one or other of their children's garments, or tie them inside their head-coverings or caps.

ALATUIR.—See AMBER.

AMBER.—Ornaments made of amber were worn by women in the earliest periods of the history of many of the peoples of ASIA, AFRICA, and EUROPE. When men discovered its electrical properties, which

were known to THEOPHRASTUS, they began to make
amulets of it, and men, women, and children wore
them on their necks. Amber dust was sometimes
mixed with honey and oil of roses and given as a
medicine to those who were suffering from ear-ache
or failure of sight ; amber dust when taken in water
relieved pains in the stomach, and helped the kidneys
and liver and the larger intestines to perform their
functions regularly and effectively. The smell of
burnt amber helped women in labour, and an amber
ball, if held in the hands, kept a man cool during the
hottest days of summer, and reduced the heat in a
man suffering from fever. A model of the phallus
made of amber was regarded as a most powerful
protection against the Evil Eye and any and every
attack of evil spirits. Beads made of amber preserved the wearer against rheumatism, toothache,
headache, rickets, jaundice, and every kind of
internal ailment ; a piece of amber placed on
the nose stopped excessive bleeding, and an amber
amulet tied to the neck made the largest goitre to
disappear. In many European countries amber is
worn as a protection against witches and warlocks,
and even ill-luck. The Arab physicians used amber
powder largely in their medicines, and in addition
to the diseases and ailments mentioned above, it
was given to pregnant women to prevent miscarriage,
and to a patient suffering from ulcers, boils, car-
buncles, etc. In Eastern Asia amber amulets are
made in the form of lions, hares, dogs, frogs, fish,
etc., and these are believed to add to the virility
of men and the fecundity of women.

AMETHYST, from the Gr. ἀμέθυστος " not drunken,"
" without drunkenness." This beautiful stone was

believed to possess many qualities valuable to man, and was greatly prized as an ornament and as an amulet. Some of the ancients thought that it was called " amethyst " because it was the colour of violet wine, and protected men from drunkenness ; but PLINY (*Hist. Nat.*, xxxvii. 40) does not believe this, and thinks that the stone and the wine have no connection. He mentions that the magicians declared that if the names of the sun and moon were written upon an amethyst, and that if it was tied to the neck with peacocks' hairs and the feathers of a swallow, it would protect a man against sorcery. The man who placed an amethyst under his tongue might drink the contents of a large vessel of wine without becoming intoxicated, and he who drank wine out of a vessel made of amethyst might drink all its contents with impunity. Worn as an amulet it cured a man of gout ; placed under the pillow an amethyst gave the sleeper pleasant dreams, and it improved his memory, and made him immune from poison. Some believed that the wearer of the stone became gentle and amiable through its influence, and that by it he was preserved from outbursts of temper and wrath. Its presence in the ring of a bishop was thought to be helpful to the wearer and also to the devotee who kissed it.

ANTIPATHES was either black coral or jet, each of which was supposed to keep the wearer from suffering.

ASBESTOS preserved a man from sorcery and the Evil Eye.

ASPHALT, or bitumen, *mûmîyâ*, was much used in medicine, and that which was taken out from the skulls of Egyptian mummies was believed to possess special magical powers. It preserved a man from sprains, fractures of the bones, blows, fallings down, headache, epilepsy, dizziness, palpitation of the heart, etc. A cross made with asphalt on a man or beast protected it from witchcraft and the Evil Eye. The AZTEKS tie little bags containing asphalt to the necks of their children to keep away sickness from them.

BERYL protected the bearer against the helplessness caused by fascination. The green variety was used in treating diseases of the eye, and the yellowish-green stone for jaundice and diseases of the liver. It is often called the " stone of St. Thomas."

CARBUNCLE.—This stone protected the wearer against fascination.

CARNELIAN is called a " blood stone," because it acted on the blood, and prevented it from rising in excess to the head. It repressed fluxes of blood, and restrained superfluous menstruation, and stopped bleeding at the nose. A carnelian ring made a man peaceful and slow to anger. Carnelian makes the skin healthy and removes blotches, pimples, and sores. Throughout the Middle Ages it was believed to protect men from fascination, and to this day JEWS, ARABS, TURKS, GREEKS and many other peoples on the shores of the MEDITERRANEAN wear amulets made of it as a defence against the Evil Eye. The opaque variety of carnelian is called SARD.

CATER'S EYE, a dull red stone with a white mark in it, which is supposed to represent the pupil of a cat's eye. It has an evil reputation, and in WESTERN ASIA is regarded as a provoker of strife ; the man who sees his wife wearing the stone expects domestic trouble.

CAT'S EYE as an amulet is supposed to protect a man from witchcraft and death. The Arabs assign to it a property which caused its wearer to become invisible in battle. Mr. Anderson states that when a man in KORDOFÂN doubts his wife's fidelity, and is about to go on a journey, he makes· her drink milk in which a cat's eye has been washed, so that if after his departure she commits adultery, there shall be no children of the union.

CATOCHITIS, a Corsican stone which sticks to the hand like gum, was supposed to guard a man from fascination (PLINY, *Hist. Nat.*, xxvii. 56).

CHALCEDONY was used in medicine in cases of fever, and was supposed to render the passage of gall stones easy. It was supposed to give a man a peaceful and equable disposition, and protect him from the Evil Eye.

CHALK and other white stones, or plaster of Paris, in Germany and neighbouring countries are regarded as a protection against evil. Crosses made on objects with chalk, and the initial letters of the names of the Three Kings, C. M. B., written with chalk on the doors of houses on the day of the Epiphany, protect them from witchcraft and the danger from fire. C=Caspar, M=Melchior, B=Baltazar.

CROSS-STONES (Staurotides) protect children and others from sicknesses caused by witchcraft. They are worn in little bags attached to the neck or in the pockets. In ITALY, the stone is called *pietra della croce*, and in Finisterre it is worn as an amulet against shipwreck.

CRYSTAL (ROCK-CRYSTAL).—According to PLINY (*Hist. Nat.*, xxxvii. 9, 10) the ancients believed that crystal was petrified ice. It was used as a burning-glass in medical operations, and in powder was administered as a medicine for scrofula, swellings of the glands, diseases of the eyes, heart disease, fever, and intestinal pains. Mixed with honey it increased the milk of the mother who was suckling a child. Little balls of crystal, set in metal bands, are found all over EUROPE, and in ENGLAND and IRELAND ; where and why these were made is not known, but they were probably used as amulets. Crystal was held in high esteem by the early Christians who regarded it as a symbol of the Immaculate Conception. And KING, in his *History of Gems* (pp. 104–8), describes a ball of crystal on which was engraved the Gnostic formula ΔΒΛΔΝΔΘΔΝΔΛΒΔ. Crystal has always been greatly prized in Scotland. Several of the Clans possessed crystal balls which were regarded as " stones of victory," and water in which they were washed was given as medicine to sick men and cattle. Crystal amulets protected their wearers against the Evil Eye, and saved them from bad dreams ; he who drinks from a crystal vessel will never suffer from dropsy, and a piece of crystal laid on the cheek will drive away toothache and will give relief, in any case, to the sufferer. Some of the Mexican Indians believe that the souls of both living and dead people dwell in crystal. And among some of the tribes in AUSTRALIA and GUINEA the magicians by means of it produce rain, for crystal is the rain-maker *par excellence*.

CORAL.—An amulet against sterility, and it protected its wearer against the Evil Eye. Powdered coral was used in medicine.

DIAMOND. — According to PLINY (*Hist. Nat.*, xxxvii. 15) the diamond rendered all poisons innocuous and drove away madness, and it was believed to protect a man against fascination, and to keep away from him night spirits and evil dreams. Wine and water in which a diamond was dipped preserved the drinker of it from gout, jaundice, and apoplexy. A diamond worn on the left arm drove away wild beasts, demons, and devils, and evil men, and by its excessive hardness it overcame the Devil himself. It cured every kind of sickness and disease, fortified the mind, and strengthened the body. The water in which the great Kôh-i-nûr diamond was dipped when in INDIA was believed to heal every sickness. As an amulet the diamond protected a man against plague, and pestilence, and the Evil Eye.

EMERALD.—In ancient times the emerald was believed to cure diseases of the eyes, and later it was worn as an amulet against fascination and the Evil Eye, and epilepsy. The sight of an emerald struck such terror into the viper and cobra that their eyes leaped out of their heads.

EYE-STONE.—A name given to quartz and the eye-agate.

FELDSPAR.—A hard greenstone which was much used in EGYPT for amulets of various kinds. The natives of Kordofân attach a piece of it to their necks to preserve them from sunstroke, headaches, and bleeding of the nose during sleep.

GAGGITIS, so called because it was first found at GAGGE in LYDIA; the name first appears in NIKANDER, *Theriaca*, v. 37. See JET, GALAKTITE. See MILK-STONE.

GARNET.—An amulet of garnet protected a man from evil and terrifying dreams, and when worn on the body prevented skin diseases. When danger approached it lost its brilliance and became dull. The ITALIANS call it *pietra della vedovanza*, " the stone of widowhood," because widows wear necklaces made of garnet beads, and hairpins ornamented with garnets. The garnet assures to its wearer love and faithfulness, and freedom from wounds.

HAEMATITE, or BLOODSTONE.—The blood-red powder scraped off this stone was used freely as a medicine by the ancients, and was believed to stop bleedings of every kind, whether external or internal. It cleared blood-shot eyes, and dried up rheum in the eyes, and provided a cure for snake-bite, and stopped bleedings in the lungs, and uterus, and gave relief to sufferers from urinary troubles. The Greeks believed that the stone had fallen from heaven. Many modern peoples of EUROPE wear bezels of bloodstone in their rings, and hold the same views as the ancients as to its curative powers ; in parts of the Sûdân bloodstone amulets are supposed to protect their wearers from sunstroke and headache, and many of the Mediterranean peoples wear it as a protection against the Evil Eye. The name of BLOODSTONE is also applied to red coral, red agate, red marble, red jasper, carnelian, and HELIOTROPE.

HYACINTH.—Amulets made of this were worn on the neck, and bezels in rings assisted women in childbirth, drove away from men evil spirits and bad dreams, protected them against fascination and lightning, strengthened the members, fortified the heart, restored the appetite, suppressed flatulence, produced sleep, and banished grief and melancholy from the mind.

IRON PYRITES.—Sir HENRY YULE found that the sailors on the IRAWADDY river in Burmah wore this substance as an amulet against crocodiles.

JADE, also known as NEPHRITE, AXE-STONE, KIDNEY-STONE and GREEN JASPER.—Amulets made of this hard and very beautiful stone assisted women in childbirth, and were regarded as rendering unfailing help to those who were suffering from intestinal troubles. Many powers were attributed to this stone. Green jade was a bringer of rain, and drove away wild and evil beasts and spirits. It cured dropsy, abolished thirst, made a man victorious in battle, protected from lightning, and relieved palpitation of the heart. The use of jade as an amulet in WESTERN ASIA dates from the IVth millennium B.C., and is very common among the TURKS, ARABS, and ARMENIANS at the present day. In CHINA, jade is worn on the neck and breast, and the business man when carrying out a weighty transaction holds his amulet in his hand and seeks counsel from it. Nephrite is found in abundance in TEWAHI PUNAMU in NEW ZEALAND, and on the west coast it is called " Punamu Stone." The MAORIS wear figures of their ancestral gods in Nephrite, suspended from their necks. The smooth, soft variety of Jade, or Nephrite, is known as JADEITE.

JASPIS, or JASPER, *i.e.* the green variety of it is almost indistinguishable from Nephrite ; when there are flecks of red in it, as we see in Gnostic gems, it is called HELIOTROPE, or Bloodstone. The red variety is often found in amulets. It was supposed to possess many magical qualities, and when powdered it was used in medicine, and we find it as an ingredient in the preparations made up for women. Like Nephrite, both the red and the jaspis were employed against fascination and the Evil Eye, and they were supposed to increase the milk in women who were suckling children, to drive away night devils, and to help pregnant women. The Egyptians associated red jaspis with the blood of Isis (see page 137), and throughout the Middle Ages it was always used to staunch the bleeding of the nose and of wounds in general, and in cases of excessive menstruation.

JET (GAGGITIS).—Many ancient writers attribute numerous powers to this stone. Burnt in the powdered form it drove away snakes and reptiles ; and healed sufferers from epilepsy, toothache, headache, and glandular swellings in the neck ; and helped women in labour (if they held a piece of it in their hands) ; and nullified spells and charms ; and alleviated pains in the stomach and assisted the dropsical. In ancient times it was held in high esteem in the BRITISH ISLES, where it was believed to protect people from thunderstorms, devils, poison, demoniacal possession, internal disease caused by devils, witchcraft, failure in bodily strength and snake bite. The Irish housewife burnt jet during her husband's absence to ensure his safety. In ITALY a jet beetle was a protection against the Evil Eye, and the amulet MANO CORNUTA was, and still is, often made of jet. The Sardinian amulet PINNA-DELLU is also made of jet, which because of its black colour is supposed to be baleful for the Evil Eye. The HEART of jet inscribed with a Latin Cross, and a Cross of jet were two amulets which were held in high esteem among Christians a century or two ago. The little disks of jet which have been found in INDIA and EGYPT also probably served as amulets against the Evil Eye.

LAPIS LAZULI.—This beautiful stone was highly prized by the earliest inhabitants of INDIA, PERSIA, (IRÂN), and MESOPOTAMIA, and kings and queens and high officials in the last-named country had their cylinder-seals, or seal cylinders made of it. Many very fine examples were discovered by Mr. WOOLLEY at UR of the Chaldees, and some of them are to be seen in the British Museum. Memorial tablets and other objects were made of lapis lazuli ; see Brit. Mus., No. 91013 (tablet of LUGAL-TARSI), No. 91452 (mace-head), No. 174 (pupil of an eye ; see the *Guide*, p. 238). The Egyptians distinguished two kinds of lapis lazuli, the real and the artificial, which was a sort of paste made from the powder of the stone. The real lapis lazuli was used for making scarabs and figures of gods, and beads were made of the blue paste. The SUMERIANS believed that the wearer of a lapis lazuli amulet carried with him the veritable presence of a god, and a text says " his god will rejoice him " (Mr. Gadd's translation). In a powdered form it was administered to patients suffering from gall-stones, melancholy, sleeplessness, and fever. The lapis STAMATOPETRA amulet, *i.e.* " Stop-stone," in use in MACEDONIA at the present time is supposed to prevent miscarriage and abortion, and to ward off calamities of every kind.

MAGNETITE.—Primitive man firmly believed that the magnetic power in this stone was caused by some living being. It possessed the strength of haematite, and dispelled melancholy, and relieved pains in the hands and feet, and assisted women in labour, and (when attached to the neck) improved the memory, and was a protection against fascination. The MEXICANS carry it in their belts so that it may give them success in their undertakings, and according to SELIGMANN prostitutes prize it highly. The stone is regarded as a living thing, and needs food and drink. It is placed in water on Friday so that it may drink, and it is then laid in the sun and given iron filings to eat. If a man pollutes it he dies. If a man rubs a magnetite knife it becomes poisonous, and he who is wounded by it will assuredly die. As the devil lives in it a man must not carry it when he goes to Mass, and as it attracts lightning it must not be carried during a storm. It heals the body when laid on a wound, but it will not cure sores in the head during rainy weather. Dr. Campbell Thompson has shown that the Assyrians called Magnetite *shadanu ṣabitu*, *i.e.* the " haematite which attracts, grasps." Before sexual intercourse the man mixed the magnetite with oil and rubbed himself with the mixture. The woman rubbed herself with *parzilli*, *i.e.* iron powder to increase her power of attraction for the man. See MAN, January, 1928, p. 14.

MALACHITE.—Amulets made of this stone are common both in the East and the West, and when attached to the necks of children, whether in the cradle or out of it, the stone protects them from the Evil Eye, and eases their pain when cutting their teeth. In some parts of EUROPE people believe that if a piece of malachite be tied over the umbilicus of a woman in labour it will facilitate the birth of her child. In ITALY, under the name of *pietra del pavone*, it is supposed to cure diseases of the eyes.

MARBLE.—Amulets made of a kind of limestone like zoned alabaster are, in INDIA, believed to protect the wearer against the Evil Eye.

MELITITE.—Ball-shaped amulets made of this stone are tied to the garments of children to ward off infantile diseases.

MILK-STONE (GALAKTITE).—According to some ancient writers the milk-stone obtained its name because milk flowed from it. Others believed that when taken in the form of a powder mixed with honey it assisted the secretions and flow of milk in women. If the stone was dipped in sea water and rubbed on the backs of sheep it produced abundance of milk in the ewes. As an amulet it protected children from the Evil Eye, and women wore it when suckling their babes ; it relieved toothache, and protected the wearer against witchcraft. Light-coloured agate is used as a milk-stone in ITALY. And as the people associate the name of the stone with that of AGATHA, the martyr, whose breasts were cut off, it is supposed to possess extra protective and beneficent powers ; for this saint is regarded as the patron of all mothers who are giving suck, and to assist in regularizing all the functions in the bodies of women. In SYRIA and PALESTINE, both Christian and Muslim mothers, when they fear a shortage of milk, dissolve little cakes made of earth taken from the " Milk Grotto " near BETHLEHEM, and bearing the seal of the Holy Sepulchre, in water and drink the mixture, believing that it will increase the secretion of milk in the breasts. They do this because of their faith in an ancient legend concerning the Virgin MARY. According to this, on the night of their flight to Egypt, JOSEPH and MARY and the

CHILD took refuge in the cave, which is now called the " Milk Grotto," and there she suckled our Lord. As she was doing this a drop of her milk fell on the ground, and from that night to the present time the dust from the Grotto has been used as a sure means of increasing the secretion of milk in women and regulating the supply of the same.   Beads made from the dust and worn on the neck have the same effect.

MOONSTONE.—Amulets made of this stone protected men against epilepsy, and when hung upon fruit trees produced abundant crops of fruit.   It is generally regarded in the East as a " lucky " stone, and like moss agate it assisted all vegetation.

NEPHRITE.   See JADE.

ONYX.—Opinion is divided as to the influence of this stone.   The onyx is generally declared to be an unlucky stone, and many people, in the East as well as in the West, look upon it with disfavour. Those who hold this view say that it incites to strife, and causes contention between friends, and gives the wearer broken sleep and terrifying dreams, and causes pregnant women to bring forth their children prematurely.   On the other hand, many INDIANS and PERSIANS wear it as an amulet to protect them against the Evil Eye.   Those who give the stone a good name say that an onyx stone placed near or on a woman in labour reduces the pains of childbirth, and conduces delivery.

OPAL.—Ancient traditions attribute to this remarkable stone a two-fold quality, that is to say, it possesses the baleful influence of the Evil Eye, and also the power to relieve the pains of those who are suffering from diseases of the eye.   And some say that as an amulet it makes the wearer immune from every disease of the eye, and that it increases the powers of the eyes and the mind. As the brilliant colours of the ruby, and carbuncle, and garnet, and emerald and amethyst are seen in its depths, admirers of the stone say that the opal possesses all the prophylactic and therapeutic powers of these stones. The so-called BLACK OPAL is highly prized, and every friend who has possessed one has assured me that it was the " luck stone " of his or her life.

PERIDOT, PERIDOTE, PERIDOTO.—A word of unknown origin, but probably a corruption of some oriental name for OLIVINE. In colour it closely resembles CHRYSOLITE, but its yellowish-green colour is much deeper than that of chrysolite. It was much prized by the ancients, and in modern times by the French jewellers, who probably obtained it from EGYPT. Ancient writers called the stone TOPAZ, and it is now known that it comes from the Jazîrat Zabûgat in the Red Sea, which some have identified with the Topaz Island of Greek writers. The peridot is a comparatively rare stone, and many of those found in shops have been taken from old rings and crosses. One of the finest known is to be seen in the shrine of the Three Kings CASPAR, MELCHIOR and BALTHAZAR in Cologne Cathedral. As an amulet the peridot is said to possess all the virtues of the topaz. Worn on the left arm it protects the wearer against the Evil Eye and because of its yellowish-green colour it was regarded as a palliative for diseases of the liver and dropsy, and it was said to free the mind from envious thoughts.

PUMICE STONE is used as a birth amulet, and is carried by women who are anxious to secure easy labour.

RUBY.—As an amulet it was believed to protect a man from witchcraft of all kinds, plague, pestilence and famine. The water in which a ruby had been washed was administered as a stomachic, and ruby-powder was one ingredient in medicines that were intended to check a flux of blood.

SALT (ROCK SALT).—Strictly speaking salt should not be included among precious, and semi-precious, stones, but on account of its colour and its pre-servative qualities many people have regarded it, if not as a holy, as a sacred substance. Its operations were regarded as both prophylactic and therapeutic. Since salt was acceptable to the gods as an offering, it was held in detestation by the spirits of evil, though from the point of view of its destructive effects on vegetation, it aided them in their wicked deeds. Salt warded off the Evil Eye from a man, and its efficacy was greatly increased if it were heated and sprinkled on human beings and cattle, and if it was mixed with pitch. In the Egyptian Aphrodite mysteries salt is associated with a phallus, which was also a warder-off of evil. Throughout Europe salt was, and probably still is, regarded as a protection against evil spirits and witchcraft, and animals and the farms they lived on were sprinkled with it, no man doubting its efficacy. In many places it is still believed that it is unlucky to spill salt, and the spiller at once takes care to cast a little over his left shoulder. How old this superstition is cannot be said, but it probably dates in the West from the time of the imposition of a salt tax in England, France, and other countries. Why the spiller of salt must cast a little over his left shoulder is obvious. The evil spirits congregated on the left side of a man, and the salt drove them away and so averted the evil which they are ever ready to do to man. The Ḳabbâlâh regards the Hebrew word for salt, MLH, as a sacred word, for the numerical values of its letters $40 + 30 + 8 = 78$ is the same as the numerical values of the letters in the great name of God, YHWH, *i.e.* $10 + 5 + 6 + 5 = 26$ multiplied by 3. Seligmann has shown by the number of examples which he has collected in his book that among all the peoples of the world, both ancient and modern, salt has played a prominent part in all the rites and ceremonies connected with birth, circumcision, initiation, marriage, death and private and public worship. And it has always been believed that it protects both the living and the dead. When Muḥammad the Prophet advised 'Alî " to begin with the salt, and end with the salt, for in it lies the means of healing seventy diseases," he only described briefly the experience of all the savage and civilized peoples of the world of whom we have any knowledge. We may note in passing that in Abyssinia salt has very special importance, for slabs of rock-salt at one time formed the currency of the greater part of the country. The Abyssinians call the slab of salt which takes the place of a coin 'AMÔLÊ. It is from 10 to 12 inches in length, and in width and thickness from $1\frac{1}{2}$ to $2\frac{1}{2}$ inches ; its weight is about 17 ounces.

SAPPHIRE.—To what stone this name was given by ancient writers is not certain, for some of them seem to have confounded it with lapis lazuli, the turquoise, and the HYACINTH. In INDIA and ARABIA it is worn as a health amulet, and as a protection against the Evil Eye, and plague and pestilence. The healthier the body the least chance have the evil spirits to do it harm.   The amulet also conduced to equability of minds.

SARD.—This stone, often confounded with carnelian, was supposed to help women in labour and assist an easy delivery.

SARDONYX.—This stone was regarded as a protection against witchcraft, and removed rheum from the eyes, and prevented premature childbirth.

SELENITE (MOONSTONE).—Was believed to assist the growth of trees and plants in orchards and gardens, and to protect a man from wandering of the mind, insanity and epilepsy.

SCHIST.—This stone was much used in making amulets by the EGYPTIAN and was supposed to possess magical properties similar to those of haematite.

SERPENTINE.—This stone owes its name to its similarity to the green, speckled skin of the serpent, and amulets made of it were worn against the bites of serpents, and the stings of noxious reptiles generally, and poisons.   It was believed that if a poisoned drink was given to a man in a vessel made of serpentine, the outside of the vessel would burst into a sweat.   On the other hand a serpentine vessel increased the effect of medicines drunk from it.   It regulated the supply of milk in nursing mothers.

STALAGMITES.—Small stones, or perhaps petrified earth, which are found on the floors of stalactite caves ; they were carried in little bags and were believed to protect the wearer from witchcraft.

SULPHUR.—Pieces of sulphur have been regarded as amulets against colds, rheumatism, and pains in the body caused by witchcraft, and when powdered and mixed with wine or water it was supposed to protect the drinker from every kind of evil influence. Fumigation of animals, and dwellings, was supposed to protect them against fascination.

TOPAZ (CHRYSOLITE).   See PERIDOT.

TRAVERTINE, the Italian TRAVERTINO (from the Latin *tibertinus lapis*, " Tibur stone "), is a yellowish deposit formed by springs, which in Italy children wear as amulets in little bags to protect them from witchcraft.

TURQUOISE, *i.e.* the " Turkish " stone, is highly prized all over ASIA and in many parts of AFRICA, not only for its beautiful greenish-blue colour, but for its prophylactic and therapeutic qualities. The ARABS call it *Fayrûz* and *Fîrûzaj*, *i.e.* the " lucky stone," and have no doubt about its benevolent action. It is mounted in rings, and necklaces and ear-rings, and head-ornaments, and when carried as an amulet it protects the wearer from poison, the bites of reptiles, diseases of the eye, and, according to information received in *Arabia*, it warns him of the approach of death by changing its colour. Many Orientals carry it to ward off the Evil Eye. In the Sûdân the water in which it has been dipped or washed is administered as a palliative to those who suffer from retention of the urine. The Buddhists associate it with the Buddha, because of the legend in which a turquoise stone enabled him to destroy a foul monster.

CHAPTER XVI.

THE IMPORTANCE OF COLOUR, SHAPE, AND FORM IN AMULETS.

Now the prophylactic and therapeutic qualities which men have attributed to amulets are not the only things which they have looked for in amulets, for certain shapes, forms, and colours have been considered almost of equal importance. Thus a certain VIOLET stone is in some countries hung on the necks of children, and it is supposed not only to protect them from sicknesses, but to make them docile and obedient to their parents. It is formed of the crystallized tears which EVE shed when she was separated from ADAM. GREEN stones, e.g. nephrite, the emerald, green jade, Amazon stones, etc., are connected with luxuriant vegetation and the rain that causes it, and fertility in man and beast, and virility and strength generally. YELLOW stones assisted men who suffered from jaundice and other diseases of the liver. RED stones were used to stop blood fluxes and the bleeding of wounds, whether caused by the surgeon or by the enemy's weapons, and to protect their wearers from fire and lightning. BROWN stones warded off sicknesses. BLACK stones were protections against the Evil Eye. WHITE stones averted the Evil Eye and carried with them the protection of heaven, whence they were said to come. Stones that sparkled and rock crystal defeated every kind of witchcraft, and those which were marked either by Nature or art with bands of a different colour, circles, etc., were greatly esteemed. Water-worn stones, and stones with holes or cavities in them made effective amulets, and circular, semicircular, and triangular stones have been almost universally chosen as means of protection against evil spirits.

It seems that in some countries amulets made of precious stones were held to be more effective than those which were made of commoner materials, because it was thought that the evil spirits were pleased with the sight of rare and beautiful gems, and that their attacks were in consequence less malicious and less deadly. Groups of nine and five precious stones are still regarded in INDIA as protections against the Evil Eye, and the twelve stones in the BREAST-PLATE OF AARON were, no doubt, intended to avert the attacks of the evil spirits from the high priest. According to Exod. xxviii. 17–20, the stones were arranged in four rows, thus:

I.	ODHEM carnelian or sard	PIṬDHÂH topaz or peridot	BÊREḲETH emerald
2.	NÔPHEK ruby or carbuncle	SAPPÎR sapphire or lapis lazuli	YAHÂLÔM jasper or onyx
3.	LESHEM jacinth	SHÊBHÔ agate	AHLÂMÂH amethyst
4.	TARSHÎSH beryl or yellow jasper	SHÔHAM chrysolite	YASHPAH jasper

On each stone was engraved the name of one of
the tribes of Israel, which, added to the natural
powers of the stones, turned the breast-plate into
a most powerful amulet.

The Hebrew *ḥôshen* חֹשֶׁן, a word of unknown
meaning, but rendered " breast-plate " above, is the
name given in the Bible to the SACRED RECEPTACLE
which was attached to the ephôdh of the high
priest Aaron, and was known as the ḤÔSHEN
MISHPÂṬ, *i.e.* " breast-piece of [divine] decision "
or " breast-piece of judgment." Aaron wore it on
his breast when he brought the tribes before God
during his ministration in the Holy of Holies. It
was made of linen, and was in size one span square,
and it was fastened to the shoulders of the ephôdh
by gold chains passing through gold rings, and to
the lower part of the ephôdh just above the girdle
by a blue ribbon passing through other gold rings.
Exod. xxviii. 22–29. But it seems from Judges
viii. 26 f that the ephôdh was a sort of idol or image,
for Gideon made an " ephôdh " of the gold rings
taken from the Ishmaelites and Midianites and that
he set it up in Ophrah. The 1,700 shekels of gold
of which it was made represent nearly £3,800 of our
money. Whatever this kind of ephôdh may have
been it certainly formed some part of the apparatus
used at that time in divination. In the linen
" breast-piece " which Aaron wore the two objects
which were used in divining the will of God were
placed (Exod. xxviii. 30) ; these objects were
called the " 'ÛRÎM and the TUMMÎM " וְהַתֻּמִּים
הָאוּרִים or, as some read the " 'ÛRÎM and the
TÂMÎM." What these objects were like is not

known, for, curiously enough, the Bible does not give any directions for making them ; and the exact meaning of their names are unknown. As they were to be kept in the breast-piece, which was only a span square, they must have been small in size, and we can only assume that they were small plaques or tablets made of stone, wood, bone or ivory. It is very probable that they were two small natural stones, precious or semi-precious, and perhaps of different colours. There is no doubt that like the SORTES of the Latin peoples, they were used in drawing or casting lots. Whether the 'Ûrîm and Tummîm (not Thummîm) were inscribed cannot be said. As these lots were only two in number only one question could be put at a time, and the answer was Yes or No. Or it might be arranged beforehand what 'Ûrîm was to indicate and what Tummîm, as we see from I Sam. chap. xiv., where Saul asked God to indicate the guilt of himself or Jonathan by 'Ûrim and that of the people by Tummîm. It is clear that the lot 'Ûrîm must have had a form or shape or colour by which it was distinguished from Tummîm, or perhaps one was labelled 'Ûrîm and the other Tummîm. The custody of 'Ûrîm and Tummîm was in the hands of the high priest, whose duty it was to manipulate the lots for those who enquired of them, and to regularize this form of divination. There is no doubt that the custom of casting lots with the view of discovering the designs of God is very ancient, and that the lots 'Ûrîm and Tummîm were used in connection with some kind of idol, or the ephôdh figure, long before the ephôdh became a linen garment for the high priest, with a front inlaid with precious stones.

The two tablets of *shôham* stone, each of which was engraved with the names of six of the tribes of Israel, which were to be fastened to the shoulders of the ephôdh (Exod. xxviii. 9), were also powerful amulets. And we may note that the " five smooth stones " which DAVID took out of the brook before he went to fight Goliath (1 Sam. xvii. 40) were believed by him to possess magical power. The number five is significant.

CHAPTER XVII.

THE SWĂSTIKA OR SVASTIKA.

The amuletic sign ⌐⌐, which is known as " swăstika," " gammadion," " fylfot " and " croix-pattée," is one of the oldest known, and was probably invented by the primitive Aryans. The native Indian name of the sign is, of course, " swăstika," which the philologists tell us means something like " fortunate," or " lucky " ; it is derived from *su*, " well," and *asti*, " being." The name " gammadion," *i.e.* the cross with Gammas, was given to it because the short lines at right angles to the arms make each resemble Gamma, a letter of the Greek alphabet. Some of the early Christian mystics saw in the two lines at right angles a symbol of Christ as the corner-stone, and the architects and designers of the Middle Ages used the Gamma freely in their reliefs and patterns. Thus four of them grouped with their angles towards each other made the form of the Greek cross ⊥⊥.

Many writers consider that the fylfot and the swăstika are one and the same sign, but some doubt it. The Oxford Dictionary says that the fylfot is an " equal-armed cross of which each arm is continued rectangularly, all clockwise or all counter clockwise," and adds " name based on ancient direction for design of painted window in which *f* may mean either the particular pattern or something to *fill the foot* of the window." Those who regard the gammadion and the swăstika as one and the same sign have confounded the simple cross ✚, which was used in the West by pagans long before the coming of Christ, with the swăstika, which is a purely Aryan symbol and, of course, of pagan origin. As the swăstika is found on monuments in the catacombs (HULME, *Symbolism*, p. 219) it is clear that the Christians of the early centuries of our era used it sometimes as the equivalent of the cross. Or it may be that they knew the meaning and significance of the swăstika, and wished to indicate by its use that they thought the dead were " fortunate."

The home of the swăstika seems to be undoubtedly India, but Mr. Greg believed that both it and the fylfot has a very ancient common origin and meaning. But what is the meaning? Max Müller thought that the swăstika, with short lines projecting to the right 卍 , " represented the vernal sun, and that the sauvastika, with short arms projecting to the left 卐 , was the symbol of the autumnal sun." Another view is that the swăstika represented Ganesa and the male principle, and the sauvastika the goddess Kālī and the female principle. Another authority says that the common sign for forked lightning was Z , and says that if this sign be crossed by another of the same shape the result will be the swăstika  . Yet another authority thinks that the swastika in its simplest form represents the two pieces of wood which were used in making fire, *i.e.* fire-sticks. The generally accepted view now seems to be that the swăstika is a solar emblem, and that the short lines at right angles to the arms indicate gyratory or wheeling motion.

It has been suggested that the four arms represent the four quarters of the heavens or earth, and also that the whole sign is an emblem of INDRA, or DYAUS, or ZEUS, or JUPITER, or THOR. In his article on the sign in *Archaeologia* (vol. xlviii. London, 1885, p. 293 f.) GREG sums up by saying that

⊔ is " an Aryan special emblem of the Supreme God." He is probably correct, but it is impossible to be certain, for we shall never know exactly what idea was connected with the sign in the minds of the Asiatics who first used it, some thousands of years ago. The JAINS, a Buddhist sect, adopted it as a symbol of the Buddha, and introduced it into China about 200 B.C.

The Chinese name for the swăstika is LEI WEN, *i.e.* "thunder-scroll," a fact which shows that the sign was associated with phenomena of the sky. The circle in which the swăstika is sometimes seen suggest that the smaller lines of the sign developed into the circle, but sometimes the circle is shown independently, thus

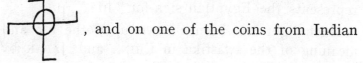 , and on one of the coins from Indian

Scythia figured by Greg we have   . On

pottery the swăstika is often shown with four dots

. Sometimes the four short lines are

made into circles, thus . On a terra-cotta

ball found by Schliemann at Troy a row of swăs-
tikas arranged between two rows of dots runs round
the middle thus :—

And on coins of Mesembria in Thrace the swăstika
follows an abbreviation of the name of the place,

thus **ΜΕΣ** (PERCY GARDNER, in *Numismatic*

Chronicle, Part I, 1880). On another coin figured
by Greg (plates xix and xx) we have the signs

in a group. This shows that the swăstika and the
cross were entirely different signs ; the second sign
represents the Egyptian sign for " life," .

Much light has been thrown upon the use and
meaning of the swăstika in CHINA and JAPAN by

T. WILSON, who in his book, *The Swastika* (Washington, 1896), seems to have collected all the available information about the sign. He says that it is cut upon the pedestals of statues of the Buddha, and that it is found also on the breasts of figures of the Bodhisattvas, *i.e.* those who will one day become Buddhas. As a character among the Chinese hieroglyphs it means "prosperity," "good luck," "wealth" and "long life." The Empress Wu (A.D. 684–704) ordered that it should be used as a sign for the sun, and so revived the meaning which it had in India several centuries before Christ, M. GOBLET D'ALVIELLA asks the question if the gammate cross can be assigned to a single birthplace, and says that its two most ancient known *habitats* are Hissarlik and the *terramares* of North Italy. He thinks it possible that both of these districts borrowed it from the valley of the Danube during the Bronze Age, and that it was regarded both as a solar symbol and a sign of life or blessing ; it may have spread both into Western Europe and into India, China, and Japan by way of the Caucasus. But it seems to the present writer, judging from the illustrations published by de Mortillet, that it is the cross which is found on the pottery, etc., from the *terramares* and not the swăstika.

CHAPTER XVIII.

THE CROSS.

One of the oldest amuletic signs in the world, perhaps even the oldest, is the CROSS, that is to say the figure which is made by two straight lines which bisect each other at right angles ✚. This is what is commonly understood by the word " cross," and not the single wooden pillar or pole to which malefactors condemned to death were tied, and which is spoken of by some writers as the *crux simplex.* It was at one time believed by many writers on ecclesiastical symbols, relics, etc., that the cross was entirely of Christian origin, but such is not the case, for it was in use among the pagan peoples of Western Asia and Europe many centuries before the death of Christ. That the pagan cross symbolized something quite different from that which the Christian cross commemorated hardly needs to be said. But judging by what we think we know of the symbolism of the pagan cross we are justified in regarding it as a forerunner of the Christian cross. On the other hand, the pagan cross may have been used as a simple ornament, and it may have symbolized nothing, or modern writers in discussing it may have been influenced by their Christian beliefs and traditions, and attributed to it a meaning and symbolism which it never possessed.

The commonest form of the cross used by pre-Christian peoples is that in which all four arms are of equal length, and which is known as the Greek or *equilateral cross*. One of the oldest known examples of it is found on an inscribed cylinder-seal in the British Museum (No. 89128) which was made during the Kassite period. The Kassite Dynasty began with Gandash (1746 B.C., and ended with Ellil-nâdin-aḫê, who ceased to reign in 1171), so then the cylinder-seal was made in the second millennium B.C. It is reproduced on Plate XI, No. 5. On the right is a figure of the Sun-god, seated, holding some object in his right hand ; before him is a rosette of unknown meaning. In the field above is an equilateral cross within a line border. The cuneiform text contains a prayer to the Sun-god, which has not yet been fully translated. Another example of the cross within a line border is published by DELAPORTE, *Cyl. Orientaux*, Plate xx, No. 297. A third example, but without the line

border is published in the *Catalogue* of

the DE CLERQ Collection, I, Plate xxxiii, No. 363. This last cross is cut in the field just before the head of a winged Centaur who is hunting in the desert, and behind him is the crescent moon . Other forms

of the Kassite cross are and .

On a wall-painting from a tomb at Thebes in the British Museum we see two small figures wearing

the equilateral cross on their breasts, and another
example is published by ROSELLINI (*Monumenti
Stor*, tav. lxx.). The objects from which these
examples are taken date from the period of the
XIXth Dynasty, *circa* 1250 B.C. To the second
millennium B.C. also belong the examples which are
described by GABRIEL DE MORTILLET, *Le Signe de
la Croix*, Paris, 1866, p. 162 f., and are reproduced
here :

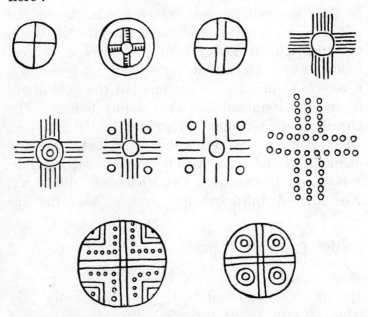

On some Assyrian sculptures we find what may
be described as a solar or radiated cross, which is
nothing more than the disk of the sun from which
proceed four arms and four rays of light ; the
arms, according to some, represent the four quarters
of heaven over which the god ANU presided. Another
form of the Cross is seen on the stele of the Assyrian
king SHAMSHI-ADAD VI (824–810 B.C.), in the

British Museum, viz., ; this is commonly known as the Maltese or Coptic or *rayed* cross. The equilateral cross is found on many of the smaller objects dug up by SCHLIEMANN at TROY, and on vases and bronze weapons found in SCANDINAVIA, GERMANY, AUSTRIA, SWITZERLAND, FRANCE and ENGLAND (see MORTILLET, *op. cit.*, p. 158, and A. W. FRANKS, *Horae ferales*, Plate xxx, fig. 49). That it at first symbolized the heavens, or some power in them, seems to be certain, and later the cross itself may have been regarded as the sign of divine protection and prosperity, riches, and life. We read that COLUMBUS and his sailors were amazed to find the cross in America, and they attributed its existence there to the teaching of the Apostle THOMAS, who visited India and worked there as a carpenter. But the authorities on Peruvian and Mexican archaeology say that these crosses are "wind crosses," and that originally they represented the four main directions whence came the winds and rains, and that at a later period they were assumed to possess a solar or stellar character.

The TAU CROSS , or Crux Commissa, which is found in the Catacombs of Rome and on monuments elsewhere of the Christian period, is sometimes called the "anticipatory cross," or "type cross," the cross of the Old Testament.[1] Writers on the Christian Cross say that it was the symbol of eternal life with the ancient Egyptians, but it never was. The well-known symbol and hieroglyphic for "life,"

---

[1] The Tau cross is the special emblem of St. Anthony.

eternal or otherwise, was ☥ ÂNKH, which has nothing to do with the Tau Cross ; and never had the phonetic value of *Tau*. Wilkinson made the mistake of thinking that ☥ was to be read *Tau*, and even in the last edition of his great work (iii. p. 364) he calls the sign *Tau*, adding " the origin of the *tau* I cannot precisely determine." In saying that the " early Christians of Egypt adopteed it in lieu of the cross " he states a fact which has been well known to the Fathers of the Church from the IInd century downwards. It is wrong, too, to call the sign ☥, *crux ansata*, the " handled cross," for whatever object the hieroglyph may represent, it was certainly not a cross or anything like it.

Writers have assumed that ☥ represents a Tau cross with a loop added, just as they have assumed that ⌯ or ⌯ NEFER (which is a conventional picture of a musical instrument) represents a Latin cross with an oval added to its lower extremity. As a hieroglyphic ☥ undoubtedly means " life " and there is no good reason for doubting that it is a conventional representation of one of the principal organs of the human body used in the process of generation or coition (see page 134). The Tau cross is said by some to represent a cross-headed yoke or gibbet and by others the hammer of THOR ; on the other hand LIPSIUS believed it to be of Phoenician origin (*De Cruce*, I. 7). As a matter of fact no one knows what object it represented, or what meaning exactly the pagans, who invented it and used it, attached to it. If it be of Egyptian origin the Tau may be

a form of the hieroglyph ⌐ which represents a female
organ of generation, and is used as a determinative,
of " birth " and therefore " life." In Ezek. ix. 4
we read that the prophet was commanded by God
to go through JERUSALEM and to " set a mark upon
the foreheads " of certain men, presumably as a
sign of their exemption from judgment. Now the
Hebrew word which is translated " mark " is *tâw*
(*hithwîthâ tâw*), and some have identified the sign
tâw with the Tau cross. TERTULLIAN in commenting
on the passage says of the sign " *ipsa* enim litera
Graecorum Tau, nostra autem T species crucis "
(*Adversus Marcian* iii. 22). This identification seems
to be fanciful, as also is the view that the mark
made with the blood of the paschal lamb on the
houses of the Israelites before they left Egypt was
the Tau cross (Exod. xii. 7).

We have now to consider the CHRISTIAN CROSS.
The New Testament makes it quite certain that
our Lord was not crucified on a single stake (crux
simplex), but on a patibulum or gibbet formed of
two bars of wood, one fastened across the other.
Some have held the view that He was nailed to the
cross whilst it lay on the ground, and that the
cross was then lifted up and set upright. Another
view is that He was made to ascend a ladder, and
was then nailed to the cross. This ladder is represented in some of the mediaeval pictures of the
Crucifixion, and from the XIIth century onward
the ladder appears on wood carvings and in stained
glass together with the other " Passion symbols,"
viz., the dice, the seamless robe, the cock, the spear,
the sword, the 30 pieces of silver, the pincers, the
three nails, the hammer, the pillar of scourging,

342 AMULETS AND SUPERSTITIONS

scourge, the reed, the sponge, the vessel of vinegar.
and the crown of thorns. Four forms of the cross were
used in the early centuries of our era, viz., the Greek

cross, the four arms being equal in length ╬ , the

Latin cross (*crux immissa* or *crux capitata*), in which

the lower limb is longer than each of the others ✝ ,

the *crux decussata*, or St. Andrew's cross ✖ , and

the *crux commissa* or Tau cross ┬ · At the same

time we find that the so-called monogram of Christ,

⳨ , was in general use among Christians.

The Latin cross was best known and most used
because the cross on which Christ was crucified is
believed to have been of this form ; the Latin cross
is also known as the " Cross of Calvary " and the
"Passion Cross." The cross which is sometimes seen
in the hands of the risen Lord is known as the
" Cross of the Resurrection," and a flag or banner
is usually attached to it. Sometimes the cross has
the form of a tree, or of a series of branches of trees ;
and some pictures of the Crucifixion suggest that each
of the two thieves suffered on the Tau cross or on
trees.

The cross did not become the supreme emblem
and symbol of Christianity until the IVth century,
i.e. until after the " Finding " of the Cross by the

Empress HELENA on May 3, 328. The true cross is said to have been found during the reign of TIBERIUS, when ST. JAMES was bishop of Jerusalem, and if this be so the Empress can only have rediscovered it. But the Coptic narrative of the Empress's labours shows that her excavations were carried out on a very large scale, and we are driven to conclude that she found something which had never before been brought to light. According to this she found three crosses, but she did not know which of the three was that on which our Lord had suffered. At length, either as a result of her own cogitations, or acting under the advice of the devout priest who was with her, she had the body of a dead man brought and laid upon one of the crosses. As contact with that cross had no effect upon the dead man, she had him placed on the second cross, and that also produced no effect on the dead man. Then she had the body removed and placed on the third cross, and the dead man came to life immediately. She sent a part of the Cross to Constantine, and the portion of it which he transmitted to the Pope is still preserved in Rome ; she reburied the greater part of the Cross in the church which she built over the site of GOLGOTHA. The Latin cross is often seen with two cross-pieces thus, and in this form it is the cross of Lorraine and of the Knights Hospitallers. And sometimes, especially among Oriental Christians, we have three cross-pieces thus. The upper cross-piece was suggested by the scroll which was nailed to the cross, and was inscribed in Hebrew, Greek, and Latin.

The original scroll was found by the Empress, together with the nails, but for some centuries nothing was heard of it and it was generally believed that it had been destroyed. It was discovered by accident in the church of St. Croce at Rome in 1492, and Pope Alexander III published a bull in which its authenticity was certified.

Silver Host-case in the form of a Cross. (Obverse : The Crucifixion.)

The early Christians assigned to the cross in any form magical powers, and they took pleasure in making the sign of the cross over themselves on every occasion possible, both because they received spiritual help from the act, and because it enabled them to prove to the onlookers that they were Christians, and to make themselves known to each other. It is said that this custom became common about A.D. 110. The cross was marked

PLATE XXII

A group of Crosses in gold, steel and Limoges enamel.

upon cattle, and traced on the walls of houses,
and models of the cross are said to have worked
miracles. To all intents and purposes the presence
of the cross carried with it the presence of Christ,
and as in Egypt the Ṭeṭ pillar was regarded
as Osiris himself, so in Egypt and Palestine and
Europe the cross WAS considered to be Christ Him-

Silver Host-case in the form of a Cross. (Reverse : The Ascension.)

self, and was actually worshipped as such. Even

the so-called monogram of Christ ⳨ = Χριστός,

or ⳨ = the initials of Ἰησοῦς Χριστός, or ⳨

= chi-ro, cut on wood or stone, or written
or painted on parchment, was believed to carry

with it the almighty power of the Blood of the Son of God. The custom of wearing amulets of the cross became common at a very early date, but the widespread cult of the cross did not begin until after the Vth century. On this point and on the history of the cross generally the reader should consult G. DE MORTILLET, *Le Signe de la Croix avant le christianisme*, Paris, 1866 ; BROCK, MOURANT, *La Croix païenne et chrétienne*, Paris, 1881 ; LIPSIUS, *De Cruce Christi ;* BLAKE, W. WILSON, *The Cross Ancient and Modern*, New York, 1888 ; ANSAULT, *Le Culte de la croix avant Jésus Christ*, Paris, 1889 ; HULME, F. E., *Symbolism in Christian Art*, London, 1908.

The group of pectoral crosses figured on Plate XXII are in my private possession. The cross in the top right-hand corner is of pure gold, and was made during the last century in West Africa for a native who had embraced Christianity. He had been a believer in Juju practices and a firm believer in the " medicine " of the native magician. But though he became a good Christian he could not cast away entirely his belief in native astrology, and in order to unite his old belief with his new one, he had the Twelve Signs of the Zodiac attached to the Christian cross which he then regarded as a powerful amulet. The cross below has the upper and lower bars and was made in Russia. The cross in the centre is a good specimen in Limoges enamel. The cross in the left-hand top corner is a Russian priest's cross decorated with Biblical scenes. The cross below it is made of steel and is beautifully " Damascened " in gold on both sides ; the legend AEI, also in gold, means " for ever," " to all eternity." It was made in

Russia. The silver cross reproduced on pages 344, 347 is really a case in which the wearer carried some relic or reserved the sacramental bread. The two halves are joined by a hinge at the top, and the ring behind shows that this amulet was worn on the breast. On the one side we have Christ on the Cross in relief, and on the other Christ triumphant ascending into heaven. The emblems of the Four Evangelists and the other scenes are in low relief.

CHAPTER XIX.

THE CRUCIFIX.

The cross, as we have seen, was used in private devotions by Christians during the Ist century of our era, and was cut upon the tombs in the IInd and IIIrd centuries, but it did not become a public symbol or badge of Christians until Constantine had it placed on the shields of his soldiers and removed the Roman eagle from them early in the IVth century. The CRUCIFIX was the natural development of the cross, but this development did not take place until the cross had become a sign of triumph and glory instead of a stumbling block and a symbol of ignominy. Representations of Christ on the Cross are found on crosses, etc., already in the Vth century, but they did not appear in churches until the VIIth or VIIIth century. Until the XIth century the body of Christ on the Cross was always clothed, and in a drawing reproduced by HULME (*op. cit.*, p. 45) He is represented as the Great High Priest. Afterwards the clothing becomes less and less, until it becomes a species of loin cloth. In the same way until the XIVth century Christ the Babe was always depicted clothed, but after this period, as a result of the decadence of Christian art, He is represented naked, or nearly so. In Hulme's drawing the Figure wears a crown of radiatory bars, and above this, on a title are, A and Ω. It is thought that this representation is as old as Charlemagne. In all the other ancient examples (the

Crucifix of John VII, the Crucifix of Charlemagne, given to Leo III) Christ wears a long tunic. In the picture of the Crucifixion given in the Syriac Evangeliarium in the Medicean Library the two thieves wear waistcoats (see ASSEMÂNÎ, *Cat. Bibl. Medic.*, Florence, 1742, tavola xxiii.). The NIMBUS, which is so often found on early scenes of the Crucifixion, is of pagan origin, and it seems to have been originally a symbol of power rather than of holiness. It possibly represented at first the rays of the sun, and it was assigned not only to God, Whose symbol was the sun, but to men of might and power like MOSES and Muḥammad, and even to Satan! The nimbus came into general use in the VIth century. Early nimbi were circular. The square nimbus was introduced in the IXth century and the triangular form of it in the XIth. The nimbus with a cross within it is always assigned to the Deity.

THE SIGN OF THE CROSS.

To what extent amulets of the Cross were worn by the early Christians cannot be said, but there are many proofs that they made the Sign of the Cross over themselves when in trouble or difficulty. Of this fact the *Paradise* of PALLADIUS contains many examples. When Satan, in the form of an Indian, came to attack St. Anthony the saint made over himself the Sign of the Cross, and ceased to tremble, and the Enemy saw the Sign of the Cross, and straightway was terrified. Anthony did the same thing when a demoniacal animal came to him, and as soon as he adjured the creature in the Name of Christ, it took to flight and fell down and burst asunder. A certain monk, when about to eat some food over which oil of radishes had been poured, made the Sign of the Cross over himself to protect himself from any untoward effect which the strong, coarse oil might have upon him. And the monks of SCETE worked miracles by the Sign of the Cross. A youth whose face had been turned behind him by Satan was brought to ABBÂ POEMEN, and when the saint made the Sign of the Cross over the young man all distortion of his features vanished. The Devil hid in a pot of water, and a certain holy woman suspecting his presence there made the Sign of the Cross over the water, and Satan fell from the pot in a flash of fire. JOHN of LYCUS made the Sign of the Cross over some oil and gave it to a blind woman to smear over her eyes ; she did so three times and three days later she recovered her sight. And the Fathers of the desert said : " The devils fear and tremble not only by reason of the Crucifixion of Christ, but even at the Sign of the Cross, wheresoever it be made apparent, whether it be depicted upon a garment, or whether it be made in the air." The pagan sorcerers seeing the wonderful effect produced by the Sign of the Cross promptly adopted it in their own magical dealings, and with such success that some of the Christian Fathers complained that even laymen could drive away devils by uttering the Name of Christ and making the Sign of the Cross. And what the magician did in those days the BAGANDA of the SÛDÂN do in our own, for the medicine-men of that country when about to work magic, take a strip of leather, and having stamped on it the Sign of the Cross, they sew nine kauri shells to it, and it is ready to produce " strong magic."

TALISMANS OF THE VIRGIN MARY.

The following is a description of a Talisman of the Virgin against fire, pestilence, the Evil Eye, and all other magical influences. The " Mappa " is reproduced in Villiers, *Amulette*, Berlin, 1928. In the centre is a heart on which is laid the Cross of St. Anthony of Padua, inscribed ALPHA, OMEGA. On the right is the Virgin's Cross inscribed with A Ω and the great Name of God YHWH and emblems of the 72 great names of God, and two crosses TT. Below is written : " Signum S. Crucis integritas B.V. Mariae. Custodia sanctorum Angelorum, nec non suffrageo SS. Trium Regū. Salvatoris nostri in Cruce sit triumphalis quotidie inter nos et inimicos nostra Visibilis et invisibilis." In the middle of the Mappa or talisman are a crowned heart and a figure of Christ on the Cross. Below are C. M. B., the initials of Caspar, Melchior and Bälthasar, the three kings who presented gifts to the Babe, and figures of the Virgin and St. Anthony of Padua. On the left is a cross inscribed with the name M.K.B.I. (Maccabaeus) in Hebrew letters and the great Name YHWH (Yahweh or Jehovah). Below is written :—Ecce Crucem Domini. Fugite partes adversae. Vicit Leo de Tribu Juda, Radix Dauid. Alleluia. O ✠ Christi, adjuua nos. O ✠ Christi defende nos. O ✠ Christi, libera nos, ab omni peccato, a fulgure, et tempestate, et a morte perpetua.

CHAPTER XX.

THE EVIL EYE.

Of all the things which have driven man in all ages to invent and to use magic, the most potent is the " Evil Eye," or the " Evil Look." And the reason for this is that the various races of men who have peopled the earth for several thousands of years were convinced that certain men and women, certain beasts and reptiles, and even apparently inanimate objects, possess the power of causing by a mere glance of the eye or a look, or by a mere aspect or appearance, injury to their fellow-creatures, and to their flocks and herds, and to their crops and orchards, and in fact to any kind of property whatsoever. This baleful look or glance of the eye has always been thought to be especially injurious to children, and to women who were about to become mothers, for it threatened the very existence of the human race. The look which the eye casts upon some person or thing in wonder, or astonishment, or surprise can be made to produce an evil effect on that person or thing by means of words which the owner of the eye may utter at the the same time. If the words are contemptuous or disparaging they, operating in connection with the look, will produce an evil effect on the person or thing which the eye is looking upon. And the same bad effect can be produced by the look or glance of the eye of the man who, while uttering words of praise or congratulation, makes a mental reservation whereby he produces the exactly opposite effect to that which his words seem to wish to make. Primitive man seems to have understood these facts quite well, though he was totally unable to describe the exact connection between the glance of the eye and the spoken words or the secretly made mental reservation. Many educated people in many parts of the world still share this belief with him, and cannot explain how the eye exercises its magical power and produces sickness, calamity, and death. Certain it is that in many parts of the East, if a customer " runs down," or speaks disparagingly or abusively of an object which a merchant wishes him to buy, that object is at once removed lest ill-luck or injury come upon it. And the same is the case if it be a person or an animal that is cried down or laughed at ; the person's friends will hustle him away, and the owner of the beast will drag it away with him from the place.

Anthropologists and others have endeavoured to find out whence the eye obtains its power to inflict evil on the persons and things which make it to wonder or surprise it, and some have concluded that the Evil Eye is produced by the mind itself, or by some quality or power which it possesses. And some eminent and most experienced oculists have told me that the eyes are integral parts of the mind. Bacon says in his Ninth Essay, " Of Envy there be none of the affections which have been noted to fascinate or to bewitch, but love and envy ; they both have vehement wishes, they frame themselves readily into imaginations and suggestions, and they come early into the eye, especially upon the presence of the objects which are the points that conduce to

fascination, if any such there be. We see likewise
the Scripture calleth envy an evil eye. Of all other
affections, it is the most important and continual
. . . for it is ever working upon some or other.
It is also the vilest affection and the most depraved ;
for which cause it is the proper attribute of the
Devil, who is called, ' The envious man that soweth
tares among the wheat by night ' " (Matt. xiii. 25).
In this extract Bacon uses the word fascination
as an equivalent for the Evil Eye ; modern writers,
as ELWORTHY observes (*Evil Eye*, p. 2), render it by
" animal magnetism." The belief in its existence
must be set down as representing one of the here-
ditary and instinctive convictions of mankind.

We may then accept the view, which is based
on the general experience of mankind, that ENVY
can, and does, impart to the eye some quality which
emanates from it and works evil upon the person
or thing on which it falls. But there is something
else which will produce the same effect as envy,
that is to say JEALOUSY, " before which who can
stand ? " as the Book of Proverbs (xxvii. 4) testifies,
and the *Song of Songs* (viii. 6) in the words " jealousy
is cruel as the grave, the coals thereof are coals of
fire [which hath] a vehement flame." Envy,
jealousy. and the Evil Eye are inseparably connected ; and when joined to words is the origin
of the evil spirits which work sickness, disaster,
ruin, and death in the world. Evil spirits and the
Evil Eye have from time immemorial been regarded
as one and the same, and it is for this reason that
among many peoples, both in the East and the
West, the Evil Eye has been regarded as a being
with a form and a personality. Sometimes it takes

the form of an animal, *e.g.* a goat or an ass (see
PALLADIUS, *Paradise,* vol. i. p. 113), or an Indian
(*ibid.* vol. i. p. 11), and in the Life of ANTHONY we
read : " It is very easy for the Enemy to create
apparitions and appearances of such a character
that they shall be deemed real and actual objects ;
and phantoms of this kind caused a phantom earthquake, and they rent asunder the four corners of
the house, and entered therein in a body from all
sides. One had the form of a lion, and another had
the appearance of a wolf, and another was like unto a
panther, and all the others were in the forms and simili-
tudes of serpents, and of vipers and of scorpions "
(*ibid.,* vol. i. p. 14). Frequently the form chosen is
feminine, as we see from TIÂMAT, and ancient
Sumerian personification of evil and LÎLÎTH, the
night-hag of the Hebrews. But the Evil Eye is often
depicted in magical writings as an eye, but in no
drawing of it do we see a representation of the " little
man in the eye " with which primitive man was well
acquainted. In the Egyptian *Liturgy of Funerary
Offerings* (ed. Budge, p. 136) the priest says to the
deceased when he presents the ninety-eighth offering : " Osiris Unas, the child which is in the Eye
of Horus hath been presented unto thee." The
" little man in the eye " is mentioned in Deut.
xxxii. 10 ; Prov. vii. 2, and the Arabic version
translates rightly *insân al-'ayn.* The " daughter of
the eye " (*bath 'ayin*) occurs in Ps. xvii. 8, and
is correctly rendered *bint al-'ayin* and *binta 'ayin*
in Arabic and Ethiopic respectively. Among some
peoples the belief is common that the " little man of
the eye," *i.e.* the figure seen in the pupil of the eye,
can leave a man and enter another person and do

harm to any person or thing he pleases. Others again hold the view that the Evil Eye has a dualistic character, and that it uses one form to perform one class of evil works, and the other to do things which have no evil effects. Various conclusions have been arrived at by those who have studied the why and the wherefore of the Evil Eye, but in no part of the world is it doubted that its influence exists and the belief in it is beyond all doubt primeval and universal. Moreover, every language, both ancient and modern, contains a word or expression which is the equivalent of " Evil Eye."

The oldest mentions of the Evil Eye are found in the texts which the Sumerians, Babylonians, and Assyrians wrote in cuneiform upon clay tablets ; the Sumerian texts date from the third millennium before Christ, and they form the base of later Babylonian and Assyrian magical literature. The Assyrians were, apparently, unable to read easily the non-Semitic Sumerian originals, and they therefore added interlinear translations in their own Semitic tongue. The Sumerian words IGI-ḪUL, literally " eye evil," are translated by the Assyrian words *i-ni li-mut-tum* (see R. C. THOMPSON, *Devils and Evil Spirits*, Tablet V. vol. ii. p. 113). In this text it is said :—" The roving Evil Eye hath looked on the neighbourhood and hath vanished far away, hath looked on the vicinity and hath vanished far away, hath looked on the chamber of the land and hath vanished far away, it hath looked on the wanderer and like wood cut off for poles it hath bent his neck."

Against this Evil Eye the great god Ea went forth, just as did the archangel Gabriel in the Christian legend published by Prof. GOLLANCZ

(*Book of Protection*, plate facing p. 18). The Evil
Eye is represented in the form of a human skeleton,
with very long hair standing upright on its head.
The Hebrews were well acquainted with the Evil
Eye and its dire effects, but it is not mentioned in
the Old Testament, although it is clearly referred
to in such passages as Deut. xv. 9, and Ps. cxli. 4.
On the other hand we have : " Eat not the bread
of him that is evil of eye (*r'a 'ayin*), neither crave
thou his dainty meats " (Prov. xxiii. 6). Still
more direct allusions to the Evil Eye are found in
the *Wisdom of Solomon*, " for the bewitching of
naughtiness doth obscure things that are honest "
(iv. 12), and in *Ecclesiasticus* xiv. 8, where the Greek
has πονηρὸς ὁ βασκαίνων ὀφθαλμῷ. Our Lord seems to
refer to the Evil Eye in Mark vii. 22 and in Matt.
xx. 15 when He speaks of the ὀφθαλμὸς πονηρός, and
St. Paul most certainly does when he says to the
Galatians (iii. 1) : " O foolish Galatians, who hath
bewitched you ? " (τίς ὑμᾶς ἐβάσκανεν). An interesting account of the views of the latei Hebrews
concerning the Evil Eye will be found in the *Jewish
Encyclopaedia*, vol. v. p. 280 f.

The Arabs have believed in the influence of the
Evil Eye in all periods of their history, and one of
their commonest names for it is the " eye of envy "
'*ain al-ḥasad ;* curiously enough they sometimes
call it, being afraid of incurring its evil effects,
'Ain al-Jamâl," *i.e.* the " beautiful eye." Muḥammad the Prophet was a firm believer in the Evil Eye,
and Asmâ' bint 'Umais states that when she asked
him if she might use spells on behalf of the family
of Ja'far he replied : " Yes, for if there were anything in the world which would overcome fate it

would be an evil eye" (HUGHES, *Dict. of Islâm,*
p. 112). And Sûrah cxiii of the Ḳur'ân is often
written on scrolls or cut on agates and carried as a
protection against the Evil Eye. No prudent
caravan leader will set out on a journey unless
every beast has attached to it a blue bead or some
amulet to protect it from the Evil Eye; and usually
every man of the caravan carries an amulet either
secreted in his clothes or turban or attached to his
body.

How far exactly the ancient EGYPTIANS believed
in the influence of the Evil Eye cannot be said at
the present time; to think that they were ignorant
of the belief in it which was current among the nations
round about them is impossible. The original
inhabitants of the Valley of the Nile probably
feared the Evil Eye as much as the Sûdânî peoples
did, but it seems to the present writer unlikely
that the worshippers of Horus the îlder and Rā
paid much heed to it. The Sun and the Moon were
the eyes of Ḥer Ur, the primeval Sky-god of the
Egyptians, the Sun ruling the day and the Moon the
night. No evil person or thing could resist the
power of the Two Eyes, or exist where it was.
Throughout the Dynastic Period the Two Eyes,
Udjatti ⲟⲟⲟ, were painted or cut upon coffins and
sarcophagi and other articles of funerary equipment
and they were painted on the bows of boats. Besides
this we have the thousands of amulets of the Eye
of the Sun and the Eye of the Moon which are to
be seen in our Museum to prove that from the Vth
dynasty onwards the cult of the Sun-god was pre-
dominant among the upper classes of Egypt. The
use of the *Udjat* amulet seems to have been universal,

and this may have been the case *because* the belief in the influence of the Evil Eye was also universal, and because the Egyptian set the influence of the Eye of the Sun-god against that of the Evil Eye. The curious fact is, if this be so, why there is so little mention of the Evil Eye, or what is supposed to be the Evil Eye, in ancient Egyptian literature. It is quite clear that *iri-t bån-t* means the Evil Eye, and it is equally clear from the text on the wall of a chamber in the temple of EDFÛ that books of spells, which were intended to destroy its existence, were recited in the temple. Finally the word *siḥu* seems undoubtedly to mean fascination, or the influence of the Evil Eye.

That the Copts, or Christian Egyptians, believed in the Evil Eye there is no doubt, for there are many allusions in the texts to those who possess it, and to those who make use of it ; the word actually used is *Bôon* or Bôn, and the professional magician who works evil by it is referred to in the Coptic version of Deut. xviii. 10 (see also SPIEGELBERG, *Kopt. Handwörterbuch*, p. 17).

The Ethiopians or Abyssinians have always held the Evil Eye, which they call " ' ÂYENAT," in great fear, and their amulets are filled with pictures of the eyes of the Persons of the Trinity, which they expect to protect them from its influence. According to a legend our Lord and His disciples when walking by the sea of TIBERIAS saw the figure of an old woman sitting on a filthy seat. Her appearance was frightful and terrifying. Her eyes glittered like gold, and her hands and her feet were like wheels, and flames of fire sixty-eight cubits long went forth from her mouth. The disciples said : " What is this thing, O Lord " ? And our Lord said unto them : " This is the eye of earth, evil and accursed. When its glance falls upon a ship sailing on the sea, that ship sinks suddenly ; when it pursues a horse, it casts down that horse and its rider ; when it looks upon a cow that is being milked, it curdles the milk, which turns into blood ; when it looks upon a woman with her child, it separates them and destroys them." And the disciples took this eye of earth, evil and accursed, and burnt her body in the fire, and scattered the ashes to the winds—east, west, south and north—so that the memorial of her might be blotted out from the earth. One form of the legend says that Christ uttered the two words " Asparapses ! Askôrâskîs ! " and that it was they that slew 'Âynat. After that the burning of her body was a simple matter (BUDGE, *History of Ethiopia*, vol. ii. p. 592).

The Greeks believed in the existence of the Evil Eye and their word for it is BÁSKANOS (βάσκανος) and the amulet to be used against it is PROBASKÁNION (προβασκάνιον). All the ancient authorities, C. FROM-MAUND, N. VALLETTA, POTTER, and others say that the Latin word *fascinatio* is derived from Báskanos. This also is the view of the late Bishop LIGHTFOOT (*Epistle to the Galatians*, p. 133 f.). Among the Greek writers who have discussed and attempted to explain the Evil Eye may be mentioned HELIO-DORUS, who flourished early in the IIIrd century after Christ and says : " When one looks at what is excellent with an envious eye he fills the surround-ing atmosphere with a pernicious quality, and transmits his own envenomed exhalations into what-ever is nearest to him " (*Thea.* i. 140).

The belief in the Evil Eye has existed in every country of EUROPE and still exists. In GERMANY it is called *übel ougen* or *böse Blick ;* in HOLLAND, *booze blik ;* in POLAND, *zte oko ;* in ITALY, *oculi maligni, mal' occhio,* and *jettatura ;* in SARDINIA, *ogu malu ;* in CORSICA, *innocchiatura ;* in SPAIN, *mal de ojo ;* in FRANCE, *mauvais œil* or *mauvais regard ;* in NORWAY, *skjoertunge ;* in DENMARK, *et ondt öje ;* in ENGLAND, *evil eye ;* in IRELAND, *droch-shuil. bad eye, ill eye ;* in SCOTLAND, *ill Ee.* In SYRIA it was, and still is, called *'aina bîshâ ;* in PERSIA, *aghashi ;* in ARMENIA, *paterak ;* in the VEDAS, *ghoram caksuh ;* in HUNGARY, *szemverés ;* in CHINA, *ok ngan* or *ok, sihi,* and the belief in the Evil Eye is common in SIAM, BURMAH, TIBET, KOREA, MALAY, MALACCA, SUMATRA, TAHITI, SAMOA, GREENLAND, ALASKA, NICARAGUA, MEXICO, BRITISH GUIANA, BRAZIL, PERU, the lands of the BANTU peoples, and the BUSHMEN and PYGMIES, parts of AUSTRALIA and NEW GUINEA. The facts given in the last paragraph are derived from *Die Zauberkraft des Auges,* Hamburg, 1922, by Dr. SELIGMANN. This learned authority shows that the peoples who have no special word for the Evil Eye make use of a number of words which convey the idea of *fascination,* and thus show that they were, and still are, well acquainted with the baleful operations of the Evil Eye.

In all ages man has believed that certain of his fellow-creatures possessed the Evil Eye, and as he made his gods in his own image he attributed to them, and to supernatural beings of all classes, the power to work evil upon him and his works by their looks whenever their envy or jealousy was aroused. Among all the early races of mankind the view that envy and jealousy and the Evil Eye were one and the same thing. Concerning the Hebrew God YHWH we read : " They provoked him to jealousy with strange [gods] ; with abominations provoked they him to anger " (Deut. xxxii. 16 ; 1 Kings xiv. 22). And when David in his pride took a census of his people YHWH sent a plague which destroyed 70,000 of the 1,300,000 men of Israel and Judah (2 Sam. chap. xxiv.). In Egyptian we find that the EYE OF HORUS, which gave life to OSIRIS, is called " Slaughterer of the enemies of Horus." And Plutarch tells us (*De Iside*, cap. xvii.) that ISIS killed the son of the King of BYBLOS by a glance of her eye. And several of the Forty-two Assessors in the Hall of Judgment of Osiris had names which show that they could kill with their eyes and the fire which came from them, *e.g.* Àriti-f-em-ṭes, " Eyes like flint knives," and Ḥepti-she, "Embracer of Fire." And it has been generally assumed throughout the world that every kind of evil spirit possesses the Evil Eye.

Certain passages in the Bible suggest that some of the men described therein were believed to possess the Evil Eye. Thus in the case of SAUL we read, " and SAUL eyed (*'ôyên*) David from that day and forward " (1 Sam. xviii. 9), and it is impossible to think that the king looked upon the young warrior with kindly feelings. And though BALAAM exclaimed : " How goodly are thy texts, O Jacob, and thy tabernacles, O Israel " (Num. xxiv. 5), it is tolerably clear that the words did not express his inner feelings. Coming down to our own times Dr. SELIGMANN mentions a number of distinguished men who were credited with the possession of the

Evil Eye. The most famous and most feared " jettatore " in Rome was His Holiness Pope Pius IX (died 1878). The aged Pope LEO XIII was held to be a " jettatore " because of the great number of the cardinals who died during his pontificate. The Italians always believed LORD BYRON and the Kaiser William II to be endowed with the Evil Eye. And the same view has been held concerning NAPOLEON III.

CHAPTER XXI.

ḲABBÂLÂH.

The word Ḳabbâlâh is mentioned frequently in books which describe amulets, charms, and talismans, but it is important to make it clear to the reader that among the early Ḳabbalists the use of magical stones and spells was unknown. The word Ḳabbâlâh means διαδοχή, and denotes TRA-DITION (παράδοδις) regarded from the point of view of RECEPTION, *i.e.* Ḳabbâlâh is something which has been handed down and is RECEIVED generally (C. TAYLOR, *Sayings of the Jewish Fathers*, Cambridge, 1877, p. 120). At first Ḳabbâlâh was understood to refer to the teaching of the Tôrâh, *i.e.* the Pentateuch, or Five Books of Moses. Later the other Books of the Bible were joined to these, and Ḳabbâlâh was regarded as the exposition of a great secret, and mystical and religious system of philosophy, which was supposed to deal with and explain the creation of the heavens and the earth, and the dealings of God with the human race. The names of the founders of Ḳabbâlâh and the date when they lived are unknown, but they were certainly mystics, and they were, in the writer's opinion, Semites, probably Hebrews who were, and they still are, great idealists. The foundations of Ḳabbâlâh are very ancient, and they were laid by men who believed that, by means of the system which they were putting together, they could bring themselves into a special relationship with God, and make Him protect them against every calamity and misfortune which can

come upon man. The Ḳabbâlâh of the Middle Ages
represents a mass of beliefs and traditions which the
Hebrews adopted from the Egyptians, Babylonians
and Assyrians, Syrians, Zoroastrians, Gnostics,
Greeks, Arabs, and even European peoples. And,
whilst readily accepting new beliefs and theories
they abandoned nothing.

Dr. Ginsburg's summary may be quoted as giving
the root of the matter : " The cardinal doctrines
of the Ḳabbâlâh are mainly designed to solve the
grand problems about—I. The nature of the Supreme
Being. II. The cosmogony. III. The creation
of angels and men. IV. The destiny of man and
the universe. V. To point out the import of the
Revealed Law, and assenting and consenting to
the declarations of the Hebrew Scriptures about the
UNITY of GOD (Exod. xx. 3 ; Deut. iv. 35, 39 ; vi. 4 ;
xxxii. 39). His INCORPOREITY (Exod. xx. 4 ; Deut.
iv. 15 ; Ps. xiv. 18. ; His ETERNITY (Exod. iii. 14 ;
Deut. xxxii. 40 ; Isaiah xli. 4 ; xliii. 10 ; xliv. 6 ;
xlviii. 12). His IMMUTABILITY (Mal. iii. 6). His
PERFECTION (Deut. xxxii. 4 ; 2 Sam. xxii. 31 ; Job
xxxviii. 16 ; Ps. xviii. 31). His INFINITE GOOD-
NESS (Exod. xxvi. 9 ; Ps. xxv. 16 ; xxxiii. 5 ; c. 5 ;
cxlv. 9), the CREATION OF THE WORLD in time
according to God's free will (Gen. i. 1) ; the moral
government of the universe and special providences ;
and to the creation of man in the image of God
(Gen. i. 27). The Ḳabbâlâh seeks to explain the
transition from the infinite to the finite ; the pro-
cedure of multifariousness from an absolute unity,
and of matter from a pure intelligence ; the operation of pure intelligence upon matter, in spite of
the infinite gulf between them ; the relationship of

the Creator to the creature, so as to be able to exercise supervision and providence ; how the Bible gives names and assigns attributes and a form to so spirited a Being ; how the existence of evil is compatible with the infinite goodness of God, and what is the Divine intention about the creation " (*The Ḳabbâlâh*, p. 86).

Among the things which the Ḳabbalists borrowed from the Gentiles was the use of amulets, charms, and talismans, although several of their Rabbis denounced their use, and proclaimed them to be vain and impotent things. A work like the present volume is no place in which to attempt to give a description of the philosophy and doctrines of the Ḳabbâlâh as a whole, and it will be impossible for anyone to do this until the original Hebrew texts, which, as Dr. Gaster says, exist chiefly in manuscript and are unprinted, have been published with commentaries by competent Hebrew scholars. The following paragraphs are only intended to give the general reader an idea of the way in which the older Rabbis and their successors employed letters and numbers as a means of interpretation. This will be readily understood when the reader remembers that the Hebrews possessed no numerical signs before the Christian era, and that they were obliged to use the letters of their alphabet as numbers. An interesting account of the permutations and combination of letters and numbers will be found in GINSBURG, C., *The Ḳabbâlâh*, London, 1865. Those who wish to study the original Hebrew texts should consult the SÊFER YĔṢÎRÂ, the text edited with a translation by M. GROSSBERG, London, 1902. This is the oldest of the Ḳabbalistic books, and is thought to have

been written about A.D. 600, but it is tolerably
certain that the substance of it was in existence
several centuries earlier. The sections of it which
deal with the permutations of numbers should be
read with the BOOK of RÂZÎÊL. This angel was
believed to have been instructed in Kabbâlâh by
God Himself. The most interesting and, perhaps,
the most important book of the Kabbalists is the
great collection of commentaries, written in Aramean,
and generally known as SÊFER ZÔHAR, *i.e.* the
" Book of Splendour." To all intents and purposes it is the foundation of Kabbâlâh from the
XIVth century onwards. Translations of extracts
from it have been given in many books, and a
French translation by PAULY, *Le Livre des Splen-
deurs*, appeared at Paris in 1894. For the literary
history of the work see GASTER's article in HASTINGS'
Encyclopaedia, vol. xii. p. 858.

On the Kabbâlâh generally see ROSENROTH,
Kabbala Denudata, Sulzbach, 1677 ; FRANCK, *La
Kabbala*, Paris, 1889 ; WAITE, *Doctrine and
Literature of the Kabbalah*, London, 1902 ; and the
important article in the *Jewish Encyclopaedia*.

The following paragraphs, which deal with the
names of God, the angels and fiends, the planets
and their influences on men and on human affairs,
magical squares, etc., all belong to what is commonly
known as " practical Kabbâlâh." The diagram of
the so-called " Kabbalistic Tree," which represents
the arrangement of the Ten Sephîrôth or " Spheres,"
strictly speaking belongs to " theoretical Kabbâlâh,"
but it is so often referred to in books that it is
necessary to reproduce it here from Ginsburg's
work (p. 100). The Spheres are a development of

the Theory of Emanations, which was probably borrowed partly from the Gnostics and partly from the Neo-Platonists. The Ḳabbalists used a great many kinds of amulets, inscribed and uninscribed, some to ward off the Evil Eye, others to protect and preserve them from calamities and give them success in business. But to all intents and purposes the Ḳabbalists were as superstitious as the Gentiles, whether pagan or Christian. Some account of their amulets will be found in the section dealing with Hebrew Amulets.

In the drawing here reproduced (see page 371) we have a representation of the so-called " Ḳabbalistic Tree." At the top are the words " EN SÔPH," which mean something like the " great original, everlasting First Cause of Causes." Below are the TEN SEPHÎRÔTH (SPHERES) or EMANATIONS from this Cause, which are connected by channels and form one complete whole which is permeated by the might of God. The Emanations are called :—

1. KETHER, *i.e.* the Crown, or Supreme Emanation.

    (DA'ATH), *i.e.* the link between Wisdom and Understanding.

2. CHOCHMAH = Wisdom (theoretical).

3. BÎNÂH = Understanding (practical).

4. GEDULLAH = Greatness = Love, Mercy, Pity (Var. ḤESED = Mercy).

5. GEBHÛRAH = Strength (Var. PAḤAD = Justice).

6. TIPHERETH = Majesty, Sovereignty, Beauty.

7. NESAKH = Conquest, Victory, Permanence.

8. HÔD = Fame, Glory, Spendour.

9. YESÔD = Foundation, Base.

10. MALKÛTH = Kingship, Kingdom.

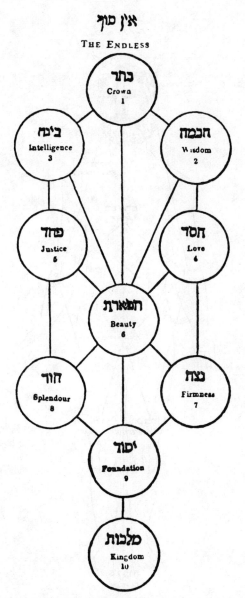

The Ḳabbalistic Tree.

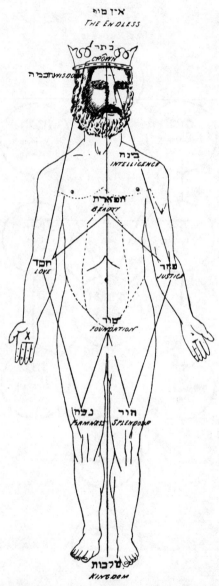

Drawing of the Archetypal or Perfect Man of the Ḳabbalists, showing the seats of the influences of the Ten Sephîrôth in his body.

The Ten Names of God which correspond with the Ten Sephîrôth are :—1. Ehyeh (Exod. iii. 14). 2. YH (YÂH). 3. Jehovah (YHWH) (Isa. xxvi. 4). 4. Êl, the Mighty One. 5. Eloah. 6. Elohîm. 7. Jehovah Ṣabâôth. 8. Elohîm Ṣabâôth. 9. Êl Ḥayy, the Mighty Living One. 10. Adônây, the Lord.

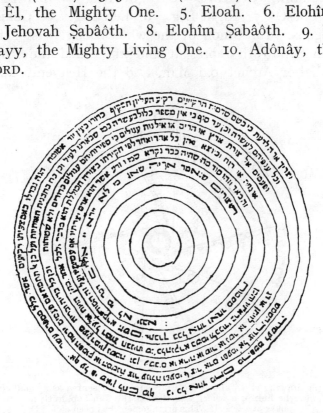

The Ten Sephîrôth arranged in ten concentric circles. (From the edition of the *Book of Yeṣîrâh*, published at Mantua in 1562.)

The Ten Classes of Angels which correspond to the Ten Sephîrôth are :—1. Ḥayyôth, ζῶον. 2. Ophannîm, κίνησις. 3. Arêlîm (Isa. xxxiii. 7). 4. Ḥashmâlîm (Ezek. i. 4). 5. Serâphîm (Isa. vi. 6). 6. Shinanîm. 7. Tarshîshîm (Dan. x. 6). 8. Sons of God (Gen. vi. 4). 9. Îshîm (Ps. civ. 4). 10. Cherûbîm.

The TEN MEMBERS of the human body which
correspond to the Ten Sephîrôth are :—1. Head.
2. Brain. 3. Heart. 4. Right Arm. 5. Left Arm.
6. Chest. 7. Right Leg. 8. Left Leg. 9. Genital
Organs. 10. Union of the whole Body. Thus the
Ten Sephîrôth represent and are called the Prim-
ordial or Archetypal Man, and the Heavenly Man.
See page 372.

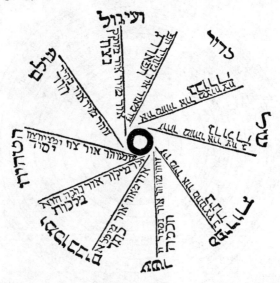

In the drawing given above the EN SÔPH is represented as a small circle,
like the hub of a wheel, and from it the Ten Sephîrôth radiate like
the spokes of a wheel. This arrangement has been called the " Sephîrôth Star " and the " Sephîrôth Wheel." (From BARON VON ROSEN-
ROTH, *Kabbala Denudata*, Sulzbach, 1677.)

In the BOOK OF YEṢÎRÂ En Sôph is represented
as a circle, and the Ten Sephîrôth are arranged
round it in concentric circles. A drawing of this
arrangement is given in the *editio princeps* and is
reproduced above.

Each of the Sephîrôth has a divine name, viz.:
1. EHEYEH (Exod. iii. 14). 2. YAH (Isa. xxvi. 4).

3. YHWH. 4. EL. 5. ELOAH. 6. ELOHÎM. 7. YHWH ṢEBÂÔTH. 8. ELOHE ṢEBÂÔTH. 9. EL-KHÂYY. 10. ADÔNÂI. The first Sephîrah is a heaven of fire; the second is the "first motion"; the third is the Firmament or the Zodiac; the fourth is Saturn; the fifth is Jupiter; the sixth is Mars or the Sun; the seventh is the Sun or Mars; the eighth is Venus; the ninth is Mercury; the tenth is the Moon.

According to Ḳabbâlâh the Great Name of God is God Himself.

The Four Angels who direct the FOUR HEAVENS are:—MICHAEL, RAPHAEL, GABRIEL and URIEL.

The Seven Angels who rule the earth are:—URIEL, RAPHAEL, RAGUEL, MICHAEL, SURIEL, GABRIEL and YERACHMÎ'EL; these appear to have been identified with the seven planets of the Babylonians.

The PRINCES over the powers of Nature, according to the old Rabbis, are:—MICHAEL (snow), GABRIEL (fire), YORKAMI (hail), RACHAB (the sea), RIDJAH (rain), and BEN NEZ (wind). According to the later Rabbis they are:—GALGALIEL (the solar disk), OPHANIEL (the lunar disk), KOCHBIEL (darkness), REHATIEL (the planets), SHAMSHIEL (daylight), LAYLAHEL (night), BARADIEL (hail), BARAKIEL (lightning), MATHARIEL (rain), SHALGIEL (snow), RUCHIEL (wind), SA'AMIEL (storm), SIKIEL (sirocco), SAWAEL (whirlwind), SA'APHIEL (hurricane), RA'AMIEL (thunder), and RA'ASHIEL (earthquake).

The Underworld was peopled by Orders of evil spirits similar in number to the Sephîrôth, but besides these Ḳabbâlâh taught that the air round about was peopled with spirits. In Mark v. 9, they are called "Legion," because they are so many.

They fly about in the air of this world like birds, and they discharge their arrows of evil at us as they please. Their precise dwelling-place is the space

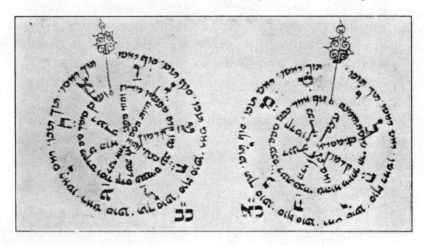

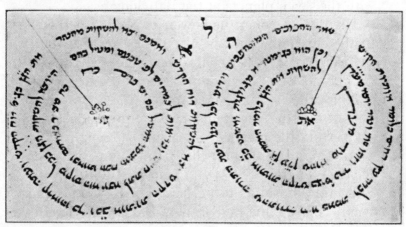

Specimen of the magical Letter-wheels and Circles which are found in Kabbalistic Manuscripts (The above are reproduced from Brit. Mus. Oriental, No. 4596, which is described in Margoliouth, *Catalogue of Hebrew MSS.*, London, 1909.)

between the clouds of heaven and surface of the earth. Compare Eph. vi. 11 and 22. The demons called by the Rabbis SHEDÎM are chiefly fallen angels and their offspring, which their intercourse with men has produced. They have wings and fly about and have a knowledge of the future. Among them must be reckoned ASHMEDAY (ASMODIUS) and LÎLÎTH, who according to the Rabbis was ADAM'S first she-devil wife. The demons called MASSIKÎM are evilly disposed and seek to destroy ; they are the causes of sicknesses and diseases. Another group of demons is called RUCHÎM or (fem.) RUCHÔTH, and many of them appear to be the souls of dead men.

Ḳabbâlâh treats of the names of God at great length. The greatest of all His names is YHWH (יהוה), the so-called TETRAGAMMATON, which is sometimes confounded with the " Shêm hammit-phôrâsh," *i.e.* " the Name which is separate or, to be distinguished from every other name " (see Buxtorf, *Lexicon, s.v.*). The pronunciation of the name YHWH is unknown, but it is vocalized by adding to it the vowels of the word for " Lord," *i.e.* ADÔNÂY ; hence the form of the name " Jehovah " in our Bibles.

The title " Shêm Hammitphôrâsh " is applied to three other Names of God, which are often used instead of the unpronounceable Name of four letters (consonants) YHWH. These Names contain Twelve, Forty-two, and Seventy-two letters (consonants) respectively.

The Name composed of TWELVE LETTERS (consonants) is formed of the names of the first three Sephîrôth and reads :—

KTRḤḤMHTBWNH.

A variant form of the Name is ḤḤMHTBWNHD'AT which omits KTR and adds D'AT.

The Name composed of FORTY-TWO LETTERS (consonants) contains the names of all the Sephîrôth and reads :—

KTRḤḤMHTBWNHGDWLHTPERT
GBWRHNSḤYSODHODMLKWT

This Name was believed to possess great mystical and magical power.

The first part of the name of SEVENTY-TWO letters consists of the Name of Forty-two letters ; preceded by the letters AYNSOP (Ên Sôph), and the last part is formed of the consonants of the Hebrew word KDOS repeated thrice, " Holy, Holy, Holy," and of the Hebrew words KONHṠMIMWARṢ, *i.e.* possessor of heaven and earth " (Gen. xiv. 19). Thus the name of Seventy-two letters reads :—

AYNSOPKTRḤḤMHTBWNHGDWLHT
PERTGBWRHNSḤYSODHODMLKWT
KDOŠKDOŠKDOŠKONHŠMIMWARS

It is said traditionally that it was by this Name that God brought the Israelites out of Egypt. Another tradition says that God brought Israel out of Egypt by means of a Name which consisted of Seventy-two Names. These, according to Dr. Bischoff, are :—

1-10   WHW·YLY·SYT·'LM·MḤŠ·LLH·'K'·KHT·
        HSY·'LD·
11-20   L'W·HH'·YSL·MBH·HRY·HKM·L'W·KLY·
        LWW·PHL·
21-30   NLK·YYY·MLH·HHW·NTH·H''·YRT·Š'H·
        RYY·'WM·
31-40   LKB·WŠR·YHW·LHḤ·KWK·MND·'NY·H'M·
        RH'·YYS·
41-50   HHH·MYK·WWL·YLH·S'L·'RY·'ŠL·MYH·
        WHW·DNY·
51-60   HḤŠ·'MM·NN'·NYT·MBH·PWY·NMM·YYL·
        HRḤ·MSR·
61-70   WMB·YHH·'NW·MḤY·DMB·MNK·'Y'·ḤBW·
        R'H·YBM·
71-72   HYY·MWM·

(For the Hebrew letters see GINSBURG, *Ḳabbâlâh*, p. 136.)

The form of the Name of Seventy-two names given above was probably composed during the Middle Ages, but it seems to be based upon a very ancient form which was evolved by the early Hebrew theologians who deduced it from various passages in the Pentateuch, which they manipulated in the manner with which we are familiar from the later Ḳabbalistic writings. On the other hand, the 72-named Name may have been invented by the Ḳabbalists, who were skilled in dealing with permutations of letters and their numerical values.

The great Name of God, YHWH, commonly called the Tetragammaton, which was never pronounced and only written, was associated with the Twelve Tribes of Israel, the Twelve Signs of the Zodiac, and the Twelve months of the year, which were divided into four groups of three names each and arranged under the four letters YHWH respectively. Thus we have :—

Letter.	Tribe.	Zodiacal Sign.	Month.
Y	Judah.	Ram.	Nisan.
	Issachar.	Bull.	Iyyar.
	Zebulon.	Twins.	Sivan.
H	Reuben.	Crab.	Tammuz.
	Simeon.	Lion.	Ab.
	Gad.	Virgin.	Elul.
W	Ephraim.	Scales.	Tishri.
	Manasseh.	Scorpion.	Marchesvan
	Benjamin.	Sagittarius.	Chislev.
H	Dan.	Capricornus.	Tebeth.
	Asher.	Aquarius.	Shebat.
	Naphtali.	Pisces.	Adar.

CHAPTER XXII.

ASTROLOGY.

From the earliest times men have firmly believed that the stars exerted controlling influences on themselves and their affairs, and in every age they have tried to find out what those influences were and how and by what means they are exercised. As far as we know the earliest astrologers were Asiatics, and among these the Sumerians and Babylonians occupied an important place. The Ḳabbalists made a system of Astrology of their own, but judging by the evidence now available, the foundations of their science were of Babylonian origin. The starry Rulers of their system were the SEVEN ASTROLOGICAL PLANETS which " ruled " the twenty-four hours of the day, and the seven days of the week, and the twelve months of the year, and the years, and the cycles of years. The Seven Astrological Planets, the sun being included and the earth omitted, were represented thus

The SUN by a circle and point ⊙.

SATURN by a cross with a half of the line circle attached ♄.

MOON by a crescent of the waxing moon ☽.

MARS by the solar disk and a ray ♂.

VENUS by a cross surmounted by the solar disk ♀.

MERCURY by the symbol of Venus with a pair of horns attached ☿.

JUPITER by three solar disks united in a mystic figure, which is supposed to represent fire and aether ♃ or ♃.

The following table, which was compiled by Dr. Bischoff, shows how the planets rule the hours of the day and night on each day of the week. It begins with zero on Sunday evening.

DAYS OF THE WEEK.

			S.	M.	T.	W.	TH.	F.	S.
1	6-7	evening	☉	☽	♂	☿	♃	♀	♄
2	7-8	,,	♀	♄	☉	☽	♂	☿	♃
3	8-9	,,	☿	♃	♀	♄	☉	☽	♂
4	9-10	,,	☽	♂	☿	♃	♀	♄	☉
5	10-11	,,	♄	☉	☽	♂	☿	♃	♀
6	11-12	,,	♃	♀	♄	☉	☽	♂	☿
7	12-1	night	♂	☿	♃	♀	♄	☉	☽
8	1-2	,,	☉	☽	♂	☿	♃	♀	♄
9	2-3	,,	♀	♄	☉	☽	♂	☿	♃
10	3-4	,,	☿	♃	♀	♄	☉	☽	♂
11	4-5	,,	☽	♂	☿	♃	♀	♄	☉
12	5-6	,,	♄	☉	☽	♂	☿	♃	♀
13	0-7	forenoon	♃	♀	♄	☉	☽	♂	☿
14	7-8	,,	♂	☿	♃	♀	♄	☉	☽
15	8-9	,,	☉	☽	♂	☿	♃	♀	♄
16	9-10	,,	♀	♄	☉	☽	♂	☿	♃
17	10-11	,,	☿	♃	♀	♄	☉	☽	♂
18	11-12	,,	☽	♂	☿	♃	♀	♄	☉
19	12-1	afternoon	♄	☉	☽	♂	☿	♃	♀
20	1-2	,,	♃	♀	♄	☉	☽	♂	☿
21	2-3	,,	♂	☿	♃	♀	♄	☉	☽
22	3-4	,,	☉	☽	♂	☿	♃	♀	♄
23	4-5	,,	♀	♄	☉	☽	♂	☿	♃
24	5-6	,,	☿	♃	♀	♄	☉	☽	♂

The Rabbis believed that the character and physical characteristics of a man were influenced by the planets which " ruled " the hour and the day during which he was born. The man born when the SUN " ruled " the hour acquired fame and honour, riches, independence, and absolute freedom of thought and action. He would possess naturally wisdom, sagacity and shrewdness, clear judgment, dexterity and eloquence of speech ; he would be magnanimous, and possess a noble pride and ardour of disposition, and he would find favour in the sight of great men.

The influence of VENUS gave a man riches, great ability, a lovable and loving disposition the love of beauty and Art, amiability towards his fellow-men, proneness to confide in people and credulity ; on the other hand he would have little strength to fight against Fate and resist temptation, and be frivolous, vain, pleasure-loving, unmoral, impetuous but irresolute.

The influence of MERCURY gave a man a fine memory, skill in writing, readiness and capability in dealing with the various circumstances of life, artistic and scientific ability, eagerness, capriciousness, dependence on the opinions of others, and proneness to consider immediate results more than lasting effects.

The influence of the MOON produced much variety in the affairs of a man and in his characteristics, causing both success and failure. Usually his domestic relationships are happy. It makes a man rather a dreamer than a worker, religious, kindly, considerate, communicative, but yet secretive, industrious and persevering, but also capricious.

The influence of SATURN produces slowness and heaviness of disposition, and the habit of pondering deeply on affairs, and of forming numerous plans and schemes, the results of which are usually un-important. It makes a man learned, energetic, hard-working, and trustworthy, and increases his dignity, and enables him to attain success ultimately.

The influence of JUPITER makes a man honest, and gives him a deep and strong moral sense. It gives him great prudence and makes him reserved and sometimes suspicious of his fellow-men. It gives him great mental energy and strength of will and character, and great ambition, and leads him to results which are usually satisfactory, but which do not always bring happiness to him.

The influence of MARS incites a man to do mighty deeds, and to perform works of valour which often terminate in the shedding of blood. It makes him reckless, and gives him an iron will and a bellicose disposition, and prompts him to do deeds of violence and to commit sins, but it often drives him on to victory. It frequently destroys in a man the benign influences which the other planets have had upon him.

If the hour and day of a man's birth be ruled by the same planet, the influence of the planet on his physical and mental attributes is greatly strengthened.

The seven astrological planets travel through the regions or " houses " of the Twelve Signs of the Zodiac, and they rule the Signs just as they rule the days of the week. The Sun rules the house of the Lion, and the Moon the house of the Crab. Mercury rules the houses of the Twins and the Virgin ; Venus the houses of the Bull and the Scales ; Mars the houses of the Ram and the Scorpion ; Jupiter the houses of the Fishes and Sagittarius ; and Saturn the houses of the Water-bearer and Capricornus. Each of the Twelve Signs of the Zodiac corresponds with one of the Twelve Months. The Ḳabbalistic astrologers did not reckon by the lunar, but by the solar, year, which they assumed roughly to consist of 365 days.

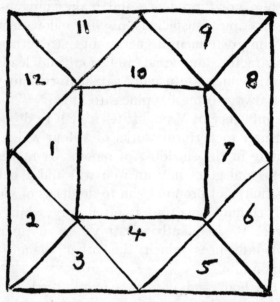

THE TWELVE " HOUSES OF HEAVEN."

 1. The House of Life.
 2. The House of Wealth.
 3. The House of Brethren.
 4. The House of Kinsfolk
        (Relatives).
 5. The House of Children.
 6. The House of Slaves.

 7. The House of Marriage.
 8. The House of Death.
 9. The House of Charity.
10. The House of Glory (Honour).
11. The House of Peace
        (Happiness).
12. The House of Hatred.

The Rabbis divided the heavens for astrological purposes into twelve " houses," which the Ḳabbalists of the Middle Ages placed in the positions shown in the accompanying diagram.

The Rabbis believed that God created seven worlds, and that these occupied the upper half of the universe, which, as we see from the drawing below, was circular ; the lower half formed " Okeanos," the World Ocean. This drawing is reproduced from the Book of the Angel Râzîêl—a comparatively late work—but it represents the views of the Rabbis of the early centuries of our era, and is clearly based upon ancient Babylonian statements or drawings, and perhaps upon both. The first or

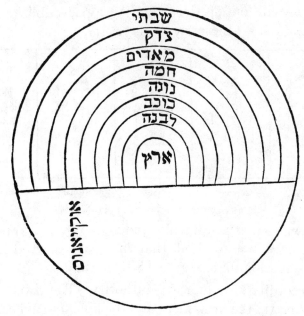

The Seven Worlds, the Earth and the World-Ocean.

lowest semicircle represents the Earth, and above it are the Seven Worlds, viz., the world of the Moon ; the world of Mercury ; the world of Venus ; the world of the Sun ; the world of Mars ; the world of Jupiter ; and the world of Saturn.

In the astrological system of the Ḳabbalist the Signs of the Zodiac were nearly as important as the Seven Astrological Stars or Planets, and in the

Book of Râzîêl they are represented as a series of twelve circles which overlap. In each circle the name of the Sign is given in Hebrew, the translation of the names being made from the Greek or Latin (see p. 387). As will be seen later each Sign of the Zodiac has its special symbol, but the Ḳabbalists and others drew up a series of symbols for other stars. A selection of these is given here from the quarto edition of Cornelius Agrippa, published in 1531. When these symbols were invented is not

| Venus. | Mercury. | Mars. | Saturn. | Jupiter. |

The Egyptian Gods of the Five Planets.

known, but it is difficult, judging by their appearance only, not to think that they were derived from the signs for these stars in Sumerian.

According to another authority (The BOOK OF ARB'AT'AL) the firmament and the kingdom of heaven wherein the various hosts of spirits live is divided into 196 provinces or districts which are ruled over by seven supreme angels, each of whom was served by subordinate officials and servants. Each angel had a seal or symbol which the Ḳabbalists and magicians wrote on amulets and used in working magic, and they are reproduced on p. 389, Nos. 1-7.

ARATRON, the first Angel, ruled 49 Provinces. He could change beasts or vegetables into stones, and transmute metals, and possessed all the powers and knowledge which his transcendental knowledge of magic gave him. He ruled 49 Kings, 42 Princes, 35 Satraps, 28 Dukes, 21 servants, 14 councillors, and 7 envoys, and he commanded 36,000 legions of spirits, each legion containing 490 beings.

BETHOR, the second Angel, ruled over 42 Provinces. He possessed the powers and attributes of

The Circles of the Signs of the Zodiac, according to the Book of Râziêl. The names are to be read from right to left : Group I. Ram, Bull, Twins, Crab. Group II. Lion, Virgin, Balance, Scorpion. Group III. Sagittarius, Capricornus, Aquarius, Pisces.

Jupiter. He ruled 42 Kings, 35 Princes 28 Dukes, 21 councillors 14 servants, seven envoys, and 29,000 legions of spirits.

PHALEG, the third Angel, was the War lord. He ruled over 35 Provinces.

OCH, the fourth Angel, presided over solar matters. He was famous for his wisdom, and perfected the science of medicine, and could change everything into gold and precious stones. He commanded

36,536 legions of spirits, and they all served him. He ruled over 28 Provinces.

HAGITH, the fifth Angel, ruled over all matters which were connected with Venus. He could transmute gold into copper, and copper into gold. He commanded 4,000 legions of spirits. He ruled over 21 Provinces.

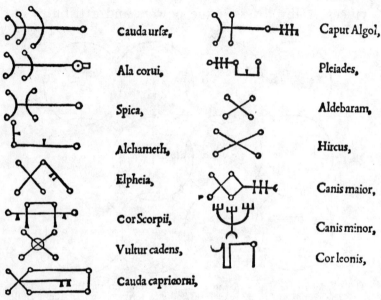

Symbols of stars and constellations in use by the Kabbalists according to Cornelius Agrippa.

OPHIEL, the sixth Angel, dealt with everything which related to Mercury. He could transmute quicksilver into a white stone. He ruled over 14 Provinces and he commanded 100,000 legions of spirits.

PHUL, the seventh Angel, ruled over 7 Provinces, and directed everything which appertained to the Moon. He could transmute anything and everything into silver, and cure dropsy, and destroy the [evil] spirits of the water.

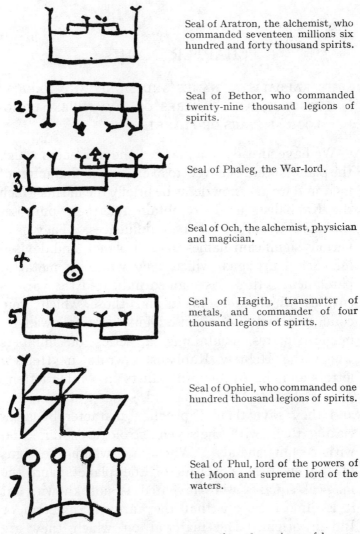

Seal of Aratron, the alchemist, who commanded seventeen millions six hundred and forty thousand spirits.

Seal of Bethor, who commanded twenty-nine thousand legions of spirits.

Seal of Phaleg, the War-lord.

Seal of Och, the alchemist, physician and magician.

Seal of Hagith, transmuter of metals, and commander of four thousand legions of spirits.

Seal of Ophiel, who commanded one hundred thousand legions of spirits.

Seal of Phul, lord of the powers of the Moon and supreme lord of the waters.

The Seals of the Seven Angels who rule over the 196 provinces of heaven. (From the collection of ancient magical books published in the German edition of Cornelius Agrippa's works, IVth edition, vol. v., Berlin, 1921, p. 111 f.)

CHAPTER XXIII.

THE ḲABBALISTIC NAMES AND SIGNS, AND MAGICAL FIGURES, AND SQUARES OF THE SEVEN ASTRO-LOGICAL STARS OR PLANETS.

We have already summarized the influences which the planets were believed to exert on the characters of men and we may now describe briefly the means which the Ḳabbalists used to obtain for their purposes the most favourable of these influences. They gave various significant names to each planet, and devised for each four signs, which they wrote on metal or parchment ; these last-named indicated the various entities which were in it and those which were connected with it. These signs were followed by magic squares, containing a series of numbers which the Hebrew Ḳabbalists wrote in Hebrew letters and the Arabic Ḳabbalists in Arabic letters. The Ḳabbalists used magical squares as amulets, and they gave them a peculiar character by associating them with the seven astrological stars, and with certain metals. When and where the signs of the entities or spirits of the planets and the magical squares were invented is not known, but it is almost certain that they are of Sumerian or Indian origin. The material on which they are based in its earliest form is undoubtedly very ancient, though the forms in which we now have both signs and magical squares are not. The Ḳabbalists call the magical square " Ḳâmê'a," which Buxtorf

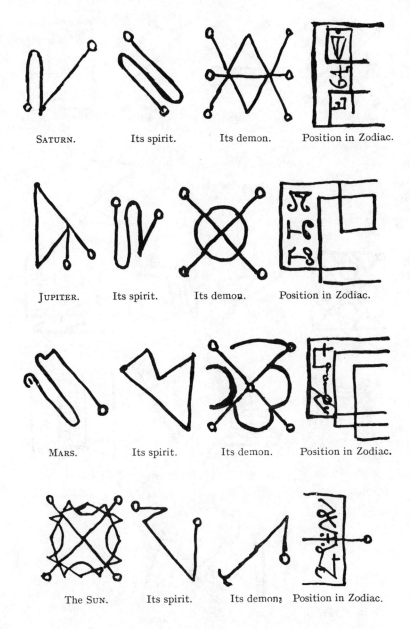

SATURN.   Its spirit.   Its demon.   Position in Zodiac.

JUPITER.   Its spirit.   Its demon.   Position in Zodiac.

MARS.   Its spirit.   Its demon.   Position in Zodiac.

The SUN.   Its spirit.   Its demon.   Position in Zodiac.

THE KABBALISTIC SYMBOLS OF THE ASTROLOGICAL PLANETS AND THEIR
SPIRITS AND DEMONS AND POSITIONS IN THE ZODIAC.

VENUS.   Its spirit.   Its demon.   Position in Zodiac.

In some lists of these symbols
Venus is given a second spirit.

MERCURY.   Its spirit.   Its demon.   Position in Zodiac.

The MOON.   Its spirit.   Its demon.   Position in Zodiac.

The older lists add a second spirit and a second demon, thus :—

Spirit.   Demon.

THE ḲABBALISTIC SYMBOLS OF THE ASTROLOGICAL PLANETS AND THEIR
SPIRITS AND DEMONS AND POSITIONS IN THE ZODIAC.

translates by *pittacium* and *amuletum*, and he says that the Ḳâmê'a was hung on the neck or breast (From Ḳâmê'a comes *caméo* (French and Italian) and our word *cameo*.) The signs and squares for the planets have been published in many books, *e.g.* CORNELIUS AGRIPPA, *Magische Werke*, Bd. II. p. 128 f.; POINSOT, *Encyclopédie des Sciences Occultes*, Paris (no date) ; SEPHARIAL, *The Book of Charms and Talismans*, London (no date), etc.

The forms reproduced on pages 391 and 392 are based upon the work of Dr. E. PAPUS (*Traité de Magie pratique*, Paris). In each set of drawings the first symbol is the sign of the planet itself, the second represents the spirit or intelligence of the planet, the third its demon, and the fourth the position of the planet in the Zodiac, which is indicated by the undecipherable characters which occur within it.

Each planet had several divine names, and each name had its number ; the numbers and names of the spirits of the planets and their demons are as follows :—

Planet.	Spirit.	Demon.
SATURN	'Agîêl (45).	Zâzêl (45).
JUPITER	Yôphîêl (136).	Hasmâêl (136).
MARS ..	Graphîêl (325).	Barṣâbêl (325).
SUN ..	Nakîêl (111).	Sôrath (666).
VENUS..	Hagîêl (49).	Ḳedemèl (175).
MERCURY	Bne Serâphîm (1252).	Taphthartharath (2080).
MOON ..	Malka bethar-shesîm (3321)	1. Sh ê dbarshe-moth Shar-thathan (3321).
		2. Hasmôdây(369)

The Moon has two demons, one subordinate to the other.

The Magical Squares of the seven astrological planets are :—

    1. THE ḲÂMÊ'A of LEAD (SATURN, 3 columns).

4	9	2
3	5	7
8	1	6

ר	ט	ב
ג	ה	ז
ח	א	ו

Whether these nine figures are added up vertically, horizontally or diagonally the total is 15, or in Hebrew letters YH, the shortened form of the Tetragrammaton YHWH. The total of the three columns of figures is 45, *i.e.* the expanded Tetragrammaton . YWD . HA . WAW . HA. When used as an amulet this square was cut upon a sheet of lead.

    2. THE ḲÂMÊ'A of SILVER or TIN (JUPITER, 4 columns).

4	14	15	1
9	7	6	12
5	11	10	8
16	2	3	13

ר	יד	יה	א
ט	ז	ו	יב
ה	יא	י	ח
יו	ב	ג	יג

Whether these sixteen figures are added up vertically. horizontally or diagonally the total is 34, or in Hebrew letters D = 4 and L = 30. These letters form a part of the Hebrew word for *tin*. The total of the four columns of figures is 136, which is the number of the Spirit and of the Demon of the planet. When cut upon coral this square protected the wearer from sorcery.

3. THE K'AMÊ'A of IRON (MARS, 5 columns).

11	24	7	20	3
4	12	25	8	16
17	5	13	21	9
10	18	1	14	22
23	6	19	2	15

יא	כד	ז	כ	ג
ד	יב	כה	ח	יו
יז	ה	יג	כא	ט
י	יה	א	יד	כב
כג	ו	יט	ב	יה

Whether these five times five figures are added up vertically, horizontally or diagonally the total is 65, or in Hebrew letters A = 1, D = 4, N = 50 and Y = 10, *i.e.* 'ADÔNÂY a name of God. The total of the five columns of figures is 325, which is the number of the Spirit and Demon of the planet.

4. THE ḲÂMÊ'A of GOLD (the SUN, 6 columns).

6	32	3	34	35	1
7	11	27	28	8	30
24	14	16	15	23	19
13	20	22	21	17	18
25	29	10	9	26	12
36	5	33	4	2	31

ו	לב	ג	לד	לה	א
ז	יא	כז	כח	ח	ל
יט	יד	יו	יה	כג	כד
יח	כ	כב	כא	יז	יג
כה	כט	י	ט	כו	יב
לו	ה	לג	ד	ב	לא

The total of the addition of these thirty-six figures in each of the three directions is 111, *i.e.* the total of the numerical values of the consonants *zâhâb paz*, "refined gold." The total of the six columns of figures is 666, which is the number of SÔRÂTH, the

Demon of the Sun. A variant square of the Sun as a lion is given by Dr. Bischoff (*op. cit.* p. 146).

5. The Ḳâmê'a of Copper (Venus, 7 columns).

22	47	16	41	10	35	4
5	23	48	17	42	11	29
30	6	24	49	18	36	12
13	21	7	25	43	19	37
38	14	32	1	26	44	30
21	39	8	33	2	27	45
46	15	40	9	34	3	28

כב	מז	יו	מא	י	לה	ר
הֹ כֹג	כג	מח	יז	מב	יא	בט
לֹ ו	ו	כד	מט	יח	יֹחֹ	יב
יֹג	לא	ז	כה	מג	מֹנ	לז
לח	יד	לב	א	לב	מר	כ
כא	לֹט	ח	לג	ב	כז	מה
כח	ג	לד	ט	מ	יה	מו

The total of the addition of these forty-nine figures in each of the three directions is 175, *i.e.* the total of the numerical values of the consonants in *sodh-Mny*, " secret council of the goddess Mĕny " (Venus). The total of the seven columns of figures is 1,225, which is the number of the Spirit or Intelligence of the planet.

6. The Ḳâmê'a of Quicksilver (Mercury, 8 columns).

8	58	59	5	4	62	63	1
49	15	14	52	53	11	10	56
41	23	22	44	45	19	18	48
32	34	35	29	28	38	39	25
40	26	27	37	36	30	31	33
17	47	46	20	21	43	42	24
9	55	54	12	13	51	50	16
64	2	3	61	60	6	7	57

ח	נח	נט	ה	ד	סב	סג	א
מט	יה	יד	נב	נג	יא	י	נו
מא	כג	כב	מד	מה	יט	יח	מח
לב	לד	לה	כט	כח	לח	לט	כה
מ	כו	כז	לז	לו	ל	לא	לג
יז	מז	מו	כ	כא	מג	מב	כד
ט	נה	נד	יב	יג	נא	נ	יו
סד	ב	ג	סא	ס	ו	ז	נז

The total of the addition of these sixty-four figures in each of the three directions is 260, *i.e.*, the total of the numerical values of the consonants in *kokab kesef ḥayyim*, " star of living silver " (*i.e.* quicksilver). The number of ṬÎRÎEL, the spirit of the planet, is 260. The total of the eight columns of figures is 2,080, which is the number of the demon of the planet, TAPHTHÂRTHARATH. As an amulet the square should be written upon a sheet of tin or quicksilver.

7. THE ḴÂMÈ'A OF SILVER (the MOON, 9 columns).

37	78	29	70	21	62	13	54	5
6	38	79	30	71	22	63	14	46
47	7	39	80	31	72	23	55	15
16	48	8	40	81	32	64	24	56
57	17	49	9	41	73	33	65	25
26	58	18	50	1	42	14	34	66
67	27	59	10	51	2	43	75	35
36	68	19	60	11	52	3	44	76
77	28	69	20	61	12	53	4	45

לז	עח	עט	כט	ע	כא	סב	יג	נד	ה
ו	לח	עט	ל	עא	כב	סג	יד	מו
מז	ז	לט	פ	לא	עב	בג	נה	יה
יי	מח	ח	מ	פא	לב	סד	נו	כד
נז	יז	מט	ט	מא	עג	לג	סה	כה
כו	נח	יח	נ	א	מב	עד	לד	סו
סז	כז	נט	י	נא	ב	מג	עה	לה
לו	סח	יט	ס	יא	נב	ג	מד	עו
עז	כח	בח	סט	כ	סא	יב	נג	ד	מה

Note the arithmetical progression in the central diagonal column of each square.

The total of the addition of these eighty-one figures in each of the three directions is 369, *i.e.* the total of the numerical values of the consonants in *ḳeren ha-zâhâb*, " golden horn." The total of the nine columns of figures is 3,321, which is the number of the supreme Intelligence or Spirit of the Moon and also of the demon thereof.

The above symbols of the Moon and Mercury are reproduced from the quarto edition of Cornelius Agrippa's *De occulta philosophia.*
For those of the Sun and the other planets see the opposite page.

According to CORNELIUS AGRIPPA it is necessary to be careful, when using a magical square as an amulet, that it is drawn when the sun, or moon, or the planet is exhibiting a benevolent aspect, for otherwise the amulet will bring misfortune and calamity upon the wearer instead of prosperity and happiness (see Part II. chap. 22).

It has already been said that in the Hebrew texts of the *Kabbâlâh* the numbers given in the magical

CHARACTERES VENERIS.

Ab amißiõe

A puella

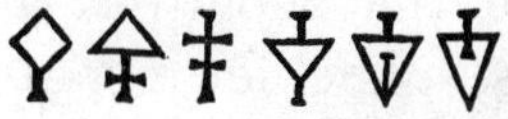

CHARACTERES SOLIS.

A fortuna maiore.

A fortuna minore.

CHARCTERES MARTIS.

A rubeo

A puero

CHARACTERES IOVIS.

Ab acquisitione.

A letitia

CHARACTERES SATVRNI.

A carcere.

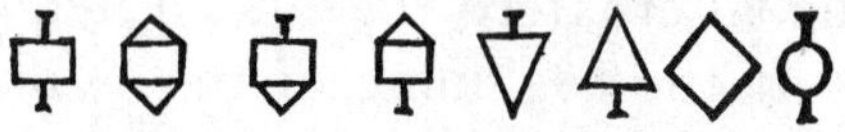

A triftitia

Characteres capitis Draconis.

Characterescaude Draconis.

r ii

squares are expressed by letters of the Hebrew alphabet. These letters are taken from certain verses of the Bible, *e.g.* Exod. xiv. 19–21, which contain the three Pillars of the Sephîrôth and the Divine Name of 72 words. The letters are then arranged in three squares, and from these a fourth square is made which contains the Divine Name of 72 letters (see GINSBURG, *Ḳabbâlâh*, p. 133 f.). The Ḳabbalists made use of a system of dealing with numbers as represented by letters which is called GEMEṬRIA or GRAMMATYÂ = γραμματεία. In this system : I. Every letter of a word is reduced to its numerical value, and the word is explained by another of the same numerical value. II. Every letter of a word is taken as an initial or abbreviation of a word. III. The initial and final letters of several words are respectively formed into separate words. IV. Two words in the same verse may be joined together. V. The letters of words are changed by way of anagram. and new words are obtained by PERMUTA-TION. The alphabet of 22 letters is divided into two equal parts, and one part is put over the other, and by changing alternately the first letter or the first two letters at the beginning of the second line 22 commutations are produced, *e.g.* :—

$$\begin{cases} \text{ABGDHWZHṬYK} \\ \text{LTŠRḲṢP‘ASNM} \end{cases}$$

or

$$\begin{cases} \text{AGDHWZHṬYKL} \\ \text{БT RḲṢP‘ASNM} \end{cases}$$

The first of these anagramic alphabets is called ALBATH, from the first words, and the second ABGATH and so on. As the texts of some Ḳabbalistic and other Hebrew amulets are reproduced in this book, the Hebrew alphabet and the names and numerical values of the letters are here given.

Final form.	Hebrew letter.	Phonetic value.	Hebrew name.	Numerical value.
	א	ʾ	Âleph	1
	ב	B, BH	Bêth	2
	ג	G, GH	Gîmel	3
	ד	D, DH	Dâleth	4
	ה	H	Hê	5
	ו	W	Wâw	6
	ז	Z	Zayin	7
	ח	CH	Chêth	8
	ט	Ṭ	Ṭêth	9
	י	Y	Yôdh	10
ך	כ	K, Kh	Kâph	20
	ל	L	Lâmedh	30
ם	מ	M	Mêm	40
ן	נ	N	Nûn	50
	ס	S	Sâmekh	60
	ע	ʿ	ʿAyin	70
ף	פ	P, PH	Pe	80
ץ	צ	Ṣ	Ṣâdhe	90
	ק	Ḳ or Q	Ḳôph	100
	ר	R	Rêsh	200
	שׂ	S	Sîn ⎫	
	שׁ	SH	Shîn ⎭	300
	ת	T, TH	Tâw	400

THE ḲABBALISTS AND THE HUMAN HAND.

We have already seen how the Ḳabbalists associated the Sephîrôth or Emanations of En Sôph with the various parts of the body of the " Primal " or " Perfect Man " (see page 372), and the following diagram shows which astrological star " rules " each part of the human hand. Venus " rules " the thumb, Mars the palm of the hand, the Moon the heel of the hand, Jupiter the first finger, Saturn the second finger, the Sun the third finger, and Mercury

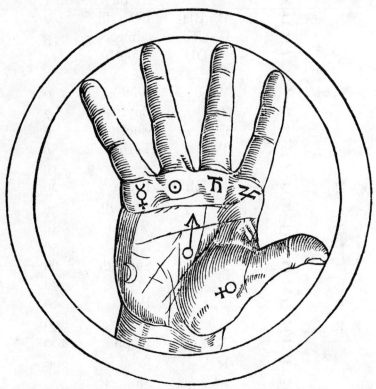

the fourth finger. See Cornelius Agrippa, chap. xxvii. (vol. ii. of the German translation, p. 160, Berlin, 1921).

KABBALISTIC SYSTEMS OF WRITING.

The KABBALISTS adopted certain well-known alphabets, Hebrew, Chaldean, etc., in writing their works, but they modified the forms of the letters and made additions to them, and then they attributed esoteric meanings to them which were known and understood by the initiated only.   It seems too that they assigned additional phonetic values to them. They probably borrowed the idea of doing this from the Egyptians, for already in the XIXth dynasty we find examples of hieroglyphic writing to which the name of " enigmatic " has been given.   Specimens of the Ḳabbalistic alphabets have been given in Cornelius Agrippa (chap. xxix) in discussing the letters and seals of the spirits, and the examples on page 404 are reproduced from his work.   No. 1 is said to have been invented by Honorius, a Theban, and to have been handed down by Peter of Apono.   No. 2 is derived from the old " square " character Hebrew letters with which the Tôrâh is written.   Whether, as Cornelius says, this character was used by Moses and the Prophets is doubtful, for from the analogy of the Stele of Mesha, King of Moab (Moabite Stele), they probably used Phoenician letters.   This writing is called the " Writing of heaven."   The small circles which are attached to the letters have probably a magical signification.   No. 3 is called the " Writing of the Angels " or the " Writing of the Kings," *i.e.* the Royal Script.   No. 4 is the " Writing of the Crossing of the River."   I cannot explain the allusion.

The Ḳabbalists also divided the Hebrew alphabet (the twenty-two letters and the final forms of five of them) into three classes, each containing nine letters.   The first nine represented the numbers 1–9, and the nine divisions of the world which are ruled by nine orders of angels. The second nine represented the numbers 10–90 and

1	A	B	C	D	E	F	G	Ḥ	I	K	L	M

N	O	P	Q	R	S	T	V	X	Y	Z	Ω

Specimens of Ḳabbalistic Scripts.

the things which are in the nine circles of heaven. The third nine contained the four last letters of the alphabet and the final forms of K. M. N. P and Ṣ. The four letters represented the numbers 100–400, and the four elements earth, air, fire, and water, and the five final forms symbolized the five unions of bodies. Each of the three divisions of nine letters was subdivided into three divisions and arranged between lines thus :—

גלש	בכר	איק
וסם	הנך	דמת
מצץ	חפף	זען

From א the lines which enclose the groups of three letters the nine following figures were constructed—

ד ח ר ⊐ ⊏ ⊑ ⅃ ⊔ ∟

The alphabet arranged in this way formed a very powerful amulet.

CHAPTER XXIV.

THE STARS OR SIGNS OF THE ZODIAC AND THEIR
INFLUENCES, THE HOUSES OF HEAVEN AND THE
DEKANS.

The SUMERIANS and BABYLONIANS believed that
the will of the gods in respect to man and his affairs
could be learned by watching the motions of the
stars and planets, and that skilled star-gazers could
obtain from the motions and varying aspects of the
heavenly bodies indications of future prosperity
and calamity. They therefore caused observations
to be made and recorded on tablets, which they
interpreted from a magical and not astronomical
point of view, and these observations and their
comments on them, and interpretations of them,
have formed the foundation of the astrology in
use in the world for the last 5,000 years. According
to ancient traditions preserved by Greek writers,
the Babylonians made these observations for some
hundreds of thousands of years, and though we
must reject such fabulous statements, we are bound
to believe that the period during which observations
of the heavens were made on the plains of Babylonia
comprised many thousands of years. During that
period the star-gazers collected unwittingly a large
number of facts of pure astronomy—and but
for the ban laid upon their work by the all-

powerful magicians, they would have developed into good astronomers. The magician desired the maintenance and extension of his own craft, and the personal benefits which accrued to him therefrom to the unremunerative increase in the scientific knowledge of the heavens.

It is now a well-ascertained fact that during the rule of the kings of the Ist Dynasty of BABYLON the star-gazers were able to calculate astronomical events with considerable accuracy, and " to reconcile the solar and lunar years by the use of epagomenal months." They had learned to distinguish between the planets and the fixed stars, and some think they had recognized the existence of the circumpolar stars which never set. They had assigned " stations " to the moon and planets, and garbled forms of the cuneiform characters which represented them are preserved in the famous *De Occulta Philosophia* of COR-NELIUS AGRIPPA of NETTESHEIM (1486–1535). Whether they were the first to formulate the ZODIAC cannot be said, but they had good knowledge of it.

In the Fifth Tablet of the Creation Series (line 2) the Signs of the Zodiac are mentioned under the name of " Lumashi," and from lines 121 ff. we learn their names, *i.e.* :—

1. UMMU-KHUBUR, *i.e.* TIÂMAT, a female monster and the origin of all evil. She possessed the Tablet of Destiny.

2. KINGU, her husband.

3. The VIPER.

4. The SNAKE.

5. LAKHAMU.

6. The WHIRLWIND.

7. The RAVENING DOG.

8. The SCORPION-MAN.

9. The HURRICANE.

10. The FISH-MAN.

11. The HORNED BEAST (CAPRICORN).

12. The WEAPON (THUNDERBOLT ?).

All these Twelve were powers of evil, and under the leadership of TIÂMAT and KINGU they set to work to defy the great gods who were beginning the work of the Creation, *i.e.* of putting an end to Chaos and Disorder. The god put forward MARDUK, the son of EA, as their champion, and he defeated and destroyed TIÂMAT and her allies and created the heavens and the earth and made man to appear on the earth. He set in heaven the Stars of the Zodiac, which are the likenesses of the great gods, he fixed the year, and divided it into twelve months, to rule over each of which he appointed three stars, and he established the Moon-god. The Signs of the Zodiac set up by MARDUK were different from the old ones, which he had disbanded, and the three stars which he appointed to each month we now know as the THIRTY-SIX DEKANS. The following is a list of the Stars or Signs of the Zodiac taken from the tablet in the British Museum (No. 77821), with a list showing the month that was associated with each star in the Persian Period. For the cuneiform characters see *Babylonian Legends of the Creation*, p. 68 (British Museum).

Month.	Name of Star.	Translation.	Modern Equivalent.
Nisannu ...	Agru ...	The Labourer ...	Goat.
Airu ...	Kakkab u Alap shame	The Star and the Bull of Heaven	Bull.
Simanu ...	Re'u kinu shame u Tu'ame Rabuti	The Faithful Shepherd of Heaven and the Great Twins	Twins.
Duuzu ...	Shittu ...	Tortoise	Crab.
Abu ...	Kalbu rabu	Great Dog (Lion)	Lion.
Ululu ...	Shiru ...	Virgin with ear of corn	Virgin.
Tashritum	Zibanitum ...	... ...	Scales.
Araḥ shamna	Aḳrabu ...	The Scorpion ...	Scorpion.
Kislimu ...	PA-BIL-SAG	The god Enurta	Bow.
Ṭebetum ...	Suḥur-mash	The Goat-Fish ...	Capricornus.
Shabatu ...	Gula ...	The Great Star ...	Water-bearer.
Addaru ...	DILGAN u rikis nuni	The Star . . . and the Band of Fishes	The Fishes.

ZODIAC CIRCLE (ζωδιακός κύκλος), *i.e.* the circle of little figures of animals (ζῴδιον), is the name given to the imaginary circular zone of the heavens in which the sun, moon, and planets have their courses. It is divided into Twelve Signs or sections, each of which has its special sign and is marked by twelve constellations. The twelve sections δωδεκατημόρια, contain 30 degrees, and are reckoned from the spring equinox in the direction in which the sun makes its progress through them in a year. The whole Zodiac moves westwards at the rate of one degree in seventy-two years. The

1. Aries.   2. Taurus.   3. Gemini.

4. Cancer   5. Leo.

6. Virgo.   7. Libra.   8. Scorpio.

9. Sagittarius.   10. Capricornus.

11. Aquarius.   12. Pisces.

THE SIGNS OF THE ZODIAC.

These were drawn by the late Mr. Anderson, a draughtsman in the British Museum, from an Egyptian coffin of the later period in the British Museum.

Twelve constellations and the symbols which represent them are :—

Constellation.	Symbol.	
Aries, the Ram ...	♈	a ram's head.
Taurus, the Bull ...	♉	a bull's head.
Gemini, the Twins ...	♊	conventional representation of two children joined together.
Cancer, the Crab ...	♋	two figures of nine.
Leo, the Lion ...	♌	the solar disk with spermatazoa attached (?).
Virgo, the Virgin ...	♍	?
Libra, the Balance ...	♎	a sign of equilibrium.
Scorpio, the Scorpion	♏ or ΛΛΛ↗	a flash of lightning with a scorpion's tail attached.
Sagittarius, the Archer	↠	an arrow.
Capricornus, the Goat	♑	?
Aquarius, the Water-bearer	♒	waves on water.
Pisces, the Fishes ...	♓	two fishes joined. Not to be confounded with Gemini.

The Egyptians borrowed the Zodiac from the Greeks, as the Greeks had borrowed it from the Babylonians, and the most authoritative form of it was found originally in the second room of the Temple Roof at Denderah in Upper Egypt. Fortunately it was removed from its dangerous position and is now preserved in the Bibliothèque Nationale in Paris. The Egyptians made certain changes in the forms of the Signs. On the back of Taurus they placed a lunar crescent with the full moon rising from it. Gemini was represented by the god Shu and the goddess Tefnut. A beetle (*scarabaeus sacer*) took the place of a crab in Cancer. The lion of Leo stands in a sort of boat, and a goddess is grasping his tail and shaking a whip at him. VIRGO is represented by a woman holding an ear of wheat. LIBRA is represented by a pair of scales, but between them is a picture of the disk of the sun resting on the horizon ; within the disk is a figure of Horus the Child (Harpokrates). SAGIT-TARIUS becomes a centaur, with two faces, one to the front and one to the back, drawing a bow. The body of the animal is winged and has two tails, one being that of a scorpion, and the hawk of Horus or Rā is perched on the tip of one of the wings. The fore paws of the animal are in a boat. The fore part of the body of CAPRICORNUS is that of a goat, with two goat's legs ; the hind part is that of a fish with fins. AQUARIUS is the Nile-god, ḤAPI, who holds in his hands two overflowing libation vases, which symbolize the Nile of the South and the Nile of the North. The god has on his head a cluster of Nile plants. In PISCES we have two well-drawn fish, swimming, one on each side of a lake or stream.

The PERSIANS, ZOROASTRIAN and others, adopted the Zodiac and used it in their religious systems, and from IRÂN it passed into INDIA. The knowledge of the Zodiac entered CHINA with the Buddhist missionaries, and in that country it became a valuable instrument of the astrologers. The Chinese appear to have had a sort of indigenous Zodiac, the Signs of which were represented by the Rat, Ox, Tiger, Hare, Crocodile, Serpent, Horse, Sheep, Monkey, Hen, Dog, and Pig. The order of the Signs is different from that of the Sumerian Zodiac, and this suggests that the native Chinese Zodiac was horary in character, and was not employed for astronomical purposes. It was used largely in Central and Eastern

China and Japan, and according to some authorities the Aztecs had some knowledge of it. Every civilized nation in the world seems to have made use of the Zodiac in some form or other, and chiefly for astrological purposes.

It is interesting to note that the Egyptians attached much more importance to the Thirty-six Dekans than to the constellations of the Zodiac. Lists of them are found in the royal Tombs at THEBES, *e.g.* those of SETI I and his son RAMESES II, and figures of the Dekan gods are cut on the Zodiac from DENDERAH. This importance was probably due to the fact that each Dekan ruled one-third of the month, *i.e.* ten days, and the Egyptian week contained ten days. Reproductions of the gods of the Dekans and their names in hieroglyph and Greek will be found in my *Gods of the Egyptians*, vol. ii. p. 312 f. The Signs of the Zodiac were employed in the decoration of Egyptian coffins, and a well-preserved set may be seen inside the coffin of SOTER, an Archon of THEBES, in the British Museum (No. 6705). On the coffin of ḤERU-NEDJ-TEF-T also we have the Signs of the Zodiac, accompanied by figures of the gods of the planets and the Dekans (No. 6678). This coffin was made in the IVth century B.C., and the other astronomical vignettes appear to have been copied from the walls of the royal tombs at THEBES.

The Signs of the Zodiac are found in cathedrals and churches in Italy and France, and also in a few churches in England ; see Miss A. M. Clerke's article in the *Ency. Brit.*, vol. xxviii. p. 998. The Twelve Apostles are at times associated with the Signs of the Zodiac, and in a curious little theological work the Christian

Life is compared to a Zodiac, and the twelve virtues which form it, the Inner Light, Readiness for death, Sacramental Confession, Abnegation, Patient Endurance, Hearing the Word of God, etc., are described at length. The *Zodiacus Christianus* is followed by an *Horologium auxiliaris tutelaris Angeli*.[1]

Among the descendants of the Arab tribes who settled in NORTH AFRICA the Twelve Signs of the Zodiac were written altogether on pieces of paper which were carried as talismans by caravan-men and dwellers in the desert. The natives of the Gold Coast, especially the workers in metal, wore metal rings round which the Signs, made of gold wire, were soldered. Travellers were in the habit of employing the native jewellers to make " Zodiac rings " for them, and a great many exist in England at the present day. The natives who were converted to Christianity by the Portuguese missionaries adopted the Cross, which they regarded as a Christian fetish, with enthusiasm, and wore it on their persons. On plate XXII is figured a gold cross, which came from the CAMEROONS, and was made specially for a prominent native Christian who wore it regularly. But the symbol of his new Faith in its simple state did not content him, and he had some doubt as to its power to save him ; after much thought he took his cross to the bazaar, and ordered the jeweller to add to it the symbols of the Signs of the Zodiac. When this had been done he felt that his cross was a real fetish with "strong medicine" in it, and wore it proudly.

---

[1] The full title is *Zodiacus Christianus locupletatus seu Signa XII Divinae Praedestinationis. Totidem Symbolis explicata ab Hierem Drexilio è Societatis Jesu.* Col: Agrippinae Apud Cornel: ab Egmond CIↃ : IↃC. XXXII.

Another interesting amulet from the Gold Coast is figured below. This is a gold boss $1\frac{3}{4}$ inches in diameter. In the centre is a circular hole which is intended to represent the sun's disk, and all round it are zigzag lines suggesting the rays of light which shoot up from it. Over the hole is the Sacred Heart

Sacred Heart surrounded by the Signs of the Zodiac.

in gold, with a geometrical border and annules, and ranged round this are the Twelve Signs of the Zodiac, carefully worked in gold wire and soldered down on an embossed ground. This amulet was intended to be worn as a pendant on the breast, but a wire-work chain and fastening were attached to it by its last owner and it can now be worn as a bracelet.

The periods of the rule of the Signs are as follows :

Spring—

Ram	March 21–April 19.
Bull	April 20–May 20.
Twins	May 21–June 20.

Summer—

Cancer	June 21–July 22.
Leo	July 23–Aug. 22.
Virgo	Aug. 23–Sept. 21.

Autumn—

Balance	Sept. 22–Oct. 21.
Scorpion	Oct. 22–Nov. 20.
Sagittarius	Nov. 21–Dec. 20.

Winter—

Capricornus	Dec. 21–Jan. 19.
Aquarius	Jan. 20–Feb. 18.
Pisces	Feb. 19–March 20.

All these dates are inclusive. The astrological year begins with the Spring, and the Signs are enumerated in the direction opposite to that of the figures on the dial of a watch. Three Signs were associated with each of the Four Elements : with Earth, Bull, Virgin and Capricornus ; with Air, Twins, Balance, and Aquarius ; with Fire, Ram, Lion, and Sagittarius ; with Water, Cancer, Scorpion and Fishes. The influences of the Twelve Signs, astrologically, may now be enumerated.

RAM.—His ruler is Mars ; his day is Tuesday ; his colour is red ; and his stone is amethyst. If his entrance into the year is delayed his influence is for evil during his whole period of 30 days. He rules the emotions, instincts, and energies of those born under him, and gives them a dominant will, swift perception, ample vital power, a quick temper, generosity and an affectionate disposition. On the other hand, they will probably have domestic differences, few or no children, a varying fortune and many enemies. Mars exercises a benign influence over them.

BULL.—His ruler is Venus ; his day is her day, Friday ; his colour is green ; and his precious stone is agate. He presides over the crops, directs labour and the profit made from it, and makes the steady worker to prosper. Venus gives to those born under him a cheerful and amiable disposition and prolificness. The Bull specially controls the neck, and makes a man stiff-necked, obstinate, reserved, slow to forget an injury, slow to abandon cherished beliefs and things. Usually a man born under the Bull enjoys a long, quiet life and has a large circle of acquaintances.

The TWINS.—Their ruler is Mercury ; their day is Wednesday ; and their stone is beryl. They rule all the affections and emotions of love in men, and they symbolize union, which is the origin of strength. Mercury controls the arms and shoulders of those born under him, and gives them knowledge and understanding of the Arts and Sciences, and the spirit of adventure, coupled with a certain instability. Their lives are usually full of ups and downs, and periods of trouble.

The CRAB.—His ruler is the Moon ; his day is Monday ; and his stone is the blue emerald. Men and women born under him have delicate constitutions and abilities of a limited order, which they use with discretion. They are somewhat arrogant and presumptuous, and inclined to paradox, and they are swayed by the last speaker on any subject. They are precise in manner and are easily moved to mirth. The Crab controls the lungs, breast and stomach of those born under him, and they have a predisposition to cancer and phthisis; but the women are usually fertile. Good fortune attends them in the latter years of their lives.

The LION.—His ruler is the Sun; his day Sunday; and his stone the yellow ruby. Those born under him are bold, courageous, generous, devoted, faithful, not easily moved, and sentimental, and they are ambitious, autocratic, greedy of honours, quick-tempered, and lovers of money and pleasure. Their passions are strong, and they express their opinions forcibly. Their gains are tempered with unexpected losses. The Sun rules their heart and back, and they are predisposed to pleurisy, palpitations, fever, rheumatic pains, pains in the joints, and disease of the bladder. They have many acquaintances and enemies who cannot injure them.

The VIRGIN.—Her ruler is Mercury; her day Wednesday; and her stone grey jasper. She makes those born under her to be sympathetic and gives them prudence, tact, intuition, skill in directing the house and business affairs generally, and a love for the Arts and agriculture. They have skill in the acquisition of property, are given to illicit affections, and their love affairs cause trouble in their families. The Virgin rules the belly, the intestines and the genital organs.

The BALANCE.—His ruler is Venus; his day is Friday; and his stone is the green emerald. The period of the Balance brings days which are comparatively equal in length. Those born under it possess equable and just dispositions, but they lack initiative and boldness, and refuse to take risks. They possess artistic instincts, and the women are addicted to love-making. The Balance rules the kidneys.

The SCORPION.—His ruler is Mars; his day is Tuesday; and his stone is the reddish topaz. He presides over a period of the year which is prolific in sicknesses. Those who are born under him are bold and persistent, but also malicious and jealous; he is the star which is the symbol of fightings and quarrellings and strife of all kinds. He controls the genital organs and the womb, and makes men liable to fistula.

SAGITTARIUS.—His ruler is Jupiter; his day is Thursday; and his stone is blue turquoise. As governor of the period when men go a-hunting, he directs the thighs of huntsmen and causes them to fall from their horses. Those who are born under his rule possess dispositions hard to understand, but they are full of energy and of love for the arts and sciences. The influence of Jupiter produces in men wisdom, honour and sagacity, humility and timidity, simplicity of manner and cheerfulness.

CAPRICORNUS.—His ruler is Saturn; his day is Saturday; and his stone is black onyx. Those born under his rule are weak-kneed, delicate, and of meagre appearance, but their apparently humble impassiveness is only a cloak for their ambition, and wish for honours, and egoism and their propensity for double dealing. They usually marry more than once, but have few children; their affections are characterized by inconstancy. They have a tendency to suffer from rheumatism and diseases of the skin, and brittle bones.

AQUARIUS.—His ruler is Saturn; his day is Saturday; and his stone is the dark sapphire. Aquarius

gives to those who are born under him thoughtful-
ness inclining to mysticism, prudence, fidelity, love
of the arts, a strong will, patience, capacity for
work, a courteous disposition, and strong, enduring
passions. They have weak shoulders and legs, and
suffer from cramp and convulsions. This Sign
affords no protection to those who travel by sea.

The FISHES.—Their ruler is Jupiter; their day
is Friday; and their stone is the blue chrysolite.
This Sign is especially malignant and has been called
the " hell of the Zodiac." It controls the feet, and
those who are born under it are liable to pustules
and arthritis. It makes them weak, cowardly,
lazy, shuffling, and it portends for them calamities,
misfortunes, losses, dishonour, ruin and death. On
the other hand some think that they may obtain
positions of trust and importance, and enjoy the
friendship of powerful and wealthy friends.

THE TWELVE HOUSES OF THE SKY.

In Astrology the course of the sun is divided into
twelve portions or " Houses," which correspond to
the twelve months and the twelve Signs of the
Zodiac. Each " House " exercises a certain influence
on men, and on all the affairs of their lives. These
influences are indicated by the names of the Houses.

1. House of Life.	7. House of Marriage.
2. House of Riches.	8. House of Death.
3. House of Kinsfolk.	9. House of Religion.
4. House of Parents.	10. House of Dignities.
5. House of Children.	11. House of Friendship.
6. House of Health.	12. House of Enemies.

All the Signs of the Zodiac pass through these Houses
in turns taking their own special influences with them.

THE DEKANS.

To each Sign of the Zodiac the god Marduk attached three stars or constellations. Each group of three Dekans rules the month of 30 days, and each Dekan rules a ten-day week (*i.e.* one-third of the month), hence the name Dekan. The following table shows the period of the rule of each Dekan in each Sign of the Zodiac, and gives the name of its planetary regent.

SIGN.	DEKAN.	PERIOD OF RULE.	PLANETARY REGENT.
RAM	1 ...	Mar. 21–Mar. 30 ...	Mars.
	2 ...	,, 31–April 9 ...	Sun.
	3 ...	April 10– ,, 19 ...	Venus.
BULL	1 ...	,, 20– ,, 30 ...	Mercury.
	2 ...	May 1–May 10 ...	Moon.
	3 ...	,, 11– ,, 20 ...	Saturn.
TWINS	1 ...	,, 21– ,, 30 ...	Jupiter.
	2 ...	,, 31–June 9 ...	Mars.
	3 ...	June 10– ,, 20 ...	Sun.
CANCER ...	1 ...	,, 21–July 1 ...	Venus.
	2 ...	July 2– ,, 11 ...	Mercury.
	3 ...	,, 12– ,, 22 ...	Moon.
LION	1 ...	,, 23–Aug. 1 ...	Saturn.
	2 ...	Aug. 2– ,, 11 ...	Jupiter.
	3 ...	,, 12– ,, 22 ...	Mars.
VIRGIN ...	1 ...	,, 23–Sept. 1 ...	Sun.
	2 ...	Sept. 2– ,, 11 ...	Venus.
	3 ...	,, 12– ,, 21 ...	Mercury.
BALANCE ...	1 ...	,, 22–Oct. 1 ...	Moon.
	2 ...	Oct. 2– ,, 11 ...	Saturn.
	3 ...	,, 12– ,, 21 ...	Jupiter.
SCORPION ...	1 ...	,, 22– ,, 31 ...	Mars.
	2 ...	Nov. 1–Nov. 10 ...	Sun.
	3 ...	,, 11– ,, 20 ...	Venus.
SAGITTARIUS ...	1 ...	,, 21– ,, 30 ...	Mercury.
	2 ...	Dec. 1–Dec. 10 ...	Moon.
	3 ...	,, 11– ,, 20 ...	Saturn.

Sign.	Dekan.	Period of Rule.	Planetary Regent.
Capricornus ...	1 ...	Dec. 21–Dec. 30	... Jupiter.
	2 ...	,, 31–Jan. 9	... Mars.
	3 ...	,, 10– ,, 19	... Sun.
Aquarius ...	1 ...	Jan. 20– ,, 29	... Venus.
	2 ...	,, 30–Feb. 8	... Mercury.
	3 ...	Feb. 9– ,, 18	... Moon.
Pisces ...	1 ...	,, 19– ,, 28	... Saturn.
	2 ...	Mar. 1–Mar. 10	... Jupiter.
	3 ...	,, 11– ,, 20	... Mars.

CHAPTER XXV.

THE STONES OF THE PLANETS AND THEIR INFLUENCES.

The old astrologers believed that precious and semi-precious stones were bearers of the influences of the Seven Astrological Stars or Planets. Thus they associated with the—

SUN, yellowish or gold-coloured stones, *e.g.* amber, hyacinth, topaz, chrysolite.

With the MOON, whitish stones, *e.g.* the diamond, crystal, opal, beryl, mother-of-pearl.

With MARS, red stones, *e.g.* ruby, haematite, jasper, blood-stone.

With MERCURY, stones of neutral tints, *e.g.* agate, carnelian, chalcedony, sardonyx.

With JUPITER, blue stones, *e.g.* amethyst, turquoise, sapphire, jasper, blue diamond.

With VENUS, green stones, *e.g.* the emerald and some kinds of sapphires.

With SATURN, black stones, *e.g.* jet, onyx, obsidian, diamond, and black coral.

The astrologers believed that each stone possessed a sort of living personality, which could experience sickness and disease, and could become old and powerless and even die. As has been shown in the section on Babylonian amulets, superstitions of this kind were common in Babylonia in the third millennium B.C., and the Rubrics in the Book of the Dead prove that the same was the case in Egypt. Thus chapter XXX B must be written on a scarab of green stone, and the text of the Isis amulet on carnelian, and that of the Ṭeṭ of Osiris on gold. The Shamîr gem (diamond ?), which was set in the magic ring of Solomon, was regarded as a living power which preserved him from all harm, and kept him on his throne. To the early Christians the diamond was the symbol of our Lord, and they regarded it as an antidote to both physical and moral evil. Both the pagan astrologers and Christians held the sapphire in high esteem, the former associating it with the planet Venus, and the latter with the Virgin Mary. It was a type of virginity and chastity. Some stones were credited with many powers. Thus the jacinth gave a man health and happiness and wealth and protected him from lightning and the thunderbolt. The turquoise, emerald, and root-of-emerald preserved a man from every kind of accident, and the emerald especially was supposed to stimulate the mental powers. But authorities on such matters did not always agree as to the effect which was produced by certain stones. Thus some thought that an amethyst preserved its wearer from drunkenness, whilst others believed that it made him dream many dreams. Red stones, the ruby, carbuncle, and red jasper were generally believed to make a man strong and sturdy ; some, however, regarded it as a healer of wounds. To stones used in medicine specific qualities were ascribed.

THE SYMBOLISM OF GEMS AND SEMI-PRECIOUS STONES.

AGATE (black).—Courage, boldness, victory in games, prosperity. Agates with unusual markings on them were greatly prized, and special value was attached to them.

AGATE (red).—Calm, peace, protection against the bites of snakes, scorpions, and other insects, and against lightning and the thunderbolt.

AQUAMARINE.—Youth, hope, health. Worn in earrings it gained affection and love for the wearer.

AMBER.—Preserved children from fits.

AMETHYST.—Peace of mind. It prevented its wearer from getting drunk and, if the circle of the sun or moon was engraved on it, from death by poison.

BERYL.—Hope.

CAT'S EYE.—Protection against the Evil Eye. Long life.

CARBUNCLE.—Determination, assurance, energy, Physical well-being.

CARNELIAN.—Friendship. A cure for depression and pessimism.

CHRYSOLITE.—Wisdom, discretion, prudence.

CHRYSOPRASE.—Gaiety, joy.

CORAL (red).—Attachment, devotion, protection against plague and pestilence. It loses its colour when a friend of the wearer is about to die.

CORUNDUM.—Stability of mind.

DIAMOND.—Candour, sincerity, fidelity and affection.

EMERALD.—Faithfulness, unchanging love. Helps the wearer to forecast events.

GARNET.—Energy, devotion, loyalty. Promotes sincerity.

HAEMATITE.—Alertness, vivacity, sexual impulse, success in litigation.

HYACINTH (JACINTH).—Fidelity.

JADE (white).—Quiets intestinal disturbances.

JADE (black).—Strength, power.

JASPER.—Joy, happiness, relief from pain.

JET.—Grief, mourning.

LAPIS LAZULI.—Capacity, ability, success, divine favour.

LOADSTONE.—Honesty, integrity, virility.

MAGNETITE.—Sexual impulse.

MOONSTONE.—See SELENITE.

OLIVINE.—Simplicity, modesty, pleasure, happiness.

ONYX.—Destroys nightmare and bad dreams. Perspicacity.

OPAL.—Fidelity, religious emotion, prayers, assurance.

PEARL.—Chastity, purity.

PERIDOT.—Thunderbolt.   An aid to friendship.

RUBY.—Love, passion.   An aid to firm friendship. Beauty.

SAPPHIRE.—Innocence, truth.   A giver of health and a preserver of chastity.

SARDONYX.—Brightness, vivacity.   A guide to honour and renown.

SELENITE.—Good Luck.

TOPAZ.—Love, affection.   An aid to sweetness of disposition.

TURQUOISE.—Courage which leads to fulfilment and success.

TURQUOISE (black-lined).—Love, and a winner of love.

CHAPTER XXVI.

THEORIES ABOUT NUMBERS AND THEIR MYSTIC AND SACRED CHARACTER.

Many ancient nations seem to have held the view which PYTHAGORAS (born B.C. about 580) enunciated to the effect that " all things are numbers " and that the elements of numbers are the elements of all things. The Pythagoreans thought the numbers which were only divisible by themselves, or by unity, to be of more importance than the others, and among these may be mentioned 1, 2, 3, 5, 7, 11, 13, 17, 19, 23, 29, 31, 41, 43, 47, 53, 59, 61, 67, 71, 73, 79, 83, 89, 97. The mathematical tables found at NIFFAR in Babylonia prove that the SUMERIANS and their kinsfolk were skilled reckoners, and there seems to be no good reason for doubting that the Greeks and many later peoples have borrowed many of their beliefs as to the mystic and sacred character of certain numbers from them. They were in fact the founders of the science of mathematics. In BABYLONIA the numbers from 60 to 1 were reserved for gods, *e.g.* 60 (the *soss*) = ANU, 50 = BEL, 40 = EA, 30 = SIN (Moon-god), 25 MARDUK, 20 = SHAMASH, 15 = ISHTAR, 10 = RAMMÂN (JASTROW, *Religion*, p. 465). The greatest sacred number in BABYLONIA was 12,960,000 (= 60^4 or $3,600^2$, *i.e.* the *sar* squared). It has been shown to be the " number of Plato " (ADAM, *Republic of Plato*, p. 264 f.). When related to time 12,960,000 days = 36,000

years, each containing 360 days, and is fundamental
in astronomy and in astrology. It governs the
universe and also man's life, especially the period
of gestation, for 216 days (?), the period of the seven
months' child, and 270 days the period for the nine
months' child, inaugurate a lucky birth, for both
are divisors of 12,960,000. Every number which
is a divisor of 12,960,000 is a lucky number, and
therefore 7, 11, and 13 are unlucky (W. CRUICKSHANK
in HASTINGS' *Encyclopaedia*, vol. ix. p. 417), according to some authorities. The numbers 3, 4, 5, 7,
10, 12, 40, 70, and 100 were sacred among many
ancient peoples, and of these 3 seems to be the most
popular mystic number. It represents the perfect
number 2 plus 1. In Vedic literature 3, 7, 21, 55,
77 and 99 are magical numbers. In the Story of
the Buddha 7 occurs very frequently, and in Iranian
(Pehlevi) texts 3 and 7 play very prominent parts.
The GREEKS and ROMANS regarded 3, 9, and 12 as
magical numbers, and it is clear that they borrowed
12 from the BABYLONIANS and SUMERIANS, who had
a duodecimal-sexagesimal system. The fundamental
cyphers of it were 5 and 7 ; $5 + 7 = 12$ and 5×12
$= 60$; the Sumerian *soss* = 60, the *ner* = 600, and
the *sar* 3,600. The numbers 3 and 9 were favourites
with the CELTS, and 3, 9, and 7 with the Slavs.

ONE.—The number 1 represented God. The
Egyptian declared in his Hymns to Rā or 'Amen, or
'Amen-Rā, that he was the " one ONE," or perhaps
" the only ONE." MOSES said, " Hear, O Israel,
the Lord our God [is] ONE " (Deut. vi. 4 ; Mark xii.
29). The PYTHAGOREANS made 1 = the Deity,
indivisible and embracing all things. The Muslim
says " Say God is ONE God " (Ḳur'ân, Sûrah cxii).

The Babylonians considered 1, 2, 6, 10, 11, 12, 13 to be unlucky numbers.

Two.—The number 2, the perfect number, is the sign of duality, and was regarded as the origin of evil, and the emblem of matter which is divisible ; it is a symbol of a revolt against unity. The Egyptians had an amulet in the form of two fingers, their country consisted of two parts, and their kingship was dual. Christian priests raise two fingers in blessing.

THREE.—The Babylonians considered 3, 4, 5, 7, 15 to be lucky numbers. The number 3 was said to symbolize birth, life, and death ; beginning, middle, and end ; and childhood, manhood, and old age. As symbolic of the Trinity it was most sacred. In BABYLONIA and EGYPT we have triads of gods, e.g. Anu, Ea, and Bêl ; Khepera, Shu, and Tafnut ; Amen, Mut, and Chonsu, etc. The Babylonians spoke of heaven, earth, and underworld, and the Egyptians of heaven, earth, and the Tuat. The Old and New Testaments contain many instances of the use of 3 as a symbolic or perfect number, e.g. God called Samuel three times, Our Lord asked Peter if he loved Him three times, David bowed before the Lord three times, Christ fell down three times on the road to Golgotha. In classical mythology we have the three-headed Cerberus, the 3 Fates, the 3 Furies, the 3 Graces, the 3 Harpies, the 3 Gorgons, etc. The Magi were 3 in number (according to one legend they were twelve), CASPAR, MELCHIOR, and BALTHAZAR. MAN consists of 3 parts : body, soul, and spirit. The Church distinguishes 3 sections in the Other World, heaven, hell, and purgatory ; in Church Architecture we have the three-light window, and in Christian Art the trefoil or triangle usually symbolizes the Trinity. Authorities on dreams assert that a dream thrice repeated " comes true," and that the man who does not obey an order given to him in a dream three times will suffer great material loss. And the dimensions of solid bodies are 3 in number.

FOUR.—In Egypt (as in Babylon) we have the 4 quarters of the earth, and in the hieroglyphic texts the number 4 is symbolic and complete. Thus we have the 4 sons of Horus, the 4 altars, the 4 Birthplaces in Abydos, the 4 cardinal points, the 4 doves of heaven, the 4 winds, the 4 rudders, the 4 *nems* vases, the 4 vessels of blood, the 4 vessels of milk, the 4 glorious gods, the 4 spirits, the 4 lighted lamps, etc. In the Bible we have the 4 rivers of Paradise, the 4 days lamentation (Judges xi. 40), the 4 barrels of water (1 Kings xviii. 33), the beasts with 4 faces and 4 wings (Ezek. i. 3), the 4 men in the fire, the 4 beasts, the 4 kings, the 4 horns, the 4 carpenters (Zech. i. 20), the 4 anchors (Acts xxvii. 29), etc. We have also the 4 Elements—Earth, Air, Fire, and Water, the 4 Evangelists, and the 4 temperaments of men (according to HIPPOKRATES). A name of God YH, contains two letters, but the Great and Most Holy Name, YHWH contains four. The *Kabbâlâh* adds many other examples of the use of the number 4.

FIVE.—The number 5 is most holy and lucky, according to some writers, and it is symbolic and a sign of completeness. In Egypt 5 men formed a gang of workmen, and among the Hebrews 5 men formed a household. In the Bible we read of the 5 righteous whom ABRAHAM hoped to find in SODOM ;

the altar had to be 5 cubits long and 5 cubits wide ;
5 were to put to flight a hundred (Lev. xxvi. 8) ;
the peace offering was to be 5 rams, 5 goats, 5 lambs ;
5 kings were slain, 5 kings hid, 5 kings were hanged
on 5 trees ; the golden emerods were 5, the golden
mice 5 ; David chose 5 smooth stones from the
brook ; there were 5 loaves and 2 fishes ; 5 sparrows
were sold for 2 farthings ; 5 of the virgins were
wise and 5 were foolish ; the pound (Luke xix. 18)
gained 5 pounds ; the Samaritan woman had had
5 husbands, etc. The Pentacle of the Templars,
the so-called " Solomon's Seal " was five pointed,
and it was regarded as a great and mighty protection.
Our senses are 5, the skull is formed by 5 bones,
the metacarpal bones are 5, and the metatarsal
bones are also 5. Those who play games of chance
look upon 5 as the heart and governor of the figures
1–9. In the Casino it is called the " protector of the
house," for it is thought to reduce the chances of
those who have the numbers 1, 3, 6, 8 and those
who have 2, 4, 7, 9 to an equality, and in any case
the chances are in favour of the Bank.

Six.—The figure 6 is said to be a perfect number,
because the days of creation were 6. It is holy
because it contains the first even number (2), and
the first odd number (3), the former representing
the male member, and the latter the *muliebris
pudenda*. The Egyptians celebrated a festival
of 6. The Bible speaks of 6 cities of refuge
(Numb. xxxv. 6). JONATHAN slew the giant of
Gath, who had 6 fingers on each hand, and 6
toes on each foot (2 Sam. xvii. 20, 21) ; the height
of GOLIATH was 6 cubits and a span (1 Sam. xvii. 4)
and the breadth of the image of gold was 6 cubits

(Dan. iii. 1). The frequent use of 6 in measurements is significant.

The ADAMITES represented the Creation in 6 days by the HEXAGRAM thus :—

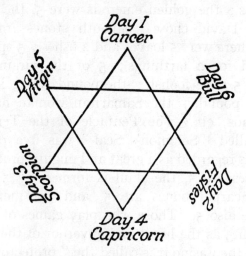

Each of the 6 small triangles should have in it the Sign of the Zodiac indicated by the name in English letters.

Day 1, or Period 1, represents the time of the crustaceans and molluscs.

Day 2 = the period of fishes.

Day 3 = the period of reptiles.

Day 4 = the period of small mammifers and birds.

Day 5 = the period of the great mammifers.

Day 6 = the period of human beings.

Those who believed in the physical significance of the Hexagram taught that communication between the living and the dead was possible, and adopted the dogma of REINCARNATION. The Hexagram is often called the Pentacle or Solomon's Seal, but it is a mistake to do so ; the true form of the Pentacle is here given ;   it is to all intents and

purposes a five-pointed star. It is first seen on pottery from Ur of the Chaldees.

SEVEN.—The number 7 is specially sacred, symbolic, perfect and mystic, and it has always been so. Indians, Persians, Sumerians, Babylonians, Assyrians, Egyptians, and the Teutonic, Celtic, and other peoples of Europe have all considered that it possesses a special significance. In that it is indivisible it has been compared to God. In the Vedic and Buddhist Literatures it plays a very important part. In Babylonian we have the 7 gates of the Underworld, the 7 evil spirits of heaven, the 7 evil spirits of earth, the 7 stages of the Tower of Babel, the 7 tablets of Creation, the Seven-fold deity, *i.e.* the children of ENMESHARA, etc. In Egyptian we have the 7 Asits, or halls of Osiris, the 7 forms of Osiris, the 7 Hathors, the 7 cows and their bull, the 7 great Spirits, the 7 cobras (Uraei), the 7 hawks, the 7-headed serpent, the 7 scorpions of Isis. The Bible supplies many examples of the use of 7. Thus we have the 7 kine of Pharaoh's dream, 7 ears of corn, 7 sabbaths, the 7 altars, 7 oxen and 7 rams of BALAAM, 7 trumpets, 7 locks of hair, 7 pillars of wisdom, 7 steps, 7 cubits, 7 weeks, 7 shepherds, 7 eyes, 7 lamps, 7 baskets, 7 loaves, 7 devils, 7 deacons, 7 churches in Asia, 7 candlesticks, 7 stars, 7 plaques (Rev. xv. 1), 7 golden vials, 7 years, 7-fold vengeance, etc. Jacob bowed 7 times, the priest sprinkled blood 7 times. Naaman was told to wash in the Jordan 7 times, silver is purified 7 times, and the erring brother is to be

forgiven 70 times 7.   God rested on the 7th day ;
Christ spake 7 words on the Cross.   The Jews have
7 holy days in the year, and their golden candlestick
had 7 branches.   The 7th day of the 7th month
was holy, and Israel feasted 7 days and remained
in their tents 7 days.   We have the 7 Sacraments,
7 deadly sins, 7 penitential psalms, the 7 sorrows,
7 joys and 7 glories of the Virgin, 7 virtues, 7 gifts
of the Spirit, 7 Councils of the Church, 7 sprinklings
of the Christian altar ;   7 champions of Christendom
(St. George, St. Andrew, St. David, St. Patrick,
St. James (Spain), St. Denys (France), St.
Anthony (Italy)) ;   the 7 wonders of the world, the
7 sages of Greece, the seven before Thebes, the 7-headed
Hydra, the 7 hills of Rome, the 7 Archangels, the
7 colours of the rainbow, the 7 planets, the 7 notes
of music, the 7 ages of man, the 7 metals of the
Alchemists, etc.   In the Middle Ages the altar in a
church was decorated with 7 precious and semi-
precious stones, viz. diamond or crystal = strength ;
sapphire, or some blue stone = wisdom ; emerald, or
some green stone = skill in adaptability ; topaz =
knowledge ; jasper or agate = splendour, beauty ;
ruby, carnelian or garnet = submission or devotion ;
amethyst = prayer and adoration.

Eight.—One of the oldest Companies of gods in
Egypt, that of Thoth of Hermopolis, contained
8 deities, i.e. four gods and four goddesses ; the
gods were frog-headed, and the goddesses serpent-
headed.   The number 8 seems to have had no
special significance among the Egyptians, but the
Sovereign Chiefs in the Tuat were 8 in number ;
8 gods bore the Boat of the Earth, the Shemti
serpent had 8 heads, 4 at each end of his body.

Hulme calls it the "number of regeneration" because most of the old baptisteries and fonts are octagonal. The Pentateuch lays it down that a male child 8 days old is to be circumcised, and in connection with a measure used in building it seems to have had a special meaning. Thus there were to be 8 boards and sockets of silver (Exod. xxvi. 25), stones of 8 cubits were used in the foundations of the temple (I Kings vii. 10), the going up in Ezekiel's building had 8 steps and 8 tables were provided for the slaughter of sacrificial animals (Ezek. xl, 31, 41).

NINE.—Among many ancient and modern nations the number 9 has been thought to be as important and complete as 3. As representing 3 × 3 it has been called a triad of triads *i.e.* each person of a triad was expanded into a triad. Hence 9 is a triply sacred and perfect number. The Companies of the gods of heaven, earth and the underworld of Egypt contained 9 gods, and Osiris had 9 Watchers and 9 Mourners. The devouring Worms of hell were 9 in number (*Book of the Dead*, chap. iB), and we have the 9 repellers of Āpep. The number 9 is mentioned rarely in the Bible, but we may note that the bedstead of Og, the King of BASHAN, was 9 cubits long (Deut. iii. 4). Then we have the 9 Muses, the 9 Archons of Greece, the 9 orders of angels, the 9 orders of devils, the 9-fold gates of Hell, the 9 days during which Satan and his angels fell from heaven, Christ appeared to His disciples 9 times after His death. The period of human gestation is 9 months. In classical and mediaeval literature we have :—9 earths, 9 heavens, 9 spheres, 9 fairies of ARMORICA, 9 rivers of hell, LARS PORSENA swore by 9 gods, 9 Gallicenae priestesses, the ark of

DEUCALION sailed for 9 days before it rested, 9 crowns in heraldry, 9 kinds of crosses, 9 points of the law, Dryden's 9 worthies (3 Jews, 3 Pagans, and 3 Christian knights), 9 days' wonder, 9 tailors (tellers ?) make a man, a cat has 9 lives, the cat-o-9-tails whip, to see 9 magpies is unlucky, the witches in *Macbeth* repeated their spell 9 times, the Crown offered as a prize by King Arthur had 9 diamonds in it, 9 knots in a piece of black wool cured a sprained ankle, a smartly dressed person is " dressed up to the nines," a person or thing was as nice as a silver 9-penny piece, leases were granted for 999 years, and are still granted for 99 years, toasts three times three were formerly very common. The results of certain multiplications of 9 reproduce the same figures :—

$$9 \times 2 = 18 \text{ and } 9 \times 9 = 81$$
$$9 \times 3 = 27 \text{ and } 9 \times 8 = 72$$
$$9 \times 4 = 36 \text{ and } 9 \times 7 = 63$$
$$9 \times 5 = 45 \text{ and } 9 \times 6 = 54$$

TEN.—There seems to be nothing mystical about 10, but there is no doubt that it was regarded as a complete and perfect number. The Papyrus of Ani makes the Pylons in the kingdom of Osiris to be 10 in number, but some of the later Recensions of the Book of the Dead make their number larger. The Ḳabbalists regarded it as a perfect number, for the Sephîrôth or Emanations from EN SÔPH were 10 ; their names will be found under the section Ḳabbâlâh. And we have, of course, the Ten Commandments. In the Bible 10 appears often as a number indicating completeness, *e.g.* 10 camels, 10 shekels, 10 asses, 10 pillars, 10 bullocks, 10 women who baked bread, 10 men, 10 concubines, 10 men slew ABSALOM, 10 knots, 10 lovers, 10 leaves, 10 tribes, 10 chariots, 10 pounds gained by one pound, etc., and we may note that DAVID's harp had 10 strings, and that the seven-headed dragon had 10 horns. Mr. Hulme (*Symbolism*, p. 15) mentions the 10 petals of the passion flower as representing 10 of the twelve Apostles, Judas, the betrayer, and Peter, the denier of our Lord being unrepresented.

ELEVEN.—There seems to be nothing mystic about the number 11, and he who dreams about it is said to be about to suffer some loss or misfortune. A company of Egyptian gods sometimes contains 11 members, and Mr. A. B. KEITH says that the gods of the Rigveda are often given as 33, and consist of 3 groups each containing 11. The Muslim rosary, when complete, contains 99 beads, *i.e.* 3 × 11 × 3, and a marker is inserted at the end of every 33 beads (3 × 11) to enable the reciter of the 99 Beautiful Names of God to rest. At the present time many rosaries are sold containing only 33 beads, and in every one which the writer has bought there was a marker at the end of the first and second 11, and the " tower," which represents ALLÂH, at the end of the third 11.

TWELVE.—The number 12, like 10, 11, etc., was held in Babylonia to be unlucky, and modern writers on numbers accept this view ; but it seems to have no symbolic meaning. The Zodiac originated, it seems, in Babylonia, and its Signs were 12, and the months of the year were 12, and the whole day contained 12 *kasbu* or double hours. The night-realm of Osiris was divided into 12 parts, and in the Book of Gates we have :—12 gods of the funerary

mountains, 12 gods of Åmentt, 12 gods in shrines
in the Tuaṭ (Underworld), 12 gods of the Lake of
Boiling Water, 12 gods with their doubles, 12 gods
of the Lake of Life, 12 gods before and 12 gods
behind the shrine, 12 gods of the measuring line,
12 gods of hidden arms and hands, 12 gods of stakes,
12 gods who control the serpent Seba-Āpep, 12
Djadjau who provide the bread of Maāt, 12 casters
of spells, 12 gods of the stars that never set, 12 goddesses of the hours, etc. In the Bible we have :—
12 sons of JACOB, 12 wells in ELIM, 12 precious
stones, 12 cakes, 12 oxen, 12 stones from JORDAN,
12 Apostles, 12 baskets of fragments, 12 legions of
angels, a crown with 12 stones, 12 gates, the 12 kinds
of fruit of the tree of life, etc. HERCULES performed
12 labours, Roman Law was written on 12 bronze
tablets, 12 pence = one shilling, and 12 inches make
one foot. In Ḳabbâbâh the number 12 represents
the Philosopher's Stones.[1]   And we may note that the
144,000 mentioned in Rev. xiv. 3 = 12 times 12,000.

THIRTEEN.—According to some, 13 is an unlucky number, and according to others it is lucky.
The superstitious dislike to be one of 13 at dinner
is derived from the Last Supper of our Lord with His
Twelve Disciples. The number 13 is associated
also with the fee of 13 pence which the hangman
was paid for each execution at Tyburn ; the payment
actually made was $13\frac{1}{2}$ pence, but the halfpenny
was regarded as the price of the rope. The value of
the Scots mark was fixed at $13\frac{1}{2}$ pence, and was
sometimes alluded to as " hangman's money."

---

[1] As a matter of fact the Philosopher's Stone was a red
powder which the alchemist used in getting rid of alloys or
impurities in metals.

In the Haxey Hood Game 13 has a special significance. The Lord of the Hood wears a red coat and a hat wreathed with flowers and carries a wand made of 13 willows tied 13 times with willow bands (*The Times*, Jan. 4, 1929, p. 15, col. 6).

FOURTEEN.—A mystic number connected with the 14th day of the moon when it is full.

FIFTEEN was a sacred number to the Kabbalists because it represented the numerical value of the two Hebrew letters YH, which form one of the names of God.

SIXTEEN, according to the PYTHAGOREANS, who regarded it as a perfect number, was of special importance, because it represented 4×4.

TWENTY-ONE, *i.e.* 3×7, each a perfect number, indicated completeness and majesty ; the salute of 21 guns probably represents an ancient ceremonial in which the number 21 played a prominent part.

TWENTY-TWO, *i.e.* 2×11, is a sacred number because the Hebrew alphabet contains 22 letters, and the Books of the Old Testament are 22 in number.

TWENTY-EIGHT, a mystic number connected with the 28 days, *i.e.* 7×4 of the moon.

THIRTY, an accursed number, because JUDAS betrayed our Lord for 30 pieces of silver ; another view is that it is lucky because JESUS began to preach His Gospel in the 30th year of His age.

THIRTY-THREE, *i.e.* 3×11, has been held to be a mystic number, because JESUS was 33 years old when He was crucified ; and ALEXANDER the Great was poisoned at Babylon when he was 33 years of age.

THIRTY-NINE.—It was laid down in Deut. xxv. 3,

that a man might be punished by a beating of 40 stripes and no more, and St. Paul says that he received from the Jews 40 stripes save one, *i.e.* 39 stripes, 3×13.

Forty seems to be nothing more than a round or general number. The Israelites ate manna 40 years, and wandered in the desert 40 years; Solomon, Jehoash, and Joash each reigned 40 years; Moses was on the mount 40 days; Jonah preached in Nineveh 40 days; our Lord fasted for 40 days, and remained in the tomb 40 hours, etc. Quarantine lasts 40 days; the period of sanctuary was 40 days, and many people still believe that if St· Swithin's day be wet 40 wet days will follow. And 40 shillings is a well-known fine in our days· It is probable that in many cases 40 was originally 42, *i.e.* 7×6.

Forty-two.—The Assessors or Judges in the Hall of Osiris were 42 in number, each one representing a nome.

Fifty.—The Law was given to Moses on Sinai 50 days after Israel came out of Egypt, and the Holy Spirit descended on the Apostles 50 days after the Resurrection. 50 is said to be the number of the Holy Spirit. 50 honorific and great names were bestowed upon Marduk after he had reconsituted the heavens and the earth.

Fifty-five, *i.e.* 5×11 appears as a magical number in Indian spells.

Sixty.—In Southern Babylonia the sexagesimal system was in general use in texts of a mathematical character.

Seventy appears to have been used, like 40, as a round or general number, and many instances of its use are to be found in the Bible, *e.g.* " the days of our years are three-score years and ten " (Ps. xc. 10) ; " after these things the Lord appointed another 70 also " (Luke x. 1). It is, however, tolerably certain that the actual number of disciples sent out was 72, and this view is supported by the statements of ecclesiastical writers. We refer commonly to the ancient Greek version of the Old Testament as the " Seventy " (LXX), but the *Book of the Bee* and other Syriac works say that the translation was made by 72 men, 6 from each of the Twelve Tribes, and give their names. And one of the great Ḳabbalistic names of God contained 72 and not 70 letters. The Egyptian priests composed a Hymn of Praise to AMEN-RĀ, in which the god was addressed by each of his great names and attributes. In the papyrus of NESI-KHONSU, in Cairo, the god himself says that he has had the Seventy Addresses to Rā recited on behalf of the princess (Budge, *Book of the Dead*, 1923, p. 660). But in the edition of the Egyptian text published by NAVILLE the Addresses are SEVENTY-FIVE in number ; for a translation see my *Gods of the Egyptians*, vol. i. p. 339 f. The words of our Lord in Matt. xviii. 22 indicate the completeness of the number $70 \times 7 = 490$.

NINETY-NINE.—The " beautiful names " of God, according to the Arabs, are 99 in number, and the beads in the Muslim rosaries are 99, *i.e.* 11×9 ; these are divided into groups of 33, *i.e.* 11×3.

ONE HUNDRED AND TEN.—The famous Egyptian writer PTAḤ-ḤETEP, the Wazîr of King ASSA (about 3200 B.C.), lived to the age of 110 years, and several Egyptian officials are known to have reached this great age. Why 110 years were regarded as the limit of human life is not clear.

The Ḳabbalists advised their followers to undertake no business on the following days of the month : 2, 5, 11, 13, 15, 18, 30.

The following were favourable days for business : 1, 3, 7, 9, 10, 12, 16, 17, 19, 20, 21, 22, 27, 23.

CHAPTER XXVII.

DIVINATION.

The word "Alchemy," *i.e.* the "Black Art," or rather the "magical craft of the Black Country," is derived from one of the names of Northern Egypt, which was called the "Black Country" because of the brownish-black colour of the soil in the Delta, as opposed to the "Red Country," which was given to Upper Egypt because of its reddish-yellow sand. We might thus think that Egypt was the oldest home of divination known to us, but such is not the case, for the literature of Egypt contains neither mention nor allusion to any of the numerous kinds of divination which were practised in Sumer and Akkad in the third millennium B.C. Until the Ptolemaïc period divination by earth, air, fire, and water was practically unknown among the indigenous peoples of the country, and there is little doubt that they only became acquainted with these branches of the art of Magic through the Greeks who borrowed many of their magical practices from the Babylonians. That Joseph used the divining cup does not prove that divining by water, or wine, or oil was common in Egypt, for Joseph was a Hebrew and his people borrowed the art from the Babylonians.

The object of divination, no matter what the means used were, is to find out what is the Will of God, and what the course of future events is going to be, whether they concern an individual or a people. The methods of divination used by primitive or uncivilized peoples were of a simple character, but among such highly civilized people as the Sumerians and Babylonians they represent much thought and reasoning powers, and some of them were almost scientific in character. The Sumerians developed a great system of omens, and the cuneiform texts show that the omen-lists were revised carefully from time to time and added to, presumably as the result of new experiences. The priests derived omens from dreams, whether dreamed by the priest or a private individual, from the planets and stars, from eclipses, from the movements of animals, from the flight of birds, from the appearance of snakes at certain places, from locusts, lions, the actions of dogs, the direction of the winds, the state of the rivers, from peculiarities in newly-born children and animals, from the birth of twins, from accidents that may happen to men, from deformities in children, from the birth of monstrosities, from the symptoms which occur in diseases, etc. According to the Sumerians and Babylonians everything that happened to the king, and to men and animals and birds and reptiles, portended something, and the priest was expected to tell the enquirer what that something was. The enormous number of omen-tablets which have been found in Babylonia and Assyria prove that the priests kept strict account of the events which followed every happening that came to their notice, and it would seem that their tablets of omens, e.g. the *Book of the Illumination of Bel*, contained the results of the experiences of an untold number of generations of priests. For further details and translations of a number of typical omens see the chapter, " Oracles and Omens," in Jastrow, *The Religion of Babylonia and Assyria*, 1898, p. 328 f.

CHAPTER XXVIII.

The ancients attached special sanctity and power to water, and in many countries, *e.g.* in Egypt, water was declared to be the " father of the gods." The Babylonian and Egyptian cosmogonies make it to be the original home of the gods, and the primeval watery abyss was the dwelling-place both of the powers of light and darkness. The Copts said that water and the wheat plant and the Throne of the Father stand in one category, and they are the equals of the "Son of God" (Budge, *Coptic Apochrypha,* p. 246). And the Ethiopians believed that the three Persons of the Trinity lived *in name only* in the primeval World-Ocean until They pronounced their own names, when they became Persons. The Babylonian Water-god was called EA, his name meaning the "house of water"; he lived in the subterranean deep which surrounds the earth, and he was the source of wisdom and learning and the personification of all knowledge. It is therefore easy to understand why the Babylonians made divination by water, and why omens derived from the state and appearance of the rivers of their country were held to be of supreme importance. As the god of wisdom and knowledge he was able to inform the enquirer into the future better than any other god. The early Egyptian texts make NU or NENU the god of the World-Ocean, but it was Ḥapi, the Nile god, the incomprehensible and unknowable god, whose form could neither be delineated nor described, who was the Egyptian equivalent of EA.

DIVINING CUPS AND BOWLS.

The cups or bowls which the Babylonians used as drinking vessels and as instruments of divination were probably made of gold or refined copper, and the same was the case in Egypt. Some of the gold bowls which Mr. Woolley found at Ur, and some of the Egyptian electrum bowls in the British Museum, were probably drinking vessels. According to Gen. xliv. 2, the cup from which Joseph drank, and by which he divined, was made of silver. Whether it was inscribed with any magical text is unknown, The use of magical bowls was perpetuated by the Hebrews who lived at Babylon and in Lower Babylonia in the centuries immediately preceding and following the birth of Christ, and large numbers of terra-cotta bowls inscribed with magical texts written in the " square " Hebrew character, Syriac and Mandaïtic have been found at Abu Ḥabbah, Tall Ibrâhîm (Cuthah), Derr, Niffar, Bâbil, Birs-i-Nimrûd. Jumjumah, etc. A large collection of them is in the British Museum. When the first specimens of these were found by Layard the natives regarded them as ancient bowls which the magicians had used when deciding cases or administering draughts of medicine. They supposed that they were filled, or partially filled, with water which the litigants drank, and that the magicians were able to tell which of them was telling the truth by the effect which the water had upon him, for the Water god would make the truth known. But the perfect state of the writing in many of these bowls suggest that they were not used for divining purposes. Moreover, they were found at the four corners of the foundations of houses, both singly and in pairs and inverted, and the latest view about them is that they were placed there to serve as traps to catch devils and evil spirits.

When the Orientals at the present day use the divining cup, or bowl, water is poured into it up to the brim, and the magician tells the enquirer to repeat the question to which he wants an answer and to look into the water. As he is doing this the magician exercises the magical power which he is supposed to possess, and so causes a scene to appear on the surface of the water, which gives the enquirer his answer, whether favourable or unfavourable to him. Sometimes the cup is filled with black water, or ink, when the scene on the surface of it becomes very plain. When no cup or bowl is available the enquirer is made to " cup " his hand and ink is poured into it. The magician walks round the enquirer a number of times repeating passages from the Ḳur'ân as he goes, and the enquirer sees on the surface of the ink what, presumably, the magician intends him to see.

The following instance of divination by water occurred at Khartûm a few years ago. A native who was going to Cairo deposited with a friend a sum of money and asked him to use it for the benefit of his wife if he did not return ; the friend accepted the trust and received from his friend a gift of money for his service. The owner of the money went to Cairo, and returned safely to Khartûm. When he asked his friend to return to him the money which he had deposited with him,

the friend denied all knowledge of the matter
and swore by Allâh that the traveller was mis-
taking him for someone else. An angry altercation
followed, and at length the man who had deposited
the money went to the Ḳâdî and told him his story.
The Ḳâdî summoned the other man, and having
heard from him an absolute denial of the charge
brought against him by his friend, determined to
elicit the truth by means of a bowl of water. He
took a sheet of paper and wrote upon it certain
verses from the Ḳur'ân, and then having filled a
clean earthenware bowl with water, he put the
inscribed paper into the water and held it there
until all the ink which was still wet on the paper was
washed off from it into the water. He then told
each man that he was to drink one-half of the
water, and solemnly warned them that the judgment
of Allâh would fall upon the liar after he had drunk
his half of the water. Each man drank, and the
Ḳâdî put the bowl on the ground, and then suddenly
the man who had received the money fell backwards
and died forthwith. Some of his friends and kinsfolk who had been watching the men drink cried
out that he had been poisoned, and fetched the
police. When they arrived they hauled the other
man off to prison and set a guard over the house of
the Ḳâdî, whom they believed to be in league with
him. In due course he was charged with poisoning
his friend, and the British authorities were inclined
to believe him guilty. But so many representations
were made to them by the Muḥammadan authorities,
who declared that the death of the man was due to
effect of the words of the Ḳur'ân which were dissolved
in the water, that at length the case was remanded,

and the matter was referred to Lord Cromer in Cairo, who was asked to give a judicial decision. With the fairness and open-mindedness which were so characteristic of him, he sent for some of the Mullahs of the Al-Azhar University in Cairo, and laid the matter before them, and said that he would abide by their decision. The Mullahs made full enquiry into the case, and their unanimous verdict was that the man who fell back dead was a liar and a thief, and that it was Allâh Himself Who had killed him by means of the holy words of the Ḳur'ân which had been dissolved in the water in the bowl. They exonerated the Ḳâdî from all blame and commended him for his fearless behaviour. Lord Cromer accepted their explanation of the cause of the man's death, and the accused man, who had been kept in prison whilst his case was being discussed in Cairo, was released.

CHAPTER XXIX.

DIVINATION BY MEANS OF THE LIVER OF AN ANIMAL.

Among the Roman Aruspices, or Haruspices, *i.e.* the diviners who made known to the people the will of the gods by means of their arts, was a class of experts who specialized in the art of prognosticating by the appearance of the entrails of the animals which were offered in sacrifice. This class of men was called EXTISPICES and the art of divining by means of the intestines of animals was known as *extispicium* (Cicero, *De Divinatione*, ii. 11). This art was introduced into Rome by the Etrurian envoys who were sent to the city on the business of the Government, and according to Cicero (*De Div.* ii. 23) was invented by the Etruscan Tages. And the Haruspices of Etruria were sent for from many distant places to interpret the sacrifices and the oracles of the gods (Livy, v. 1, 6 ; xxvii. 37, 6). There is, however, now reason to believe that *extispicium* was not an indigenous art in Etruria, but was introduced there as a result of the well-known connection between Etruria and the East which existed in prehistoric times.

In the Book of Ezekiel (xxi. 21) we have a description of the King of Babylon consulting his diviners as to the probability of making a successful campaign against Jerusalem. The prophet says : " For the King of Babylon stood at the parting (*i.e.* mother) of the way, at the head of the two ways, to use divination : he made [his] arrows bright, he consulted with images (TERÂPHÎM), he looked in the liver." The TERÂPHÎM have already been discussed (see page 213). The arrows used for purposes of divination were kept in a case, which, unless the king had his own private apparatus, was produced by the priest. Usually the arrows were two in number, but sometimes a third was added. When there were two, one had a mark upon it, meaning " Yes," and the other a mark meaning " No." The third was blank, and this arrow indicated that the enquirer must do as he pleased, and that the oracle passed no opinion on the question of the enquirer, and neither approved nor disapproved. Enquiry by arrows was known as " Telomancy." We now come to the prophet's words, " he looked in the liver," and they seem to indicate that the king was an expert in *extispicium*. In any case they show that the art of divining by the liver of a sacrificial victim was practised in Babylon as early as the VIth century B.C. That it was practised in Nineveh a century earlier is proved by the clay model of a liver inscribed with omens which was found during the excavations at Ḳuyûnjik, and is now in the British Museum (No. Rm. 620 ; see *Guide*, page 211).

The excavations made at Boghazköi have also brought to light a considerable number of clay models of an animal's liver inscribed in cuneiform, with remarks in the Babylonian and Hittite languages. It was from this region that the art of divination by the liver passed westwards into Eastern Europe and Etruria. The famous Etruscan bronze liver which is now at Piacenza is described in the *Mitteilungen* of the German Archaeological Institute at Rome, Section xx. And see the remarks of Boissier in his *Note sur un document babylonien se rapportant à l'extispicine,* 1899. The rough drawing here given indicates sufficiently well its shape and appearance. But the true home of the art of divination by the liver of an animal is Babylonia, and the Babylonians declared that it was not invented by them but by the gods. The Sun-god was believed to have arranged the

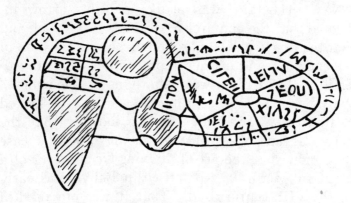

Model of an animal's liver in bronze at Piacenza.

entrails of the sacrificial lamb in such a way that they would indicate to men the will of the gods, and, moreover, that he set marks upon them which could not be mistaken by the skilled extispex. The omen-tablets show that Sargon (Sharrukin) of Agade, the first king of the Dynasty of Akkad (2637–2582 B.C.), and Narâm-Sin, son of Manishtusu 2557–2520 B.C.), made use of omens derived from the livers of sheep, and it is probable that there was never a time when the extispex did not exist in Southern Babylonia. Each generation of extispices added to the collection of omens which they had inherited from their predecessors, and these already in the second millennium B.C. formed a very large section of Babylonian literature. The series of the omens which were copied for Ashurbanipal, King of Assyria (668–626 B.C.), and were stored in the Royal Library, and those which were made for the Library of Nebo in Nineveh, were counted by the score, perhaps even hundreds, and without the catalogues which the king had made the expert would have found it impossible to consult them.

The Babylonians believed that the seat of all passions and emotions was not the heart, but the liver, and that each passion, emotion, and feeling had its own special section in the liver, and the extispex based his prophecies on the appearances which these sections exhibited. It is clear that different extispices might read these appearances in different ways, and therefore the priesthoods of all the great temples took care to make provision for the training of expert extispices. Therefore models of livers were made in clay, and squares were marked on them, and inscriptions added. By means of these models young men were taught the art of divination by the liver, but it is very probable that real livers were sometimes used by the expert to illustrate his teachings in the lecture room.

The oldest clay model of a liver which was used for teaching purposes, or perhaps in actual magical ceremonies, is that which is preserved in the British Museum (No. 92668, *Guide*, page 120). I purchased this in Baghdâd in 1888 from a native of Môṣul called Dâwûd Khalaf, who said that it was found at Abû Ḥabbah where the Trustees of the British Museum were at that time carrying out excavations under the direction of the late Mr. Hormuzd Rassam. For some time the opinions of authorities were divided as to what the object represented, but the matter was decided by the late Canon Isaac

OBVERSE.
Baked clay model of the liver of a sheep in the British Museum.

Taylor, Rector of Settrington, who unhesitatingly declared it to be the model of a human liver, because its general characteristics resembled those of the Etruscan bronze liver which he had seen and examined at Piacenza during a recent visit to Italy. A photographic facsimile of it was published in *Cuneiform Texts from Babylonian Tablets in the British Museum*, Part VI, London, 1898, together with a transcript of the texts upon both sides of it by Dr. T. G.

REVERSE.
Baked clay model of the liver of a sheep in the British Museum.

Pinches. In the Preface it is remarked that the texts inscribed upon the unique object (Bu. 98–4–26, 238), which has been thought to represent a human liver, probably refer to Babylonian magic. The first published study of the liver model was by

Boissier, *Note sur un document babylonien se rapportant à l'extispicine*, 1899. Another description of it was made by M. Jastrow, *Religion Babyloniens und Assyriens*, Bd. II. pages 218, 221, and he published a reproduction of it in the *Bildermappe* which accompanied that work (Nos. 102, 103). It was again reproduced by Klauber, *Politische-religiöse Texte*, xxxi. f, and see Ebeling, *Keilschrifttexte aus Assur religiösen Inhalts*, No. 444.

There is now no doubt that this model represents the liver of a small ruminant, probably a sheep. It shows the organ as viewed from behind. It indicates the four lobes into which the liver is divided, and the most distinctive features, viz., the *processus pyramidalis* (*i.e.* the pointed projection) the gall-bladder, and the small excrescence called *processus papielaris*. The surface of the model is divided into about 50 squares and other compartments, inscribed with significations, *i.e.* the supposed consequences of the appearance of certain marks which might be observed on the indicated parts of the liver, though there is nothing to show what these marks were. Presumably this model was used to explain only one particular kind of mark, according to the position in which it occurred, and this would be known to the user, though it is no longer ascertainable. The other side of the model is but little inscribed, and obviously the mark in question was less frequently observed there.

In recent years Mr. C. J. Gadd, of the British Museum, has made an intensive study of the models in connection with his work on the omens, and he has discovered several important facts connected with the construction of the model which have been generally overlooked. He has found that there are three channels bored in the thickness of the clay ; all these meet in the deep angle or cavity at the base. From these the first emerges in the middle of the large left lobe, and perhaps, therefore, represents the *ductus hepaticus*. The second runs straight up through the model and emerges just above the excrescence which represents the *processus papielaris*, while the third emerges just to the left of the pointed projection, and no doubt represents the *vena portae*.

According to the style of the writing this model belongs to the period of the Ist Dynasty of Babylon about 2050–1750 B.C.

CHAPTER XXX.

THE INSCRIBED BRONZE DIVINING DISK OF
PERGAMON.

This very important object was discovered at Pergamon in Asia Minor in 1899, and is preserved in the Museum in Berlin. It is in a good state of preservation, and its diameter is 0·12 cm. It

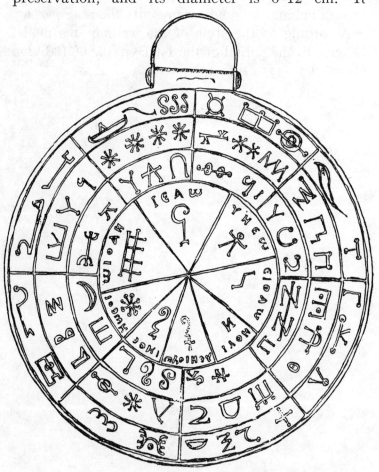

formed a part of the apparatus which the magicians of Pergamon used for purposes of divination and for obtaining Oracles in the first half of the third century of our Era. The inscriptions on the convex side are arranged in concentric-circles and contain a large number of magical hieroglyphs, but among them are several letters of the Greek alphabet, and a whole circle of Greek vowels, the Egyptian hieroglyph for B, the symbols of the sun and moon, etc. The system employed by the magician is unknown. It has been carefully described by DR. R. WÜNSCH in the *Jahrbuch* of the German Archaeological Institute, Ergänzungshaft, No. 6, 1905. A drawing of the complete apparatus, which consisted of ten parts, has been prepared by PROF. CONZE of Pergamon, and see Abbildung 13 in DR. T. HOPFNER, *Griechisch-Ägyptischer Offenbarungszauber*, Leipzig, 1924, page 146.

CHAPTER XXXI.

DIVINATION BY EARTH OR SAND (GEOMANCY).

Geomancy was common among many of the peoples of Africa and Western Asia,[1] and it is practised at the present day in several towns and villages in both continents. The magician made the enquirer into the future to sit down upon the ground and to throw handfuls of dust or sand up into the air, and when the dust or sand had fallen on the ground, the magician inspected the little heaps or ridges and proceeded to identify them with some of the astrological symbols of the seven planets, and the Signs of the Zodiac, and certain important stars, and according to their shapes and positions he decided what the course of future events were to be. At the present time the sand is spread over a square board or flat stone, and the enquirer takes up handfuls of it at random and throws them up into the air. When the sand has fallen the magician examines the shapes and forms which it has taken and makes his deductions as to their meaning as before.

Another form of enquiry by earth is made in the following way : the enquirer sits upon the ground, and taking a dry reed in his right hand prods the earth with it several times in all directions, and then the magician examines the holes and groups them in such a way in his mind that they seem to

---

[1] Mr. Sidney Smith has found among the fragments of the Ḳuyûnijḳ Collection a portion of a tablet with a series of numbers of holes arranged in the same kind of way as those shown on page 462.

FIGVRA.	NOMEN.	ELEMENTVM.	PLANETA.	SIGNVM.
* * * *	Via Iter	Aqua	☽	♌
* * * * * * * *	Populus Congregatio	Aqua	☽	♑
* * * * * *	Coniunctio Coadunatio	Aër	☿	♍
* * * * * *	Carcer Conſtrictus	Terra	♄	♓
* * * * * *	Fortuna maior Auxilium maius. Tutela intrans	Terra	☉	♒
* * * * * *	Fortuna minor Auxilium minus Tutela exiens	Ignis	☉	♉
* * * * * *	Acquiſitio Comprehenſum intus.	Aër	♃	♈
* * * * * *	Amiſſio Comprehenſum extra.	Ignis	♀	♎
* * * * * * *	Letitia Ridens Sanus Barbatus.	Aër	♃	♉
* * * * * * *	Triſtitia Damnatus Tranſuerſus	Terra	♄	♏
* * * * *	Puella Mundus facie	Aqua	♀	♎
* * * * *	Puer Flauus Imberbis	Ignis.	♂	♈
* * * * * * *	Albus Candidus	Aqua	☿	♋
* * * * * * *	Rubeus Ruffus	Ignis	♂	♊
* * * * *	Caput Limen intrans Limen ſuperius	Terra	☊	♍
* * * * *	Cauda Limen exiens Limen inferius	Ignis	☋	♐

Table of geomantic signs with their meanings and the Planet and Sign of the Zodiac, and Element with which they were associated.

form figures of the magical symbols of the planets and stars. Though the enquirer makes the holes in the earth apparently at random, it was believed that the reed with which he made them was directed and guided by the spirits that lived in the

Geomantic signs on the fragment of a terra-cotta tablet in the Ḳuyûnjiḳ Collection in the British Museum.

earth ; and that they made them into groups which the magician was able to interpret, and from which he could deduce omens. Sometimes the enquirer made a number of points on paper with the reed or a pen. Thus if the enquirer made four holes in the ground or four points on paper ⁚ the magician interpreted them as meaning a " road " or a " way." With this group was associated the element Earth, the planet Moon, and the Sign of the Zodiac Leo. With the group ∴· meaning " great good fortune," were associated the element Earth, the planet Sun, and the Sign of the Zodiac Pisces. With the group ⁚⁚ " greediness " were associated the element Air, the planet Jupiter, and the Sign of the Zodiac Mercury. Several other examples are given on page 461, where a list, compiled by Cornelius Agrippa, is reproduced from page cxc of his *De Occulta Philosophia*. Following this is an important list of the characters representing the seven astrological stars which are formed from geomantic figures (see above, page 388) ; it is reproduced from page cxcv of the second part of Agrippa's work.

CHAPTER XXXII.

LUCKY AND UNLUCKY DAYS.

The ancient astrologers and magicians kept among their archives careful notes of the times of the day and of the days themselves on which striking or important events happened. In due course they tabulated the results of their experience, and were able to state definitely which days were lucky and which unlucky. According to one tradition the Babylonians possessed records of calculations which extended over a period of 720,000 years! The list of lucky and unlucky days was the forerunner of the Calendar, and it served as a Calendar until about 2000 B.C., when the Babylonians and Assyrians divided the year into twelve months, each containing 30 days. As the months were lunar their position in the Calendar changed from year to year, and every few years an intercalary month was added to restore the months to their normal places in the Calendar. Tablets inscribed in cuneiform with a list of the lucky and unlucky days are exhibited in the British Museum.

The Egyptians also divided their year into twelve months, each containing 30 days, which was based on a list of lucky and unlucky days throughout the year. A copy of this list is written on the back of the Papyrus of Amen-em-apt in the British Museum (No. 10474), and a portion of another is given in the papyrus Sallier IV. In these lists the word lucky is represented by ⚰ (literally " good "), and unlucky by ⚰ (literally " bad "). The day is supposed to be divided into three portions, each containing four or eight hours. Certain days were lucky throughout, and others unlucky throughout. Sometimes only one or two-thirds of a day were lucky or unlucky, and the list in papyrus 10474 distinguishes clearly which they are, and whether they are in the morning or afternoon of the day. In some parts of Upper Egypt I have seen natives using calendars compiled by Copts, in which certain days are indicated as being unlucky for sowing or reaping or performing agricultural labours generally, and on comparing several of these with the ancient Egyptian list I have noticed that they were also held to be unlucky by the dynastic Egyptians.

The teaching of the astrologers of the Middle Ages was that the Lucky Days of the week were :—

MONDAY, or Moon's day, a day of peace and happiness.

WEDNESDAY, or Mercury's day, a day of success in business.

THURSDAY, or Jupiter's day, a day for courage.

SUNDAY, or the Lord's Day, a day of happiness and rest.

The Unlucky Days were :—

TUESDAY, or Mars's day, a day for quarrels, litigation, and discord.

FRIDAY, or Venus's day, the Passion of Christ. Cessation of all work.

SATURDAY, or Saturn's day, a day of danger and death.

LUCKY AND UNLUCKY HOURS.

	LUCKY.	UNLUCKY.
S.	3 p.m. to 4.30 p.m.	4.30 p.m. to 6 p.m.
M.	1 p.m. to 3 p.m.	7.30 p.m. to 9 p.m.
T.	12 noon to 3.30 p.m.	3 p.m. to 4.30 p.m.
W.	10 a.m. to 12 noon	12 noon to 1.30 p.m.
Thur.	9 a.m. to 10.30 a.m.	1.30 p.m. to 3 p.m.
Fri.	7 a.m. to 9 a.m.	10 a.m. to 12 noon.
Sat.	6 a.m. to 7.30 a.m.	9 a.m. to 10 a.m.

The lucky and unlucky days of the week, according to the Arabs, are :—

SUNDAY.—A day for planting and building, because on this day God created the 7 spheres, the 7 planets, the 7 hells, the 7 earths, the 7 seas, the 7 members of man, and the 7 days of the week.

MONDAY.—A day for business and travelling. Idrîs went up to heaven. Moses went to Sinai and on this day the Unity of God was revealed.

TUESDAY.—A day of blood. This day Eve first menstruated. Cain killed Abel; and John the Baptist, Zachariah, and George (St. ?) were killed.

WEDNESDAY.—A day of calamity and catastrophe.

THURSDAY.—A favourable day for business. On this day Abraham obtained the freedom of Sara from Pharaoh. On this day Pharaoh's butler entered the prison of Joseph, and Muḥammad returned to Mecca.

FRIDAY.—A day for marriage. On this day the Prophets married and Adam consorted with Eve, Joseph with Zuleikha, Solomon with Balkîs, Muḥammad with Khadîja and 'Aisha, and 'Alî with Fâṭimah.

SATURDAY.—A day for fraud and trickery. On this day Joseph's brethren sold him to the Ishmaelites.

CHAPTER XXXIII.

THE HAND OF FÂṬIMAH.

In all ages and among all peoples, the hand has been a symbol of strength and power, and a picture of it has been regarded as a representation of God. In the Egyptian text of the *Book of Gates* on the alabaster coffin of Seti I in Sir John Soane's Museum, the "Great Hand" means the supreme Power which rules heaven and earth. And in the Vignettes which illustrate the text we see this "Great Hand" grasping the chain to which the Four Sons of Horus are fastened, and which fetters the serpents of the Underworld and Āpep the god of Evil and everlasting enemy of Rā the Sun-god. In mediaeval pictures the Supreme Being is represented by a hand which projects from the clouds. Sometimes the hand is open, and rays of light issue from the fingers, but it is often seen in the act of benediction, *i.e.* with two fingers raised. In the Bible the raising of the hand to a god is regarded as an act of worship (see I Kings xix. 18 ; Job xxxi. 27, etc.). The Assyrians used a collection of prayers to which they gave the name " Nish ḳâti," *i.e.* " the lifting of the hand " (King, *Babylonian Magic and Sorcery*, London, 1896). In Western Asia the act of raising the hand was universally regarded as symbolical of invocation to a deity, whether in attestation of an oath, or in offering up prayer and supplication. And the words " lifting of the hand " actually introduces the actual prayer of Nebuchadnezzar II to Marduk in the *East India House Inscription*. Little models of the outstretched hand have been found in many countries, and these were used as amulets ; figures of the hand were attached to royal sceptres and spears and other weapons, always with the idea of con-

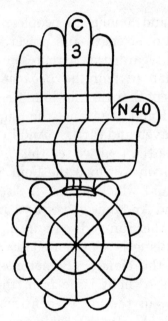

The hand of Fâṭimah.

ferring power on the holders of the sceptres and the users of the weapons. In pictures a hand with the thumb and the third and fourth fingers closed, and the first and second finger outstretched, indicates " blessing " ; but a closed hand with the first and fourth fingers outstretched represents the " horns of the Devil." Nevertheless models of such a hand were worn as amulets. A closed hand with the first

finger alone outstretched was in some countries
regarded as a sure protection against the Evil Eye.
Among the Arabs and Abyssinians the right hand is
held to be the " hand of honour " and the left the
" hand of dishonour," because it is used in the performance of acts which, though necessary, are
regarded as unclean. The hands must be washed
before prayers and before meals. And note the
words in Ps. xxvi. 6 : " I will wash mine hands in
innocency."

Among the Arabs figures and drawings of
the right hand of the lady Fâṭimah, *i.e.* the
" Weaver," were held to be powerful amulets.
Fâṭimah was a daughter of Muḥammad by his first
wife Khadîjah, and she married 'Alî, the cousin
of Muḥammad, by whom she had three sons, Ḥasan,
Ḥusain and Muhain. She is called " Al-Zahra,"
the " bright blooming " (a name of Venus), and
" Al-Batûl " *i.e.* " clean maid " or " Virgin," even
after her motherhood. Muḥammad held her to
be one of the four perfect women, the other
three being his wife Khadîjah, Asia, the wife of
Pharaoh, and the Virgin Mary. According to the
commentators the hand of Fâṭimah represents the
whole religion of Islâm and its fundamental duties,
viz., to keep the Fast of Ramaḍân, to make the
pilgrimage to Makkah, to give alms to the poor,
and destroy the unbelievers, and to perform strictly
and regularly the prescribed ablutions. Her
hand too symbolized the family of Muḥammad,
the thumb represented the Prophet himself, the
first finger Fâṭimah, the second finger 'Alî her
husband the third and fourth fingers their sons
Ḥasan and Ḥusain. And the fourth finger also

symbolized many spiritual and moral excellencies and good qualities.

The illustration on page 468 shows how the right hand of Fâṭimah was drawn in mediaeval manuscripts. In each division was a letter of the alphabet and a number. To find the character, disposition, and qualities of an individual by means of it the enquirer wrote down the letters which formed his name. He then wrote down under them the numbers which were written in the divisions from which the numbers were taken. Thus if the letter was N he wrote by it 40 ; if it was C he wrote 3, and so on. He then added up the figures, and the total represented the special number of the individual. To find out what this number signified the enquirer then consulted a long list of numbers to each of which was attached some characteristic or quality, thus :—

3 Mysticism, contemplation, love of the divine.

15 Affection for what is beautiful and idealistic.

21 Brutality, violence, harshness.

36 Large-mindedness, endowed with great ideas.

70 Love of science.

If a man wishes to find out if he is going to be successful in any undertaking, or if he is going to vanquish a rival, he must write down the baptismal names of himself and his rival in letters and the numerical value of each letter below it according to the values given by the Double Zodiac. He must then add up each group of figures and divide each total by 9. He must then consult the table of numbers of which extracts have been given above, and the number which is the same as that remaining

over after the divisions of totals of the name number
by 9, will tell him whether he or his rival will be
successful. A list of numbers in the table will be
found in the *Encyclopédie des Sciences Occultes*, Paris
(no date), p. 523. The Introduction to this volume
is by M. C. Poinsot. The Hebrews also had a
magical hand in which permutations of the ineffable
Name of God, etc., were written, see Seligmann,
Dr. S., *Die Zauberkraft des Anges*, Hamburg, 1922,
p. 16.

CHAPTER XXXIV.

CONTRACTS WITH THE DEVIL.

The magical literature of the Middle Ages contains many legends of men who in order to obtain wealth or power or possession of a certain woman, made a contract with the Devil who, having given them what they coveted, came at the end of the period agreed upon and seized them and carried them off to hell. The contract was said to be written on parchment or paper with the blood of the man who applied to the Devil for assistance, and when he had signed his name the Devil carried off the document and placed it among his archives. That men could and did make contracts with the Devil was commonly believed in the East and in the West, for it was argued that if men could obtain their heart's desire from the Archangels of God, why should they not be able to do so from the Devil himself, or from his chief ministers? Usually the man who made the contract paid the penalty and the Devil got his due, but a few instances are known in which certain Christian saints have succeeded in cheating him out of his prey. For when the powers of evil were carrying away his soul to hell, the saints intervened and snatched it from their hands (or paws), and conveyed it elsewhere. Few, if any, of the mediaeval legends make the Devil give back the bond or contract and release the man from his obligation to him, probably because no one believed that the Devil would act like a charitable creditor.

One interesting instance of the Devil's charity in this respect is on record, and that is found in the Ethiopian SENKESÂR or Book of Saints of the Ethiopian Church. The Ethiopians, like the Egyptian Christians (Copts), believed in a personal Devil who was able to take any and every form or shape at will, and who could travel with equal ease through earth, air, and water. In the pictures which illustrate their manuscripts he is usually represented as a huge black man, with large fiery eyes and terrible teeth, with an enormously long body and long thin legs, and paws with claws. On his head is a pair of horns, and he has a long tail. The lesser fiends who perform his will have animals' heads and also tails ; they, like their master, possessed an over-poweringly filthy smell, by which their comings and goings could be detected. But the Devil, whether called Diabolos, or Satan, or Masṭêmâ, took form of a man at will, and possessing great cunning and skill in trafficking and bargaining with men frequently succeeded in buying their souls from them.

According to the SENKESÂR (month of Maskaram, day XIII, Budge's translation, vol. i. p. 46) a certain young man fell in love with his master's daughter, and as, apparently, his suit was not favoured by her parents, he consulted a magician and asked him to entreat Satan to give him the maiden. The magician agreed to do this, and having written a petition on a piece of paper, he gave it to the young man and told him to go to the cemetery of the pagans at midnight, and to stand by one of the tombs there, and to hold up his right hand with the paper in it. The young man obeyed these instructions, and a Satan appeared and took the paper out of his hand

and conducted him to the Satan-in-chief, who said :
" Dost thou believe in me, O young man ?   Wilt
thou deny thy Christ and not turn again to Him
after I have fulfilled thy desire ? "   The young man
promised to do what the Satan told him, and then
the Satan said to him : " Write with thine own
hand on the piece of paper that thou wilt do this,"
and the young man wrote and denied Christ.

Then Satan began to work on the heart of the
maiden, and he filled her with lust so completely
that she said to her father : " If thou wilt not give
me in marriage to thy servant then assuredly I will
kill myself." Fearing that she would carry her
threat into execution the father consented to the
marriage and the couple were married forthwith
and set up housekeeping together.   Then the parents
of the maiden wept sorely and they entreated God
to remove their sorrow, and Christ heard their petition
and showed the maiden that the man whom she
loved was not a Christian.   Presently she noticed
that he never partook of the Sacrament, and when
she pressed him to go with her to the Table of the
Lord, he refused and told her of what he had done
in order to obtain possession of her, and how he had
denied Christ and given a bond to the Devil.   Then
was the young wife filled with grief, and she blamed
herself and went to Saint Basil and told him her
story and asked him to save her.   Basil sent for the
young man and having heard his version of the
story asked him if he wished to repent and return to
Christianity.   The young man said that that was
his wish, and Basil replied : " Be of good cheer, and
fear not."   Having made the sign of the Cross over
him Basil took him to his cell and lodged him in a

small chamber and told him to pray for three days. At the end of this period Basil went to him and asked him what had happened during the three days. The young man replied that he had suffered greatly through the Satans who threatened him with loud cries and showed him the paper which he had signed. After speaking words of encouragement to him Basil gave him bread and water and took him back to the chamber and prayed over him. After a further period Basil visited him, and the young man told him that he had been hearing the cries of the devils round about him, but had not seen them. Basil continued this treatment of the young man for forty days, and visited him every third day. When the forty days were ended the young man said to Basil : " O my holy father, last night I saw thee waging war against Satan on my behalf, and thou didst vanquish him straightway," and the holy man rejoiced exceedingly, for he knew that his own prayers and those of the young man, which were coupled with repentance, were having great effect on the devils. He then summoned all the monks from all the monasteries of Caesarea and Cappadocia, of which places he was the bishop, and all the priests, and they prayed for the salvation of the young man all that night. On the following day he brought the young man to his church, and the people of the city came there also, and he commanded all of them to lift up their hands to heaven and to pray and make entreaty to God and say : " Have mercy upon us " ; and they all did as he commanded them. And they continued to cry out and to say : " Lord have mercy upon us," and at length the piece of paper on which the young man had denied Christ and promised allegiance to Satan and signed with his name fell down from the roof in the presence of all the people. Then Basil went and took up the paper, and unrolled it, and read what was written upon it in the presence of all the people. And he blessed the young man and administered the Sacrament to him. And he called the wife of the young man and blessed them both and they departed to their home rejoicing and exulting in their salvation. And they praised God and thanked Saint Basil, who by his prayers had delivered the young man from the thrall of Satan.

Another section of the same book (p. 76) tells the story of a young man of Antioch, who applied to Cyprianus the magician for help in a somewhat similar case. But the magic of Cyprianus was unable to stir up lust in the maiden Justina, for when the Satans went to her they always found her praying. The Satans tried to deceive Cyprianus, but he discovered their imposture, which disgusted him so much that he burnt his books of magic and was baptized by the Archbishop of Antioch. He became a monk, and was made a deacon and then a priest, and finally he became Bishop of Carthage, and made Justina abbess in a house of virgins. Decius ordered them to worship idols, but they refused to do so, and after they had suffered severe tortures the Emperor had the bishop and Justina beheaded.

The Book of the Miracles of the Virgin Mary contains many stories which show that Our Lady not only had the power to rescue souls from the Satans when they were carrying them to hell, but that she frequently used it. In the large richly illustrated Codices of her Miracles we see her fighting with the Satans for the possession of the souls of

those in whom she was personally interested, and
according to the Vignettes she was in such cases
always successful. The Virgin did not interfere
in the case of the unrepentant sinner, as we see from
drawing No. 1. Here we see the dying man lying
on his rope bed, with one devil seizing his wrists
and another his feet, and as soon as he dies they will
carry his soul off to hell.   In No. 2 we see two devils

No. 1.

carrying away the souls of two men which they had
wrenched from their bodies. But whilst they were
doing this the Virgin appeared, and grasping the
two souls, who are given human forms, she delivered
them from the claws of the devils. The text makes
it clear why she exercised her power on this occasion.
The two souls were the souls of two brothers who
were scribes, and who at one time of their life
had made a copy or copies of her Book of Miracles.

They had fallen into sin subsequently and on their death, the devils seized their souls as their lawful possessions. But Mary, because they had written her Book of Miracles, could not allow them to be destroyed, and she therefore rescued them. Nos. 3 and 4 illustrate the story of the cannibal of Kemer, who was a strong and a very cruel and brutal man. He killed and ate his wife and children and all his servants, in all seventy-eight people. Now he was

No. 2.

a Christian. Then he set out to find other victims, and one day he saw a beggar and determined to eat him ; but when he came up to him he found that he was a leper. The leper begged for water in the Name of God, and in the names of martyrs, but the cannibal laughed at him. Finally the leper begged for water in the name of Mary, and the cannibal handed him his water bottle, but before the leper could satisfy his thirst, the bottle was snatched from his hands by the cannibal. In due course he died and the devils appeared and seized his soul and took it to Satan. Mary, remembering that the cannibal had given the leper half a drink of water in her name, tried to snatch the soul from the devil,

No. 3.

but failed to secure it (No. 3). Then she appealed to the Father, and begged for the salvation of the soul of the cannibal because he had given water to the leper. The Father ordered an archangel to weigh the draught of water against the seventy-eight people whom the cannibal had killed and eaten. The Scales of Justice were brought forth, and the merit of giving a draught of water to the leper was weighed against the sin of the murders of the seventy-eight people whose heads are seen pro-

No. 4.

jecting from the right pan of the Scales. When the archangel held up the Scales it was found that the merit of the cannibal outweighed his sins. Thereupon his soul was given to Mary, and in No. 4 we see her sheltering it within her cloak.

CHAPTER XXXV.

ENVOÛTEMENT.

This word, which is often used in French books on magic, means the act of making a figure of wax of a certain person as exact as possible as regards face (the Latin *in* + *vultus*) and form and special characteristics, with the intention, after having performed upon it certain baleful acts and ceremonies, of making the person represented by the wax figure to suffer all the pains and indignities which the magician inflicts on the wax figure. Whilst the magician is attacking the wax figure he repeats spells and incantations which effect the transmission of aches and pains and sufferings to the human being wheresoever he may be. Thus, if a needle was thrust through the knee joints of the wax figure the human being which it represented would suffer agonies in his knees ; if a needle was thrust through the heart of the wax figure the human being would die. But envoûtement could be practised with a good as well as a bad object. For there is on record the case of a seaman who during a fight at sea was shot in the eye with an arrow, and as a result he suffered indescribable agony. But his friends made a figure of him with the arrow in his eye, and took it to a famous shrine of the Virgin Mary in Syria. The figure of the Virgin drew the arrow out of the eye of the figure, and at the same moment the arrow which was in the eye of the seaman, who was still on the sea, fell out from it, and the pain ceased from that moment.

One of the oldest examples of the use of wax figures for the purpose of injuring a human being is found in a papyrus inscribed with the account of a conspiracy hatched against Rameses III (see Déveria, *Le Papyrus Judiciare de Turin*, Paris, 1868). The king had become unpopular, and several of the Court ladies and the higher officials wished to get rid of him and to appoint in his room one Pen-ta-urt. They took into their service a certain magician called Hui, who was famed for his knowledge of the occult, and having put into his hands a Book of Magic from the Royal Library at Thebes, they told him to bring about the death of the king and his friends. Hui made figures of the king and his officials in wax, and, presumably, wrote their names upon them, and he made amulets on which he inscribed words of power, and he cast a spell on a certain man and made him take these things into the palace, where they were expected to influence adversely the king's health. But the plot became known, and the ringleaders of the conspiracy were arrested and tried for high treason by eleven judges. Ultimately about forty men and six women were executed, and several other conspirators were permitted to commit suicide.

Another interesting example of the use of the wax figures is given in the Papyrus of Nesi-Amsu in the British Museum (ed. Budge, *Archaeologia*, vol. lii). In order to overthrow Āpep, the god of evil and the everlasting enemy of Rā the Sun-god, a series of chapters of spells and curses had to be recited, and certain ceremonies performed. The rubrics order that a figure of Āpep be drawn in green ink upon a piece of new papyrus, and that a wax figure be made of Āpep, and his name was to be inscribed upon it in green ink. This figure, wrapped round with the piece of new papyrus, is to be thrown into a fire made of a special kind of herb, and whilst burning is to be kicked with the left foot four times, and when burnt its remains are to be mixed with excrement and thrown into another fire. Figures of Āpep were to be burnt in this manner at frequent intervals during the day and night, and another rubric says : " Thou shalt act thus when tempests rage in the eastern sky, to prevent the arrival of red clouds there and to prevent rain or storm." To burn Āpep was a meritorious act, for the rubric continues : " It is good for a man to do this, good for him upon earth and in the Underworld. Power will be given to him to attain to honours which are beyond him, and he will be, in truth, delivered from all evil things."

And wax figures of the king's enemies were made, and their names were written upon the wax with green ink, and then they were placed in cases and burnt. During this process they were to be spit upon, and trampled upon and defiled with the left foot, and gashes were to be made in them with a knife ; after this they were to be thrown into a fire made with special herbs, and the fire was to be quenched with the urine of a crocodile.

To destroy the fiends which were the servants of Āpep figures of four serpents were made in wax One had the face of a cat, another the face of a duck, another the face of a white cat, and the fourth the face of a hawk. They were tied up and fettered, knives were stuck in their backs, and then they were cast on the ground and treated in the same manner as the wax figures of Āpep. This monster had about thirty distinct forms, and each had its own name, and in the ritual was cursed with terrible curses. Besides that of a crocodile Āpep was given the form of a serpent, which had its tail in its mouth, and a knife stuck in its back. The ceremony of burning the waxen Āpep was performed many times during the month by day and by night in the great temple of Amen-Rā at Thebes, and it is quite certain that the Egyptian priesthood, as well as the people, believed that the frequent repetition of the " Book of Overthrowing Āpep " was of vital importance for the well-being of Egypt and her people. Now there was another aspect in which Āpep was regarded. He was the arch-enemy of Rā the Sun-god, but the king of Egypt was the " son of Rā " ; therefore Āpep was the arch-enemy of Pharaoh, and all the fiends and devils who served Āpep in the Under-world, and all the evil men and rebels who served him on earth were also enemies of Pharaoh, and wax figures of them were made and burned and cursed as were the figures of Āpep.

A wax figure of a man which was made for a magical purpose was found in Egypt a few years ago and is now in the British Museum (No. 37918) ; the wax casing encloses a lock of human hair and a piece of inscribed papyrus. Figures of the Four Sons of Horus were also made in wax, and either laid on the coffin or inserted among the swathings of the mummy. Some are in white wax (B.M., No. 15563, etc.) and some in red (B.M., No. 8889, etc.).

As we have seen wax was used in working White as well as Black Magic, but sometimes a piece of paper was used instead of wax. Thus the Muslim who wants to harm or kill a man when he has no wax takes a piece of paper and draws on it the figure of the person he wishes to injure, and he writes the name of that person either on or by the figure. He then nails the paper to a door or wall upside down, and proceeds to recite over it certain verses from the Ḳur'ân. The recitation over he takes an iron needle and makes it red hot in the fire and stabs the paper with it, taking care that the hole made by the needle is in the breast of the figure. At the same time he pronounces a spell or incantation and says to the needle, " Pierce his body even as this needle pierces this paper, and take away sleep from him." Thereupon the person whose figure is on the paper feels the stab in his body, coupled with the burning pain caused by the red-hot needle, and suffers agony as long as the needle remains stuck in the paper. As soon as the needle is withdrawn from the paper the man finds relief, but if it is left there indefinitely he dies. Carra de Vaux in HASTINGS' *Encyclopaedia*, vol. iii. p. 460.

The use of wax figures for magical purposes passed from Egypt viâ Greece and Italy into England, and in the Middle Ages much harm was wrought by their means, and people were terrified at the thought that sickness and even death could be inflicted on them by foes a long way off. It will be remembered that much alarm was caused in London during the reign of Queen Elizabeth because a wax figure of Her Majesty, with a pin stuck in the breast, had been found in Lincoln's Inn Fields. As no one had any doubt but that harm to Her Majesty's person had been planned by some villain, Dr. John Dee

(1527–1608), the famous astrologer, and as some said magician, was summoned to the Queen's presence to deal with the matter. For modern instances of the use of wax figures with diabolical intent see Elworthy, *Evil Eye*, London, 1895, pp. 53–56.

That the Hebrews at times used envoûtement is proved by the following passage from the magical book entitled " The Sword of Moses " (see Gaster, *Studies and Texts*, vol. i. p. 324, No. 68).

" If you wish to kill a man, take mud from the two sides of the river and form it into the shape of a figure, and write upon it the name of the person, and take seven branches from seven strong palms, and make a bow from reed (?) with the string of horse-sinew, and place the image in a hollow, and stretch the bow and shoot with it, and at each branch (shot) say the words of No. 68 (*sic*) ; and may NN be destroyed."

CHAPTER XXXVI.

MISCELLANEOUS.

1. METALS identified with the Planets :—Gold with the Sun, Silver with the Moon, Iron with Mars, Mercury with Mercury, Tin with Jupiter, Copper with Venus, Lead with Saturn.

2. COLOURS identified with the Planets :—Gold with the Sun, Silver with the Moon, or colour which changes (shot), Green with Venus, Red with Mars, Blue with Jupiter, Black with Saturn.

3. Colours identified with the Signs of the Zodiac : Fire with the Ram, Dark green with the Bull, Chestnut with the Twins, Silver with Cancer, Gold with the Lion, Variegated with the Virgin, Water-green with the Balance, Vermilion with the Scorpion, Sky-blue with Sagittarius, Black with Capricorn, Grey with Aquarius, Sea-blue with the Fishes.

4. GOOD COLOURS.—Violet symbolizes intelligence, knowledge ; Blue, chaste affection ; Green hope, confidence ; Rose, sweetness of disposition ; White, purity, truth and joy ; Red, ardour, health and strength ; Amaranth, constancy, fidelity ; Lilac, freshness, first-born ; Violet and Green and Yellow, triumph.

5. BAD COLOURS.—White and black, death, sorrow ; Black, sadness, grief ; Orange, luxury ; Yellow, falsity, treason, ambition, avarice ; Brown, penitence and grief ; Purple, pomp, pride ; the colour of dead leaves, grief, decay, ruin.

6. THE APPARATUS OF THE MAGICIAN.—One of

the stories told in the Westcar Papyrus (Berlin, p. 3033) shows that the Egyptian magician Ubaner kept the materials which he used in working magic in a box made of ebony and white gold, and that one of the substances which he used was wax. His servant brought this box to him one day, and he took wax from it and made the model of a crocodile seven spans long, and he recited over it magical words which gave it the power to turn into a living crocodile. The servant took the model and threw it into the river, and it became a monstrous and hideous crocodile which devoured the lover of the magician's wife when he went to bathe at dawn. The Egyptian king Nectanebus made models of ships and men in wax, and set them in a tank of water. Then he took an ebony rod in his hand, and having uttered certain magical formulae in the name of Amen of Lybia the models of his own ships and men would begin to move about, and attack and sink the models of the ships of his enemies. The powers of the rod of Moses which destroyed the rods of the Egyptian magicians and gave victory to the Israelites is too well known to need description. It had the power of the rod of the water diviner, for when Moses struck the rock with it water gushed forth. The medical magicians also used a rod during the performance of their cures, and their god also used a rod, a drawing of which is given on page 489. This is copied from a vase in Paris which was dedicated by Gudea, king of Babylonia about 2350 B.C., to the Sumerian god Ningishzida, the son of Ninazu, the Master-physician. This rod probably had two serpents carved upon it, or perhaps figures of two serpents in bronze were coiled about it ; in any case it is the symbol of the great guild of physicians in England at the present day. The snake sloughs its skin annually, and so suggested the ideas of renewed life and immortality to the ancients.

7. MAGICAL PLANTS.—Many of the ancient herbalists knew that the juices of certain plants possessed properties which produced extraordinary effects when introduced into the human body, and that some might be used as aphrodisiacs, and others as narcotics, and others as stimulants. And the magicians when they were acquainted with them naturally used them in their lotions and philtres to produce both good and evil effects. Certain plants were associated with the planets and were supposed to supplement or strengthen the influences of the Seven Astrological Stars, but they were probably more useful to the physician than the astrologer.

The rod of Ningishzida.

8. MAGICAL MIRRORS were, and are to this day, made of vessels filled with clear water drawn from a well or river ; sometimes the mirror is made with ink held in the hollow of the left hand of the enquirer into the future, who must be seated. The magician walks round him several times repeating spells as he walks, and at intervals he bids the enquirer look steadily into the ink. When he had done so for some few minutes small ripples pass over the surface of the ink, and when these have died down the scene required makes itself visible. The Kabbalists used

seven metal mirrors, each of which bore the name of one of the planets ; thus the mirror of the Sun was made of gold, *i.e.* the solar metal, and could only be consulted with advantage on a Sunday, *i.e.* the day of the Sun. The mirror of the Moon was made of silver and could only be consulted with advantage on Monday, and so on for the other days of the week. The five other metals were iron (Tuesday), mercury (Wednesday), tin (Thursday), copper (Friday), lead (Saturday).

9. MANDRAKES (LOVE APPLES).—These are mentioned in the Bible (Gen. xxx. 14), and there is no doubt that ancients used decoctions of the plant both as aphrodisiacs and as narcotics. The roots assume extraordinary shapes and forms, and frequently resemble the legs of men and women and phalli. The magicians used it largely in making their love philtres, and the modern Cairene drug seller gives it to young couples who are going to be married and who wish to have large families of *boys*. Formerly little figures made from mandragora roots could be bought in Baghdâd, where they found a ready sale, and they were worn as amulets which stimulated virility and fecundity, and made their wearers prosperous. For a remarkable series of drawings of the roots of the mandragora, see Mr. C. Singer's article on the " Juliana Anicia Codex " in the *Journal* of Hellenic Studies, vol. xlvii (1927), p. 4 ff. The plant has a foetid and somewhat nauseating smell.

10. DIVINATION BY THE DEAD.—Probably the oldest instance of divination by the dead is found in the Epic of Gilgamish, the King of Ur, whose one quest in life was to find the secret of immortality.

He had failed to find it on earth and he tried to find it in the kingdom of the dead. He applied to the priests, but they one and all failed him, and he thought that if only he could hold converse with his beloved friend Enkidu, he would be able to find out what he wished to know. He appealed to Bêl and Sin to raise up the spirit of Enkidu for him, but each god refused. Then he appealed to Ea, who ordered Nergal, the god of war, to produce the spirit of Enkidu. Nergal opened a shaft in the ground through which the spirit of Enkidu passed up into this world " like a breath of wind." Gilgamish began to question the spirit of Enkidu but he gained little information from him and certainly no satis-faction. What the spirit of Enkidu was like we shall never know, but Gilgamish must have seen something, or he could not have asked his questions. The priest of Nergal was probably a medium, who burnt incense and by suggestion or hypnotism made Gilgamish see some kind of figure. The witch of Endor also was probably a medium and used the same means as the priest of Nergal, and showed Saul a figure of Samuel in the smoke of the incense. It is something of this sort which is done to-day in parts of North-east Africa where men, and women, in difficulties, seek for information from their dead kinsfolk.   And necromancers like Cecrops, Apol-lonius of Tyana, Jamblichus, Porphyry and others who made divination by the dead probably used a similar method.

11. PALMISTRY.—The art of obtaining information about the future from the palm of the hand is very old, and the modern form of it which is now in use in the countries of the Near East and in Europe is

based upon the systems which were formulated by the Chinese and Indians. (See Prof. H. A. Giles, " Palmistry in China," in the *Nineteenth Century*, 1904.) Two phases of the art are known, and these are called " Chirognomia " and " Chiromantia," the latter dealing with the hand from an astrological point of view. Some have attempted to show that the art is of divine origin, relying on the words of Job xxxvii. 7, " He sealeth up the hand of every man ; that all men may know his works." Many of the older palmists attached special importance to the shape and form of hands, of which some seventy varieties were enumerated, and their readings differed very considerably from those obtained from the lines and prominences of the inner side of the hand. All agree that the thumb is the most important part of the hand, and say that the first phalange symbolizes will-power and the second logic ; the ball of the thumb is called the Mount of Venus. The line round about the thumb is the *line of life*. Every phalange of the four fingers symbolizes some quality, physical or mental. The mount of Jupiter is at the base of the first finger and symbolizes arrogance, haughtiness, pride, and the like. The mount of Saturn is at the base of the middle finger, the *digitus infamis* of the Romans, and symbolizes fate, destiny. The mount of Apollo is at the base of the third finger and symbolizes art, music, easy circumstances in life, etc. The Mount of Mercury is at the base of the fourth finger and indicates learning. The mount of Mars and the mount of the Moon are on the heel of the hand, and symbolize violence and light-mindedness respectively. The *line of the heel* joins the *line of life* under the first finger ; parallel to it is the *line of the heart ;* the *line of fate* runs up the centre of the hand, and parallel to it, on the heel side of the hand, is the *line of fortune.* The curved line from below the fourth finger to the base of the first is called " the girdle of Venus." The left hand is usually chosen for examination by palmists, but neither the left nor right hands of any two persons are identical as far as their lines and mounts are concerned.   Expert palmists attach great importance to the little crosses and triangles and markings which appear in many hands, and to the lines which are found on the phalanges of the four fingers, and very few agree about the qualities which they think they indicate.   Many think that the lines and ridges on the back of the hand are important witnesses as to character and disposition, and some deduce much information from the lines on the wrist.   Mediaeval writers based their works on Hartlieb, *Die Kunst Ciromantia,* Augsburg (XVth century), but modern writers like Desbarolles, D'Arpentigny, Frith, and Allen seem to have borrowed largely from the section of the work of Cornelius Agrippa which deals with Palmistry.   A fresh impetus was given to the study of Chiromancy by Mr. Cheiro, who gave many lectures and published a cheap, popular book on the subject.

12. LUCKY STONES OF THE TWELVE MONTHS OF THE YEAR.—January, Garnet ; February, Amethyst; March, Bloodstone ; April, Diamond ; May, Emerald ; June, Agate ; July, Turquoise ; August, Carnelian ; September, Chrysolite ; October, Beryl ; November, Topaz ; December, Ruby.   The stones specially fitted for amulets for the twelve months are : January, Onyx ; February, Jasper ; March,

Ruby ; April, Topaz ; May, Carnelian ; June, Emerald ; July, Sapphire ; August, Diamond ; September, Heliotrope ; October, Agate ; November, Amethyst ; December, Beryl. But several other lists are known. See Villiers and Pachinger, *Amulette*, pp. 92, 93.

13. AMULETS MADE OF PARTS OF THE HUMAN BODY.—These were the phallus, the *pudenda muliebris*, the hand, the little finger of the right hand, one other finger. BONE DUST was used in medicine and food, and bone-ashes were mixed with water and drunk. HUMAN fat was used as ointment in Black Magic, and SKULLS were used as drinking vessels. HUMAN skin was nailed on seats of judgment, and at one time cigarette cases made of it could be bought in Paris.

INDEX.

INDEX

In the transliteration of Oriental proper names and words, Ḥ represents a sharp but smooth gutteral aspirate; Ṭ is a strongly articulated palatal T; Ṣ is a strongly articulated S, something like ss in *hiss*; Ḳ is a strongly articulated gutteral K; an apostrophe before a letter (*e.g.* 'A) is the spiritus lenis of the Greeks, and an inverted comma (*e.g.* ʿA) is a strong gutteral, like the Hebrew **ע**, which is unpronounceable by Europeans. Long vowels are marked by a circumflex.

A.a.A = AHYH.asher.AHYH, 270.

Åāḥ, the Egyptian Moon-god, 141.

Åakhunåten, *i.e.* Åmen-hatep IV, 136.

Aaron, high priest, 215, 270, 290, 327, 328.

Aaron, the great blessing of, 219.

Ab, the month, 379.

Âb, a mythological fish, the Fighter, 152.

Ab Abr Abra formula, 221.

Abatûr, the throne of, 241.

'Abbâdâ Kĕ Dâbrâ (Abracadabra), 220.

ʿAbd al-Hamid, ex Sultân of Turkey, 74.

Abel, brother of Cain, 466.

'Abgâr, his letter to Christ, 132.

'Abgath, the alphabet of, 404.

ʿAbhd Îshô', 278.

Abit, the praying mantis, 132.

Ablanathanalba, palindrome (?), 206, 207, 209, 211, 312.

Ablutions of Mandaeans, 239.

Ablutions of Muslims, 469.

Abortion, amulet against, 317.

ABRACADABRA formula, 220.

Abraham, 270, 430, 466.

Abrahàm, Isaac and Jacob, 307.

Abraham, Stele of, 129.

Abrakala, 222.

Abrasax = 365, 208f.

Abraxas, 208f.

Abraxas IAΩ, 207.

Abraxaster amulets, 205f.

Absalom, 437.

'Absare Dengel, amulet of, 182.

ʿAbtu Fish, 85, 152.

Abtûr-Tura, 285.

Abu, 409.

Abu Bakr and the Kur'ân, 51.

Abû Fara (?), 195.

Abu Ḥabbah, 452, 446.

Abu Hurairah, 47.

Abydos, 169.

Abyss, the primeval, 4.

Abyssinia, 177, 197, 323.

Abyssinians, 213, 235, 469.

Adad, 91, 124.

'Adaḳ bar-Ḥâthôi, 248.

'Adaḳ bath-Ḥâthôi, 248.

Adam, the first man, 195, 270, 274, 326, 377, 466.

Adam, creation of, 10; Bismillâh written on his side, 70.

Adam, his seal as a magical sign, 224, 226, 227.

Adam Ḳadmôn, 210.

Adam and Eve, 194.

Adam and Eve and Lîlîth, 236.

Adam of the Ophites (Gnostics), 210.

Adamites, 432.

Adar, the month, 379.

Kirschmann, Dr., 306.
Kishar, 4.
Kislimu, 409.
Knights Hospitallers, 343.
Knot, amulet of the, 150.
Knots, blowers on, 62.
Knots, the Eleven, 62.
Knowledge, transcendental, 200.
Kochbiel, 375.
Kôh-i-Nûr, 313.
Kolâstâ, 240.
Koldewey, Dr., 99–101.
Koraish tribe, 51.
Kordofân, 311, 313.
Korea, 363.
Ḳubbah Idrîs, 25, 79.
Ḳûfah, 51, 53.
Kullah, 118.
Kummu, the sick room of a temple, 103, 119.
Ḳur'ân, 31, 34, 44, 280 ; as amulet, 235 ; materials on which written, 27, 51 ; number of letters, verses and words in, 52.
Ḳur'ân amulet cases, 28.
Ḳûurnah, 77, 240.
Ḳûyûnjik, 451.

Laban, 152, 214, 301.
Labartu, 104ff. See Lamashtu.
Labour, women in, 318, 324.
Labourer, 409.
Ladder of Jacob, 148.
Ladder of Râ, 148.
Ladder of the Crucifixion, 341.
Ladder amulet, 148.
Lagash, 118.
Lake of boiling water, 438.
Lake of Life, 438.
Lake, Sacred, at Karnak, 163.
Lakhamu, 408.
Lâlâ, 288.
" La Muscotte " Opera of, 31.

Lamashtu, the devil-woman, 92, 97 ; 104, 117 ; amulets of, 116 ; bribes of, 115 ; her five names, 117.
Lamassu, 120.
Lamb-parchment, 341.
Lâmbros, 279.
Lamentations of Isis, 163.
Lamp, 113, 114.
Lamp-bearers of Satan, 10.
Lankester, Prof. Ray, 298.
Lapis lazuli, 87, 317, 327.
Lapis lazuli, artificial, 317.
Lars Porsena, 435.
Last Judgment, 128.
Latarak, 120, 121.
Law, the Hebrew, 260 ; the Revealed, 367.
Law, Roman, 438.
Layard, Sir H., 113, 283, 288, 446.
Laylahel, 315.
Lead, amulets, of, 34.
Lead, inscribed sheets of, 253.
Lead, magical square of, 394.
Learning, 492.
Leather amulets, 18.
Leaves, amulets of, 18.
Lefâfa Sedeḳ, 196 ; crosses from, 179.
Legend of the Creation, 3.
Legion (Devils), 375.
Legrain, M. G., 136, 164.
Leḥâshîm (amulets), 215.
Leo, Zodiacal Sign, 205, 410, 411, 463 ; his influences on men, 418, 421.
Leo III, Pope, 351.
Leo XIII, Pope, 365.
Leopard, 109 ; gall of, 17.
Leopard amulets, 18.
Lepers and cannibal, 478.
Lepidotus fish, 298.
Le Puy, relic at, 26.
Le Roux, M. Hugues, 198, 199.
Leshem, 327.
Letter Circles and Wheels, 376.

Moses and the brazen serpent, 205.
Moss agate, 307.
Môṣul, 26, 272, 453.
Mother (Evil Eye), 279.
Mother-of-pearl, 70.
Mother-alphabet, 251.
Mother-of the Book, 52.
Mother of-everything (Tiâmat), 4.
Motion, the First, 375.
Mount Carmel, 250.
Mount Gerizim, 259, 269.
Mount of Apollo, 492.
Mount of Jupiter, 492.
Mount of Mars, 492.
Mount of Mercury, 492.
Mount of the Moon, 492.
Mount of Saturn, 492.
Mouse (?), 126.
Mueller, Max, 332.
Mughtasils, 239. 240.
Muhain, 469.
Muḥammad the Prophet, 26, 33, 46, 51, 73, 79, 302, 351, 359, 466, 469 ; bewitched, 67.
Muḥammad 'Alî Pâshâ, 165.
Muḥammadans, 10.
Mulilu, 118.
Mullah, a blesser of amulets, 70.
Multifariousness, 367.
Mûm yâ, 309.
Mummies, Egyptian, 309.
Mummu, envoy of Ea, 4.
Mummy of Apis, 85.
Musawwir, 302.
Muses, the Nine, 435.
Mushrush, 101.
Music, 434, 492.
Musk in ink, 70.
Muslims, 56, 60, 68, 80 ; of Persia, 26.
Mussel shells, 18.
Mut, goddess, 150, 157.
Mutonium, 15.
Mycerinus, King, 139.

Myrrh, 298.
Mysticism, 420, 470.

Naaman, 433.
Nablûs, 258.
Nabû, 17, 124.
Nahr al-Kabîr, 250.
Nail-fetish, 18.
Nails, the Three, 341.
Nakîêl, 373.
Name, the, equivalent of God or man, 7.
Name, the Essential, 46.
Name amulet, 147.
Names on ring of Solomon, 281.
Names, Gnostic, 203.
Names, the Ninety-nine Beautiful, 47.
Nancy, relic at, 26.
Naphtali, 379.
Napoleon III, 365.
Narâm-Sin, 452.
Narcotics, 489.
Nâr Marratu, 116.
Naruda, goddess, 120, 121.
Nassau, Dr., 15.
Neb-er-djer, 7.
Nebo, Library of, 453.
Nebseni, Papyrus of, 140–41.
Nebtshet, 157.
Nebti amulet, 156.
Nebuchadnezzar II, 468.
Nebun, 168.
Neck amulets, 306.
Necklaces, 155.
Necromancy, 213.
Nectanebus, 306.
Nefer amulet, 144, 340.
Nefer-Tem, 157.
Nefrite, 202.
Ne-gab stone, 116.
Negative Confession, 162, 180.
Neith, 150, 157.
Nekhebit, 157, 292.
Nekht-neb-f, 168.
Nenu, 7, 445.

Pebbles for counting prayers, 79.

Pechuel Loesila, 17.

Pectoral, 155 ; amulet, 150.

Pectoral, the Egyptian, 140.

Pegasus, 126.

Pegogha, 279.

Pehlevi language, 428.

Pehlevi gems, inscribed, 125.

Peleus, wedding of, 292.

Pen, copper, 228.

Penates, 152.

Pepi I, 148.

Pentacle, the, 40, 281, 431, 432, 433.

Pentacle with the Tetragrammaton, 203.

Pentagram, 209, 233, 298.

Pentateuch, 81, 235, 366, 379, 435.

Pentaurt, 482.

Perat, 269.

Pérétié, M., 109.

Perfume-Rings, 301.

Pergamon, divining disk of, 458.

Peridot, Peridote, Peridoto, 321, 327.

Permanence, emanation of En-Sôph, 370.

Permutations of letters and numbers, 261, 368, 400.

Persia, 31, 33, 53, 59, 70, 125, 137, 200, 306, 317, 320, 363.

Persians, 27, 28, 252, 412.

Personality in stones, 423.

Persons of the Trinity, 301.

Pert-em-hru, 162, 235.

Peru, 363.

Pessimism, 425.

Pestilence, 219, 322 ; amulets against, 21.

Peter, St., 437.

Peter of Apono, 403.

Phagrus fish, 152.

Phaleg, 387.

Phalli on rings, 296.

Phallus and Phallic Amulets, 15, 20, 308, 322, 490, 494.

Phallus of Osiris swallowed by a fish, 151.

Phallus with frog, 144.

Phallus with snake's head, 110.

Phantoms, 357.

Pharaoh, 433, 469 ; his butler, 466 ; his magicians, 212 ; his royal ring, 295.

Philistines, 216.

Philosopher's Stone, 438.

Philtres, love, 490.

Phoebus, 209.

Phoenicia, 137, 250.

Phoenicians, 250f ; cylinder seals of, 121 ; letters of the, 403.

Phoenix, 151.

Phul, 388.

Phylactery, 12 ; the Samaritan name of, 262.

Phylactery, metal case for, 265.

Phylacteries, Hebrew, 216.

Phylacteries, Samaritan, 258 f.

Piacenza, 451, 452.

Pictographs, Indian and Sumerian, 201, 202.

Pietra del pavone, 318.

Pietra della croce, 311.

Pietra della vedovanza, 314.

Pig, 151 ; not used in " medicine," 17 ; the wild, 97.

Pig, Zodiacal Sign, 412.

Pig and Lamashtu, 114.

Pilcher, Rev. E. T., 236.

Pilgrimage, (the Hajj), 469.

Pillar of scourging, 341.

Pillar of the Muslim Rosary, 79, 80.

Pillars, the Five, 45.

Pillars of the Sephîrôth, 400.

Pillow (headrest) amulet, 138.

Pimples, 310.

Pincers, 341:

Pinches, Dr. T. G., 455.

Pinehas, 270.

A CATALOGUE OF SELECTED DOVER BOOKS
IN ALL FIELDS OF INTEREST

A CATALOGUE OF SELECTED DOVER BOOKS
IN ALL FIELDS OF INTEREST

THE NOTEBOOKS OF LEONARDO DA VINCI, edited by J.P. Richter. Extracts from manuscripts reveal great genius; on painting, sculpture, anatomy, sciences, geography, etc. Both Italian and English. 186 ms. pages reproduced, plus 500 additional drawings, including studies for Last Supper, Sforza monument, etc. 860pp. 7⅞ x 10¾. USO 22572-0, 22573-9 Pa., Two vol. set $15.90

ART NOUVEAU DESIGNS IN COLOR, Alphonse Mucha, Maurice Verneuil, Georges Auriol. Full-color reproduction of Combinaisons ornamentales (c. 1900) by Art Nouveau masters. Floral, animal, geometric, interlacings, swashes — borders, frames, spots — all incredibly beautiful. 60 plates, hundreds of designs. 9⅜ x 8¹/₁₆. 22885-1 Pa. $4.00

GRAPHIC WORKS OF ODILON REDON. All great fantastic lithographs, etchings, engravings, drawings, 209 in all. Monsters, Huysmans, still life work, etc. Introduction by Alfred Werner. 209pp. 9⅛ x 12¼. 21996-8 Pa. $6.00

EXOTIC FLORAL PATTERNS IN COLOR, E.-A. Seguy. Incredibly beautiful full-color pochoir work by great French designer of 20's. Complete Bouquets et frondaisons, Suggestions pour étoffes. Richness must be seen to be believed. 40 plates containing 120 patterns. 80pp. 9⅜ x 12¼. 23041-4 Pa. $6.00

SELECTED ETCHINGS OF JAMES A. McN. WHISTLER, James A. McN. Whistler. 149 outstanding etchings by the great American artist, including selections from the Thames set and two Venice sets, the complete French set, and many individual prints. Introduction and explanatory note on each print by Maria Naylor. 157pp. 9⅜ x 12¼. 23194-1 Pa. $5.00

VISUAL ILLUSIONS: THEIR CAUSES, CHARACTERISTICS, AND APPLICATIONS, Matthew Luckiesh. Thorough description, discussion; shape and size, color, motion; natural illusion. Uses in art and industry. 100 illustrations. 252pp. 21530-X Pa. $3.00

TEN BOOKS ON ARCHITECTURE, Vitruvius. The most important book ever written on architecture. Early Roman aesthetics, technology, classical orders, site selection, all other aspects. Stands behind everything since. Morgan translation. 331pp. 20645-9 Pa. $3.75

THE CODEX NUTTALL. A PICTURE MANUSCRIPT FROM ANCIENT MEXICO, as first edited by Zelia Nuttall. Only inexpensive edition, in full color, of a pre-Columbian Mexican (Mixtec) book. 88 color plates show kings, gods, heroes, temples, sacrifices. New explanatory, historical introduction by Arthur G. Miller. 96pp. 11⅜ x 8½. 23168-2 Pa. $7.50

HOUDINI ON MAGIC, Harold Houdini. Edited by Walter Gibson, Morris N. Young. How he escaped; exposés of fake spiritualists; instructions for eye-catching tricks; other fascinating material by and about greatest magician. 155 illustrations. 280pp. 20384-0 Pa. $2.75

HANDBOOK OF THE NUTRITIONAL CONTENTS OF FOOD, U.S. Dept. of Agriculture. Largest, most detailed source of food nutrition information ever prepared. Two mammoth tables: one measuring nutrients in 100 grams of edible portion; the other, in edible portion of 1 pound as purchased. Originally titled Composition of Foods. 190pp. 9 x 12. 21342-0 Pa. $4.00

COMPLETE GUIDE TO HOME CANNING, PRESERVING AND FREEZING, U.S. Dept. of Agriculture. Seven basic manuals with full instructions for jams and jellies; pickles and relishes; canning fruits, vegetables, meat; freezing anything. Really good recipes, exact instructions for optimal results. Save a fortune in food. 156 illustrations. 214pp. 6⅛ x 9¼. 22911-4 Pa. $2.50

THE BREAD TRAY, Louis P. De Gouy. Nearly every bread the cook could buy or make: bread sticks of Italy, fruit breads of Greece, glazed rolls of Vienna, everything from corn pone to croissants. Over 500 recipes altogether. including buns, rolls, muffins, scones, and more. 463pp. 23000-7 Pa. $3.50

CREATIVE HAMBURGER COOKERY, Louis P. De Gouy. 182 unusual recipes for casseroles, meat loaves and hamburgers that turn inexpensive ground meat into memorable main dishes: Arizona chili burgers, burger tamale pie, burger stew, burger corn loaf, burger wine loaf, and more. 120pp. 23001-5 Pa. $1.75

LONG ISLAND SEAFOOD COOKBOOK, J. George Frederick and Jean Joyce. Probably the best American seafood cookbook. Hundreds of recipes. 40 gourmet sauces, 123 recipes using oysters alone! All varieties of fish and seafood amply represented. 324pp. 22677-8 Pa. $3.50

THE EPICUREAN: A COMPLETE TREATISE OF ANALYTICAL AND PRACTICAL STUDIES IN THE CULINARY ART, Charles Ranhofer. Great modern classic. 3,500 recipes from master chef of Delmonico's, turn-of-the-century America's best restaurant. Also explained, many techniques known only to professional chefs. 775 illustrations. 1183pp. 6⅝ x 10. 22680-8 Clothbd. $22.50

THE AMERICAN WINE COOK BOOK, Ted Hatch. Over 700 recipes: old favorites livened up with wine plus many more: Czech fish soup, quince soup, sauce Perigueux, shrimp shortcake, filets Stroganoff, cordon bleu goulash, jambonneau, wine fruit cake, more. 314pp. 22796-0 Pa. $2.50

DELICIOUS VEGETARIAN COOKING, Ivan Baker. Close to 500 delicious and varied recipes: soups, main course dishes (pea, bean, lentil, cheese, vegetable, pasta, and egg dishes), savories, stews, whole-wheat breads and cakes, more. 168pp. USO 22834-7 Pa. $1.75

How to Solve Chess Problems, Kenneth S. Howard. Practical suggestions on problem solving for very beginners. 58 two-move problems, 46 3-movers, 8 4-movers for practice, plus hints. 171pp. 20748-X Pa. $3.00

A Guide to Fairy Chess, Anthony Dickins. 3-D chess, 4-D chess, chess on a cylindrical board, reflecting pieces that bounce off edges, cooperative chess, retrograde chess, maximummers, much more. Most based on work of great Dawson. Full handbook, 100 problems. 66pp. 7⅞ x 10¾. 22687-5 Pa. $2.00

Win at Backgammon, Millard Hopper. Best opening moves, running game, blocking game, back game, tables of odds, etc. Hopper makes the game clear enough for anyone to play, and win. 43 diagrams. 111pp. 22894-0 Pa. $1.50

Bidding a Bridge Hand, Terence Reese. Master player "thinks out loud" the binding of 75 hands that defy point count systems. Organized by bidding problem—no-fit situations, overbidding, underbidding, cueing your defense, etc. 254pp. EBE 22830-4 Pa. $3.00

The Precision Bidding System in Bridge, C.C. Wei, edited by Alan Truscott. Inventor of precision bidding presents average hands and hands from actual play, including games from 1969 Bermuda Bowl where system emerged. 114 exercises. 116pp. 21171-1 Pa. $2.25

Learn Magic, Henry Hay. 20 simple, easy-to-follow lessons on magic for the new magician: illusions, card tricks, silks, sleights of hand, coin manipulations, escapes, and more —all with a minimum amount of equipment. Final chapter explains the great stage illusions. 92 illustrations. 285pp. 21238-6 Pa. $2.95

The New Magician's Manual, Walter B. Gibson. Step-by-step instructions and clear illustrations guide the novice in mastering 36 tricks; much equipment supplied on 16 pages of cut-out materials. 36 additional tricks. 64 illustrations. 159pp. 6⅝ x 10. 23113-5 Pa. $3.00

Professional Magic for Amateurs, Walter B. Gibson. 50 easy, effective tricks used by professionals —cards, string, tumblers, handkerchiefs, mental magic, etc. 63 illustrations. 223pp. 23012-0 Pa. $2.50

Card Manipulations, Jean Hugard. Very rich collection of manipulations; has taught thousands of fine magicians tricks that are really workable, eye-catching. Easily followed, serious work. Over 200 illustrations. 163pp. 20539-8 Pa. $2.00

Abbott's Encyclopedia of Rope Tricks for Magicians, Stewart James. Complete reference book for amateur and professional magicians containing more than 150 tricks involving knots, penetrations, cut and restored rope, etc. 510 illustrations. Reprint of 3rd edition. 400pp. 23206-9 Pa. $3.50

The Secrets of Houdini, J.C. Cannell. Classic study of Houdini's incredible magic, exposing closely-kept professional secrets and revealing, in general terms, the whole art of stage magic. 67 illustrations. 279pp. 22913-0 Pa. $3.00

CATALOGUE OF DOVER BOOKS

EAST O' THE SUN AND WEST O' THE MOON, George W. Dasent. Considered the best of all translations of these Norwegian folk tales, this collection has been enjoyed by generations of children (and folklorists too). Includes True and Untrue, Why the Sea is Salt, East O' the Sun and West O' the Moon, Why the Bear is Stumpy-Tailed, Boots and the Troll, The Cock and the Hen, Rich Peter the Pedlar, and 52 more. The only edition with all 59 tales. 77 illustrations by Erik Werenskiold and Theodor Kittelsen. xv + 418pp. 22521-6 Paperbound $4.00

GOOPS AND HOW TO BE THEM, Gelett Burgess. Classic of tongue-in-cheek humor, masquerading as etiquette book. 87 verses, twice as many cartoons, show mischievous Goops as they demonstrate to children virtues of table manners, neatness, courtesy, etc. Favorite for generations. viii + 88pp. 6½ x 9¼. 22233-0 Paperbound $2.00

ALICE'S ADVENTURES UNDER GROUND, Lewis Carroll. The first version, quite different from the final *Alice in Wonderland,* printed out by Carroll himself with his own illustrations. Complete facsimile of the "million dollar" manuscript Carroll gave to Alice Liddell in 1864. Introduction by Martin Gardner. viii + 96pp. Title and dedication pages in color. 21482-6 Paperbound $1.50

THE BROWNIES, THEIR BOOK, Palmer Cox. Small as mice, cunning as foxes, exuberant and full of mischief, the Brownies go to the zoo, toy shop, seashore, circus, etc., in 24 verse adventures and 266 illustrations. Long a favorite, since their first appearance in St. Nicholas Magazine. xi + 144pp. 6⅝ x 9¼. 21265-3 Paperbound $2.50

SONGS OF CHILDHOOD, Walter De La Mare. Published (under the pseudonym Walter Ramal) when De La Mare was only 29, this charming collection has long been a favorite children's book. A facsimile of the first edition in paper, the 47 poems capture the simplicity of the nursery rhyme and the ballad, including such lyrics as I Met Eve, Tartary, The Silver Penny. vii + 106pp. (USO) 21972-0 Paperbound $2.00

THE COMPLETE NONSENSE OF EDWARD LEAR, Edward Lear. The finest 19th-century humorist-cartoonist in full: all nonsense limericks, zany alphabets, Owl and Pussycat, songs, nonsense botany, and more than 500 illustrations by Lear himself. Edited by Holbrook Jackson. xxix + 287pp. (USO) 20167-8 Paperbound $3.00

BILLY WHISKERS: THE AUTOBIOGRAPHY OF A GOAT, Frances Trego Montgomery. A favorite of children since the early 20th century, here are the escapades of that rambunctious, irresistible and mischievous goat—Billy Whiskers. Much in the spirit of *Peck's Bad Boy,* this is a book that children never tire of reading or hearing. All the original familiar illustrations by W. H. Fry are included: 6 color plates, 18 black and white drawings. 159pp. 22345-0 Paperbound $2.75

MOTHER GOOSE MELODIES. Faithful republication of the fabulously rare Munroe and Francis "copyright 1833" Boston edition—the most important Mother Goose collection, usually referred to as the "original." Familiar rhymes plus many rare ones, with wonderful old woodcut illustrations. Edited by E. F. Bleiler. 128pp. 4½ x 6⅜. 22577-1 Paperbound $1.50

EARLY NEW ENGLAND GRAVESTONE RUBBINGS, Edmund V. Gillon, Jr. 43 photographs, 226 rubbings show heavily symbolic, macabre, sometimes humorous primitive American art. Up to early 19th century. 207pp. 8⅜ x 11¼.
21380-3 Pa. $4.00

L.J.M. DAGUERRE: THE HISTORY OF THE DIORAMA AND THE DAGUERREOTYPE, Helmut and Alison Gernsheim. Definitive account. Early history, life and work of Daguerre; discovery of daguerreotype process; diffusion abroad; other early photography. 124 illustrations. 226pp. 6⅙ x 9¼.
22290-X Pa. $4.00

PHOTOGRAPHY AND THE AMERICAN SCENE, Robert Taft. The basic book on American photography as art, recording form, 1839-1889. Development, influence on society, great photographers, types (portraits, war, frontier, etc.), whatever else needed. Inexhaustible. Illustrated with 322 early photos, daguerreotypes, tintypes, stereo slides, etc. 546pp. 6⅛ x 9¼.
21201-7 Pa. $6.00

PHOTOGRAPHIC SKETCHBOOK OF THE CIVIL WAR, Alexander Gardner. Reproduction of 1866 volume with 100 on-the-field photographs: Manassas, Lincoln on battlefield, slave pens, etc. Introduction by E.F. Bleiler. 224pp. 10¾ x 9.
22731-6 Pa. $6.00

THE MOVIES: A PICTURE QUIZ BOOK, Stanley Appelbaum & Hayward Cirker. Match stars with their movies, name actors and actresses, test your movie skill with 241 stills from 236 great movies, 1902-1959. Indexes of performers and films. 128pp. 8⅜ x 9¼.
20222-4 Pa. $3.00

THE TALKIES, Richard Griffith. Anthology of features, articles from Photoplay, 1928-1940, reproduced complete. Stars, famous movies, technical features, fabulous ads, etc.; Garbo, Chaplin, King Kong, Lubitsch, etc. 4 color plates, scores of illustrations. 327pp. 8⅜ x 11¼.
22762-6 Pa. $6.95

THE MOVIE MUSICAL FROM VITAPHONE TO "42ND STREET," edited by Miles Kreuger. Relive the rise of the movie musical as reported in the pages of Photoplay magazine (1926-1933): every movie review, cast list, ad, and record review; every significant feature article, production still, biography, forecast, and gossip story. Profusely illustrated. 367pp. 8⅜ x 11¼.
23154-2 Pa. $7.95

JOHANN SEBASTIAN BACH, Philipp Spitta. Great classic of biography, musical commentary, with hundreds of pieces analyzed. Also good for Bach's contemporaries. 450 musical examples. Total of 1799pp.
EUK 22278-0, 22279-9 Clothbd., Two vol. set $25.00

BEETHOVEN AND HIS NINE SYMPHONIES, Sir George Grove. Thorough history, analysis, commentary on symphonies and some related pieces. For either beginner or advanced student. 436 musical passages. 407pp. 20334-4 Pa. $4.00

MOZART AND HIS PIANO CONCERTOS, Cuthbert Girdlestone. The only full-length study. Detailed analyses of all 21 concertos, sources; 417 musical examples. 509pp.
21271-8 Pa. $6.00

CATALOGUE OF DOVER BOOKS

THE MAGIC MOVING PICTURE BOOK, Bliss, Sands & Co. The pictures in this book move! Volcanoes erupt, a house burns, a serpentine dancer wiggles her way through a number. By using a specially ruled acetate screen provided, you can obtain these and 15 other startling effects. Originally "The Motograph Moving Picture Book." 32pp. 8¼ x 11. 23224-7 Pa. $1.75

STRING FIGURES AND HOW TO MAKE THEM, Caroline F. Jayne. Fullest, clearest instructions on string figures from around world: Eskimo, Navajo, Lapp, Europe, more. Cats cradle, moving spear, lightning, stars. Introduction by A.C. Haddon. 950 illustrations. 407pp. 20152-X Pa $3.50

PAPER FOLDING FOR BEGINNERS, William D. Murray and Francis J. Rigney. Clearest book on market for making origami sail boats, roosters, frogs that move legs, cups, bonbon boxes. 40 projects. More than 275 illustrations. Photographs. 94pp. 20713-7 Pa $1.50

INDIAN SIGN LANGUAGE, William Tomkins. Over 525 signs developed by Sioux, Blackfoot, Cheyenne, Arapahoe and other tribes. Written instructions and diagrams: how to make words, construct sentences. Also 290 pictographs of Sioux and Ojibway tribes. 111pp. 6⅛ x 9¼. 22029-X Pa. $1.75

BOOMERANGS: HOW TO MAKE AND THROW THEM, Bernard S. Mason. Easy to make and throw, dozens of designs: cross-stick, pinwheel, boomabird, tumblestick, Australian curved stick boomerang. Complete throwing instructions. All safe. 99pp. 23028-7 Pa. $1.75

25 KITES THAT FLY, Leslie Hunt. Full, easy to follow instructions for kites made from inexpensive materials. Many novelties. Reeling, raising, designing your own. 70 illustrations. 110pp. 22550-X Pa. $1.50

TRICKS AND GAMES ON THE POOL TABLE, Fred Herrmann. 79 tricks and games, some solitaires, some for 2 or more players, some competitive; mystifying shots and throws, unusual carom, tricks involving cork, coins, a hat, more. 77 figures. 95pp. 21814-7 Pa. $1.50

WOODCRAFT AND CAMPING, Bernard S. Mason. How to make a quick emergency shelter, select woods that will burn immediately, make do with limited supplies, etc. Also making many things out of wood, rawhide, bark, at camp. Formerly titled Woodcraft. 295 illustrations. 580pp. 21951-8 Pa. $4.00

AN INTRODUCTION TO CHESS MOVES AND TACTICS SIMPLY EXPLAINED, Leonard Barden. Informal intermediate introduction: reasons for moves, tactics, openings, traps, positional play, endgame. Isolates patterns. 102pp. USO 21210-6 Pa. $1.35

LASKER'S MANUAL OF CHESS, Dr. Emanuel Lasker. Great world champion offers very thorough coverage of all aspects of chess. Combinations, position play, openings, endgame, aesthetics of chess, philosophy of struggle, much more. Filled with analyzed games. 390pp. 20640-8 Pa. $4.00

CATALOGUE OF DOVER BOOKS

CREATIVE LITHOGRAPHY AND HOW TO DO IT, Grant Arnold. Lithography as art form: working directly on stone, transfer of drawings, lithotint, mezzotint, color printing; also metal plates. Detailed, thorough. 27 illustrations. 214pp.
21208-4 Pa. $3.50

DESIGN MOTIFS OF ANCIENT MEXICO, Jorge Enciso. Vigorous, powerful ceramic stamp impressions — Maya, Aztec, Toltec, Olmec. Serpents, gods, priests, dancers, etc. 153pp. 6⅛ x 9¼.
20084-1 Pa. $2.50

AMERICAN INDIAN DESIGN AND DECORATION, Leroy Appleton. Full text, plus more than 700 precise drawings of Inca, Maya, Aztec, Pueblo, Plains, NW Coast basketry, sculpture, painting, pottery, sand paintings, metal, etc. 4 plates in color. 279pp. 8⅜ x 11¼.
22704-9 Pa. $5.00

CHINESE LATTICE DESIGNS, Daniel S. Dye. Incredibly beautiful geometric designs: circles, voluted, simple dissections, etc. Inexhaustible source of ideas, motifs. 1239 illustrations. 469pp. 6⅛ x 9¼.
23096-1 Pa. $5.00

JAPANESE DESIGN MOTIFS, Matsuya Co. Mon, or heraldic designs. Over 4000 typical, beautiful designs: birds, animals, flowers, swords, fans, geometric; all beautifully stylized. 213pp. 11⅜ x 8¼.
22874-6 Pa. $5.00

PERSPECTIVE, Jan Vredeman de Vries. 73 perspective plates from 1604 edition; buildings, townscapes, stairways, fantastic scenes. Remarkable for beauty, surrealistic atmosphere; real eye-catchers. Introduction by Adolf Placzek. 74pp. 11⅜ x 8¼.
20186-4 Pa. $3.00

EARLY AMERICAN DESIGN MOTIFS, Suzanne E. Chapman. 497 motifs, designs, from painting on wood, ceramics, appliqué, glassware, samplers, metal work, etc. Florals, landscapes, birds and animals, geometrics, letters, etc. Inexhaustible. Enlarged edition. 138pp. 8⅜ x 11¼.
22985-8 Pa. $3.50
23084-8 Clothbd. $7.95

VICTORIAN STENCILS FOR DESIGN AND DECORATION, edited by E.V. Gillon, Jr. 113 wonderful ornate Victorian pieces from German sources; florals, geometrics; borders, corner pieces; bird motifs, etc. 64pp. 9⅜ x 12¼.
21995-X Pa. $3.00

ART NOUVEAU: AN ANTHOLOGY OF DESIGN AND ILLUSTRATION FROM THE STUDIO, edited by E.V. Gillon, Jr. Graphic arts: book jackets, posters, engravings, illustrations, decorations; Crane, Beardsley, Bradley and many others. Inexhaustible. 92pp. 8⅛ x 11.
22388-4 Pa. $2.50

ORIGINAL ART DECO DESIGNS, William Rowe. First-rate, highly imaginative modern Art Deco frames, borders, compositions, alphabets, florals, insectals, Wurlitzer-types, etc. Much finest modern Art Deco. 80 plates, 8 in color. 8⅜ x 11¼.
22567-4 Pa. $3.50

HANDBOOK OF DESIGNS AND DEVICES, Clarence P. Hornung. Over 1800 basic geometric designs based on circle, triangle, square, scroll, cross, etc. Largest such collection in existence. 261pp.
20125-2 Pa. $2.75

THE RED FAIRY BOOK, Andrew Lang. Lang's color fairy books have long been children's favorites. This volume includes Rapunzel, Jack and the Bean-stalk and 35 other stories, familiar and unfamiliar. 4 plates, 93 illustrations x + 367pp.
21673-X Paperbound $3.00

THE BLUE FAIRY BOOK, Andrew Lang. Lang's tales come from all countries and all times. Here are 37 tales from Grimm, the Arabian Nights, Greek Mythology, and other fascinating sources. 8 plates, 130 illustrations. xi + 390pp.
21437-0 Paperbound $3.50

HOUSEHOLD STORIES BY THE BROTHERS GRIMM. Classic English-language edition of the well-known tales — Rumpelstiltskin, Snow White, Hansel and Gretel, The Twelve Brothers, Faithful John, Rapunzel, Tom Thumb (52 stories in all). Translated into simple, straightforward English by Lucy Crane. Ornamented with headpieces, vignettes, elaborate decorative initials and a dozen full-page illustrations by Walter Crane. x + 269pp.
21080-4 Paperbound $3.00

THE MERRY ADVENTURES OF ROBIN HOOD, Howard Pyle. The finest modern versions of the traditional ballads and tales about the great English outlaw. Howard Pyle's complete prose version, with every word, every illustration of the first edition. Do not confuse this facsimile of the original (1883) with modern editions that change text or illustrations. 23 plates plus many page decorations. xxii + 296pp.
22043-5 Paperbound $4.00

THE STORY OF KING ARTHUR AND HIS KNIGHTS, Howard Pyle. The finest children's version of the life of King Arthur; brilliantly retold by Pyle, with 48 of his most imaginative illustrations. xviii + 313pp. 6⅛ x 9¼.
21445-1 Paperbound $3.50

THE WONDERFUL WIZARD OF OZ, L. Frank Baum. America's finest children's book in facsimile of first edition with all Denslow illustrations in full color. The edition a child should have. Introduction by Martin Gardner. 23 color plates, scores of drawings. iv + 267pp.
20691-2 Paperbound $3.00

THE MARVELOUS LAND OF OZ, L. Frank Baum. The second Oz book, every bit as imaginative as the Wizard. The hero is a boy named Tip, but the Scarecrow and the Tin Woodman are back, as is the Oz magic. 16 color plates, 120 drawings by John R. Neill. 287pp.
20692-0 Paperbound $3.00

THE MAGICAL MONARCH OF MO, L. Frank Baum. Remarkable adventures in a land even stranger than Oz. The best of Baum's books not in the Oz series. 15 color plates and dozens of drawings by Frank Verbeck. xviii + 237pp.
21892-9 Paperbound $2.95

THE BAD CHILD'S BOOK OF BEASTS, MORE BEASTS FOR WORSE CHILDREN, A MORAL ALPHABET, Hilaire Belloc. Three complete humor classics in one volume. Be kind to the frog, and do not call him names . . . and 28 other whimsical animals. Familiar favorites and some not so well known. Illustrated by Basil Blackwell.
156pp. (USO) 20749-8 Paperbound $2.00

THE ART DECO STYLE, ed. by Theodore Menten. Furniture, jewelry, metalwork, ceramics, fabrics, lighting fixtures, interior decors, exteriors, graphics from pure French sources. Best sampling around. Over 400 photographs. 183pp. 8⅜ x 11¼.
22824-X Pa. $4.00

THE GENTLEMAN AND CABINET MAKER'S DIRECTOR, Thomas Chippendale. Full reprint, 1762 style book, most influential of all time; chairs, tables, sofas, mirrors, cabinets, etc. 200 plates, plus 24 photographs of surviving pieces. 249pp. 9⅞ x 12¾.
21601-2 Pa. $6.00

PINE FURNITURE OF EARLY NEW ENGLAND, Russell H. Kettell. Basic book. Thorough historical text, plus 200 illustrations of boxes, highboys, candlesticks, desks, etc. 477pp. 7⅞ x 10¾.
20145-7 Clothbd. $12.50

ORIENTAL RUGS, ANTIQUE AND MODERN, Walter A. Hawley. Persia, Turkey, Caucasus, Central Asia, China, other traditions. Best general survey of all aspects: styles and periods, manufacture, uses, symbols and their interpretation, and identification. 96 illustrations, 11 in color. 320pp. 6⅛ x 9¼.
22366-3 Pa. $5.00

DECORATIVE ANTIQUE IRONWORK, Henry R. d'Allemagne. Photographs of 4500 iron artifacts from world's finest collection, Rouen. Hinges, locks, candelabra, weapons, lighting devices, clocks, tools, from Roman times to mid-19th century. Nothing else comparable to it. 420pp. 9 x 12.
22082-6 Pa. $8.50

THE COMPLETE BOOK OF DOLL MAKING AND COLLECTING, Catherine Christopher. Instructions, patterns for dozens of dolls, from rag doll on up to elaborate, historically accurate figures. Mould faces, sew clothing, make doll houses, etc. Also collecting information. Many illustrations. 288pp. 6 x 9. 22066-4 Pa. $3.00

ANTIQUE PAPER DOLLS: 1915-1920, edited by Arnold Arnold. 7 antique cut-out dolls and 24 costumes from 1915-1920, selected by Arnold Arnold from his collection of rare children's books and entertainments, all in full color. 32pp. 9¼ x 12¼.
23176-3 Pa. $2.00

ANTIQUE PAPER DOLLS: THE EDWARDIAN ERA, Epinal. Full-color reproductions of two historic series of paper dolls that show clothing styles in 1908 and at the beginning of the First World War. 8 two-sided, stand-up dolls and 32 complete, two-sided costumes. Full instructions for assembling included. 32pp. 9¼ x 12¼.
23175-5 Pa. $2.00

A HISTORY OF COSTUME, Carl Köhler, Emma von Sichardt. Egypt, Babylon, Greece up through 19th century Europe; based on surviving pieces, art works, etc. Full text and 595 illustrations, including many clear, measured patterns for reproducing historic costume. Practical. 464pp. 21030-8 Pa. $4.00

EARLY AMERICAN LOCOMOTIVES, John H. White, Jr. Finest locomotive engravings from late 19th century: historical (1804-1874), main-line (after 1870), special, foreign, etc. 147 plates. 200pp. 11⅜ x 8¼. 22772-3 Pa. $3.50

JEWISH GREETING CARDS, Ed Sibbett, Jr. 16 cards to cut and color. Three say "Happy Chanukah," one "Happy New Year," others have no message, show stars of David, Torahs, wine cups, other traditional themes. 16 envelopes. 8¼ x 11.
23225-5 Pa. $2.00

AUBREY BEARDSLEY GREETING CARD BOOK, Aubrey Beardsley. Edited by Theodore Menten. 16 elegant yet inexpensive greeting cards let you combine your own sentiments with subtle Art Nouveau lines. 16 different Aubrey Beardsley designs that you can color or not, as you wish. 16 envelopes. 64pp. 8¼ x 11.
23173-9 Pa. $2.00

RECREATIONS IN THE THEORY OF NUMBERS, Albert Beiler. Number theory, an inexhaustible source of puzzles, recreations, for beginners and advanced. Divisors, perfect numbers. scales of notation, etc. 349pp. 21096-0 Pa. $4.00

AMUSEMENTS IN MATHEMATICS, Henry E. Dudeney. One of largest puzzle collections, based on algebra, arithmetic, permutations, probability, plane figure dissection, properties of numbers, by one of world's foremost puzzlists. Solutions. 450 illustrations. 258pp. 20473-1 Pa. $3.00

MATHEMATICS, MAGIC AND MYSTERY, Martin Gardner. Puzzle editor for Scientific American explains math behind: card tricks, stage mind reading, coin and match tricks, counting out games, geometric dissections. Probability, sets, theory of numbers, clearly explained. Plus more than 400 tricks, guaranteed to work. 135 illustrations. 176pp. 20335-2 Pa. $2.00

BEST MATHEMATICAL PUZZLES OF SAM LOYD, edited by Martin Gardner. Bizarre, original, whimsical puzzles by America's greatest puzzler. From fabulously rare Cyclopedia, including famous 14-15 puzzles, the Horse of a Different Color, 115 more. Elementary math. 150 illustrations. 167pp. 20498-7 Pa. $2.50

MATHEMATICAL PUZZLES FOR BEGINNERS AND ENTHUSIASTS, Geoffrey Mott-Smith. 189 puzzles from easy to difficult involving arithmetic, logic, algebra, properties of digits, probability. Explanation of math behind puzzles. 135 illustrations. 248pp. 20198-8 Pa. $2.75

BIG BOOK OF MAZES AND LABYRINTHS, Walter Shepherd. Classical, solid, and ripple mazes; short path and avoidance labyrinths; more —50 mazes and labyrinths in all. 12 other figures. Full solutions. 112pp. 8⅛ x 11. 22951-3 Pa. $2.00

COIN GAMES AND PUZZLES, Maxey Brooke. 60 puzzles, games and stunts —from Japan, Korea, Africa and the ancient world, by Dudeney and the other great puzzlers, as well as Maxey Brooke's own creations. Full solutions. 67 illustrations. 94pp. 22893-2 Pa. $1.50

HAND SHADOWS TO BE THROWN UPON THE WALL, Henry Bursill. Wonderful Victorian novelty tells how to make flying birds, dog, goose, deer, and 14 others. 32pp. 6½ x 9¼. 21779-5 Pa. $1.25

EAST O' THE SUN AND WEST O' THE MOON, George W. Dasent. Considered the best of all translations of these Norwegian folk tales, this collection has been enjoyed by generations of children (and folklorists too). Includes True and Untrue, Why the Sea is Salt, East O' the Sun and West O' the Moon, Why the Bear is Stumpy-Tailed, Boots and the Troll, The Cock and the Hen, Rich Peter the Pedlar, and 52 more. The only edition with all 59 tales. 77 illustrations by Erik Werenskiold and Theodor Kittelsen. xv + 418pp. 22521-6 Paperbound $4.00

GOOPS AND HOW TO BE THEM, Gelett Burgess. Classic of tongue-in-cheek humor, masquerading as etiquette book. 87 verses, twice as many cartoons, show mischievous Goops as they demonstrate to children virtues of table manners, neatness, courtesy, etc. Favorite for generations. viii + 88pp. 6½ x 9¼. 22233-0 Paperbound $2.00

ALICE'S ADVENTURES UNDER GROUND, Lewis Carroll. The first version, quite different from the final *Alice in Wonderland,* printed out by Carroll himself with his own illustrations. Complete facsimile of the "million dollar" manuscript Carroll gave to Alice Liddell in 1864. Introduction by Martin Gardner. viii + 96pp. Title and dedication pages in color. 21482-6 Paperbound $1.50

THE BROWNIES, THEIR BOOK, Palmer Cox. Small as mice, cunning as foxes, exuberant and full of mischief, the Brownies go to the zoo, toy shop, seashore, circus, etc., in 24 verse adventures and 266 illustrations. Long a favorite, since their first appearance in St. Nicholas Magazine. xi + 144pp. 6⅝ x 9¼. 21265-3 Paperbound $2.50

SONGS OF CHILDHOOD, Walter De La Mare. Published (under the pseudonym Walter Ramal) when De La Mare was only 29, this charming collection has long been a favorite children's book. A facsimile of the first edition in paper, the 47 poems capture the simplicity of the nursery rhyme and the ballad, including such lyrics as I Met Eve, Tartary, The Silver Penny. vii + 106pp. (USO) 21972-0 Paperbound $2.00

THE COMPLETE NONSENSE OF EDWARD LEAR, Edward Lear. The finest 19th-century humorist-cartoonist in full: all nonsense limericks, zany alphabets, Owl and Pussycat, songs, nonsense botany, and more than 500 illustrations by Lear himself. Edited by Holbrook Jackson. xxix + 287pp. (USO) 20167-8 Paperbound $3.00

BILLY WHISKERS: THE AUTOBIOGRAPHY OF A GOAT, Frances Trego Montgomery. A favorite of children since the early 20th century, here are the escapades of that rambunctious, irresistible and mischievous goat—Billy Whiskers. Much in the spirit of *Peck's Bad Boy,* this is a book that children never tire of reading or hearing. All the original familiar illustrations by W. H. Fry are included: 6 color plates, 18 black and white drawings. 159pp. 22345-0 Paperbound $2.75

MOTHER GOOSE MELODIES. Faithful republication of the fabulously rare Munroe and Francis "copyright 1833" Boston edition—the most important Mother Goose collection, usually referred to as the "original." Familiar rhymes plus many rare ones, with wonderful old woodcut illustrations. Edited by E. F. Bleiler. 128pp. 4½ x 6⅜. 22577-1 Paperbound $1.50

VISUAL ILLUSIONS: THEIR CAUSES, CHARACTERISTICS, AND APPLICATIONS, Matthew Luckiesh. Thorough description and discussion of optical illusion, geometric and perspective, particularly; size and shape distortions, illusions of color, of motion; natural illusions; use of illusion in art and magic, industry, etc. Most useful today with op art, also for classical art. Scores of effects illustrated. Introduction by William H. Ittleson. 100 illustrations. xxi + 252pp.
21530-X Paperbound $2.50

A HANDBOOK OF ANATOMY FOR ART STUDENTS, Arthur Thomson. Thorough, virtually exhaustive coverage of skeletal structure, musculature, etc. Full text, supplemented by anatomical diagrams and drawings and by photographs of undraped figures. Unique in its comparison of male and female forms, pointing out differences of contour, texture, form. 211 figures, 40 drawings, 86 photographs. xx + 459pp. 5⅜ x 8⅜.
21163-0 Paperbound $5.00

150 MASTERPIECES OF DRAWING, Selected by Anthony Toney. Full page reproductions of drawings from the early 16th to the end of the 18th century, all beautifully reproduced: Rembrandt, Michelangelo, Dürer, Fragonard, Urs, Graf, Wouwerman, many others. First-rate browsing book, model book for artists. xviii + 150pp. 8⅜ x 11¼.
21032-4 Paperbound $4.00

THE LATER WORK OF AUBREY BEARDSLEY, Aubrey Beardsley. Exotic, erotic, ironic masterpieces in full maturity: Comedy Ballet, Venus and Tannhauser, Pierrot, Lysistrata, Rape of the Lock, Savoy material, Ali Baba, Volpone, etc. This material revolutionized the art world, and is still powerful, fresh, brilliant. With *The Early Work,* all Beardsley's finest work. 174 plates, 2 in color. xiv + 176pp. 8⅛ x 11.
21817-1 Paperbound $4.00

DRAWINGS OF REMBRANDT, Rembrandt van Rijn. Complete reproduction of fabulously rare edition by Lippmann and Hofstede de Groot, completely reedited, updated, improved by Prof. Seymour Slive, Fogg Museum. Portraits, Biblical sketches, landscapes, Oriental types, nudes, episodes from classical mythology—All Rembrandt's fertile genius. Also selection of drawings by his pupils and followers. "Stunning volumes," *Saturday Review.* 550 illustrations. lxxviii + 552pp. 9⅛ x 12¼.
21485-0, 21486-9 Two volumes, Paperbound $12.00

THE DISASTERS OF WAR, Francisco Goya. One of the masterpieces of Western civilization—83 etchings that record Goya's shattering, bitter reaction to the Napoleonic war that swept through Spain after the insurrection of 1808 and to war in general. Reprint of the first edition, with three additional plates from Boston's Museum of Fine Arts. All plates facsimile size. Introduction by Philip Hofer, Fogg Museum. v + 97pp. 9⅜ x 8¼.
21872-4 Paperbound $3.00

GRAPHIC WORKS OF ODILON REDON. Largest collection of Redon's graphic works ever assembled: 172 lithographs, 28 etchings and engravings, 9 drawings. These include some of his most famous works. All the plates from *Odilon Redon: oeuvre graphique complet,* plus additional plates. New introduction and caption translations by Alfred Werner. 209 illustrations. xxvii + 209pp. 9⅛ x 12¼.
21966-8 Paperbound $6.00

CONSTRUCTION OF AMERICAN FURNITURE TREASURES, Lester Margon. 344 detail drawings, complete text on constructing exact reproductions of 38 early American masterpieces: Hepplewhite sideboard, Duncan Phyfe drop-leaf table, mantel clock, gate-leg dining table, Pa. German cupboard, more. 38 plates. 54 photographs. 168pp. 8⅜ x 11¼.   23056-2 Pa. $4.00

JEWELRY MAKING AND DESIGN, Augustus F. Rose, Antonio Cirino. Professional secrets revealed in thorough, practical guide: tools, materials, processes; rings, brooches, chains, cast pieces, enamelling, setting stones, etc. Do not confuse with skimpy introductions: beginner can use, professional can learn from it. Over 200 illustrations. 306pp.   21750-7 Pa. $3.00

METALWORK AND ENAMELLING, Herbert Maryon. Generally coneeded best all-around book. Countless trade secrets: materials, tools, soldering, filigree, setting, inlay, niello, repoussé, casting, polishing, etc. For beginner or expert. Author was foremost British expert. 330 illustrations. 335pp.   22702-2 Pa. $4.00

WEAVING WITH FOOT-POWER LOOMS, Edward F. Worst. Setting up a loom, beginning to weave, constructing equipment, using dyes, more, plus over 285 drafts of traditional patterns including Colonial and Swedish weaves. More than 200 other figures. For beginning and advanced. 275pp. 8¾ x 6⅜.   23064-3 Pa. $4.50

WEAVING A NAVAJO BLANKET, Gladys A. Reichard. Foremost anthropologist studied under Navajo women, reveals every step in process from wool, dyeing, spinning, setting up loom, designing, weaving. Much history, symbolism. With this book you could make one yourself. 97 illustrations. 222pp.   22992-0 Pa. $3.00

NATURAL DYES AND HOME DYEING, Rita J. Adrosko. Use natural ingredients: bark, flowers, leaves, lichens, insects etc. Over 135 specific recipes from historical sources for cotton, wool, other fabrics. Genuine premodern handicrafts. 12 illustrations. 160pp.   22688-3 Pa. $2.00

DRIED FLOWERS, Sarah Whitlock and Martha Rankin. Concise, clear, practical guide to dehydration, glycerinizing, pressing plant material, and more. Covers use of silica gel. 12 drawings. Originally titled "New Techniques with Dried Flowers." 32pp.   21802-3 Pa. $1.00

THOMAS NAST: CARTOONS AND ILLUSTRATIONS, with text by Thomas Nast St. Hill. Father of American political cartooning. Cartoons that destroyed Tweed Ring; inflation, free love, church and state; original Republican elephant and Democratic donkey; Santa Claus; more. 117 illustrations. 146pp. 9 x 12.
22983-1 Pa. $4.00
23067-8 Clothbd. $8.50

FREDERIC REMINGTON: 173 DRAWINGS AND ILLUSTRATIONS. Most famous of the Western artists, most responsible for our myths about the American West in its untamed days. Complete reprinting of Drawings of Frederic Remington (1897), plus other selections. 4 additional drawings in color on covers. 140pp. 9 x 12.
20714-5 Pa. $5.00

CATALOGUE OF DOVER BOOKS

THE FITZWILLIAM VIRGINAL BOOK, edited by J. Fuller Maitland, W.B. Squire. Famous early 17th century collection of keyboard music, 300 works by Morley, Byrd, Bull, Gibbons, etc. Modern notation. Total of 938pp. 8³/₈ x 11.
ECE 21068-5, 21069-3 Pa., Two vol. set $15.00

COMPLETE STRING QUARTETS, Wolfgang A. Mozart. Breitkopf and Härtel edition. All 23 string quartets plus alternate slow movement to K156. Study score. 277pp. 9³/₈ x 12¼.
22372-8 Pa. $6.00

COMPLETE SONG CYCLES, Franz Schubert. Complete piano, vocal music of Die Schöne Müllerin, Die Winterreise, Schwanengesang. Also Drinker English singing translations. Breitkopf and Härtel edition. 217pp. 9³/₈ x 12¼.
22649-2 Pa. $5.00

THE COMPLETE PRELUDES AND ETUDES FOR PIANOFORTE SOLO, Alexander Scriabin. All the preludes and etudes including many perfectly spun miniatures. Edited by K.N. Igumnov and Y.I. Mil'shteyn. 250pp. 9 x 12.
22919-X Pa. $6.00

TRISTAN UND ISOLDE, Richard Wagner. Full orchestral score with complete instrumentation. Do not confuse with piano reduction. Commentary by Felix Mottl, great Wagnerian conductor and scholar. Study score. 655pp. 8¹/₈ x 11.
22915-7 Pa. $11.95

FAVORITE SONGS OF THE NINETIES, ed. Robert Fremont. Full reproduction, including covers, of 88 favorites: Ta-Ra-Ra-Boom-De-Aye, The Band Played On, Bird in a Gilded Cage, Under the Bamboo Tree, After the Ball, etc. 401pp. 9 x 12.
EBE 21536-9 Pa. $6.95

SOUSA'S GREAT MARCHES IN PIANO TRANSCRIPTION: ORIGINAL SHEET MUSIC OF 23 WORKS, John Philip Sousa. Selected by Lester S. Levy. Playing edition includes: The Stars and Stripes Forever, The Thunderer, The Gladiator, King Cotton, Washington Post, much more. 24 illustrations. 111pp. 9 x 12.
USO 23132-1 Pa. $3.50

CLASSIC PIANO RAGS, selected with an introduction by Rudi Blesh. Best ragtime music (1897-1922) by Scott Joplin, James Scott, Joseph F. Lamb, Tom Turpin, 9 others. Printed from best original sheet music, plus covers. 364pp. 9 x 12.
EBE 20469-3 Pa. $7.50

ANALYSIS OF CHINESE CHARACTERS, C.D. Wilder, J.H. Ingram. 1000 most important characters analyzed according to primitives, phonetics, historical development. Traditional method offers mnemonic aid to beginner, intermediate student of Chinese, Japanese. 365pp.
23045-7 Pa. $4.00

MODERN CHINESE: A BASIC COURSE, Faculty of Peking University. Self study, classroom course in modern Mandarin. Records contain phonetics, vocabulary, sentences, lessons. 249 page book contains all recorded text, translations, grammar, vocabulary, exercises. Best course on market. 3 12" 33¹/₃ monaural records, book, album.
98832-5 Set $12.50

COOKIES FROM MANY LANDS, Josephine Perry. Crullers, oatmeal cookies, chaux au chocolate, English tea cakes, mandel kuchen, Sacher torte, Danish puff pastry, Swedish cookies — a mouth-watering collection of 223 recipes. 157pp.

22832-0 Pa. $2.25

ROSE RECIPES, Eleanour S. Rohde. How to make sauces, jellies, tarts, salads, potpourris, sweet bags, pomanders, perfumes from garden roses; all exact recipes. Century old favorites. 95pp.

22957-2 Pa. $1.75

"OSCAR" OF THE WALDORF'S COOKBOOK, Oscar Tschirky. Famous American chef reveals 3455 recipes that made Waldorf great; cream of French, German, American cooking, in all categories. Full instructions, easy home use. 1896 edition. 907pp. 6⅝ x 9⅜.

20790-0 Clothbd. $15.00

JAMS AND JELLIES, May Byron. Over 500 old-time recipes for delicious jams, jellies, marmalades, preserves, and many other items. Probably the largest jam and jelly book in print. Originally titled May Byron's Jam Book. 276pp.

USO 23130-5 Pa. $3.50

MUSHROOM RECIPES, André L. Simon. 110 recipes for everyday and special cooking. Champignons a la grecque, sole bonne femme, chicken liver croustades, more; 9 basic sauces, 13 ways of cooking mushrooms. 54pp.

USO 20913-X Pa. $1.25

THE BUCKEYE COOKBOOK, Buckeye Publishing Company. Over 1,000 easy-to-follow, traditional recipes from the American Midwest: bread (100 recipes alone), meat, game, jam, candy, cake, ice cream, and many other categories of cooking. 64 illustrations. From 1883 enlarged edition. 416pp.

23218-2 Pa. $4.00

TWENTY-TWO AUTHENTIC BANQUETS FROM INDIA, Robert H. Christie. Complete, easy-to-do recipes for almost 200 authentic Indian dishes assembled in 22 banquets. Arranged by region. Selected from Banquets of the Nations. 192pp.

23200-X Pa. $2.50